The Unmaking of Special Rights

NEW HORIZONS IN INTERNATIONAL RELATIONS

Series Editor: Patrick James, *Dornsife Dean's Professor, School of International Studies, Dana and David Dornsife College of Letters, Arts and Sciences, University of Southern California, USA*

New Horizons in International Relations is a book series that embraces the wide range of topics, theoretical frameworks and methods that combine to produce the field of International Relations. The series welcomes studies that are paradigm-based, studies that emphasize a visual approach and also those that fit within the new tradition of analytic eclecticism. In addition, this book series is well-disposed toward interdisciplinary research. Items with a pedagogical focus are welcome along with those that might be characterized more purely as works of theory or empirical analysis.

With oversight from the Series Editor, Patrick James, the Dana and David Dornsife Professor of International Relations at the University of Southern California, the book series is seeking out projects from scholars at all career stages. As a former President of the International Studies Association, the Series Editor hopes to include a wide range of subject matter, theoretical outlooks and methods among the books that appear. The volumes under the auspices of *New Horizons in International Relations* will be essential reading for professors and students, along with those in the policy world.

For a full list of Edward Elgar published titles, including the titles in this series, visit our website at www.e-elgar.com.

The Unmaking of Special Rights

Differential Treatment of Developing Countries in Times of Global Power Shifts

Klaus Dingwerth

Professor of Political Science, School of Economics and Political Science, University of St.Gallen, Switzerland

Clara Weinhardt

Assistant Professor of International Relations, Faculty of Arts and Social Sciences, Maastricht University, the Netherlands

Julian Eckl

Post-doctoral Research Fellow, School of Economics and Political Science, University of St.Gallen, Switzerland

Till Schöfer

Freie Universität Berlin, Germany

Simon Herr

University of St.Gallen, Switzerland

NEW HORIZONS IN INTERNATIONAL RELATIONS

Edward Elgar PUBLISHING

Cheltenham, UK • Northampton, MA, USA

Cover image: Eve Wangui Gichuhi

Published by
Edward Elgar Publishing Limited
The Lypiatts
15 Lansdown Road
Cheltenham
Glos GL50 2JA
UK

Edward Elgar Publishing, Inc.
William Pratt House
9 Dewey Court
Northampton
Massachusetts 01060
USA

A catalogue record for this book
is available from the British Library

Library of Congress Control Number: 2023951250

This book is available electronically in the **Elgar**online
Political Science and Public Policy subject collection
http://dx.doi.org/10.4337/9781035325986

MIX
Paper from responsible sources
FSC® C013056

ISBN 978 1 0353 2597 9 (cased)
ISBN 978 1 0353 2598 6 (eBook)

Printed and bound in Great Britain by
TJ Books Limited, Padstow, Cornwall

Contents

Figures

Tables

Acknowledgements

This book is the product of a collaborative effort the five of us undertook over the last five years. Because the analytical framework we follow in our study is a product of joint reflection, discussion, writing, and rewriting, and because we collectively reviewed every single chapter multiple times, our book is best described as a co-authored monograph. At the same time, and as usual in projects of this kind, we have divided the empirical work along the issue areas we cover. As a result, the primary responsibility for each empirical chapter rests with individual team members whom we identify at the beginning of each chapter.

Like all academic books, this one would not have been possible without the support of numerous institutions as well as individuals. Special thanks are due to the GFF Project Funding of the Basic Research Fund at the University of St.Gallen for providing seed money for a larger grant proposal, and to the Deutsche Forschungsgemeinschaft (DFG, Grant No. WE 6012/1-2) as well as the Swiss National Science Foundation (SNSF, Grant No. 100017L_175887) for their generous funding of the research project on which this book is based. Moreover, we thank our host institutions and our colleagues at these institutions for their generous support over the years. At the Hertie School in Berlin, at Maastricht University, and at the University of St.Gallen, we were provided the work environment and the intellectual exchanges that allowed us to develop the ideas we present in this book. We also owe gratitude to the Global Public Policy Institute in Berlin where about a decade ago two of us – Clara and Klaus – met and where the first ideas for this collaborative project took shape.

Once the project was up and running, a steady flow of research assistants supported us in various ways. In Berlin and Maastricht, Farida Hassan, Anna-Lena Braun, Francisco Almeida, Talisha Schilder, and Simon Pompé helped with the research on the international trade regime. In St.Gallen, Giulia Alario, Philia Heuberger, Rebecca Kessler, Philippe Phan, and Jonatan Schäfer supported our work on the international climate and health regimes. Moreover, Cornelia Kappeler and Thomas Rempfler provided administrative support at the University of St.Gallen, as did Grit Heidemann-Schirmer and Sanne Winkens-Gärtener at the Hertie School and at Maastricht University. Finally, our colleague Vanessa Boanada Fuchs provided input at the early stages of our project. A big thanks to all of them!

In addition, we are grateful to all colleagues who, on various occasions, commented on draft versions of our initial project proposal, on individual chapters, or even on the entire manuscript; shared ideas, knowledge, and contacts; helped us identify relevant sources; or made time available for expert interviews. They include Ilias Alami, Felix Anderl, Déborah Barros Leal Farias, Paula Castro, Cynthia Couette, Christina Davis, Sandra Destradi, Angela Geck, Jennifer Hadden, Tine Hanrieder, Monika Heupel, Chris Höhne, Kristen Hopewell, Nele Kortendiek, Matthias Kranke, Björn Kümmel, Andreas Kruck, Max Lesch, Anke Moerland, Jean-Frédéric Morin, Hermann E. Ott, Myriam Prys-Hansen, Xiaoyu Pu, Henning Schmidtke, Jan Aart Scholte, Omar Serrano, Harro van Asselt, Remco van de Pas, Rolf Wüstenhagen, Lily Young, Bernhard Zangl, Lisbeth Zimmermann, and two anonymous reviewers. We also thank all participants who provided feedback on presentations of our research at the Political Science Research Seminar in St.Gallen in 2019 and 2021; the research colloquium on 'Europe and the Crisis of Rule-Based Global Order' at Maastricht University in 2020 and 2021; the joint DVPW/SPSA/ÖVPW Conference in Zürich in 2019; the EWIS workshop in 2021 (virtual); the ECPR General Conference in 2021 (virtual); the SASE Annual Conference in Amsterdam in 2022; the ISA Annual Conventions in Toronto in 2019, Las Vegas in 2021 (virtual), Nashville in 2022, and Montreal in 2023; at TU Dresden in 2020; at the (virtual) German IR Conference at Albert-Ludwigs-Universität Freiburg in 2020; and at the SNIS Conference in St.Gallen in 2023. We also thank the policy-makers who agreed to share their insights and made time to talk to us.

Last, but not least, we thank Alex Pettifer, Nina Booth, and the entire team at Edward Elgar Publishing for their trust in our work, for taking our book under the wings of their ambitious *New Horizons in International Relations* series, and for their truly excellent support throughout the publication process.

Berlin, Maastricht, and St.Gallen, July 2023

Abbreviations

ACP	African, Caribbean, and Pacific
ACTA	Anti-Counterfeiting Trade Agreement
ADP	Ad Hoc Working Group on the Durban Platform for Enhanced Action
AFRO	WHO African Region
AMS	Aggregate Measure of Support
AOA	Agreement on Agriculture
AOSIS	Alliance of Small Island States
APC	African, Caribbean and Pacific Countries
ASEAN	Association of Southeast Asian Nations
AU	African Union
AWG-KP	Ad Hoc Working Group on Further Commitments for Annex I Parties under the Kyoto Protocol
AWG-LCA	Ad Hoc Working Group on Long-Term Cooperative Action
BASIC	Brazil, South Africa, India, and China
BITs	Bilateral investment treaties
BRICs	Brazil, Russia, India, and China
BRICS	Brazil, Russia, India, China, and South Africa
C2P	Capacity to pay
CARICOM	Caribbean Community
CBD	Convention on Biological Diversity
CBDR	Common but differentiated responsibilities
CBDR-RC	Common but differentiated responsibilities and respective capabilities
CCNR	Central Commission for the Navigation of the Rhine
CCP	Chinese Communist Party
CDIP	Committee on Development and Intellectual Property
CDM	Clean Development Mechanism

CDP	Committee for Development Policy
CEITs	Countries with economies in transition
CELAC	Community of Latin American and Caribbean States
CHF	Swiss franc
COA	Committee on Agriculture
COP	Conference of the Parties
CTD	Committee on Trade and Development
CWN	Capacity, willingness, and need
DAG	Development Agenda Group
EC	European Communities
ENB	Earth Negotiations Bulletin
EPA	Economic Partnership Agreements/European Partnership Agreements
EU	European Union
EURO	WHO European Region
FAO	Food and Agriculture Organization
FIELD	Foundation for International Environmental Law and Development
G-20, 33, 77, etc.	Group of 20, 33, 77, etc.
GATS	General Agreement on Trade in Services
GATT	General Agreement on Tariffs
GCF	Green Climate Fund
GDP	Gross domestic product
GEF	Global Environmental Facility
GHG	Greenhouse gas/gases
GNP	Gross national product
Gt	Gigatonne
HDI	Human Development Index
IMF	International Monetary Fund
IEA	International Energy Agency
IMO	International Maritime Organization
INC	International Negotiating Committee
IP	Intellectual property

IPCC	Intergovernmental Panel on Climate Change.
IPR	Intellectual property rights
IR	International relations
LDC Fund	Least Developed Countries Fund
LDCs	Least Developed Countries
LMDC	Like-Minded Developing Countries
LUCF	Land use change and forestry
MEF	Major Economies Forum on Energy and Climate
N4S	Need for support
NAMAs	Nationally appropriate mitigation actions
NBA	National Basketball Association
NDCs	Nationally determined contributions
NGO	Non-governmental organization
NHL	National Hockey League
NIEO	New International Economic Order
OECD	Organisation for Economic Co-operation and Development
OPEC	Organization of the Petroleum Exporting Countries
PTA	Plurilateral trade agreement
RCA	Relative comparative advantage
RCEP	Regional Comprehensive Economic Partnership
SBSTA	Subsidiary Body for Scientific and Technological Advice
ppm	Parts per million
SCCF	Special Climate Change Fund
SDT	Special and differential treatment
SIDS	Small Island Developing States
SPLT	Substantive Patent Law Treaty
SSG	Special Safeguard
SSM	Special Safeguard Mechanism
SP	Special Product
TFA	Trade Facilitation Agreement
TRIPS	WTO Agreement on Trade-Related Aspects of Intellectual Property Rights
TWN	Third World Network

UN	United Nations
UNAIDS	Joint United Nations Programme on HIV/AIDS
UNDP	United Nations Development Programme
UNEP	United Nations Environment Programme
UNESCO	United Nations Educational, Scientific and Cultural Organization
UNFCCC	United Nations Framework Convention on Climate Change
UNIDO	United Nations Industrial Development Organization
UNSC	UN Security Council
US	United States
USD	United States dollar
W2C	Willingness to contribute
WHO	World Health Organization
WIM	Warsaw International Mechanism
WIPO	World Intellectual Property Organization
WTO	World Trade Organization

1. The unmaking of special rights

Klaus Dingwerth, Clara Weinhardt, Julian Eckl, Simon Herr, and Till Schöfer

1.1 INTRODUCTION

We tend to think that rules are rules by virtue of their general application: because they apply to everyone in the same way. Yet, that is not the case. Once we look around, we will realize that special rights abound. What holds for some does not necessarily apply to all. The motives for treating those subject to a rule differently vary considerably. We can roughly sort them in to two groups.

In some cases, special rights *follow from the advantaged position* some actors hold. Here, some actors manage to reserve legal privileges for themselves because they have the power to do so. Even though democratic societies had accepted the idea of a universal suffrage – that every citizen may have their vote counted – many of them continued to exempt women from the right to vote for a long time. In international politics, UN members are elected for membership in the UN Security Council and, when their campaign succeeds, serve a two-year term. However, five member states that were particularly powerful when the UN was founded hold a permanent seat as well as the right to veto substantive decisions of the Council. If a normative justification for such privileges is given, it often rests on the notion that great powers also hold 'special responsibilities' that other states lack (Bukovansky et al. 2012).

In other cases, special rights are *granted to compensate for a disadvantaged position*. Here, differentiation follows from the normative idea that some forms of inequality are undesirable and should therefore be alleviated in some ways. In North American sports, the National Basketball Association (NBA) and the National Hockey League (NHL) allow teams that failed to qualify for the play-off matches in the previous season to have first choice among the most promising college players for the next season. In this way, differences in the competitiveness of teams are reduced rather than aggravated over time. Here, special rights may also reflect the self-interests of stronger teams, as the audience may lose interest in NHL or NBA matches if smaller teams become uncompetitive. In international politics, the relative financial contributions of economically weaker countries to the United Nations (UN) regular budget are lower than those of wealthier countries. For instance, the share of a country's financial contribution that depends on economic capacity is reduced proportionally for countries with a per capita income below the world average.

Other special rights for those in a disadvantaged position go even further. Electoral gender quotas, for example, strive for equal – and not just 'less unequal' – representation of women in national parliaments. Here, notions of distributive justice that focus on outcomes provide an important normative justification for granting special rights: the aim is to overcome existing inequalities. Where the principle of 'the same rule for all' does not lead to just results, differential treatment is thus necessary to establish substantive equality. In international politics, the movement to establish a 'New International Economic Order' (NIEO) in the 1970s prominently sought to correct existing injustices by eliminating the gap between developed and developing countries.

Taken together, the examples shed light on several key aspects of special rights. First, they point out that, if we look around carefully, special rights are pervasive. Rules frequently do *not* apply to everyone in the same way. Instead, they are carefully crafted to allow for differential treatment. Second, the special rights for some usually imply special obligations for others. Lowering financial contributions for some implies that others are obliged to contribute a higher share. Third, the justifications for granting special rights differ in important ways. Often, they are rooted in conceptions of justice. Yet, what is considered just can differ substantially and may range from claiming 'special responsibilities' based on unequal power positions to alleviating or correcting past or present inequalities.

In this book, we are interested in special rights (and corresponding obligations) that relate to the compensation for a disadvantaged position, namely in international norms of differential treatment for developing countries. The idea that developing countries are disadvantaged and should therefore be treated differently is a key pillar of the liberal international order of the post-war and postcolonial era, and special rights for developing countries have been institutionalized in multiple international regimes.

In our study, we examine to what degree this pillar continues to persist today. The main development we look at in this regard is global power shifts: the rise of Brazil, China, India, and other so-called rising powers. The growing economic weight of these countries challenges existing systems of special rights based on the binary distinction between developed and developing countries. Against this background, we ask: When and how have states contested the system of special rights for developing countries in view of the global power shift to Brazil, China, and India? And when and how have they adjusted such systems in response? In these questions, 'when' refers to the conditions under which we would expect contestation and adjustment to take place, whereas 'how' hints at the evolution and transformation of special rights. Moreover, we make an analytic distinction between the contestation and the adjustment of special rights. Two reasons guide this distinction. First, there is a temporal sequence in that contestation challenges the stability and robustness of a norm and, as such, often precedes more comprehensive forms of adjustment. Second, any contestation of international norms, whether discursive or behavioural, can already impact the interpretation of these norms. However, while contestation involves actors making demands, such demands may or may not be heeded. Here, the notion of adjustment focusses on those demands that correspond to the adoption of changes in the law or in wider social practices around which differential treatment is organized in a given regime.

Our general suspicion that systems of differential treatment may confront contestation as well as a pressure to adjust to new circumstances is motivated by four considerations. First, the countries designated as 'rising powers' have benefited from differential treatment for developing countries in the past. The developed countries, however, increasingly perceive rising powers as competitors in global markets. As a result, developed countries are likely to become more and more reluctant to grant Brazil, China, and India special rights. Second, at least some developing countries may concur that granting special rights to rising powers is not in their interest and runs counter to the idea of helping disadvantaged nations or creating a level playing field. Therefore, pressures could rise not only 'from above', but also 'from below'.

Third, rising powers themselves face complex incentives. While the material benefits associated with developing country status might make it attractive to maintain the lower social rank, moving up the status rank goes hand in hand with higher prestige. Considerations of status or prestige may thus lead rising powers themselves to relinquish some of their special rights and to accept the 'special responsibilities' that come with the status of a major power.

Fourth, and more generally, historical observations should lead us to expect that the global power shifts we currently witness will leave their traces in contemporary systems of differential treatment for developing countries. The development of these systems has been tied to world political transformations before (cf. Buzdugan and Payne 2016; 2020). Initially, the period of decolonization in the 1960s shifted the numerical balance in the international institutions created after 1945 towards 'newly independent states' and gave rise to calls for distributive justice. The normative push for a NIEO in the 1970s added further impetus to the request for special rights of developing countries. This facilitated the introduction of differential treatment provisions in global regimes, most prominently in the emergent environmental regimes and the global trade regime. Conversely, the end of the Cold War – coupled with the rise of neoliberal thinking – in the early 1990s had the opposite effect. In the trade regime, for instance, neoliberal ideology discredited differential treatment as unwelcome market distortion, which led to its weakening in the Uruguay Round negotiations (1986 to 1994). And as neoliberal ideas spilled over to other policy areas, they also informed discussions in global environmental governance, a field that has traditionally been open to the inclusion of differential treatment provisions for developing countries (Bernstein 2001; see also Farias 2023; Farias and Roger 2023).

To address our central questions, we examine challenges to as well as changes of differential treatment for developing countries between 1995 and 2020. Our empirical focus is on differential treatment norms in three international regimes. In the *trade regime*, we study the principle of special and differential treatment (SDT) which typically grants developing countries either permanent exemptions, flexibilities regarding liberalization obligations, or longer transition periods (see Chapters 2, 5, and 6). In the *climate regime*, we examine the principle of common but differentiated responsibilities (CBDR) which assigns different rights and obligations to developed countries and developing countries, both in terms of greenhouse gas emissions and financial assistance (see Chapters 3, 7, and 8). In the *health regime*, we focus on financing that is channelled through the World Health Organization (WHO). Here, we argue that differential treatment can be conceptualized as differentiation based on capacity, willingness, and need (CWN). Member states (and other actors) are expected to contribute according to capacity and willingness, and the financial resources raised are expected to be distributed based on need (see Chapters 4 and 9).

In the remainder of this introductory chapter, we proceed in four steps. In the next section, we summarize our central argument of an 'unmaking of special rights'. Subsequently, we define what we mean by international norms of differential treatment and systematically distinguish between different forms of 'unmaking' and 'resilience' of such norms (section 1.3). Finally, sections 1.4 and 1.5 lay out the explanatory framework and the methodological considerations that guide our study, respectively.

1.2 THE ARGUMENT IN A NUTSHELL

The central empirical argument we put forth in this study comes in three parts. First, we observe that the system of differential treatment for developing countries that we used to know is increasingly unmade. By 'unmaking', however, we do not mean that international norms of differentiation disappear, dissolve, or erode entirely. Rather, the unmaking of special rights refers to our observation that the system of differential treatment that we used to know is giving way to something new. This is particularly evident in the climate and trade regimes, in which differential treatment was traditionally built on the clear-cut distinction between developing countries as rights-holders and developed countries as duty-bearers.

Second, however, the unmaking of special rights takes on a variety of different forms. In the climate regime, for example, a main development is that differential treatment has become more nuanced and *individualized*, with each state's targets defined 'in the light of national circumstances'. In the trade regime, on the other hand, existing rules have remained in place, while new ones limit differential treatment to a narrower category of LDCs or to other sub-groups of developing countries. We conceive of this trend as a *fragmentation* of the system of differential treatment. In the health regime, which was more individualized than the other two from the outset, a type of change predominates that we did not anticipate in our original conceptualization of change but uncovered inductively: an *informalization* that goes hand in hand with the increasing relevance of voluntary budget contributions. While informalization also plays a role in the climate regime, it is particularly pronounced in the health regime and makes differential treatment, as such, increasingly voluntary and discretionary.

Third, pockets of resilience exist in all regimes, though to a different extent. In some cases, key aspects of the system of special rights are thus *preserved* despite pressures to expand or unmake them. In these cases, rising powers typically *graduate* – often gradually – and hence benefit to a lesser degree from differential treatment, thereby allowing the broader system of differential treatment to be maintained. And in a few cases, notably climate finance, we also witness developments that can be described as an *expansion* of special rights for developing countries. The tension between patterns of unmaking and resilience also sheds light on the ongoing processes of contestation over the differential treatment of developing countries.

How do we account for these patterns of unmaking and resilience that we observe across the three regimes that we study? Making use of an eclectic explanatory framework that draws on insights from three standard approaches of international relations (see section 1.4) meant that we have not found a mono-causal explanation. Our findings nonetheless suggest a predominant pathway of change: whenever 'developing countries' have become less united in their coalitions over time, and special rights less legitimate in light of global power shifts, the unmaking of the status quo became more likely. In addition, institutional factors not only affected the timing of unmaking, but also shaped the extent to which existing systems of differential treatment came under pressure to adjust to global power shifts. The more rigid a pre-existing approach, the more likely that it became subject to contestation.

Beyond our empirical cases, our findings speak to the growing academic literature on the consequences of global power shifts for the international order (Stephen 2017; Kruck and Zangl 2020). Yet, when we read or hear about global power shifts, the next big question is commonly what such shifts will mean for 'the West'. Will America decline? Will the liberal international order that Western powers have built in the wake of World War II survive? By contrast, our study takes a different perspective. Rather than asking what global power shifts mean for 'the West', we examine what they imply for a system of internationally recognized rules that explicitly sought to benefit developing countries – and hence various countries within the Global South. In doing so, we shed light on the evolution of a central, but under-researched pillar of the international order, namely special rights for developing countries.

In addition, our findings also speak to scholarly calls to unpack the category of the 'Global South' (Haug et al. 2021; see also Eckl and Weber 2007). Here, we find that the implications of the changes in differential treatment that we observe across the three regimes affect different groups of developing countries differently. Rising powers do not necessarily have the same stake in special rights of developing countries compared to other, smaller, developing country members of these global regimes. More specifically, our findings suggest that the unmaking of differential treatment for developing countries as a group will hit countries that are neither LDCs nor rising powers hardest. In contrast to LDCs, these countries have lost (and are likely to continue to lose) some of their access to preferential treatment. In contrast to rising powers, they may (still) lack the resources to adapt to a new international order with fewer and weaker special rights for developing countries.

Lastly, the differences that we observe across regimes shed new light on the evolving, multifaceted principles of global order as multilateral institutions adjust to global power shifts. In what Acharya (2017) refers to as a 'multiplex world order', differential treatment of developing countries is becoming increasingly multifaceted. Patterns of contestation and change follow not only from different pre-existing institutionalizations of these special rights in different regime contexts, but also reflect issue-area-specific constellations of interest. Moreover, how the rise of Brazil, China, and India affects developing country coalitions differs not only across regimes; it can also play out differently across issues within these regimes. Taken together, this suggests that the resulting fragmentation of the evolving global order reflects patterns of contestation that cut across 'North–South' conflict lines in some cases while reinforcing them in others.

1.3 CONCEPTUALIZING DIFFERENTIAL TREATMENT FOR DEVELOPING COUNTRIES

What exactly is differential treatment, and where does it come from? Like sovereignty or human rights, differential treatment of developing countries is a central pillar of the international normative order. Its historical origins lie in the post-World War II era in which the parallel processes of the Cold War and decolonization led to the categorization of countries into the 'First', 'Second', and 'Third' world, closely linked to the notion of a 'developed West' and an 'underdeveloped Third World' (Doty 1996: 151). The distinction between 'developed' and 'developing countries' subsequently began to become part of many international institutions, as more and more former colonies demanded recognition of the structurally disadvantaged position they faced.

In comparison to sovereignty or human rights, however, the special rights of weaker states have received little scholarly attention. Our study seeks to fill this gap. In the following sections, we propose an analytical framework that helps us trace when and how differential treatment of developing countries is changing. To capture and explain such change, we conceptualize *what* is changing (this section), *how* it is changing (cf. below), and *when* this is the case (section 1.4). The 'what' part of our research centres around international norms of differential treatment. We start with what we mean by 'differential treatment' and then go on to discuss our perspective on 'international norms'.

1.3.1 Differential Treatment: Systems of Special Rights and Obligations in World Politics

The first part of our central concept is *differential treatment.* We understand differential treatment schemes as bundles of norms that grant special rights to (groups of) disadvantaged parties and assign special obligations to (groups of) advantaged parties. Differential treatment schemes entail positive discrimination based on the acknowledgement that formally equal treatment would be either unjust or ineffective in view of other substantive goals. Differential treatment thus differs from other forms of special rights that reflect existing power asymmetries, such as the restriction of the veto right to the most powerful countries in the UN Security Council.

In the environmental law literature, Philippe Cullet (2003: 15, see also Cullet 1999; 2016) has proposed to reserve the concept of differential treatment for 'instances where, because of pervasive differences or inequalities among states, the principle of sovereign equality is side-lined to accommodate extraneous factors, such as divergences in levels of economic development or unequal capacities to tackle a given problem'. Cullet specifies furthermore that differential treatment 'refers to non-reciprocal arrangements which seek to foster substantive equality' (Cullet 1999: 551). While 'substantive equality' may be one possible motivation of differential treatment norms, we opt for a broader definition. This definition neither implies a specific justice-based motivation nor rules out those instances where the relevant actors may act based on a combination of justice considerations and self-interest. According to our definition, differential treatment exists where two conditions (a) and (b) are fulfilled:

(a) States are differentiated – either explicitly or implicitly – in terms of being in a 'disadvantaged' or 'advantaged' position in a given realm of world politics; *and:*

(b_1) The states perceived to be in a 'disadvantaged' position are either explicitly given or implicitly understood to have more extensive rights; *and/or:*

(b_2) The states perceived to be in an 'advantaged' position are either explicitly given or implicitly understood to have more extensive obligations.

We refer to countries with more extensive rights (b_1) as 'rights-holders' regarding differential treatment, while countries with more extensive obligations (b_2) are defined as 'duty-bearers' regarding differential treatment. However, as our analysis will show, there can be a gap between implicit assumptions that inform rule-making and empirical consequences of the rules states agree upon. Put differently, it is not always clear who will *empirically* benefit from differential treatment and who will have to contribute to it. Considering this tension and foregrounding the empirical consequences of rules, we will at times speak of 'beneficiaries' of differential treatment (rather than 'rights-holders') and of 'contributors' to differential treatment (rather than 'duty-bearers'). This wording is particularly relevant for the chapters on financial issues, for situations in which we analyse informal rules, and for those contexts in which change is a matter of degree (e.g. when a country benefits less than previously but remains a rights-holder). Finally, while we acknowledge that both sets of concepts have normative connotations, our intention in using them is primarily descriptive. In our effort to reconstruct how systems of differential treatment of developing countries adjust to global power shifts, we thus remain mostly agnostic about whether specific (groups of) countries *should* hold rights or obligations that others do not hold or whether they *should* contribute to or be able to benefit from financial assistance.

Beyond this general definition, differential treatment can be institutionalized in multiple different ways. We distinguish between *substantive* and *procedural* characteristics of differential treatment in this regard. The former captures what the special rights entail, the latter how a regime determines who counts as rights-holder or duty-bearer. Regarding substance, the legal literature commonly distinguishes between three categories of differential treatment (Rajamani 2006: 93–114). *Central obligations* refer to legal or political agreements that formulate differentiated rights and obligations for countries, for example in the form of different emissions' reduction targets. *Implementation flexibilities* cover prolonged implementation and/or reporting schedules, the

Table 1.1 *Central features of differential treatment*

Dimension	Description	Options
Substantive	Types of rules that provide for differential treatment	• Central regime obligations • Implementation flexibilities • Assistance
Procedural	Basis for the distinction between duty-bearers (or contributors) and rights-holders (or beneficiaries)	• Self-declaration (or auto-election) • Negotiated lists • Negotiated definitions or formulas

Source: Building on Rajamani 2006.

adoption of different base years in relation to which targets are measured, or a soft approach to noncompliance. *Assistance* includes financial support, technology transfer, and technological assistance as well as capacity building.

Differential treatment may also differ regarding the *procedures* to determine who counts as a rights-holder or duty-bearer regarding differential treatment in world politics. Building on Rajamani (2006: 165–168), we distinguish between three main approaches. While some regimes ground their decisions on a *list approach* (as in the climate regime), others build on *self-declaration* (as in the trade regime). Moreover, a third group of rights are based on specific *definitions* or *formulas* (as in the health regime). As we will see, this distinction has major implications for the possibility of graduation from the status as rights-holder to the status of duty-bearer. Definitions and formulas pave the way for an eventual graduation of rising powers while the status quo is otherwise preserved. By contrast, differentiation that is based on a list approach or on the self-declaration of states as 'developing countries' will often create pressure towards more profound adjustments that are far more difficult to obtain.

1.3.2 International Norms: Bundles of Interacting Social Expectations

The second part of our definition emphasizes that differential treatment for developing countries can best be understood as a set of *international norms*. In the international relations' literature, norms are commonly defined in terms of 'shared assessments' that incorporate a moment of 'normality' (in the sense of standardized behaviour) as well as of 'normativity' (or as 'oughtness' in the sense of socially desirable or morally appropriate conduct). International norms can then be defined as 'standards for the appropriate behaviour of states' (Finnemore and Sikkink 1998: 893), to a lesser degree also of non-state actors. Such standards may be codified in law and hence become *legal norms*. Yet, they do not need to and hence may also maintain their status as *social norms*.

Our understanding of such social norms further builds on recent strands in the constructivist literature that caution against a static conception of the content of international norms. This scholarship starts from the assumption that norms, even where they have become widely accepted, retain an element of instability (Stimmer 2019; Deitelhoff and Zimmermann 2020; Wiener 2008), not least because their meaning is subject to divergent interpretations. Seen this way, norms are understood as 'processes' driven by actors who – through discourses as well as behaviour – constantly shape and reshape their meaning (Krook and True 2012: 109; Sandholtz and Stiles 2008: 7; Stimmer and Wisken 2019).

In this context it is also important to point out that norms rarely come in isolation. Rather, they come at different levels of concreteness and are accompanied by specifying rules. This implies that the norms we discuss here should for the most part be thought of as bundles of norms that can be contested at an abstract or at a more concrete level. By the same token, we treat terms like rules and principles as conceptually equivalent to norms since they also refer to standards of behaviour.

Conceptualizing differential treatment as norms thus implies that they can be highly formalized and codified in international regimes, but also take shape in informal practices that reflect on shared understandings of oughtness or normality. In this way, our conceptualization departs from the legal perspectives that so far dominate scholarship on special rights for developing countries. This has a methodological implication as well: to assess both the status quo of differential treatment and how it may be changing over time, it is crucial to go beyond the analysis of law to include more informal processes of contestation (and change) through discourses or practices (Bode and Huelss 2018: 395). Doing so allows us to capture more subtle changes in differential treatment in meaning or interpretation.

In spite of this process-oriented understanding of international norms, we find it analytically useful to distinguish between contestation and adjustment. This pays tribute to the fact that the actors themselves can formulate far-reaching demands for change that may or may not be met through legal and/or practical changes, although the utterance of such demands does already impact on the interpretation of the contested norms.

To sum up, our conceptualization of international norms of differential treatment allows us to do four things. Based on the central features of differential treatment we describe, we can: i) *assess* the status quo of systems of differential treatment prior to the global power shift to rising powers and how they change over time, ii) systematically *compare* differences across international regimes, and iii) *explore* which aspects of differential treatment norms (see Table 1.1) are adjusted to global power shifts. Finally, iv) due to our understanding of international norms as social norms, we *anticipate* that these adjustments are not confined to legal changes only but could also manifest themselves in more informal processes of contestation.

1.3.3 The Unmaking and Resilience of Differential Treatment Norms

In this book, we argue that systems of special rights for developing countries are increasingly unmade in the wake of global power shifts. By 'unmaking', however, we do not mean that international norms of differentiation disappear, dissolve, or erode entirely (see also Percy and Sandholtz 2022). Rather, the unmaking of special rights refers to our observation that the system of special rights that we used to know is giving way to something new. As a result, we seek to describe not only the holes that are being punched in the 'old way' of doing things as states adjust the status quo, but also to sketch the contours of the 'new way' we identify. So, what could the new system look like?

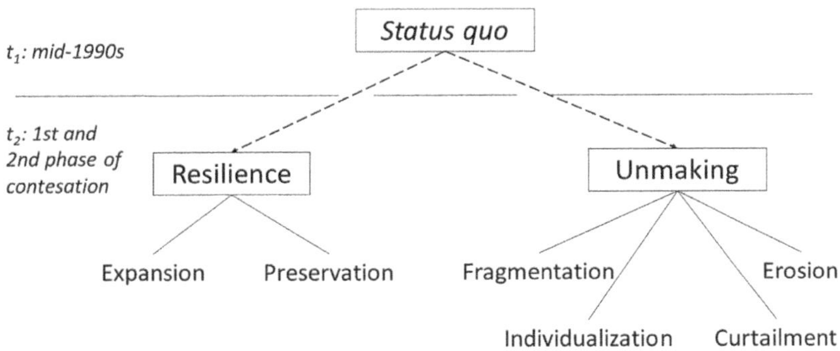

Figure 1.1 The spectrum of normative change

Figure 1.1 gives an overview of the different options. Based on a description of the status quo before the rise of emerging powers (t_1), we distinguish between situations at later stages (t_2) that we describe as 'resilience' and as an 'unmaking' of systems of special rights, respectively.

In the category of resilience, we include an expansion as well as the preservation of differential treatment schemes. An expansion would, for example, occur when rights-holders benefit more strongly from differential treatment. It may result from the fact that the coalition of states favouring differential treatment gains bargaining power as some of its members – notably Brazil, China, and India – become stronger. By contrast, preservation may either result from institutional 'gridlock' (Hale et al. 2013) or from the willingness of rising powers to graduate and hence no longer claim special rights for themselves.

However, differential treatment may also be unmade, since the states that 'grant' special rights may stop accepting the legitimacy of treating developing countries as a group as rights-holders – a group that includes rising powers. In relation to unmaking of special rights, we distinguish between four more specific forms. First, a *fragmentation* of special rights occurs when (some) special rights are increasingly limited to group(s) of rights-holders that are smaller than the group of developing countries. Here, 'increasingly limited' can mean that some rights are re-negotiated to apply to a smaller group. Such negotiations will often be difficult, however. As a result, fragmentation frequently implies what institutionalist scholars call layering: the old rules remain in place, but the newly added rules no longer apply to developing countries as a group. As some rights continue to apply broadly while others are reserved for smaller groups the landscape of differential treatment becomes more fragmented.

Second, we speak of an *individualization* of differential treatment when the system of differential treatment for developing countries is reorganized based on more fine-grained rules that assign each contracting party specific rights and obligations. Differential treatment is not abolished in these situations either: some states continue to contribute or receive more than others. Like in the previous case, however, the individualization detaches differentiation from a state's binary status as either a 'developing country' or a 'developed country', and the distinction between these categories loses some of its centrality as an ordering principle in international society. In fact, and in contrast to fragmentation, country categories become secondary or stop playing a role altogether.

Third and fourth, we include the *erosion* and *curtailment* of special rights as further forms of unmaking. Here, the legitimacy of differential treatment would be questioned as such so that we would end up with an 'unmaking' in the stronger sense – either more gradually and/or in only some areas of an international regime (curtailment) or more fully and across the entire institution (erosion). In sum, the forms of resilience and unmaking outlined in Figure 1.1 thus constitute a continuum. That continuum ranges from the possibility that differential treatment norms will expand (as Brazil, China, and India gain power) to the possibility of their erosion (as the states that 'grant' special rights stop accepting the legitimacy of differential treatment of developing countries altogether).

Like so often, however, the reality lies somewhere in between. In our study, we thus find many instances of fragmentation and individualization, combined with some instances of *preservation* and individual cases that can be described as a limited *expansion* of differential treatment norms. Weighing up the evidence, however, the balance of resilience vs. unmaking tilts towards the latter.

1.4 GLOBAL POWER SHIFTS AND DIFFERENTIAL TREATMENT: ACCOUNTING FOR VARIATION

In line with our abductive approach (cf. below: section 1.5), the previous sections have laid out a relatively comprehensive conceptual framework. What remains is the explanatory framework that can help us answer when (and how) contestation and adjustment occur. So, under which conditions would we *generally* imagine systems of special rights for developing countries to become contested and adjust to global power shifts? Standard approaches to theorizing international relations provide divergent answers. In the following sub-sections, we focus on rationalist, constructivist, and institutionalist theories. While rationalist theories highlight material interests and relative power, constructivist approaches would see the legitimacy of special rights and the status considerations of states as major explanatory factors. Both concur, however, that the strength and unity of bargaining coalitions are central. Finally, institutionalist theories emphasize how the specific ways in which systems of special rights have been institutionalized in the past enable or constrain normative change.

1.4.1 Rationalism: The Importance of Bargaining Power

Rationalist approaches expect adjustment of international institutions to result from the interplay of economic interests and political bargaining among states or coalitions of states (Zangl et al. 2016; Kruck and Zangl 2019; 2020). They start with the intuition that domestic interests and political contests over power determine outcomes in international politics. From this perspective, asking how international norms of differential treatment are adjusted to global power shifts already presumes that such shifts will affect the constellation of interests and power among relevant actors (Kruck and Zangl 2020). Three thoughts render this assumption plausible. They foreground the specific perspective of duty-bearers, the specific perspective of rights-holders, and the generic perspective of challengers of the status quo.

First, while all states may have an incentive to benefit from differentiation, being a net contributor appears rational only if short-term contributions can be expected to turn into a benefit in the long-run. This would, for instance, be the case if implementation flexibilities or exemptions help to foster the expansion of (or stabilize) markets for one's own goods and services. By enlarging the pie, special rights would then benefit not only those at the receiving end of concessions or assistance, but also those who make the concessions.

Such a link may appear plausible not least because market expansion has been a key motive for setting up and transforming international organizations throughout history. Applied to our study, the implication would be that developed countries would, as a rule, grant concessions to developing countries as long as doing so holds a promise to foster new markets or to manage conflicts resulting from market expansion (Murphy 1994). Yet, the willingness of developed countries to grant concessions ends where rights-holders of differential treatment become competitors. In the latter situation, rationalist approaches would therefore expect that established powers will seek to exclude rising powers from the benefits they have been granted in the past.

Second, systems of differential treatment must be acceptable not only to duty-bearers but also to rights-holders. At first, it may seem intuitive that rights-holders will always favour special rights. Yet, decisions go beyond the question of whether to include special rights and obligations in an agreement. Notably, once a decision to include such provisions has been adopted, debates will focus on the specific design of a system of differential treatment. Regarding this decision, the potential rights-holders of differential treatment schemes will favour those rules that match their individual preferences best. Notably, such preferences may diverge with respect to where the line between rights-holders and duty-bearers is drawn. All else equal, states that are on the receiving end of special rights will thus prefer a larger pool of duty-bearers and a smaller set of rights-holders. While more duty-bearers 'enlarge the pie' that can be distributed, fewer rights-holders mean that each rights-holder obtains a larger share. Regarding the rise of Brazil, China, and India as emerging markets, both aspects matter. Thus, other developing countries may benefit when Brazil, China, and India are no longer entitled to claim special rights and become duty-bearers instead.

Third, power matters. Thus, the fact that states have certain interests does not mean they will get what they want. Instead, their chances of getting what they want will depend on their bargaining power. Often, this bargaining power will itself depend on the ability of states to form coalitions with like-minded actors. Jointly, they may then be able to force those with competing interests to give in or make concessions. Regarding rising powers specifically, commentators have noted that these powers' ability to move existing international rules closer to their own preferences crucially depends on two factors: on their ability to undermine existing institutions, and on the credibility of their threats to do so (Zangl et al. 2016). In our case, however, the logic is usually the other way around: it is often developed countries who are the challengers – and hence need to be able to undermine the status quo – and rising powers (or developing countries) whose special rights are being challenged.

In sum, rationalist approaches ask two major questions: How does the constellation of interests in special rights for developing countries change once Brazil, China, and India begin to rise? And how does the changing constellation of interests – together with the power dynamics – affect the bargaining strength and unity of state coalitions in relation to special rights? In response to these questions, rationalist approaches suggest that, all else equal, international norms of differential treatment for developing countries will be unmade if the coalitions of states that challenge the existing system of special rights become more powerful relative to the coalitions of states that support that system. Conversely, if the strength and unity of coalitions on both sides remains relatively stable (or changes in favour of those supporting the existing system), resilience would seem a more likely outcome.

1.4.2 Social Constructivism: The Importance of Legitimacy

Social constructivist approaches start from a different assumption, namely that all social activity – and therefore also international policy-making – is embedded in normative or justificatory orders (Boltanski and Thévenot 2016; Forst 2017). From this point of view, existing differential treatment schemes need not only (or even primarily) be in line with state interests. Instead, they have to resonate with broader social norms of international or world society and with the identity constructions of the actors constituting that society. Three aspects are particularly relevant in this regard: the social construction of the 'developed/developing country' distinction, including the idea of solidarity among developing countries tied to it; the discursive contestation over the legitimacy of rising powers' claim to special rights; and the status considerations of rising powers themselves.

First, as a central ordering principle of world politics, the *developed/developing country distinction* 'has structured much of the thinking and practice in world politics over the past 80 years' (Alami and Dixon 2020: 3). The dichotomy has formed not only an analytical category ('sense-making'), but also (re)shaped our understanding of world politics ('world-making'). In brief, constructivists thus hold that labels like developed/developing or North/South (Eckl and Weber 2007), but also concepts such as rising powers as well as the lumping together of countries such as 'the BRICS', serve as 'means of making mental maps and claiming the future' (Sidaway 2012: 56). The contestation of differential treatment norms can be seen as a specific discursive terrain in which such maps are made and remade – and, maybe more importantly, one in which they are currently in flux (Farias 2019).

In brief, adopting a constructivist lens would thus imply that we remain sensitive to the possibility of discursive challenges to the validity of the distinction between 'developed' and 'developing countries'. The at least partial success of such challenges would be a necessary condition for the unmaking of special rights for developing countries as a group. Moreover, much like the rationalist approach, a constructivist lens would emphasize coalition unity. Yet, it would see the reason for such unity not in states' material interests, but rather in their identities as developing countries and in the idea of solidarity among developing countries.

Second, constructivist accounts put the *notion of legitimacy* centre stage. They maintain that even where they are backed by powerful interests, international orders require a certain level of social acceptance as rightful (Clark 2007). If we wish to understand how international norms of differentiation are made, unmade, or remade, we will need to examine the discursive processes in which legitimacy is collectively negotiated. Because legitimacy is always 'norm-referential', constructivist scholars will usually examine the processes in which the general validity, the specific meaning, and the concrete application of the norms that legitimate systems of special rights are contested (Stimmer 2019; Deitelhoff and Zimmermann 2020; Wiener 2009; Wiener and Puetter 2009).

Here, a social constructivist lens would thus lead us to assume that the unmaking of the system of special rights unfolds, at least in part, as a discursive process. Moreover, because discourses are conceived as 'webs of meaning', normative change does not occur in isolation. Instead, we would expect it to unfold in close interaction with other changes in the more immediate or broader ideational environment of which differentiation treatment norms are a part. Such changes – for instance, efforts to introduce a new norm or to link existing norms in new ways – may originate at different levels. They can 'trickle down' from fundamental norms to organization principles and standards, but they can also 'work their way up' from (multiple) standards to organizing principles and fundamental norms (Wiener 2018: 27–75). Where they 'trickle down' from meta-norms of global governance, we can expect relatively similar changes across different issue areas. By contrast, where normative changes 'work their way up', the developments will be more idiosyncratic in each regime.

What processes of contestation might global power shifts trigger on that basis? Notably, we can expect that the legitimacy of granting special rights to rising powers will be questioned and that, more generally, the legitimacy of existing systems of special rights will be affected by such contestation. As the examples given at the beginning of this chapter highlight, the justifications that undergird schemes of differential treatment vary considerably. They may, for instance, be based on the different roles actors play in a social system, on relevant disadvantages some actors face either temporarily or permanently, on different capabilities actors have, or on different current or historical contributions to a given policy problem. In the context of global power shifts, however, the values that 'rising powers' score on many of these criteria will change significantly over time. As a result, norms of differential treatment for developing countries as a group are likely to be unmade when the specific justifications on which such norms have been built in the past come under pressure. Challengers may then either question the general validity of systems of special rights or their specific application in a given international regime (Deitelhoff and Zimmermann 2020).

Third and finally, global power shifts also involve struggles about *status in international politics*. To the extent that rising powers seek recognition of their status – or are ascribed that status by others – we would expect existing systems of special rights to change more or less rapidly and severely. The reason is that where rising powers have a strong desire to be recognized in their new roles, they will commonly need to accept the norm of 'special responsibility' (Bukovansky et al. 2012) that comes with that role. This norm would normally require them to refrain from claiming special rights for themselves (although it would be consistent with seeking an extension of such rights for their fellow G-77 (Group of 77) members). Instead, status recognition is most likely to be tied to the acceptance of special obligations – and hence to the shift from 'rights-holder' to 'duty-bearer' within a differential treatment scheme.

In sum, because the epistemological stance most constructivists adopt favours interpretation rather than hypothesis-testing (Bevir and Blakely 2020), the core assumptions of constructivist approaches are less easily translated into specific hypotheses. Nonetheless, we can derive some building blocks for our empirical analysis. On a more general note, constructivist approaches suggest that international norms of differentiation will change when the normative order in which these norms are embedded changes, and they highlight discursive contestation as a central mode of change. More specifically, we can identify three specific areas in which discursive change will affect the contours of special rights for developing countries. In brief, significant adjustments to such systems will require at least one of the following: that the binary distinction between developed and developing countries – and with it, the idea of solidarity among developing countries – is successfully challenged; that the major justifications for differential treatment norms or for the application of those norms to rising powers lose some of the legitimacy they held in the past; and/or that rising powers actively seek a new status in the international order that is incompatible with a claim to hold special rights.

1.4.3 Institutionalism: The Importance of Opportunity Structures

So far, the theoretical approaches we have outlined would suggest that the processes of adjustment will need to find a balance between material interests (weighted by the power of coalitions) and legitimacy as well as status concerns. This would leave us with two kinds of 'win-sets' or 'zones of discursive agreement': those that result from the material interests of states, and those that result from notions of legitimacy states (and possibly other actors in world politics) hold. Based on this conception, we could expect that only such systems of differential treatment that are included in both win-sets stand a chance of being realized at all. Yet, these considerations presume that re-negotiations of existing norms and rules take place in isolation from the institutions we already have. From all we know about institutions, however, this assumption is flawed.[1]

Institutionalist theories thus assume that institutions have a 'life of their own'. For our purpose, an important starting point lies in the assumption that, once they have come into being, institutions act as important filters in processes of normative and regulatory change. Two mechanisms are particularly relevant in this context. The first mechanism is typically linked to institutional opportunity structures *within a regime's focal institution.* Here, rules can make normative change more or less likely. Some rules will make change more difficult – for example, when beneficiaries of the status quo hold a veto – and may thus give rise to calls for a more fundamental overhaul of the regime in the long-run. Others, by contrast, will favour a smoother transition – for instance, when they allow for a graduation of rising powers that leaves other elements of the system in place.

We can generally expect three types of rules to be key in this regard. First, the specific procedures for categorizing countries as 'duty-bearers' and 'rights-holders' matter. While differentiation based on lists or self-declaration requires political negotiations that will often be difficult, differentiation based on clear definitions and formulas makes adjustment largely automatic. Second, the presence or absence of sunset clauses matters. For example, differentiation organized in the form of transition periods exempts developing countries temporarily. In such a case, a renewal needs to be negotiated. By contrast, where sunset clauses are absent, it is not the prolongation but the *termination* of special rights that requires a new legal agreement. And third, the specific decision-making rules matter that apply to special rights and obligations: a successful (re-)negotiation may require the consent of a majority, of a supermajority, or even of all parties to an agreement.

The second mechanism is typically related to institutional opportunity structures *outside of a regime's focal institution.* Here, the theoretical notion of 'contested multilateralism' is helpful. It clarifies how the presence of outside options allows states to put pressure on norms and rules in a 'host regime'. In brief, Julia Morse and Robert Keohane define contested multilateralism as a situation that meets three criteria. First, the situation must include 'a multilateral institution (…) within a defined issue area and with a mission and a set of established rules and institutionalized practices'. Second, a group of states must be dissatisfied with the status quo of the existing institution, form a coalition (or use an already existing coalition), and 'shift the focus of its activity to a challenging institution with different rules and practices'.[2] Third, the activities of the challengers must result in conflict between the multilateral institutions in question or in a significant modification of the rules and institutionalized practices of the *status quo* institution' (Morse and Keohane 2014: 388).

In sum, institutionalist approaches stress that the specific institutionalization of differential treatment norms that predated the rise of Brazil, China, and India is likely to affect when and how such norms will become contested and be adjusted. More specifically, pressures on existing systems of special rights are 'filtered' in two important ways: first, by the specific ways in which international norms of differential treatment have been institutionalized within a given institution; and second, by the presence or absence of institutional layering and fragmentation that provides challengers with alternative options for pushing their agenda. In general, the institutional opportunity thesis therefore holds that systems of differential treatment will be adjusted in line with the challengers' demands if the existing institutional structure within or outside the regime's focal institution provides opportunities for change that challengers may exploit. Conversely, we would expect little or no adjustment where such opportunities are weak or absent.

1.5 METHODOLOGICAL APPROACH

What is our strategy to investigate when and how international norms of differential treatment have changed in the context of global power shifts? The previous section has already hinted that our approach is neither purely deductive nor purely inductive. Instead, we begin our empirical analysis based on a relatively small number of rather modest conceptual and theoretical reflections. We test and enrich these propositions in our case studies and subsequently tie together and reflect on them in the concluding chapter. As this research strategy mixes exploration and explanation, it could be subsumed under the broader umbrella of 'abductive' approaches to qualitative social research. In line with this approach, we seek to pay equal attention to description and explanation. While both are analytical tasks, the social sciences tend to prioritize explanation at the cost of solid description. As a result, we often rush to explain phenomena before we have fully grasped or mapped them. To avoid this pitfall, we aim to balance the 'when' and the 'how' of special rights and their unmaking in the three international regimes we examine.

This leads us to case selection. We address four points in this context. First, we will prepare the ground by explaining why our analysis proceeds at two levels – why some cases are situated at the *level of individual regimes* and why some cases are situated at the *level of specific conflicts* within those regimes. Second, we elaborate on the periodization that forms the basis for the *before-after design* of our paired case studies. Third, we discuss what rationale informed the *selection of individual regimes*. Finally, we will account for the considerations that led to the *selection of specific conflicts*.

With a view to the two levels at which we analyse change, we follow Joachim Blatter and Markus Haverland's (2012: 110) argument that,

> a full-fledged explanation based on the fact that causality plays out in time takes into account a longer period of time through which the overall causal process evolves, and much shorter periods of time in which causal conditions add up and/or interact in decisive ways for the further development of the causal process.

For us, the regime level allows us to examine the 'longer period of time through which the causal process evolves'. We do this through our analyses of the regime-level processes during which systems of special rights adjust to global power shifts between 1995 and 2020 (Chapters 2–4). By contrast, the study of specific conflict situations enables us to zoom in on 'much shorter periods of time' and to examine the interplay of different causal factors in specific situations (Chapters 5–9). The regime-level and the conflict-level chapters have one thing in common: both are based on a before-after design and thus comprise a systematic comparison of the time period before the rise of Brazil, China, and India and the time period thereafter.

Second, the distinction between our two time periods – a period 'before' and a period 'after' the rise of Brazil, China, and India – requires some elaboration. While any periodization will be contested to some extent, and while we discuss context-sensitive distinctions in each case study chapter, various developments between 2004 and 2013 can serve as a basis for a reasonably robust distinction. After a period of declining growth rates in the late 1990s, for instance, China's annual economic growth almost doubled from 7.6 per cent in 1999 to a staggering 14.2 per cent in 2007. In 2005, moreover, China surpassed the US as the largest emitter of greenhouse gases among states. Similarly, India maintained high growth rates of around 7.8 per cent between 2004 and 2007, a period in which US growth declined from 3.8 to 1.8 per cent.[3]

Moreover, the global financial crisis of 2007 and 2008 hit all countries hard. Yet, China and India (though not Brazil) managed to weather the crisis relatively well. Even though rising powers faced their own financial or political crises, this period has thus been described as 'a significant phase of power dispersal in the global economy away from the traditional Western centres of power' (Alami and Dixon 2020: 3). Finally, the accession of Xi Jinping to the leadership of the Chinese Communist Party (CCP) in 2012 and to the Chinese Presidency in 2013 is relevant because it marked the beginning of a new and more assertive foreign policy strategy. As a result, 2013 can be viewed as the end of a longer transition phase, with the financial crisis of 2007/2008 as a major catalyst (and hence turning point). We thus differentiate between two main time periods: a first one that begins in 1995 and ends around 2007–2008, and a second one that begins around 2008–2009 and lasts until 2020. While the exact cut-off year is regime- and context-specific, the key point is that the former period roughly demarcates the time 'before', and the latter 'after' the rise of Brazil, China, and India had become widely seen as a global power shift.

This brings us to the third point regarding case selection: the choice of trade, climate, and health as the regimes in which we implement this research strategy builds on two considerations. Here, examining the fate of differential treatment norms in the international trade (Chapter 2) and climate (Chapter 3) regimes allows us to incorporate evidence from two 'classical' cases of differential treatment while the inclusion of the health regime (Chapter 4) allows us to broaden our view beyond the usual suspects. This way, we can understand better how widespread systems of differential treatment are and to what extent and how they came under pressure as some of their traditional 'rights-holders' began to rise. Moreover, by including these three regimes, we can cover three divergent starting points regarding procedural characteristics. At the outset, the trade regime was dominated by self-declaration, the climate regime was primarily based on a list approach, and the health regime relied strongly on a formula approach. Our selection of regimes allows us to track how each procedural alternative developed over time.

Finally, the focus on specific conflicts over differentiation within each issue area is guided by three additional considerations. First, our interest is limited to conflicts over differential treatment norms. Second, to hold contextual factors related to the object of a conflict constant, we limit our search to pairs of conflicts – one before and one after the rise of Brazil, China, and India – over the same point of contention (Zangl 2008). Third, we aim for variation in relation to substantive characteristics of differential treatment norms. Thus, the case studies on trade in agriculture (Chapter 5) and on climate mitigation (Chapter 7) address conflicts over differentiated central obligations. By contrast, the case studies on transition periods related to intellectual property protection deal with implementation flexibilities (Chapter 6). Moreover, the case studies on climate finance (Chapter 8) cover special rights and obligations related to assistance. Finally, the case studies on financing for global health (Chapter 9) cover both central obligations and implementation flexibilities while the resources of the WHO can be used for either the provision of global public goods or for the provision of assistance. This variation allows us to cast the net wide and observe changing norms of differentiation not only in different issue areas, but also in relation to different types of differentiated legal obligations.

The methods we employ to reconstruct these changes are similar across the empirical chapters. They are best described as theory-guided process-tracing based on the analysis of primary sources and secondary literature. The theoretical guidance for the analysis comes from the analytical framework we outlined in this chapter. In terms of the primary sources, all chapters share a common basis in relying on the official outcomes of international meetings as well as on the existing records of negotiations. In some regimes, these are verbatim records, in others these are official summaries, in yet others these are summaries provided by an independent observer organization. Beyond this common basis, individual chapters use a mix of additional sources, including news reports, interviews with delegates and decision-makers, as well as participant observation. We reflect upon the insights gained from these different sources in the concluding chapter.

1.6 STRUCTURE OF THE BOOK

The following three chapters provide our regime-level analysis. In Chapter 2, Clara Weinhardt and Till Schöfer examine the implications of the rise of new powers in the Global South for a central principle of the global trade order: SDT of developing countries in the World Trade Organization (WTO). To trace the evolution of SDT in light of global power shifts, they analyse legal developments and processes of contestation. Their central observation is that resilience at the level of the legal framework goes hand in hand with the gradual unmaking of differential treatment for developing countries in the practices of day-to-day negotiations. Notably, special rights have increasingly been reserved for the narrow developing country sub-group of LDCs. The resulting fragmentation has contributed to the unmaking of the North–South distinction as a central ordering principle in global trade politics.

In Chapter 3, Klaus Dingwerth and Simon Herr examine the principle of CBDR. This principle has guided international climate politics as a fundamental norm ever since the adoption of the UN Framework Convention on Climate Change (UNFCCC) in 1992. In the context of global power shifts, however, the operationalization of this principle has become increasingly contested and eventually been subjected to a reinterpretation. Notably, the exemption of developing countries has gradually given rise to a more individualized as well as a more informalized system of differential treatment. At the same time, differential treatment has expanded in the area of climate finance.

Chapter 4 by Julian Eckl concludes the regime-level analysis with a focus on financing as the key area of differential treatment in the global health regime. It conceptualizes differential treatment in this context as a bundle of norms revolving around CWN. His analysis reveals that there have been repeated contestations to this norm bundle, ranging from an attempted unmaking to an attempted expansion of CWN. Against the background of these contestations, CWN has been subject to adjustments, but these have often contributed to a preservation of the *status quo ante* and hence to resilience. In particular, the attenuated and partial graduation of rising powers has increasingly been accepted while it was initially heavily contested. These developments have, however, been accompanied by an informalization that has ambivalent consequences and weakens differential treatment in a manner that was not anticipated in our initial conceptualization of change. In essence, it makes differential treatment increasingly voluntary and discretionary.

Chapters 5 to 9 each engage in the analysis of two specific conflicts over differential treatments in the three issue areas. In Chapter 5, Clara Weinhardt and Till Schöfer examine the agency that Brazil, China, and India have had in shaping the evolution of SDT in the WTO era by focussing on the case of agriculture negotiations. Analysing sectoral dynamics, country submissions, and interviews comparing the WTO Ministerial Conference in Cancún (2003) with Buenos Aires (2017), they argue that while rising powers sought to strengthen differential treatment for developing countries in Cancún they (inadvertently) contributed to its unmaking in Buenos Aires. A main reason was that their rise has led to increasingly divergent economic interests, particularly with the emergence of China and India as major subsidizers in global agricultural trade. Moreover, divergent interests have undermined South–South solidarity as rising powers claim access to special rights themselves. This has eroded the normative legitimacy of differential treatment in general and has allowed the erstwhile influential G-20 coalition of developing countries to disappear from the scene by the 2010s. Lastly, the inability of WTO members to formally reform differential treatment for developing countries has facilitated the delegitimation of SDT. These findings help to reassess how the contested status of rising powers in the WTO has led to a partial unmaking of special rights for developing countries and contributes to the recent deadlock in WTO negotiations.

Chapter 6 by Till Schöfer re-examines the coalitions and justificatory discourses that have shaped the evolution of differential treatment for LDCs in the WTO Agreement on Trade-Related Aspects of Intellectual Property Rights (TRIPS) throughout the WTO's ongoing negotiating round. Doing so allows the author to shed new light on debates about differential treatment as a central ordering principle in the trade regime. Empirically, Schöfer focusses on the conflict over the extension of transition periods – both for developing countries in general and, later, solely for LDCs – that featured prominently in WTO debates on intellectual property. Based on TRIPS Council minutes and supplementary interviews, he finds that special rights for the group of developing countries are unmade. At the same time, stronger coordination between Brazil, China, and India on TRIPS implementation flexibilities, coupled with growing opposition to a developed country TRIPS-plus push outside the WTO, has helped to prevent an erosion of more limited special rights for LDCs. In terms of the negotiation dynamics, forum-shopping and interests-based factors have played an important role in explaining the resulting fragmentation that characterizes recent developments on differential treatment in trade.

Chapters 7 and 8 examine conflicts over differential treatment in the climate regime. In Chapter 7, Klaus Dingwerth zeroes in on the unmaking of special rights in climate mitigation. Here, parties to the UNFCCC agreed at their first annual conference in 1995 that developing countries would be exempt from commitments to limit their greenhouse gas emissions. In 2011, the same parties – plus a few new additions – put an end to this exemption and launched negotiations for creating a new legal instrument that would be 'applicable to all parties' at COP-17 (Conference of the Parties) in Durban. The author reconstructs the complex dynamics that have led to both decisions. He argues that both outcomes are best understood as resulting from the intersection of specific coalition dynamics, specific institutional contexts, and a long-lasting contestation of differential treatment norms by some industrialized states.

In Chapter 8, Simon Herr examines the dynamics of two conflicts that have led to the gradual expansion of differential treatment in the area of climate finance. The first conflict arose in 2001 and led to the establishment of the Special Climate Change Fund (SCCF), the Adaptation Fund, and the Least Developed Countries (LDC) Fund. The second conflict peaked in 2009 and resulted in the establishment of yet another fund, the Green Climate Fund (GCF). The outcomes of both conflicts have led to increased financial transfers from North to South, and they have adjusted the ways in which decision-making about such transfers is organized in favour of the interests of rights-holders. This gradual expansion, the author argues, was possible because the G-77 and China remained united on questions of climate finance and because industrialized countries had to offer concessions if they wanted developing countries to accept commitments on climate mitigation.

Chapter 9 by Julian Eckl analyses two key moments during which the norm of capacity to pay (C2P) was contested – but ultimately remained resilient. The analysis shows that the norm, as such, enjoys broad support. However, reviewing the scale methodology (as an operationalization of the norm) and updating data (as a practical consequence of the methodology) have turned out to be contentious. In the first conflict, the G-77 and China were opposed to any changes that would redistribute financial obligations from developed to developing countries. At the WHO, the contestations resulted in implementation flexibilities. In the second conflict, the idea was accepted that such change was a legitimate consequence of the global economic shift as long as it was only induced by updated data. This altered understanding is noteworthy since the assessment rates of Brazil, China, and India had risen considerably at the time of the second case study. At the same time, China and India in particular remained beneficiaries of differential treatment. In both conflicts, the G-77 and China have proven a stable coalition that continues to include Brazil, China, and India. A common identity as developing countries, the institutional separation of the discussions on the scale methodology, and attenuated graduation are among the factors that have contributed to this stability and to the overall outcome.

Finally, in Chapter 10, Clara Weinhardt, Julian Eckl, and Klaus Dingwerth conclude by summarizing, comparing, and reflecting upon the most relevant observations we have made in the preceding chapters. First, they discuss our finding that systems of differential treatment for developing countries as a group are increasingly unmade, but that significant pockets of resilience remain. Second, the conclusion revisits the main theoretical expectations we have formulated in this introduction and discusses how we can best account for the pattern of unmaking and resilience we observe. Here, the authors illustrate the added value of our eclectic explanatory framework that goes beyond reducing the driving forces of change in global order to rationalist, ideational, or institutional perspectives alone. Third, the conclusion summarizes and compares the different forms of unmaking and resilience we observe across the three regimes before, fourth, concluding with a reflection on implications and avenues for future research. In doing so, the authors focus on debates on: i) global power shifts and international institutions, ii) global order and Global South countries, and iii) our comparative perspective on (nascent) debates on differential treatment in international politics.

NOTES

1. See also Zangl et al. (2016: 174) who argue that adjustment happens in ‘a path-dependent manner and will therefore not fully reflect states’ (current) common interests or the (current) power distribution among them’.
2. Lipscy (2017) importantly adds that the incentives to do so will vary across issues and with problem structure, as some issues like international finance call for a unified governance approach to function properly.
3. Based on World Bank Data, available at https:// data .worldbank .org/ (last accessed 16 June 2021).

PART I

Regime-level trends

2. The gradual unmaking of special and differential treatment in the trade regime

Clara Weinhardt and Till Schöfer

2.1 INTRODUCTION

Special rights of developing countries have, for decades, been a central feature of the trade regime.[1] As more and more colonies became independent and joined the trade regime in the 1950s and 1960s, calls to address their structurally disadvantaged position rose. This led to the introduction of special and differential treatment (SDT) for developing country members in the trade regime. Under SDT, developing countries receive flexibilities and exemptions from trade liberalization commitments, while developed countries are supposed to provide developing countries with more favourable access to their own markets. However, in the past decade, developed country members of the World Trade Organization (WTO) have increasingly called for a reform of differential treatment. This is because the United States (US) and other major developed country members are unwilling to grant special rights to countries such as Brazil, China, and India that traditionally belong to the group of developing country members. In 2017, the US Trade Representative Robert Lighthizer prominently complained at the WTO that '[t]here is something wrong, in our view, when five of the six richest countries in the world presently claim developing country status' (Lighthizer 2017).[2] The rise of economic powers in the Global South has thus engendered pressure to adjust the existing system of special rights for disadvantaged regime members.

Against this background, this chapter examines whether and how the global power shift towards rising powers has affected the evolution of special and differential treatment for developing countries in the WTO era. By mapping key changes in the SDT norm in the multilateral trade regime, we find that in the case of trade, *resilience* at the level of the legal framework goes hand in hand with the *gradual unmaking* of differential treatment for developing countries in the practices of day-to-day negotiations. In other words, we have not yet witnessed a reform of the overarching legal framework of differential treatment in the WTO in light of the rise of Brazil, China, and India. However, regime members have begun to adjust the way they incorporate differential treatment in newly negotiated decisions and agreements on specific issues. We observe three main patterns in this gradual unmaking of the status quo. First and foremost, special rights are increasingly limited to group(s) of rights-holders that are smaller than the group of developing countries – and exclude rising powers. Notably, this *fragmentation* implies that newly negotiated special and differential treatment provisions tend to be reserved for the narrow developing country sub-group of Least Developed Countries (LDCs). Second, more individualized forms of differentiation emerge, albeit only at the margins of the world trade regime. Third, in recent years, informalization increasingly leads to the selective use of the developing country status in WTO negotiations.

Within the larger framework of this book, this chapter shows that the global power shift has profoundly affected the system of special rights for developing countries in the trade regime. However, it has done so in unexpected ways: increasing bargaining power among the developing countries group has not led to the expansion of schemes of differential treatment, nor have we seen a single-format unmaking. Instead, special rights are unmade differently, and at different levels, for different groups of developing countries. This chapter shows that resilience at the level of the legal framework, i.e. the lack of reform of special rights' foundational framework at the WTO, does not prevent normative change at the level of day-to-day negotiations. Contestation – both discursively and in negotiation practices – has meant that the system of special rights is gradually changing. Our conceptualization of special rights as social norms (see Chapter 1) thus sets our findings apart from legal scholarship: while they emphasize individualization as the main trend in the legal evolution of SDT (Pauwelyn 2013; Lamp 2017), the fragmentation we observe signals more diverse types of unmaking.

The chapter is structured as follows: section 2.2 introduces the main characteristics of the special and differential treatment norm institutionalized in the WTO, as well as the distinction between the legal framework and day-to-day negotiation levels.[3] We then assess changes in differential treatment across two distinct time periods: 1995–2008 (section 2.3) and 2009–2019 (section 2.4). This periodization was chosen because the 2007/2008 financial crisis is commonly seen as a turning point after which the new realities of a multipolar world became apparent, since rising powers were more resilient throughout the crisis (see, for example, Christensen 2015). We thus roughly distinguish between a period 'before' and 'after' the rise of Brazil, China, and India. Doing so allows us to reconstruct how their rise has shaped the evolution and contestation of special rights for developing countries in the trade regime. In terms of sources, the chapter draws on WTO decisions and agreements concluded between 1995 and 2019, complementary secondary sources, and a set of five interviews conducted in Geneva in October 2019 and in August/September 2021 with trade officials and trade experts.

2.2 SPECIAL AND DIFFERENTIAL TREATMENT FOR DEVELOPING COUNTRIES: THE STATUS QUO PRIOR TO THE GLOBAL POWER SHIFT

This section delineates the main characteristics of SDT that were incorporated in the WTO upon establishment in 1995. This institutionalization resulted from the 1986–1994 Uruguay Round of trade negotiations and hence provides the background for our observations of changes over the subsequent decades. The agreements establishing the WTO codify the differentiated rights and obligations of developing and developed country members in the world trade regime. These agreements incorporate the earlier General Agreement on Tariffs and Trade, or GATT, from 1947 and its subsequent revisions.

In the following, we rely on this book's conceptualization of differential treatment norms that distinguishes between substantive and procedural dimensions (see Chapter 1: section 1.3.1). Lastly, we discuss how this level of the legal framework of differential treatment relates to the level of day-to-day negotiations.

2.2.1 The Substantive Dimension of Differential Treatment

The system of special rights endorsed in the WTO agreements cover – similar to other global regimes (Rajamani 2006: 93; 2012a: 611) – three categories: central obligations, implementation flexibilities, and assistance. In practice, these categories of differential treatment translate into exemptions and flexibilities regarding liberalization obligations, longer transition periods when implementing these obligations, and the provision of financial or technical assistance. Conversely, developed countries were supposed to take on 'more extensive obligations' by means of providing (non-reciprocal) preferential market access to developing countries.[4] These 'more extensive rights' for developing countries partly date back to the 1979 Enabling Clause and are part of the GATT (1994: Article XXXVI). The institutionalization of differential treatment thus partly predates the creation of the WTO.

Yet, the creation of the WTO also introduced a substantive reinterpretation of differential treatment under the SDT norm. During the GATT era, special rights were primarily limited to 'blanket' exemptions from liberalization and the vague obligation of developed countries to provide preferential market access to developing countries. The agreements establishing the WTO introduced longer transition periods for the implementation of the negotiated agreements and provisions on technical and financial assistance as new categories. Longer transition periods for developing country members were included in almost all WTO Agreements, with the exception of the Agreements on Pre-Shipment Inspection and on Anti-Dumping Procedures (Michalopoulos 2000: 20). Many agreements also contained explicit references to the provision of assistance for developing or LDC members. For instance, the Agreement on Trade-Related Aspects of Intellectual Property Rights (TRIPS 1994) contains provisions that call upon developed country members to provide assistance to facilitate technology transfer. These technical assistance promises were born out of the fact that many developing countries at the time did not have the necessary capacity to implement new liberalization initiatives (Michalopoulos 2000: 14). While blanket exemptions for developing countries were thus faded out, flexibilities regarding liberalization commitments continued to exist.

This shift away from exemptions was the result of increased criticism in the 1980s. On the one hand, developing countries realized that being exempt from liberalization commitments undermined their bargaining power vis-à-vis the developed world (Hudec 2010; Hoda 2009: 43–44). This led to a greater willingness of developing countries to participate in trade bargains in the Uruguay Round in order to pursue their trade priorities – mainly in agriculture and textiles – at the negotiating table. On the other hand, a growing neoliberal consensus questioned the hitherto reliance on exemptions from liberalization commitments as viable strategy for economic development (VanGrasstek and Sauvé 2006: 854; Kessie 2007: 19). By 1995 the constitutional basis of WTO was established and incorporated special rights for developing countries comprising flexibilities regarding central obligations, longer transition periods, and financial and technical assistance.

2.2.2 The Procedural Dimension of Differential Treatment

The SDT norm in the trade regime centres on the distinction between developed and developing countries, allowing countries to self-declare their status. This implies that no graduation mechanism exists.

2.2.2.1 Who counts as a rights-holder?

Systems of differential treatment not only define what differentiated rights and obligations consist of, but also determine who counts as a rights-holder or duty-bearer. Here, two aspects are central: first, which group of countries is considered disadvantaged, and hence, a rights-holder of special rights? Second, what criteria should be used, if any, to determine who belongs to the groups of countries deemed as rights-holders or duty-bearers? While the trade regime's focus on developing and developed countries is common in world politics, the way in which status questions are institutionalized remains unique.

The main distinction between rights-holders and duty-bearers is a loose binary distinction between the groups of developed and developing countries.[5] Special legal consideration of developing countries was justified with reference to the particular needs of 'those contracting parties the economies of which can only support low standards of living and are in the early stages of development' (GATT 1947: Article XVIII: I, cited in Broude 2006: 255). Similarly, the 1979 Enabling Clause states that (GATT 1979: para. 3c; italics added)

> [a]ny differential and more favourable treatment provided under this clause ... shall in the case of such treatment accorded by developed contracting parties to developing countries be designed and, if necessary, modified, to respond positively to the *development, financial and trade needs* of developing countries.

The focus on developing countries as rights-holders means that special rights apply to a majority of regime members: when the WTO was created in 1995, more than two-thirds of its 128 members counted as developing countries.

While the distinction between developed and developing counties has been a common feature of differential treatment norms in world politics, the trade regime is quite distinct in its differentiation approach. There are no criteria that define who belongs to the group of developing or developed countries. Instead, differential treatment relies on what Rajamani (2006) refers to as the auto-election approach (see Chapter 1: section 1.3.1): states can simply self-declare their status as developing country members of the WTO. This approach dates back to the 1970s. To some extent, the Cold War separation of global politics into three worlds informed these categories – the 'First World' of free industrialized countries, the 'Second World' of communist industrialized countries, and the 'Third World' of underdeveloped, non-industrialized countries (Weinhardt 2020). Against this background, the practice of self-declaration in the world trade regime was seen as a political means to strengthen solidarity across 'Third World' countries (Heron 2013: 22).

Apart from developed and developing country members, there is one other legal category that is formally recognized as holding the right to differential treatment in the multilateral trading system: the group of LDCs (cf. e.g. GATT 1979: para. 8). The Enabling Clause (1979) stipulates that its provisions apply to '[s]pecial treatment on the least developed among the developing countries in the context of any general or specific measures in favour of developing countries' (GATT 1979: para. 2d). It is notable that differential treatment for LDCs was not designed as a competing norm, but as complementary to the central norm of SDT for all developing countries. However, differential treatment designed only for LDCs plays a minor role in the status quo scenario of the mid-1990s. The agreements establishing the WTO contain 72 different SDT provisions for developing countries as a group, but only 17 provisions applicable to LDCs (Michalopoulos 2000: 17).[6] The basic principle is that developing countries as a group hold special rights – without further differentiation among them.

2.2.2.2 No graduation criteria

The practice of self-declaration also implies that there are no clear criteria that indicate when members graduate from their status as developing countries. Graduation has to be negotiated. Again, this practice dates back to the GATT era and has, from the onset, opened the door for political contestation. In the early days of the GATT, former colonies often cautioned that members of the 'First World' unfairly benefited from differential treatment. Brazil, for instance, complained in a GATT General Council debate that 'some countries which were in an advanced stage of development now considered themselves developing countries' (GATT General Council 1971: 10). As an example, Israel and Spain at the time claimed access to preferential trading schemes under the SDT norm as developing countries. In the 1980s, the focus shifted towards 'Third World' developing countries, in particular in East Asia, that posted high economic growth rates (Alessandrini 2010: 119–121; Preeg 2012: 125). However, attempts to introduce graduation mechanisms from developing country status never took hold. [7] By 1995, none of the 'Third World' developing country members had ever self-declared their graduation towards developed country status.

2.2.3 Differential Treatment and the Set-up of WTO Negotiations

While the agreements establishing the WTO provide the constitutional framework for differential treatment in the trade regime, the practices of negotiation rounds partly shape its application and evolution. The WTO serves as a negotiation forum in which its members can negotiate further liberalization measures – in addition to those laid down in the agreements establishing the WTO. To do so, the WTO launches so-called major negotiation rounds, which span several years. The Uruguay Round which led to the establishment of the WTO, for instance, lasted from 1986 until 1994. Each round is organized around biennial Ministerial Conferences, in which trade ministers represent all regime members. These Ministerial Conferences constitute the 'topmost decision-making body of the WTO' (WTO n.d.-a). Decisions are normally taken by consensus, without voting. To prepare for these negotiations, ambassadors and delegates of regime members regularly come together in trade negotiation committees. These committees focus on the specific areas of the round, such as agriculture or trade in services.

Each negotiation round follows a specific mandate, which results from a Ministerial Conference. WTO members, for example, initiated the current negotiation round, the Doha Development Round, at their fourth Ministerial Conference in Doha in 2001. The outcomes of these conferences can come in the form of various different types of decisions and agreements. These include, for instance, new liberalization agreements in areas that were so far not covered, or updates of existing deals.

Taken together, this implies that differential treatment is, first, part of the agreements establishing the WTO. This level of the legal framework, however, is complemented by the body of new decisions and agreements that are added during an ongoing negotiation round. Differentiated rights and obligations in the WTO context are thus characterized by a multitude of different agreements and decisions, rather than one central manifestation of the SDT norm. The WTO Secretariat itself estimated that WTO Agreements so far include 139 provisions of differential treatment for developing countries (WT/COMTD/W/239 of 12 October 2018).[8]

2.3 PROCESSES OF CONTESTATION IN THE EARLY WTO ERA (1995–2008): RESILIENCE OF DIFFERENTIAL TREATMENT

How did differential treatment for developing countries change in light of the nascent rise of Brazil, China, and India? In this initial period of WTO negotiations, Brazil, China, and India's distinct economic positions were not yet as apparent as they became in the aftermath of the global financial crisis of 2007/2008. However, economic heterogeneity within the developing country group has always existed and was beginning to increase. China, in particular, took on a distinct economic position: it's gross domestic product (GDP) at purchasing power parity accounted for USD 9.41 trillion, or 14.5 per cent of the world's GDP, in 2006. India and Brazil's GDP were USD 3.63 trillion and USD 1.58 trillion at the time (Cost and Wildrick 2007: 14). While Brazil, China, and India together held a share of around 24 per cent of world GDP, Africa's share accounted for only 2.1 per cent (figures for 2006, OECD 2011). These signs of the global power shift in the making could have contributed to the unmaking of a system of special rights that relied on the binary distinction between developed and developing countries. In particular, the rise of Brazil, China, and India could have led to questions concerning their status as rights-holders. However, we find that differential treatment remains largely resilient in this initial period of multilateral trade negotiations. There are no substantive changes at the level of the legal framework – and hence the design of differential treatment – nor does the SDT norm transform substantively through processes of contestation in day-to-day negotiations. However, the onset of normative change becomes apparent during China's accession negotiations prior to 2001 in the discussions surrounding its contested status as a developing country.

2.3.1 The Legal Framework of Differentiation: No Reform, Contestation Without Effect

The early WTO era does not witness explicit attempts to reform the overarching legal framework of differential treatment. As a result, contestation geared towards the unmaking of differential treatment of developing countries cannot be observed. Conversely, when members of the world trade regime advocated for the necessity to adjust the foundation of these special rights, these attempts were geared towards their expansion. In short, the period that we classify as largely 'before the rise' of Brazil, China, and India is characterized by resilience at the level of the legal framework. In the following sub-sections, we discuss relevant legal developments and reform debates. Notable developments relate to the procedural dimension of the SDT norm – and how to define its rights-holders – as well as to the substance of differentiated rights and obligations.

2.3.1.1 Reluctance to define developing country status

A key aspect of the differentiation approach in the trade regime is the absence of a definition that could be used to determine developing country status (see section 2.2). Instead, countries can self-declare the status they allegedly have. This approach has occasionally led to conflicts, even in this earlier period of the multilateral trade regime, 'before the rise' of Brazil, China, and India. The self-declared developing country status of emerging countries became part of legal disputes at the WTO's Appellate Body, the organization's dispute settlement body. However, what is remarkable is that each time the Appellate Body could have ruled on developing country status, it carefully avoided taking a position that could be construed as a definition of developing country status. Similarly, when China joined the WTO, its status did not explicitly become part of its accession protocol. This indicates resilience via the preservation of the auto-election approach.

Questions related to the definition of developing country status were invoked in a total of three legal disputes among WTO members in this period. However, each time the Appellate Body avoided taking a position on this issue. It thus side-lined the complainant's concerns about the ways in which the auto-election approach allows rising powers to self-declare themselves as rights-holders of differential treatment. In a case on US steel safeguards

(2002/3, DS248), China for instance argued in favour of SDT treatment as a developing country member and contested the US's reliance on criteria stemming from the Generalized System of Preferences to determine its status. US–Chinese frictions thus centred on the US' implicit attempt to articulate formal criteria for China's status as a rights-holder of SDT, but the Appellate Body avoided ruling on this aspect of the dispute. During an Appellate Body case involving South Korea (2001, DS161 Korean Beef Case), the European Union (EU) representative in turn disagreed with South Korea self-declaring as a developing country member. However, the Appellate Body again did not rule on this aspect. In the absence of new case law on developing country status, the auto-election approach thus remained legally unchanged.[9]

Similar patterns of avoiding reinterpretations of the overarching legal framework of differential treatment – i.e. avoiding defining developing country status more clearly – became apparent during China's WTO accession negotiations in the late 1990s and early 2000s. China attempted to officially join the WTO with the status of a developing country. However, this demand became one of the key planks of contention in its accession negotiations, given the status is tied to less extensive liberalization obligations compared to developed country members. The US, in particular, claimed that China's position as a major global trader prevented it from entering the WTO with developing country status (Bhala 2000: 1489), and thus with access to SDT. The Peterson Institute for International Economics at the time summarized the US position as follows: '[t]he United States has argued … that significant parts of China are sufficiently developed that it would be folly to permit China the additional leeway granted developing countries' (Noland 1995). Conversely, the EU and Japan were more willing to recognize the developmental challenges of China.[10] In 1996, the EU tried to ease political tensions and to defuse at least the rhetoric over China's status as a developing country: it dropped the firm reference to developing country status and began to talk in terms of a case-by-case, or sectoral, approach to China's accession.

China then accepted a compromise: it gave up its demand for comprehensive developing country status, and agreed to negotiate transition periods only for industrial sectors genuinely in need of SDT owing to serious adjustment difficulties (Bhala 2000: 1489; Eglin 1997: 494). However, this did not prevent China from self-declaring its status as a developing country member, as summarized by the head of the Chinese delegation at a working group meeting in 2001:

> As we have emphasized consistently at various occasions in the past, although great progress has been made on China's economic development in the past two decades, we still firmly believe that China is a developing country. The position we have taken to accede to the WTO as a developing country is not only a reflection of the actual economic level of China at the present stage, but also our political choice. (WTO 2001)

Nevertheless, WTO members avoided any legal decision that would affect the legal framework of differential treatment, which proved highly resilient. In the end, China was not allowed to officially join as a developing country member and its accession protocol did not clearly define its membership status.

While the definition of developing country status remained unchanged in this initial period, some notable developments took place at the margins: conflict emerged about whether or not to allow developed countries to differentiate among countries within the developing country group. This conflict relates to the level of the legal framework of differential treatment because the GATT framework itself did not clearly specify whether differentiation between rights-holders – the group of developing countries – is permissible (see Ukpe and Khorana 2021: 5–6). The Appellate Body then positioned itself on this question of internal differentiation within the developing country group. Its 7 April 2004 report on a dispute between India and the European Union confirmed that WTO members' voluntary preferential market access schemes do not need to include all developing country members – as long as they are open to all similarly situated developing countries (Pratap 2004). However, since this ruling only applied to voluntary measures of differential treatment in the form of preferential market access schemes, it did not undermine the dominant practice of linking differential treatment measures to the entire group of (self-declared) developing country members.

2.3.1.2 Reform debates focus on the possible expansion of special rights

In contrast, discussions on the reform of differential treatment focussed on how to render SDT more effective. A major concern of developing countries in this period was the insufficient implementation of SDT provisions that were already concluded in the early 1990s. In particular, the myriad of differentiation provisions contained in 1994 legislation raised important questions about the practical implementation of these measures. Many provisions had barely ever been used, as demonstrated by the Customs Valuation Agreement, whose nebulous Annex III:5 has never been invoked. Similarly, the lack of clarification regarding the definition of SDT in the General Agreement on Trade in Services (GATS) Article V made implementation hazy. These examples indicate that SDT provisions were often added in an ad hoc and under-defined manner in 1994 legislation, allowing several measures to yield little or no practical consequences. This raised concerns amongst developing country members at the turn of the century. Indeed, the 'built in agenda', which sought answers to such issues, became a prominent theme in WTO negotiations in the late 1990s.

Arguably, these reform proposals were geared towards the expansion of differential treatment in the world trade regime. As recalled by the G-90 developing country coalition[11] on the occasion of the WTO's Sixth Ministerial Conference: 'in paragraph 44 of the Doha Work Programme, [WTO] Members agreed to *strengthen* the Special and Differential Treatment provisions and make them more precise, effective and operational' (G-90 2005: para. 9; italics added). Furthermore, they proposed an extension of the existing legal framework to ensure the proper implementation of differential treatment: 'we call for the elaboration and conclusion of a development framework agreement in order to implement the mandate of incorporating the development dimension into the architecture of the WTO and the multilateral trading system' (G-90 2005: para. 13). However, in the end, we see no meaningful changes to make SDT more effective. Reform proposals did not find majority support, especially as established powers remained sceptical. The legal framework of the SDT norm as such proves highly resilient – and largely unaffected by global power shifts – in this initial period.

2.3.2 Day-to-day Negotiation Practices: The Application of SDT Remains Resilient

When considering the day-to-day negotiation practices, normative change could have become apparent – despite resilience at the level of the legal framework. Yet, we find that newly negotiated agreements and decisions in this period continue to primarily treat developing countries as a homogenous group that includes rising powers. There are few signs of the type of individualization and fragmentation of special rights that we witness in the later period. Notably, resilience in negotiation practices is facilitated by high levels of legitimacy concerning the existing system of differential treatment – which seems largely unaffected by the nascent rise of Brazil, China, and India. After a short review of the normative context, this section discusses developments related to the substantive and procedural dimension of the SDT norm in WTO negotiation practices.

2.3.2.1 Normative support for the existing system of special rights remains high

The legitimacy of granting differential treatment to developing country members remained largely intact in the 1990s and early 2000s – despite steady criticism. The launch of the Doha Development Round in 2001 reflected this general endorsement of the SDT norm and was accompanied by the recognition that the 'majority of WTO members are developing countries', coupled with the promise 'to place their needs and interests at the heart of the Work Programme' (WT/MIN(01)/DEC/1 of 20 November 2001: para. 2). More explicitly, the Doha Ministerial Declaration (2001) 'reaffirm[ed] that provisions for special and differential treatment are an integral part of the WTO Agreements' (para. 41) and, for instance, reiterated in its section on agriculture that 'special and differential treatment *for developing countries* shall be an integral part of all elements of the negotiations' (para. 13; italics added). The drivers behind this new development focus were twofold: on the one hand, negotiation breakdown and clashes involving anti-globalization protestors at the previous Seattle Ministerial Conference (1999) warranted the presentation of the newly established WTO as a functioning organ of equitable trade legislation. On the other, the September 11 attacks of 2001 raised concerns that a lack of regional economic development could foster the type of political radicalization that would in turn engender potential terrorism (Kleimann and Guinan 2011). The early 2000s subsequently marked a clearly unique moment for a solidaristic, or at least development-oriented, approach to global trade policy-making.

2.3.2.2 Substantive dimension: no major changes

In light of strong normative support, SDT continued to feature prominently in the decisions and agreements reached in the late 1990s and 2000s: out of 12 agreements and decisions, 11 contain SDT provisions. However, a major breakthrough in the negotiation round did not occur. The substantive agenda issues, including those linked to the development promise of the Doha Round, remained unresolved. A favourable normative environment thus did not translate into a meaningful expansion of special rights for developing countries at the level of negotiations. The breakdown of the WTO Ministerial Conference in Cancún in 2003 prominently illustrates that a favourable normative environment did not suffice to move beyond the status quo. In Cancún, rising powers, and in particular India and Brazil, were responsible for setting up a broad developing country coalition, the G-20, to push for an extension of special rights in agriculture (Hopewell 2016). In parallel, a second broad coalition of developing countries, the G33, promoted new SDT mechanisms that would allow developing countries to protect their markets against liberalized trade flows. While rising powers were able to effectively block proposals by the established powers (Heldt 2017: 20), they were not powerful enough to push their own SDT-related agenda through (for a detailed discussion of the conflict in Cancún, see Chapter 5: section 5.3). While most WTO decisions and agreements concluded during this initial period contain SDT provisions, we thus observe the *preservation* rather than the *expansion* of special rights for developing countries. The decisions and agreements that were not concluded, in particular regarding agriculture, stand for the failed expansion of special rights for developing countries. In 2007/2008, WTO negotiations again broke down in response to disagreements between the EU, the US, Brazil, China, and India over market opening in agriculture and industrial goods.

2.3.2.3 Procedural dimension: developing countries as main rights-holders

Regarding the procedural dimension of the SDT norm, there are few signs of adaptation concerning the binary developed/developing country distinction as a basis for differentiation in the few newly negotiated agreements and decisions. Such changes regarding the procedural dimension of differential treatment could come either in the form of fragmentation or individualization. The former would imply a shift towards competing, narrower sub-groups of developing countries, while the latter stands for individually differentiated commitments within the developing country group.

First, there are few signs of fragmentation. The North–South distinction is much more prevalent compared to competing groups of 'disadvantaged' WTO members, specifically the group of LDCs: in the initial years, there were only four decisions that limited differential treatment to the group of LDCs out of 26 legal documents. This share rose slightly in the 2000s, accounting for 25 per cent of differential treatment. Taken together, we find that LDC-only legislation made up only 15 per cent of documents with SDT in the first time period.[12]

Second, most manifestations of the SDT principle treat developing countries as a homogenous group. The 1995 Agreement on Agriculture, for instance, grants all developing countries a 10 per cent *de minimis* exemption for the provision of domestic support, while developed countries only receive a 5 per cent *de minimis*. This binary differentiation does not become subject to further negotiations in this period, and thus remains unchanged in negotiation practices. Similarly, one of the few decisions reached, the Transparency Mechanism for Regional Trade Agreements (2006), relies on the binary distinction between developed and developing country members. The latter group has access to differential treatment in the form of extended transition periods. The transparency mechanism stipulates that the time period in which information on regional trade agreements needs to be submitted to the WTO is twice as long for those agreements concluded between developing country members only – as opposed to agreements that included developed countries (WTO 2006: para. C).

One partial exception to the rule is provided by China, which had to accept less extensive – and hence individualized – rights compared to other developing countries when it acceded to the WTO in 2001. In areas in which China considered itself to be competitive enough for instance, it agreed to accept more extensive obligations compared to other developing countries. This was reiterated by the head of the Chinese delegation in 2001, who stated that 'where China has already had the capability to implement the obligations as all WTO

Members, we deem not necessary for China to enjoy preferential treatments to the developing countries as provided for in the relevant WTO agreements' (WTO 2001). In effect, China negotiated developing country exemptions and flexibilities in some areas, but had to take on more extensive obligations on issues such as the protection of intellectual property rights, phasing out industrial subsidies, transparency, safeguards, etc. compared to other developing countries that joined earlier or later (Bhala 2000: 1487; Kanungo 2011: 309). Conversely, Brazil and India's liberalization commitments, as set out in the Uruguay Round Agreements, are in line with those of other developing country members, and were not re-negotiated during subsequent trade negotiation rounds. The partly individualized differential treatment of China is thus primarily the result of its late accession to the WTO, rather than representative of a more general trend in this initial period of multilateral trade negotiations.

2.3.3 Summary of Developments (1995–2008)

This initial period of the WTO era shows few signs of normative change concerning the evolution of differential treatment for developing countries in light of the nascent rise of Brazil, China, and India. Neither does greater heterogeneity among developing countries lead to reform debates about the existing system of differentiated rights and obligations, nor do day-to-day negotiations reveal a changing pattern regarding their substantive or procedural dimension. The group of developing countries remains the central set of rights-holders of special rights in the WTO, and attempts to differentiate rights-holders within this group remain marginal and mostly focussed on China. Special and differential treatment is thus largely characterized by resilience. At the same time, the attempts of developing countries – often led by Brazil, China, and India – to expand differential treatment are unsuccessful. Deadlock in Cancún is symptomatic of the decisions and agreements that WTO members failed to reach, and that would have substantively expanded the special rights of developing countries. This pattern of deadlock intensifies in the latest decade of WTO decision-making to the extent that it starts to contribute to the unmaking of special rights.

2.4 PROCESSES OF CONTESTATION IN THE LATEST WTO DECADE (2009–2020): THE GRADUAL UNMAKING OF SPECIAL RIGHTS

In the aftermath of the global financial crisis of 2007/2008 the economic rise of Brazil, China, and India became much more apparent. While the countries gained in economic power, and hence clout at the negotiating table, their rise – paradoxically – contributed to the *unmaking* of special rights for developing countries. Contestation increased sharply: Should rising powers still be allowed to benefit from special rights reserved for developing countries? We find that the notable absence of reforms regarding the practice of self-declaration – and hence resilience at the level of the legal framework – goes hand in hand with the delegitimization of the status quo of differential treatment in day-to-day negotiation practices. This, in turn, contributes to the unmaking of the status quo in the practice of WTO negotiations in three ways: first, the system of special rights becomes highly fragmented, with SDT provisions focussing increasingly on the narrow sub-group of LDCs. Second, more individualized forms of differentiation become more prominent, albeit only in selected issue areas. Third, informalization becomes more important, as it allows rising powers to gradually take on more obligations without graduating from developing country status.

2.4.1 The Legal Framework of Differentiation: No Reform, but High Levels of Contestation

In this more recent decade of multilateral trade policy-making, the rise of Brazil, China, and India goes hand in hand with increased pressure to reform the existing system of special rights for developing countries. Notably, developed country members push for the introduction of clear criteria to define developing country status. Such contested reform proposals ultimately seek to prepare the ground for the graduation of rising powers from their (hitherto self-declared) status as rights-holders regarding differential treatment. Yet, while the level of the legal framework of differential treatment becomes hotly contested, its legal framework remains resilient and is not adapted to the global power shift – in contrast to the climate regime (see Chapter 3). The auto-election approach remains formally unchanged and rising powers are able to remain developing country members, and hence rights-holders, of differential treatment. Thus far, the WTO officially continues to declare that (WTO n.d.-b):

> There are no WTO definitions of "developed" and "developing" countries. Members announce for themselves whether they are "developed" or "developing" countries. However, other members can challenge the decision of a member to make use of provisions available to developing countries.

The absence of notable legal developments, however, does not imply that the normative foundation of differential treatment remains uncontested. As this section shows, central themes in ongoing reform debates are critiques of auto-election, calls for graduation, and attempted definitions of developing country status. Contestation related to the legal framework of SDT thus focusses on procedural aspects, and earlier debates about how to make the SDT norm more effective (see section 2.3.1) are crowded out.

2.4.1.1 Calls for graduation and reform

Increased contestation of the existing institutionalization of differential treatment became apparent both in tone and substance, especially from 2017 onwards. This highly polarized debate primarily pitted the US and its traditional 'Quad' allies – the EU, Canada, and Japan – against rising powers, and among them most prominently India and China: the former an advocate for a reform of differential treatment (WT/GC/W/757 of 16 January 2019), while the latter a defender of the status quo that allowed them to self-declare their status. A common thread of reform proposals is their focus on graduation and the dismantling of the auto-election approach, which in turn goes hand in hand with a shrinking of the developing country group. A 45-page proposal from 2019 explicitly calling for a more differentiated WTO reaffirms this American rejection of the existing institutionalization of the SDT norm (WT/GC/W/757 of 16 January 2019) and marks the high point of critique and contestation. The proposal explicitly suggests moving away from the auto-election approach – a demand that goes beyond earlier calls for rising powers to take on more responsibilities. In a similar vein, a 2018 EU concept paper on WTO modernization complains that 'the system remains blocked by an antiquated approach to flexibilities which allows over 2/3 of the membership including the world's largest and most dynamic economies to claim special treatment' (European Commission 2018b: 2).

In the first time period, the Appellate Body shied away from explicitly discussing how to define developing country status. Notably, WTO members themselves began to propose the introduction of clear-cut criteria that delimited the group of rights-holders under differential treatment in more recent years. In 2019, US President Trump issued a memorandum dedicated to developing country status in the WTO, in which China is explicitly singled out as a country that continues to insist on the status even when 'virtually every current economic indicator belies China's claim' (White House 2019). This was followed by a US proposal to the General Council that includes clear criteria for graduation from access to differential treatment (WT/GC/W/764 of 15 February 2019). These criteria for graduation are: i) membership in the OECD or G20; ii) classification as high-income by the World Bank;[13] or iii) accounting for 0.5 per cent or more of global merchandise trade. According to these criteria, 34 self-declared developing country members of the WTO were to graduate to developed country status. What the US proposed is a top-down definitions-based approach that allows for no grey-areas: WTO members either count as rights-holders or duty-bearers regarding SDT.

Conversely, rising powers and other self-declared developing countries fiercely defend the existing differentiation approach and reject graduation from the developing country status. Their opposition has so far prevented a reform of the framework for differential treatment in the WTO. In response to the US reform proposals, a group of 52 developing countries – including India and China – submitted a joint statement at the General Council of the WTO in which they defended their status as developing countries (WT/GC/202 of 9 October 2019). More recently, a group of rising powers that self-declare as developing country members tabled a 39-page communication dedicated to their defence of the status quo (WT/GC/W/765/Rev.2 of 4 March 2019). In this communication, they also present a number of divergent criteria to substantiate their claim (WT/GC/W/765/Rev.2 of 4 March 2019). Among those indicators are economic indicators such as per capita income or the proportion of the world's poor, indicators related to their agricultural sectors – such as the number of farmers per hectare – or those related to the research and development capacity of their countries. According to these criteria, the gap between rising powers and developed country members of the WTO remains relatively large. This is, in part, due to a greater emphasis on per capita indicators, which downplay the aggregate economic relevance of a country in the global economy, and are, for instance, more suitable for assessing poverty levels.

Why has reform of the legal framework been so difficult in the trade case? The 'politics of numbers' (Broome and Quirk 2015) makes it difficult to settle on 'objective' criteria that could delimit the group of rights-holders of differential treatment. The hitherto fruitless reform discussions in the world trade regime differ in substance from those adopted in the climate regime (see Chapter 3). The informalization and individualization that the Paris Agreement stands for allows rising powers a more flexible approach that cuts across their roles as rights-holders and duty-bearers to differentiation. The agreement explicitly moves away from designating the status of regime members in a clear-cut way, and instead allows all countries to self-designate the mitigation levels they seek to achieve in line with their differentiated capabilities. Conversely, the focus of the US proposal on automatic and full graduation of rising powers from rights-holder status does not leave any room for compromise. This stance has arguably not been conducive to facilitating an adaptation of the SDT norm to global power shifts. The particular format of the reform proposals thus partly explains why we primarily see resilience at the level of the legal framework.

Lastly, these difficulties in reforming differentiation in the trade regime illustrate how institutional path dependencies shape the evolution of differential treatment. The reliance on the auto-election approach as a starting point meant that the changed power position of Brazil, China, and India was not automatically incorporated into the norm. The absence of sunset clauses that restrict the validity of the auto-election approach (in contrast to the climate case; see Chapter 7) and consensus decision-making furthermore increases the 'stickiness' of the status quo. This institutionalization contrasts sharply with the case of public health financing that relies on a definitions-based approach, according to which contributions gradually increase if regime members gain in power (see Chapter 4). If, as a counterfactual thought experiment, the SDT norm had been institutionalized in the 1970s with clear graduation criteria – similar to the LDC category – it is possible to conceive that Brazil, China, and India (or at least China) would have been excluded at some point from the range of rights-holders of differential treatment. Similar developments have, for instance, taken place in the regime of development finance, where China and other rising powers are increasingly declared as ineligible for concessional loans given their economic status as upper middle-income countries.

2.4.2 Day-to-day Negotiation Practices: The Gradual Unmaking of the SDT Norm

The ways in which the global power shift has affected the evolution of the SDT norm in the world trading system in this later period becomes most notable at the level of day-to-day negotiating practices. Here, we observe the gradual unmaking of the status quo of special rights for developing countries in three ways: first, the dominant trend is that differential treatment becomes highly fragmented, with newly negotiated SDT provisions focussing increasingly on the narrow sub-group of LDCs. Second, more individualized forms of differentiation become more prominent, albeit only in selected issue areas. Related to this trend, there are some signs of informalization. Arguably, the absence of reforms of the legal framework, and the resulting delegitimization of the status quo, drive these changes. The following sub-section, first, discusses dwindling normative support for the existing system of differential treatment, before delineating the main forms of unmaking. Note that all three trends relate to the procedural dimension of differential treatment, as we observe only minor changes regarding negotiation dynamics on the substance of differentiated rights and obligations.

2.4.2.1 The delegitimization of the status quo

The early 2000s were characterized by a context conducive towards the normative agenda of developing countries. In the course of the following two decades, however, shifts in shares of global trade – as well as the fallout of the 2007/2008 global financial crisis – eroded this initial support. The (re-)emergence of economic nationalism in the 2010s further served to undercut 'solidaristic' multilateral initiatives. At the time of writing, a zero-sum approach towards multilateral policy-making has taken hold (again) and undermines the core principle of North–South responsibility that differential treatment relies upon. Notably, this revived protectionism includes an incipient US–China trade war, which – under the Trump administration and beyond – made long-held American concerns about Chinese trade policy more explicit (cf. Hopewell 2020). This confrontation in turn provided a geopolitical context that allowed for the delegitimization of the existing system of differential treatment at the WTO. The US and other major developed countries became unwilling to negotiate new SDT provisions that apply to developing countries as a group as long as this group includes rising powers. A WTO official made this argument explicit in an interview:[14]

> China, India, Brazil, but also now more advanced economies like South Korea and Singapore, they have been treated as developing countries ever since and developed members, they are less willing to recognize the need for S&D [SDT] by these countries. And that is also the main reason why the negotiations on S&D, they have stalled over the last years because there is no differentiation among developing countries in these negotiations on S&D and … in all negotiations, the developed members are not willing to give the same S&D to all developing countries if it's significant S&D.

The dwindling normative support for the differential treatment agenda also counteracted earlier calls for its expansion. This shrinking room for manoeuvre became apparent in the WTO's 2015 Ministerial Conference in Nairobi. As recalled by a trade negotiator, status questions 'came to a point where members began to question the entire Doha framework, the architecture'.[15] At the time, developed countries, and in particular the US, sought to openly abandon the Doha Development Agenda – and its promise to deliver on development (Wilkinson et al. 2016). Given the repeated deadlock and the emergence of new issues, the US advocated for initiating a new negotiation agenda instead. While resistance to this proposal meant that the Doha Development Round has not formally been abandoned, the agenda has lost its support among developed country regime members.

In recent years, the deadlock over the Doha Development Round has been further compounded by a crisis of trade multilateralism. Reaching new decisions and agreements on special rights for developing countries has become even more difficult, given that attention has shifted to the much more basic task of safeguarding – or reviving – the WTO's negotiation function (cf. Tu and Wolfe 2021).

2.4.2.2 Substantive dimension: no major changes, but hardening of the deadlock

Due to the deadlock, the number of decisions and agreements reached in this later WTO period remains low, despite a slight increase in legislative activities in the mid-2010s. The dearth of substantive outcomes in ongoing trade talks makes it difficult to assess changes regarding the different categories of differential treatment provisions, but the relative number of WTO decisions and agreements that include differential treatment have definitely decreased in this more recent decade (Weinhardt and Schöfer 2022). Yet, differentiation remains important to decision-making in the trade regime. Repeated calls by developing country members to consider their special needs, e.g. in the ongoing negotiations concerning an e-commerce agreement, illustrate that differential treatment as such has not gone away.

The hardening of the deadlock in WTO negotiations, moreover, implies a significant obstacle to negotiating differential treatment provisions in newly negotiated agreements and decisions. In the late 2000s and 2010s, the standstill of negotiations intensified, especially after the failure to reach an agreement in the Doha Development Round negotiations in 2007 and 2008. At the time, it became clear that the power shift to Brazil, China, and India had begun to undermine the negotiation function of the WTO. Disagreement among major powers, which now included those from the Global South, made it difficult to reach further liberalization agreements (Muzaka and Bishop 2015). In 2008, for instance, negotiations broke down primarily because of disagreement between the US and India (supported partly by China) over a Special Safeguard Mechanism for developing countries in agriculture (see Chapter 5). This failure to reach an agreement signalled a turning point. Since then, it has become commonplace in policy circles to occasionally announce the 'death' of the Doha Development Round. While these negotiations have so far always been 'revived', these revivals have come 'in a way that is of questionable value to developing and least developed countries' (Wilkinson et al. 2016: 247). The Doha mandate provides few opportunities for revitalizing trade multilateralism as opposed to adding new issues to the agenda.

2.4.2.3 Procedural dimension: the shift towards LDCs as rights-holders

Turning to the procedural dimension of differential treatment, the gradual unmaking of the status quo becomes most apparent. WTO members have begun to vote with their feet: with reforms at the level of the legal framework pending, they increasingly limit newly negotiated SDT provisions to narrower sub-groups of developing countries. Doing so allows developed country members to exclude rising powers from the group of rights-holders – despite their reluctance to give up their status as developing country members. While 'LDC-only' legislation made up only 15 per cent of documents with SDT in the first period, by the 2010s this subset of provisions accounted for more than 60 per cent of all SDT-inclusive publications (see Figure 2.1). In the last ten years, LDCs have thus become the primary rights-holders regarding new differential treatment provisions. This trend accelerated dramatically in the 2010s as Brazil, China, and India gained in power. This contrasts sharply with the initial period of WTO decision-making, in which the rights-holders, regarding differential treatment, remained primarily equated with the group of developing countries.

Given that the level of the legal framework remains unchanged, we increasingly witness the fragmentation of systems of special rights for developing countries: SDT provisions that apply to developing countries as a group – and mostly predate the 2010s – co-exist with newly negotiated SDT provisions that are increasingly restricted to LDCs.

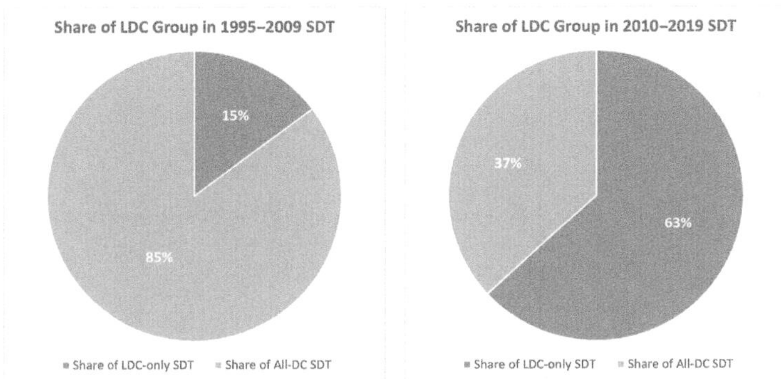

Source: Authors' own depiction. See Weinhardt and Schöfer 2022.

Figure 2.1 Shares of LDC-only SDT in WTO decisions and agreements

The shift towards LDCs implies a significant shrinking of the group of rights-holders regarding differential treatment and thus has significant distributional consequences. In contrast to the category of developing country members, membership in the LDC group does not follow the principle of auto-election but derives from a set of clearly defined UN-authorized criteria.[16] While roughly two-thirds of the 164 WTO members self-declare as developing countries, only 46 of them qualify as LDCs. The shift towards LDCs thus significantly reduces the number of developing countries that have access to differential treatment in newly negotiated agreements, instead of only excluding Brazil, China, and India.

Yet, the reluctance of rising powers to graduate from the developing country status has in part facilitated the shift towards LDC-only SDT. Granting SDT to all self-declared developing country members has simply become too costly in the eyes of major developed country members of the WTO. While developing countries' share of aggregate exports was only around 20 per cent at the time of the creation of the WTO, it has more than doubled in the meantime – to over 40 per cent (see Figure 2.2). This has increased the costs of granting SDT to all WTO members that self-declare as developing countries.

Figure 2.2 *Relative shares of total aggregate exports among WTO members (1995–2018)*

In contrast, the graduation criteria built into LDC status ensure that the group remains marginal over time – at around 1 per cent of aggregate exports of WTO members (see Figure 2.2). This makes it much less costly – and contested – to grant SDT to these smaller economies. A WTO official reiterated this point in an interview: 'LDCs, … in terms of world trade they account for less than … about 1 per cent of world exports, so it's relatively easy for other members to make concessions to the LDCs.'[17]

Another trade expert similarly claimed that the focus on LDCs 'is also a strategy, an acceptance by the richer WTO members to not allow SDT for anyone else than LDCs', adding that 'developed countries are less willing to grant SDT to countries other than LDCs, because LDCs are not a threat anyway to them'.[18] At the same time, developing countries themselves see rising powers such as China or India not only as leaders of developing country coalitions, but also as competitors for SDT (cf. Weinhardt 2020: 405). The trend of granting SDT towards narrower and potentially competing sub-categories of developing countries both reflects and reinforces increased divisions among the group of developing countries. As emphasized by a Geneva-based trade expert, the sense of solidarity that prevailed in the 1960s and 1970s among developing countries has decreased, given that 'that common identity is much weaker today'.[19]

Taken together, these developments in the practices of WTO negotiations illustrate the (gradual) unmaking of the developed/developing country distinction as a basis for differentiation in the world trade regime. The global power shift towards the Global South has thus contributed to the increasing fragmentation of the systems of special rights for competing sub-groups of developing countries in the WTO.

2.4.2.4 Procedural dimension: individualization at the margins

There are some legal developments at the margins of the world trade regime that indicate the parallel emergence of more *individualized approaches* as a basis for differentiation. This contrasts with the climate regime (see Chapter 3), where individualization becomes central to the evolution of special rights in the light of global power shifts.

In the trade regime, the Trade Facilitation Agreement (TFA) (2014) stands out. It introduced a novel approach towards differentiation that signifies the most radical departure from the existing SDT approach. The TFA developed a fine-tuned format of categorizing differentiation provisions by introducing a *list approach* (see Chapter 1: section 1.3.1) that distinguishes not only at country, but also at sectoral level – and makes differentiation voluntary. It differs from fragmentation because all (self-declared) developing countries – rather than merely narrower sub-groups – can equally claim access to the flexibilities it foresees. The main SDT tool employed by the TFA rests in its use of transitional time periods and financial assistance for different categories of listed measures (labelled A, B, C). WTO members then voluntarily self-designate different TFA provisions as belonging to one of these three categories, enabling them to decide on the necessity – and kind – of differential treatment to implement them.[20]

What this tripartite scheme effectively does is to move beyond the generalization of developing countries as a homogenous bloc and towards a more individualized form of differentiation: developing countries can apply different types of differential treatment to different liberalization measures based on their individual preferences. Given that countries can voluntarily declare what level of differentiation they seek to apply, it has allowed rising powers to take on more substantial liberalization commitments compared to others without giving up their status as developing country members at the WTO. China, for instance, is among the developing country members that have decided to designate almost all TFA measures as Category A (direct implementation), which means that they hardly make use of any of the flexibilities offered as part of differential treatment.[21]

However, it is notable that this individualized approach has so far not been broadened to other areas of the WTO regime. This can partly be explained with the rather unusual constellation of interests regarding SDT in this case. Despite the contested nature of the effectiveness of SDT, the general rationale behind developing country claims to special rights remains the assumption that countries at different stages of economic development do not benefit from trade liberalization measures in the same way. More specifically, countries that are currently at a disadvantaged structural position are expected to benefit from protectionist measures as they integrate into global markets. Longer transition periods to implement WTO obligations – or permanent exemptions from or flexibilities regarding these obligations – are meant to guarantee the policy space necessary to improve a country's competitiveness before opening up. Yet, in the case of the TFA, this rationale does not apply in a straightforward way: developing countries have little to gain from exemptions or flexibilities regarding the TFA's obligations. This is because the agreement is meant to reduce trade costs that stem, for instance, from burdensome border procedures at ports that slow down the import of goods. In principle, the TFA should thus be beneficial to all countries.[22]

The potential gains from the TFA for all countries, in turn, explain why WTO members – including rising powers – agreed to an individualized SDT approach. The expectation was that (larger) developing countries would face few incentives to delay the envisaged trade facilitation measures, as long as implementation costs could be covered. It is questionable how far this rationale can be extended to other areas of negotiations in the WTO, where Brazil, China, and India consider exemptions, flexibilities, or implementation flexibilities as important tools to maintain policy space. For instance, in agricultural negotiations, China and India defend their special rights as developing countries. They continue to perceive the flexibilities they hold as beneficial given the important role that the sector plays for domestic employment and food security (see Chapter 5). An individualized TFA-style approach towards SDT – one that requires larger developing country members to self-designate areas in which they voluntarily give up special rights – is thus unlikely to succeed here. A trade representative in Geneva claimed along these lines that 'if you speak about reducing market access barriers, so your own tariffs, your own subsidies, there self-designation is more difficult.'[23]

2.4.2.5 Informalization and the selective use of the developing country status

The individualization that the TFA stands for is closely related to a wider, albeit so far limited, trend towards informalization. Informalization implies that differentiated rights and obligations are not formally laid down in law. Instead, differentiation becomes more voluntary in nature, and hence informal.

Similar to the climate regime (see Chapter 3), Brazil, China, and India could thus decide by themselves which special rights they want to give up. In the trade regime, resilience at the level of the legal framework implies that informalization can only emerge despite – and in parallel to – formally recognized differentiated rights and obligations. This occurs to some extent in the practice of WTO decision-making regarding the auto-election approach.

While the majority of (emerging) developing countries fiercely resist any reform proposals, and defend their developing country status, a small number of developing county members have declared that they will not make use of the status in future negotiations. In the case of Singapore and South Korea, promises in September and October 2019 to refrain from future use of the developing country status have acted as responses to the US-led critique of the current auto-election approach (Ministry of Trade and Industry – Government of Singapore 2019; Chung and Roh 2019). Brazil has also followed suit: similar statements of intent regarding disuse of future SDT provisions have consequently been employed to secure US support for Brazilian OECD membership from 2019 onwards (Mano 2019). However, since these promises only concern *future* WTO negotiations, existing benefits under SDT remain seemingly untouched. Moreover, rising powers may only decide to make such promises when SDT does not fit their economic trajectory anymore. As one Brazilian trade delegate emphasized:

> The instruments of flexibility associated with that [developing country] status were not of use for us anymore. On the contrary, they were counterproductive for us. They were counterproductive because those that were using SDT were perhaps those that had the money to subsidize and the money to use for industry and agriculture subsidization, which should hurt us on the more systemic level of the global economy.[24]

China signalled in December 2021 that it is also considering refraining from using its developing country status in future negotiations on selected issues. China's ambassador to the World Trade Organization, Li Chenggang, mentioned in an interview with Reuters that '[w]e will not ask for a blank cheque for special and differential treatment (SDT). We will carefully assess our needs' (Farge 2021). This would constitute a shift in the country's approach towards informalization of its special rights. Yet, it is too early to assess whether this promise will indeed go hand in hand with changes at the level of day-to-day negotiations.

There have also been other attempts to introduce elements of voluntary, individualized differentiation decoupled from country status in WTO agreements and decisions. One prominent example is the recent decision on duty free and quota free market access for LDC cotton exports (WT/MIN(15)/46 and WT/L/981 of 21 December 2015). The agreement explicitly calls upon the group of developed country members to provide such preferential market access, but also states that developing countries 'declaring themselves in a position to do so' should take on similar obligations. A footnote to the agreement explicitly clarified that 'China declares itself in a position to do so' (WT/MIN(15)/46 and WT/L/981 of 21 December 2015: para. 2, note 2). Indeed, rising powers have acted this way even prior to the 2015 decision on cotton: [25] India was the first developing country to extend duty free, quota free access to all LDCs in 2008 (Ministry of Industry and Commerce – Government of India 2017); China, Turkey, South Korea, and Chinese Taipei have since then also launched substantial preferences schemes for LDCs (WTO 2014: 199). These instances of 'voluntary' differentiation, however, so far remain legal developments at the margins. They do not undermine the right of (self-declared) developing country members to claim differential treatment in other areas of trade policy-making.

2.4.3 Summary of Developments (2008–2019)

In contrast to the earlier period, the global power shift towards Brazil, China, and India led to increased and one-sided contestation of the status quo of special rights. Previously, both expansion and unmaking had been options for reform. In this latter period, the former had dissipated. At the centre of contestation lies the auto-election approach that allows rising powers to self-declare their status as developing countries, and hence rights-holders regarding differential treatment. Despite multiple reform proposals, there is no agreement on how to adapt the existing system of differential treatment to greater heterogeneity among developing countries. Resilience at the level of the legal framework goes hand in hand with the unmaking of special rights at the level of day-to-day negotiations. The predominant trend has been – given the absence of widespread graduation or individualization – the rise of fragmentation of differential treatment for developing countries. In particular, differential treatment is increasingly granted to the narrow sub-group of LDCs, as compared to the entire group of developing countries – that in turn continues to include rising powers. Inadvertently, this contributes to the unmaking of the status quo of special rights for developing countries as a group. This unmaking has significant distributional consequences because in addition to emerging countries, a large number of WTO developing country members are excluded from newly negotiated special rights that are reserved for the marginal group of LDCs.

2.5 CONCLUSION

This chapter has shown that differential treatment for developing countries has been profoundly affected by the power shift to Brazil, China, India, and others in the Global South. While the norm of special and differential treatment for developing countries has remained – perhaps surprisingly – resilient to change at the level of the legal framework, we observe its gradual unmaking at the level of day-to-day negotiations. This unmaking becomes apparent with regard to three main trends: first, differential treatment provisions increasingly focus on the economically marginal sub-group of Least Developed Countries (LDCs). The result is an increasing fragmentation of special rights for different groups of developing countries within the trade regime. Second, more individualized forms of differential treatment emerge at the margins, while, third, informalization increasingly leads to the decoupling of status questions from differentiated rights and obligations. While differential treatment has thus not disappeared, it has become narrower in scope, and more 'layered'.

The gradual unmaking of differential treatment in the world trade regime at the level of newly negotiated agreements and decisions is driven by a seemingly paradox development. On the one hand, the economic rise of Brazil, China, and India has increased their bargaining power in the WTO. This has made it possible for them to resist a reform of the SDT norm at the level of the legal framework that would formally exclude them from the range of future rights-holders. On the other hand, it is precisely this resilience that has contributed to the unmaking of the norm at the level of day-to-day negotiations. In the eyes of developed countries, the reluctance of Brazil, China, and India (or more precisely, India and China) to give up their right to self-declare as developing country members has made it illegitimate to grant special rights to the entire group of developing countries. Hence, we observe the shift towards LDCs as rights-holders regarding differential treatment in newly negotiated agreements and decisions. This shift, moreover, reflects the increasing costs of granting special rights to the entire developing country group. Given that emerging economies have not formally graduated from the developing country status, the global market share of this group of allegedly disadvantaged regime members has reached over 40 per cent in the past decade, as compared to 20 per cent in the initial period of multilateral trade negotiations. Lastly, institutional path dependencies played a role in shaping the evolution of differential treatment. The auto-election approach has proven very rigid and difficult to reform, given the lack of a sunset clause and the adverse incentives it provides for rising and established powers. Normative considerations, political economy dynamics, and institutional factors have thus collectively shaped the evolution of the SDT norm.

Taken together, these findings shed new light on the implications of the rise of Brazil, China, and India for global governance in general, and the trade regime in particular. Instead of focussing on the implications of their rise for the liberal international order (Ikenberry 2018; Mearsheimer 2019), we shed light on more subtle, less studied ways in which it affects the differentiated nature of global order: the rise of Brazil, China, India, and other rising powers has contributed to the unmaking of the status quo of differential treatment for developing countries as central to WTO politics. Moreover, the greater willingness of Brazil, as compared to India and China, to informally give up special rights shows that rising powers have responded differently to the pressure to adjust. Our findings also illustrate how developing country status has become politicized, as who holds it is not only a question of social prestige (Paul et al. 2014), but also material benefits. Lastly, our faceted assessment of resilience and gradual unmaking challenges the prevailing view in the legal trade literature that overemphasizes the shift towards individualization that we have seen in the Trade Facilitation Agreement (cf. Pauwelyn 2013).

At a more practical level, the distributional consequences of this gradual unmaking affect developing country members differently. Rising powers have so far been able to defend the status quo of special rights they negotiated prior to their rise – although they seem unable to negotiate new differential treatment provisions for themselves. Conversely, the large ‘middle bracket’ of developing countries that are neither emerging economically nor part of the LDC group bear the brunt of the unmaking of special rights: they have little to gain from competition with rising powers for special rights, and suffer from the dearth of newly negotiated differential treatment provisions for developing countries as a group.

NOTES

1. Parts of this chapter build on Clara Weinhardt and Till Schöfer (2022). Differential Treatment for Developing Countries in the WTO: The Unmaking of the North–South Distinction in a Multipolar World. *Third World Quarterly*, *43*(1), 74–93.
2. While these states are not named in the speech, the Third World Network (TWN) (2017) suggests that this list of countries comprises China, India, Brazil, South Africa, and Indonesia.
3. Note that a very limited number of sections of this chapter were previously published in Weinhardt and Schöfer (2022).
4. Examples are preferential trading schemes for developing countries such as the US’s Generalized System of Preferences or the EU’s preferential trading scheme Everything but Arms.
5. Note that at times different terms are used, such as ‘developing territories’ or ‘developed contracting parties’.

6. Note, however, that the Uruguay Round Agreements included a separate 'Decision on Measures in Favour of Least Developed Countries' that puts special emphasis on SDT for LDCs only.
7. In a speech on multilateral trade negotiations in the United States in 1980, Heinrich von Moltke, representative of the European Communities, for instance referred to a 'logical quid pro quo, … the clause of "gradual return"' that is closely linked to SDT and 'means that less developed-contracting parties commit themselves to take on their full rights and obligations under the GATT in line with the improvement of their economic and trading situation' (European Commission 1980).
8. We cite official WTO documents according to their WTO document number and date of publication. WTO documents can be accessed online at https://docs.wto.org/ (last accessed 11 July 2023).
9. In the later time period, the US contested Indonesia's developing country status in a 2010–2014 case on clove cigarettes (DS406), but the panel ultimately sided with Indonesia without taking a clear stance regarding its membership status.
10. At the time, for instance, China was also among the developing countries that benefited from the EU's preferential market access scheme, the Generalized System of Preferences (Eglin 1997: 508).
11. The G-90 comprises the African, Caribbean and Pacific (ACP) Group of States, the African Union (AU), and the LDCs.
12. Authors' own calculations. Texts were counted as LDC-only if the document as a whole was explicitly targeted at this sub-group.
13. The World Bank defines high-income countries as those with a gross national income per capita of USD 12,696 or more (as of February 2022). Note that this threshold is periodically adjusted.
14. Trade Official Interview, 28 October 2019.
15. Trade Delegate Interview, 17 September 2021.
16. These criteria are a gross national income below USD 1,025 per capita, low levels of human assets as defined by the Human Assets Index and high economic vulnerability, measured by the Economic Vulnerability Index.
17. Trade Official Interview, 28 October 2019.
18. Trade Expert Interview, 28 October 2019.
19. Trade Expert Interview, 29 October 2019.
20. Differentiation is between clauses that they are able to implement immediately after the TFA's entry into force (Category A), those that they will implement after a transitional period (Category B), and those that can only be implemented after both technical assistance and a transitional period (Category C).
21. China implemented 94.5 per cent of the TFA's obligations immediately (Category A), without making use of the possibility of longer transition periods or financial aid. For an overview of the current state of play of the implementation of the TFA, see: www.tfadatabase.org (last accessed 12 October 2023).
22. Trade Official Interview, 28 October 2019. Note that this does not imply that gains from the TFA will be distributed equally. Developed countries that have

a higher share of world exports are likely to benefit more compared to most developing countries (Wilkinson et al. 2016: 1039).

23. Trade Official Interview, 28 October 2019.
24. Trade Delegate Interview, 30 August 2021.
25. A similar formulation was already contained in the WTO's 2005 Hong Kong Ministerial Declaration that also called upon 'developing-country Members declaring themselves in a position to do so' (WT/MIN(05)/DEC of 22 December 2005) to also grant preferential market access to LDCs.

3. The reinterpretation of common but differentiated responsibilities in the climate regime

Klaus Dingwerth and Simon Herr

3.1 INTRODUCTION

The international climate regime is fundamentally differentiated. Yet, the interpretation of its underlying principle of 'common but differentiated responsibilities and respective capabilities' (CBDR or CBDR-RC) has changed significantly over time. When the UN Framework Convention on Climate Change (UNFCCC) was created in 1992, differential treatment primarily meant that so-called Annex I countries – the Organisation for Economic Co-operation and Development (OECD) members back then plus the Eastern European 'countries with economies in transition' at the time – were asked to limit their greenhouse gas emissions. By contrast, all other countries were exempted from such an obligation. This approach was further institutionalized in the 1997 Kyoto Protocol which specified quantified emission limitations for Annex I countries.

Within the regime, the general need for differentiation is widely accepted. However, who should have special rights and obligations and in relation to what exactly has been contested from the very start (Rajamani 2008b: 910–911). The prospect (and later reality) of the rise of Brazil, China, and India has always been a central driver of this contestation. As the emissions of rising powers grew, and as industrialized countries increasingly perceived these countries as competitors in global markets, they became more vocal in their request that 'advanced developing countries', 'major economies', or 'major emitters' (Khor and Raman 2020: 1) make meaningful contributions to global efforts to curb greenhouse gas emissions. Rising powers resisted the pressure for some time but made concessions after the 2007 climate conference in Bali and in the run-up to the 2015 Paris Agreement. Since then, developing countries are no longer exempt from central regime obligations. Instead, all states now define their own NDCs, though they are expected to do so 'in the light of different national circumstances'.

At a descriptive level, we thus make two main observations. On the one hand, the principle of CBDR has remained central to the regime. Enshrined in the 1992 UNFCCC, it has guided international climate politics as a *fundamental norm* of the regime ever since, and a major purpose of climate negotiations continues to lie in the attempt to find agreement on this burden-sharing principle (Bushey and Jinnah 2010: 1). On the other hand, the *operationalization* of this principle became increasingly contested in the context of global power shifts. As a result of such contestation, we observe a major reinterpretation of the CBDR principle (McGee and Steffek 2016; Tabau and Lemoine 2012: 204; Thompson 2020: 64–65). Following the terminology of Chapter 1, and roughly in line with authors who see a 'gradual erosion of certain forms of differential treatment in the climate regime' (Rajamani 2012a: 619), we classify this reinterpretation as an *unmaking of special rights for developing countries as a group*. This unmaking mainly results from a *gradual intensification of informal and individualized differentiation* in the international climate regime (Dingwerth 2023).

In the remainder of this chapter, we trace the evolution of differentiation norms in the international climate regime in more detail. Our analysis focusses on the ways in which the rise of Brazil, China, and India has affected the contestation, and eventual reinterpretation, of these norms. We develop our argument in four steps. In a first section, we outline how 'common but differentiated responsibilities' were expressed in the 1992 UNFCCC. Two further sections examine the processes of contestation that unfolded in the early (1992–2006) and more recent (2007–2021) phases of the climate regime. Our focus is on contestation and normative change related to three questions: Which states should be assigned to which category of duty-bearers and rights-holders? Which mitigation obligations should developing countries be asked to shoulder? And which forms of assistance should developed countries be required to contribute? The final section concludes.

3.2 THE ORIGINAL FRAME: SPECIAL RIGHTS AND OBLIGATIONS IN THE UN FRAMEWORK CONVENTION ON CLIMATE CHANGE

The UNFCCC emphasizes CBDR as one of its core principles. Following from the central placement of the principle, differential treatment norms pervade virtually all subareas of the regime. They include differentiated central obligations, implementation flexibilities, and provisions for assistance (Biermann 1998; Cullet 2003: 95–134; Gupta 2014; Rajamani 2006: 176–251). Most importantly, the Convention assigns developed countries listed in Annex I 'the strongest quantitative commitments to tackle climate change, as well as more rigorous reporting obligations'. By contrast, non-Annex I parties to the UNFCCC 'have only qualitative obligations, more lenient reporting requirements, and are eligible for financial and technological assistance to help them address climate change' (Depledge 1992: 274).

Historically, the inclusion of the principle of CBDR-RC in the UNFCCC followed similar developments in neighbouring fields. At a very general level, Lavanya Rajamani (2012a: 610) notes that the 'increasing currency of development rhetoric' that was characteristic of the early 1990s facilitated the shift towards a sustainable development agenda. Moreover, previous international environmental treaties, notably the 1987 Montreal Protocol on Substances that Deplete the Ozone Layer and the 1989 Basel Convention on the Control of Transboundary Movements of Hazardous Wastes and Their Disposal, had laid the ground by including similar norms. Shortly thereafter, UN General Assembly Resolution 44/228 adopted in 1989 affirmed that those who had caused environmental harm had a special responsibility for 'containing, reducing and eliminating' it (A/RES/44/228 of 22 December 1989; Rajamani 2012: 608). Finally, Principle 7 of the Rio Declaration, which was negotiated in parallel to the UN Framework, stipulated that, 'in view of the different contributions to global environmental degradation, states have common but differentiated responsibilities', and it further added that 'the developed countries acknowledge the responsibility that they bear in the international pursuit of sustainable development in view of the pressures their societies place on the global environment and of the technologies and financial resources they command' (A/CONF.151/5/Rev.l of 13 June 1992).

3.2.1 Common but Differentiated Responsibilities in the Preamble and in Article 3

Article 2 of the 1992 UNFCCC lays down the objective of the treaty. It lies in 'the stabilization of greenhouse gas concentrations in the atmosphere at a level that would prevent dangerous anthropogenic interference with the climate system'. The preamble to the Convention adds further principles and procedures that structure international efforts towards that goal. In doing so, the Convention text recognizes 'that the global nature of climate change calls for the widest possible cooperation by all countries', hence stressing the *common* task.

However, it also introduces *differentiated* rights and obligations at several key points. States should participate in the collaborative effort 'in accordance with their common but differentiated responsibilities and respective capabilities and their social and economic conditions'. Further clarifying the grounds on which differentiation may be claimed, the preamble acknowledges that 'the share of global emissions originating in developing countries will grow to meet their social and development needs'. Moreover, it specifically recognizes the different historical emissions of state parties as a motive. This justification based on historical contributions to global warming distinguishes CBDR from differential treatment provisions in other non-environmental fields of international law (Boyte 2010: 70–71), including international trade (cf. Chapter 2) and international health (cf. Chapter 4).

The two central justifications point out that developed countries are more responsible for and more capable of responding to climate change. The preambular clauses require them 'to take immediate action … as a first step towards comprehensive response strategies at the global, national and, where agreed, regional levels'. The objectives of developing countries, by contrast, 'should reflect the environmental and developmental context to which they apply', implying that obligations may vary to reflect the specific circumstances of individual states.

Article 3 of the Convention then explicitly defines CBDR-RC as a key principle of the agreement. It asks developed countries to 'take the lead in combating global warming', while 'the specific needs and special circumstances of developing country Parties' should be 'given full consideration'. The addition of 'respective capabilities' was particularly important to developed countries as it allowed them to link the special responsibility more directly to their greater technological and financial capacities and thereby weaken the link to their historical debt (Deleuil 2012: 271).

In sum, legal scholars emphasize that CBDR is neither a general principle of international law, nor a rule of customary law. Instead, it is binding *among parties* and according to the texts of the treaties that incorporate it. Even there, however, the wording of the principle remains 'somehow unsettled, always general'. As a result, the principle of CBDR serves as one guidance to the interpretation of treaty obligations among other preambular clauses (Deleuil 2012: 275–276; see also Honkonen 2009: 259). This openness helps to understand the contestations as well as the normative changes we sketch in this chapter.

3.2.2 Specific Differentiated Rights and Obligations Defined in the Convention

In operational terms, two questions need to be distinguished: Who is assigned special rights and obligations? And what rights and obligations exactly? With respect to the former question, the Convention highlights the differentiated responsibilities of 'developed' and 'developing' countries. Yet, neither the Convention text nor subsequent decisions by the Conference of the Parties (COP) define who counts as a developing country. Instead, the Convention uses annexes and then refers to 'developed country Parties and other developed Parties included in Annex I'. This suggests that both categories – developed countries and parties included in Annex I – were thought to be linked but not necessarily identical (see also Rajamani 2006: 168). To some extent, it was therefore up to the political process to draw the line in specific cases. For example, when Israel acceded to the UNFCCC in 1996, its gross domestic product (GDP) per capita exceeded that of other Annex I parties like Greece, New Zealand, Portugal, and Spain. Nonetheless, Israel became a non-Annex I party to the Convention (ENB 12/38 of 22 July 1996: 3).[1]

Moreover, the UNFCCC distinguishes between Annex I countries, Annex II countries (a subset of Annex I countries), and non-Annex I countries. De facto, OECD members at the time of the adoption of the UNFCCC are included in both annexes. Based on their inclusion in Annex I, these states have special obligations to limit greenhouse gas emissions. Based on their inclusion in Annex II, they are also required to assist developing countries. As a second group, the 'countries undergoing a transition to market economies' are included in Annex I (but not in Annex II). They hold obligations to limit their greenhouse gas emissions but no additional obligations to provide financial assistance. Finally, some 140 state parties were listed in neither of the two annexes. These countries do not have special obligations and may claim assistance as 'developing countries'. Traditionally, this status applies to the members of the G-77 (Group of 77) and thus also to Brazil, China, and India (Rajamani 2006: 169; see also Ella 2017).

Differentiation, however, is not limited to the annexes. Distinguishing between 'adverse effects of climate change and/or the impact of … response measures', Article 4.8 thus explicitly recognizes the 'special needs and concerns' of different sub-groups of developing countries that share certain characteristics. Among them are, for example, 'small island countries', 'countries with areas with fragile ecosystems', and – perhaps surprisingly – countries that heavily rely on fossil fuel production, processing, export, and consumption. In addition, Article 4.9 requests all parties to 'take full account' of the special needs of Least Developed Countries (LDCs), a category that is well defined and delineated in the UN system (see also Dingwerth 2023).

With respect to the substantive content of special rights and obligations, the UNFCCC translates the principle of CBDR into a three-part scheme (Honkonen 2009: 259–260). Among the *central regime obligations*, ten relatively general commitments are binding for all parties (Article 4.1). These include, for instance, the requirement to develop and publish national inventories of greenhouse gas emissions, to formulate and implement national climate programmes, or to promote and cooperate in scientific research related to climate change. In addition, another seven commitments are binding only for 'the developed country Parties and other Parties included in Annex I' (Article

4.2). Notably, Article 4.2(a) obliges Annex I countries to adopt policies and measures to limit their greenhouse gas emissions. The article also hints at the possibility of differentiation *among* Annex I countries when it allows parties to consider differing starting points (or 'base years') as well as economic circumstances.

Next, the UNFCCC also includes provisions that fall into the second differential treatment category of *implementation flexibilities*. For instance, Article 4.6 recognizes 'a certain degree of flexibility' in the implementation of commitments by countries with economies in transition. In addition, states have different reporting obligations. While Annex I parties are obliged to submit their first implementation report within six months of entry into force of the Convention, countries 'not so listed' have three years for their first communication, and LDCs may submit their first report 'at their discretion' (Article 12.5). Finally, the provision that 'developed countries' should 'take the lead' can also be interpreted as an implicit sunset clause. On this reading, it would imply that the 'common' responsibilities are 'differentiated' primarily in the form of different starting dates for different types of states. As we will see, and as we also discuss in more detail in our conflict case study in Chapter 7, different interpretations of this 'lead-taking' norm were at the heart of major conflicts in the history of the international climate regime.

Finally, *assistance* is primarily regulated by Annex II and by the Global Environmental Facility (GEF) as the financial instrument of the UNFCCC. The Convention specifically requires Annex II parties to cover the 'agreed full costs' for the communication commitments of developing countries (Article 4.3) and ties the implementation of developing country commitments to the provision of financial assistance (Article 4.7). It further requires developed countries to assist 'the developing country Parties that are particularly vulnerable … in meeting costs of adaptation' to the adverse effects of climate change (Article 4.4) and asks for financial assistance in technology transfer (Article 4.5). Finally, Article 11 establishes a Financial Mechanism 'for the provision of financial resources on a grant or concessional basis' and identifies the GEF as the interim operating entity to channel the respective funds. We discuss the contestation of the GEF and conflicts over reforming the institutional landscape of climate finance in depth in Chapter 8.

3.3 PROCESSES OF CONTESTATION IN PHASE 1 (1992–2006)

To reconstruct how the rise of Brazil, China, and India shaped the contestation of differential treatment, we distinguish between a period 'before' and 'after' that rise. This distinction follows the general approach we adopt in this book. At the same time, the precise delineation of the two periods and the underlying justifications are case specific. In our case, we adopt 1992 (rather than 1995) as our starting year. With the adoption of the UNFCCC, this date marks the beginning of the international climate regime. Moreover, we identify the years between 2005 and 2007 as a turning point.

Our choice is based on material factors as well as on developments within the climate regime. In *material terms*, political justifications for differentiation relate to economic capabilities, annual greenhouse gas emissions, and historical emissions. Around 2005, China surpassed the United States (US) as the state with the largest territorial emissions per annum (Thompson 2020: 64–65; see also Table 3.1: column 5). Moreover, Annex I parties had accounted for most global greenhouse gas emissions in 1995. By 2005, their share dropped to 47 per cent. In addition, our distinction between the two phases also resonates with developments within the international climate regime itself. Here, the affirmation of a clear distinction between Annex I and non-Annex I countries in the 1997 Kyoto Protocol is characteristic of Phase 1. Subsequently, the period from 2005 and 2007 marks a shift towards a 'post-Kyoto' architecture (Gupta 2014: 99–143; see also Jinnah 2017: 290). This shift culminated in the replacement of the Kyoto Protocol with the Paris Agreement in 2015.

In this section, we address key developments and conflicts in Phase 1. We proceed in three steps. In a first sub-section, we focus on the contestation of the institutional logics that regulated who had access to special rights and how graduation from the developing country status was organized. A second sub-section revolves around which mitigation obligations developing countries were asked to shoulder. It highlights debates over 'voluntary commitments' as well as over binding obligations in a 'second commitment period' of the Kyoto Protocol. Finally, a third sub-section discusses how obligations in the field of assistance were contested in the early climate regime.

3.3.1 Contestation over Country Categories

International norms of differentiation are central as well as pervasive in the climate regime. Like in other international regimes we examine in this book, the most central distinction is between 'developed' and 'developing' countries. Beyond that distinction, however, the climate regime comprises additional layers of differentiation that are often overlooked.[2] On the one hand, this layer includes informal norms that go beyond being listed in Annex I or Annex II. For instance, as Lavanya Rajamani has observed, 'by their use of language such as "if necessary", "as appropriate", "in so far as possible", and "all practicable steps"', the legal agreements and decisions of the international climate regime 'grant states considerable room for manoeuvre' (Rajamani 2006: 163). Moreover, the Convention recognizes a diverse bundle of claims for differential treatment – from being a 'small island developing state' to being

Table 3.1 *Key indicators for capacity (1), current emissions levels (2–5), and historical emissions (6) for selected state parties to the UN Framework Convention on Climate Change*

	(1) GDP per capita (current USD)			(2) GHG emissions per capita (tCO2e per capita – Total excluding land use change and forestry (LUCF))			(3) GHG emissions total (MtCO2e – Total excluding LUCF)			(4) Country rank of total GHG emissions (based on country's total emissions)			(5) Country share of global GHG emissions (based on country's total emissions in MtCO2e) (%)			(6) Country share of global historical GHG emissions' (MtCO2e; since 1850)		
	1995	2005	2015	1995	2005	2015	1995	2005	2015	1995	2005	2015	1995	2005	2015	1995	2005	2015
Annex I and Annex II																		
OECD	22140	30188	35612	13.79	13.40	11.47	13620	15638	14626	n/a	n/a	n/a	44.16	41.87	32.93	56.51	56.87	53.43
EU	19466	27333	30470	10.75	10.23	8.08	4317	4735	4119	n/a	n/a	n/a	14.0	12.68	9.27	21.08	21.23	20.08
Germany	31658	34507	41087	12.93	11.25	10.37	1056	928	847	6	6	8	3.42	2.48	1.91	5.88	5.34	4.73
Japan	43440	37218	34524	10.18	10.05	9.95	1278	1284	1265	5	5	5	4.14	3.44	2.85	2.92	3.10	3.09
Spain	15472	26419	25732	7.64	9.72	7.01	303	424	326	20	18	25	0.98	1.14	0.73	0.76	0.82	0.83
USA	28691	44115	56839	23.51	23.02	18.72	6261	6802	6004	1	2	2	20.30	18.21	13.51	28.14	26.75	24.71

	(1) GDP per capita (current USD)			(2) GHG emissions per capita (tCO2e per capita – Total excluding land use change and forestry (LUCF))			(3) GHG emissions total (MtCO2e – Total excluding LUCF)			(4) Country rank of total GHG emissions (based on country's total emissions)			(5) Country share of global GHG emissions (based on country's total emissions in MtCO2e) (%)			(6) Country share of global historical GHG emissions' (MtCO2e; since 1850)		
	1995	2005	2015	1995	2005	2015	1995	2005	2015	1995	2005	2015	1995	2005	2015	1995	2005	2015
Only Annex I																		
Hungary	4495	11201	12707	7.03	7.17	5.93	73	72	58	52	60	71	0.24	0.19	0.13	0.32	0.30	0.27
Turkey	2898	7456	11006	3.97	4.47	5.52	232	303	434	24	25	17	0.75	0.81	0.98	0.47	0.54	0.62
Russia	2666	5323	9313	15.49	16.54	17.18	2298	2373	2476	3	3	4	7.45	6.35	5.57	7.26	6.94	6.54
Non-Annex I																		
Saudi Arabia	7691	13791	20628	13.69	15.39	20.82	255	366	660	22	21	13	0.83	0.98	1.49	0.64	0.70	0.81
Mexico	3928	8278	9617	4.8	5.53	5.5	440	586	670	15	12	12	1.43	1.57	1.51	1.05	1.15	1.23
South Korea	12565	19403	28732	9.48	11.39	13.44	427	549	686	16	15	11	1.39	1.47	1.54	0.49	0.68	0.83

	(1) GDP per capita (current USD)			(2) GHG emissions per capita (tCO2e per capita – Total excluding land use change and forestry (LUCF))			(3) GHG emissions total (MtCO2e – Total excluding LUCF)			(4) Country rank of total GHG emissions (based on country's total emissions)			(5) Country share of global GHG emissions (based on country's total emissions in MtCO2e) (%)			(6) Country share of global historical GHG emissions' (MtCO2e; since 1850)		
	1995	2005	2015	1995	2005	2015	1995	2005	2015	1995	2005	2015	1995	2005	2015	1995	2005	2015
Israel	18104	20567	35777	10.65	10.98	10.68	59	76	90	64	57	55	0.19	0.20	0.20	0.07	0.10	0.11
Brazil	4748	4790	8814	4.18	4.78	5.3	678	889	1083	8	7	6	2.20	2.38	2.44	1.36	1.53	1.68
China	610	1753	8067	3.54	5.52	8.65	4267	7194	11859	2	1	1	13.8	19.2	26.7	7.00	8.61	11.74
India	374	715	1606	1.51	1.72	2.34	1457	1970	3064	4	4	3	4.73	5.27	6.90	3.79	3.94	4.20

Source: Information on GDP per capita is based on World Bank data (https://data.worldbank.org/, June 2021). Information on GHG emissions was taken from Climate Watch (https://www.climatewatchdata.org, June 2021), with CAIT (for annual emissions) and PIK (for historical emissions) as data sources.

'particularly vulnerable' or a 'least developed country'. Because this list of legitimacy claims was not based on clear criteria and because the boundaries of the categories were rarely defined with precision, the range of parties with a legitimate claim to differential treatment has, to a certain extent, always been subject to negotiations and dispute. Two aspects proved crucial in this regard: whether further categories could be added to the list, and whether and when states could 'graduate' from a specific category and hence lose their legitimate claim to special rights.

On the first point, the fact that the UN Framework Convention allowed several categories of developing countries to invoke 'special circumstances' provided a justification for new groups to stake their own claims. For instance, Iceland's reference to the special needs of 'small economies', while faced with some objections, eventually succeeded. After several years of negotiations, the Subsidiary Body for Scientific and Technological Advice (SBSTA) to the UNFCCC proposed to allow states whose 'total carbon dioxide emissions of the Party were less than 0.05 per cent of the total carbon dioxide emissions of Annex I Parties in 1990' (FCCC/SBSTA/2000/CRP.13 of 18 November 2000) to exempt new industrial development projects from their carbon budgets under specified circumstances.[3] The decision illustrated that states conceived the list of acceptable reasons as contingent on political agreement and could therefore be re-negotiated any time.

On the other hand, however, the list approach adopted by the UNFCCC meant that the legal basis of the differentiation regime was relatively fixed. Thus, whereas some of the major international environmental agreements of the past – most notably the Montreal Protocol on Substances that Deplete the Ozone Layer – contained detailed information on how countries would graduate and thereby be assigned (more) commitments, similar criteria were absent from international climate change law. Unsurprisingly, then, the question of graduation and especially the burdens to be shouldered by 'advanced developing countries' gave rise to fierce and lasting disputes throughout the history of the climate change negotiations. Early test cases – and hence important precedents for other cases that would arise in the future – included the placement of Turkey on the annexes as well as the accession of Mexico and South Korea to the OECD in 1994 and 1996, respectively.

3.3.1.1 The placement of Turkey

The case of Turkey illustrates the intricacies of differentiation associated with the list approach (see also Depledge 2009: 280–281). As a member of the OECD, Turkey was initially included in Annex I and Annex II. Yet, the Turkish government objected to being placed in both annexes, arguing that Turkey's placement 'did not conform to the country's economic circumstances' (ENB 12/97 of 16 November 1998: 10; see also Rajamani 2006: 169).

While some countries supported the removal of Turkey from both annexes, others rejected the idea because of the 'precedent it would set' (ENB 12/123 of 8 November 1999: 7). The issue was eventually settled at COP-7 (2001) when Turkey was removed from Annex II but not from Annex I (ENB 12/189 of 12 November 2001: 8). Turkey did not accede to the UNFCCC until 2004, making it the 189th state party to ratify the agreement.[4]

In a wider context, the contestation over the placement of Turkey illustrates that implicitly basing the annexes on membership in the OECD left some 'fuzzy margins' (Rajamani 2006: 169–171) and was prone to generate critical 'anomalies' over time (Bodansky 1993: 507; see also Boyte 2010: 86). For example, as Daniel Bodansky (1993: 507) noted at the time, placing Turkey – as an OECD member – on Annex II would have obliged the country 'to provide financial resources to Saudi Arabia', which could claim developing country status under the Convention. Yet, Saudi Arabia's GDP per capita in 1992 just about doubled the GDP per capita of Turkey.

3.3.1.2 The OECD accessions of Mexico and South Korea

While the placement of Turkey was eventually resolved with its removal from Annex II, two new challenges arose when Mexico (in 1994) and South Korea (in 1996) joined the OECD. The logic according to which countries had been placed in the two annexes to the Convention suggested that accession to the OECD would lead to a graduation from developing country status. In legal terms, however, Article 16 of the UNFCCC stipulated that amendments to the annex had to be 'subject to the same procedure as that for the proposal, adoption and entry into force of annexes to the Convention'. In practice, this meant that states had to seek consensus on amendments and that, only where all efforts to forge such a consensus had failed, 'a three-fourths majority vote of the Parties present and voting at the meeting' was available as a last resort (see also Depledge 2009).

Politically, moreover, there was 'no consensus among the [UNFCCC] parties as to whether some of these new OECD members should become Annex I countries' (Breidenich et al. 1998: 318). In the case of Mexico, such an addition was not in the interests of the G-77 and China because of the precedent it would set in a context in which some developed countries had already called for legally binding commitments for 'advanced developing countries'. In the absence of consensus, Mexico joined the OECD in May 1994, but it remained 'a "developing country" in the context of the climate change negotiations' (Rowlands 1995a: 236, fn. 2).

While relatively low scores on key development economic indicators facilitated this solution in the case of Mexico (Sheinbaum and Masera 2000: 260), the situation was more difficult with South Korea. Like other members of the G-77, the Korean government had originally opposed the creation of a new category of 'advanced developing countries'. Furthermore, with respect to its own situation, it had argued 'that it cannot be subject to any specific commitments to limit the greenhouse gases because of its current economic and industrial structure', including its dependence on coal (Kim 1995: 77–78). At the same time, some commentators expected that 'once Korea becomes an OECD member, it will be very difficult for Korea to avoid its inclusion in Annex I'. Korean commentators thus proposed that the government should seek to negotiate a 'grace period' or a differentiation of commitments among Annex I countries as possible options (Kim 1995: 83–84). The latter proposal is particularly interesting because it responds to an important strategic implication associated with the possibility of Korea's graduation. Notably, it suggested that, if the Korean government continued to oppose commitments for 'advanced developing countries', 'it will not be easy for Korea to change its position after being included in Annex I' (Kim 1995: 84).

In the end, neither Annex I nor Annex II were amended.[5] Instead, the Korean government established an 'Inter-Ministerial Committee on the Framework Convention on Climate Change' in 1998. Chaired by the Prime Minister, it 'declared in 1998 its official negotiation position that Korea would consider a mandatory commitment for the 2018–2022 period, and for the interim period would consider establishing a non-binding voluntary target and accomplishing it' (Lee and Oh 2002: 201). This commitment translated into a 'Comprehensive National Action Plan for the Framework Convention on Climate Change' in 1999 and a 'detailed action plan' in 2000 (Lee and Oh 2002: 201).

In sum, Mexico and South Korea had left the G-77 (as the 'club of developing countries') to join the OECD (as the 'club of advanced industrialized economies'). Yet, they had been able to do so without incurring any of the formal obligations of Annex I or Annex II parties.[6] De jure, they had not graduated – in part, because the annexes to the UNFCCC were hard to amend. De facto, however, both countries raised their climate ambition over time. As OECD members, they accepted an informal obligation to do more than other non-Annex I parties and thereby set an important precedent for subsequent debates over graduation in the climate regime.

3.3.2 Contestation over Developing Country Commitments

Another major point of contestation in the early climate regime revolved around developing country commitments. Did the notion of differentiated responsibilities imply that all developing countries be fully exempt from mitigation commitments? Or did it mean that *some* developing countries needed to contribute *less*? These questions arose in part in relation to the prospect of rising greenhouse gas emissions in some developing countries. Already in 1995, for instance, Ian Rowlands (1995b: 189) commented that, 'in 1990 ...,

Southern states were responsible for just over 30 per cent of all energy-related carbon dioxide emissions in the world'. For addressing the challenge of global warming, this figure could not be neglected, let alone if one took the developmental ambitions of this group of states into account. Researchers thus projected that annual developing country emissions would exceed those of developed countries by 2020 (Goldemberg 1995). As an example, Rowlands adds that 'the Chinese government had plans to expand its coal consumption five-fold between 1990 and 2020', a plan that, if realized, 'would add nearly 50 per cent to the 1990 level of *global* carbon emissions' (Rowlands 1995b: 189; italics in the original). Contestation over the emissions of developing countries thus not only emerged once the emissions of individual countries began to rise steeply – it was already a central issue in the 1990s when the prospect of such a rise became visible.

In view of this prospect, major Annex I parties sought an interpretation of CBDR in which at least some developing countries would agree to contribute. They promoted three specific ideas in support of this objective. First, the idea of voluntary commitments proposed to put an end to the full exemption of developing countries from mitigation commitments. At the same time, and much like the notion of 'willingness to contribute' in the global health regime (cf. Chapter 4), it left rising powers with control over the commitments they wished to make. Second, the idea of evolving contributions was based on the possibility of establishing objective criteria to determine when and how much developing countries would need to chip in. Finally, the notion of co-contingent contributions built on the idea that the mitigation efforts of rising powers and Annex I parties would depend on each other. On this account, developed countries would need to keep their promises and 'take the lead'. But once they fulfilled that promise, developing countries would have to follow.

In pushing these ideas in the climate negotiations, the Annex I parties made recurring attempts to drive wedges between Brazil, China, India, and other developing countries. Lavanya Rajamani notes that, at COP-1 (1995), 'several industrial countries sought to bring up the issue of "different commitments for different categories of developing countries"' (Rajamani 2006: 217; see also ENB 12/21 of 10 April 1995: 10–11). This applies, for example, to the so-called 'German Elements Paper' which envisaged binding commitments for 'advanced developing countries', a term that was initially meant to refer to OECD accession candidates but, due to its openness, provided an entry point for graduation more generally (A/AC.237/L.23/Add.1 of 27 September 1994; see also Chapter 7).

At negotiations in 1997, the US delegation further announced that 'it would not assume binding obligations until there was "meaningful participation from key developing nations"' (Rajamani 2006: 217). This message was based on the Byrd–Hagel Resolution which the US Senate had passed with 95 votes in favour and not a single vote against a few months earlier. The resolution noted that 'greenhouse gas emissions of Developing Country Parties are rapidly increasing and are expected to surpass emissions of the United States and other OECD countries as early as 2015'. Based on this assessment, the resolution requested that (US Congress 1997):

> the United States should not be a signatory to a protocol, or other agreement regarding the United Nations Framework Convention on Climate Change of 1992, at negotiations in Kyoto in December 1997, or thereafter, which would (A) mandate new commitments to limit or reduce greenhouse gas emissions for the Annex I Parties, unless the protocol or other agreement also mandates new specific scheduled commitments to limit or reduce greenhouse gas emissions for Developing Country Parties with the same compliance period, or (B) would result in serious harm to the economy of the United States.

Despite this stance, however, parties agreed to the Kyoto Protocol in 1997. In contrast to the position formulated by the US Senate, the Kyoto Protocol confirmed the 'firewall' between Annex I and non-Annex I parties. Notably, Article 3 introduced 'quantified emission limitation and reduction commitments' for Annex I parties, but not for other states. Overall, Annex I parties promised to reduce their emissions by 5 per cent compared to their 1990 (or other base year) levels for the five-year period from 2008 to 2012. In addition, the Kyoto Protocol specified how Annex I parties intended to distribute the burden of emissions reductions among themselves. Introducing a new element of differentiation within the category of Annex I parties, it detailed the commitments each Annex I party had agreed to for a 'first commitment period' ranging from 2008 to 2012. EU countries, for example, accepted an 8 per cent reduction of their average annual emissions compared to 1990. The US agreed to a 7 per cent reduction. The Russian Federation and New Zealand committed to return to their base year levels. Finally, some countries accepted limiting their increases of greenhouse gas emissions to 1 per cent (Norway), 8 per cent (Australia), or 10 per cent (Iceland).

The acceptance of the Kyoto Protocol by the US government at COP-3 (1997) was based on the introduction of three so-called 'market mechanisms' on which the US delegation had insisted: the possibilities for Annex I parties to implement emissions reduction projects jointly (Article 6), to earn emissions reductions achieved through projects that Annex I parties financed in developing countries under a new Clean Development Mechanism (CDM, Article 12), and to trade emissions (Article 17). Nonetheless, the Protocol deviated from positions that key players in the US as well as elsewhere held. This tension, it was clear, would remain until some of the economically advanced developing countries started accepting voluntary targets for themselves.

Politically, proposals to dismantle the clear-cut distinction between Annex I and non-Annex I parties proved unsuccessful. As a result, developed countries shifted attention to *voluntary commitments*. The US, for example, pushed for greater participation by countries like China and India, and the EU supported the creation of mechanisms that could incorporate voluntary commitments on the part of developing countries. Beyond the US and EU, calls for such mechanisms also received support from Russia which, at COP-4 (1998), argued 'that within 15 years, emissions from non-Annex I countries would exceed those of Annex I countries' (ENB 12/97 of 16 November 1998: 2–3). Moreover, support from the Alliance of Small Island States (AOSIS) illustrates that rising powers also faced pressure from other G-77 members (Bodansky et al. 2017: 106–109, 166). Nonetheless, a proposed article on voluntary commitments was dropped in the final night of the negotiations in Kyoto. Among the non-Annex I countries, Argentina, the AOSIS, Israel, the Philippines, and South Korea had supported the article. By contrast, Brazil, China, and India remained opposed to voluntary commitments (Oberthür and Ott 2000: 293).[7]

Only a year after the Kyoto Protocol had confirmed the 'firewall' between developed and developing countries, however, Argentina formally expressed a will to 'belong to the group holding future responsibilities'. This announcement made at COP-4 (1998) spurred renewed debate on the matter. Fearing it could set a precedent for other developing countries, the G-77 objected to the Argentinian COP President's argument that 'developing countries share some responsibility for climate change' (ENB 12/97 of 16 November 1998: 2). Nonetheless, Argentina communicated a voluntary emissions reduction target at the following COP in 1999, a move that Japan, the US, Australia, and the EU all welcomed (ENB 12/123 of 8 November 1999: 13). In the context of the larger debate, the decision demonstrated that voluntary commitments for non-Annex I parties were no longer merely a theoretical possibility. Unsurprisingly, the request that other (advanced) non-Annex I countries adopt similar commitments remained prominent in subsequent years (Bodansky et al. 2017: 109; ENB 12/260 of 20 December 2004: 8).

Beyond calls for voluntary commitments, Annex I parties began to tie the extent of their future promises to action by non-Annex I parties, thereby implying that differentiation was subject to a sunset clause defined by the end of the first commitment period of the Kyoto Protocol in 2012. The EU joined the US call for more commitments by major developing countries. New Zealand, a member of the JUSSCANNZ coalition that also included Japan, the US, Switzerland, Canada, Australia, and Norway, declared that 'Annex I Parties' constituencies need assurances that developing countries would adopt binding commitments *in a third commitment period*'. As a potential solution, it proposed a double conditionality between the efforts of developed and (key) developing countries (ENB 12/76 of 13 December 1997: 2, 5, and

13; italics added). When major non-Annex I parties kept rejecting both voluntary and co-contingent obligations, the incoming Bush administration justified its opposition to the Kyoto Protocol based on the perception that 'it exempts 80 percent of the world' (Bush 2001). The unwillingness of the US to ratify the Kyoto Protocol unless key developing countries made commitments added further to the pressure on Brazil, China, and India to accept central regime obligations in the (near) future (Dubash and Rajamani 2015: 666; Hallding et al. 2011: 35; Hochstetler 2012: 57).

Rising powers, on their part, had long countered the discursive challenges associated with references to 'advanced developing countries', 'key developing countries', 'major economies', or 'major emitters' and rejected the idea of creating a third category beyond Annex I and non-Annex I parties (see also Ella 2017; Thompson 2020: 64–65). Nonetheless, the emphasis they – alongside other G-77 members – put on the right to development as well as on historical responsibility (Gupta 2014: 73–74, 168) was gradually complemented with statements that indicated a possibility to accept future commitments. The Indian government, for example, argued that any voluntary commitment 'would have to be consistent with its national development plans and priorities' and covered by 'new and additional financial resources from the developed world' (Sengupta 2020: 169; see also Dubash and Rajamani 2015; Vihma 2011). This signalled that a possible solution to the conflicts concerning developing country commitments might lie in establishing a credible link between mitigation and climate finance. Moreover, when Argentina adopted a voluntary target in 1999, China informed the international community that 'it would not undertake commitments until it achieves a "medium development level"' (ENB 12/123 of 8 November 1999: 13). While moving the date for accepting quantified emissions targets into a more distant future, this statement hinted at the possibility of such acceptance. Moreover, it tied that possibility to a criterion that no longer depended on backward-looking, cumulative historical emissions but on capabilities alone.

Until 2005, however, developing countries did not step forward to accept commitments for future periods of the Kyoto Protocol. Moreover, the announcement of the Bush administration in 2001 that the US would not ratify the Kyoto Protocol reduced the incentives for other Annex I parties to join the agreement. It eliminated the potential for emissions trading with the US, and it enhanced the risk that the US would remain a free rider. Because 55 ratifications were needed, and because ratifications had to incorporate at least 55 per cent of all emissions of Annex I parties for 1990, US withdrawal also put into question whether the Kyoto Protocol would even enter into force. Eventually, Russia's ratification in 2004 answered that question, and the Protocol became effective in early 2005. By that time, however, the approach on which the Kyoto Protocol was based had lost considerable legitimacy among developed countries (as well as some developing countries) and the search for an alternative had already begun. In May 2006, the UNFCCC Secretariat hosted a 'dialogue on long-term cooperative action to address climate change by enhancing implementation of the Convention'. This dialogue eventually gave rise to the establishment of an Ad Hoc Working Group on Long-Term Cooperative Action under the Convention (AWG-LCA) in 2007 (see also Honkonen 2009: 262–263). Climate negotiations thus proceeded along two parallel tracks. While the 'Kyoto Protocol track' sought to make the Protocol work for future commitment periods after 2012, the 'Convention track' examined the options for creating a new 'comprehensive agreement' that would transcend the Kyoto Protocol. In retrospect, the establishment of the AWG-LCA marks the beginning of a transition towards a new international climate policy architecture, a development we discuss further below.

3.3.3 Contestation over Assistance

The question of developing country commitments is directly related to developed countries' obligations to assist. Article 4.7 of the UN Framework Convention thus conceded that, 'the extent to which developing country Parties will effectively implement their commitments under the Convention will depend on the effective implementation by developed country Parties of their commitments under the Convention related to financial resources and transfer of technology.'

As the third category of differential treatment, assistance obligations in the international climate regime include support for adaptation, mitigation, technology transfer, and capacity-building. Contestations over assistance, however, followed a broader set of questions to which developed and developing countries have given varying answers throughout the history of the climate regime. A first question is related to the evolving justifications for support from developed to developing countries ('why assist?'). This includes both backward-looking questions of historical responsibility as well as forward-looking questions of greater effectiveness, efficiency, and equity in the climate regime. A second question revolved around the scale of funding which developed countries would need to make available ('how much?'). A third question asked which countries ('to whom?') and projects ('for what?') should hold a right to which kinds of assistance and in return for which concomitant commitments. Finally, a fourth question related to the institutions and rules that should channel and govern assistance ('through which structures?').

3.3.3.1 Justifications

Regarding the justifications of assistance under the climate regime, Phase 1 (1992–2006) was characterized by both backward- and forward-looking arguments captured in the UN Framework Convention (Articles 4, 11, and 21) and Kyoto Protocol (Articles 10 to 12) and expressed during negotiations. During the first phase, developing countries emphasized backward-looking justifications of assistance. These justifications drew on developed countries' historical responsibility for climate change (Coventry 2019: 203; Vanderheiden 2015: 39). In negotiations, the arguments of developing countries also went beyond the issue of climate change and pointed to the colonial past, the economic and hegemonic dominance of developed countries in international relations, and the importance of development (see also Rajamani 2012a: 610). In brief, developing countries regarded climate change as a problem created by developed countries and mostly suffered by developing countries. They called for a right to development and regarded funding for adaptation as a historical right (Coventry 2019: 212–213; Cullet 1999: 568; Gupta 2014: 161, 172; Prys-Hansen et al. 2019: 282–283; Rajamani 2006: 4–5).

Developed countries, by contrast, relied on forward-looking arguments for assistance. Instead of framing assistance in terms of historical injustices, they underlined differences in present capabilities (Cullet 1999: 560; 2003: 21–27; Horta et al. 2002: 9). By assisting developing countries, developed countries sought to enable additional parties to shoulder commitments under the climate regime and to thereby enhance the effectiveness in the response to climate change. By helping to fund mitigation projects in developing countries (under the Kyoto Protocol's CDM, for example) rather than at home, moreover, developed countries furthermore tried to reap efficiency gains (e.g. Gupta 1995: 20; Prys-Hansen et al. 2019: 276).

The foundational documents of the climate regime do not fully resolve the tension between developing and developed country perspectives. On the right to development, for instance, the UN Framework Convention recognizes a right to 'sustainable development' in its preamble. Yet, it does not specify which actors are primarily responsible for rendering development sustainable (Rajamani 2003: 25–32; 2012a: 606–614). The Convention further clarifies that the implementation of mitigation actions in developing countries would be tied to funding from developed countries. However, it leaves open who should shoulder exactly how much of the costs of making development sustainable. As a result, the justifications, but also the extent, specific goals, and exact eligibility criteria related to special rights and obligations in the field of assistance remained contested.

3.3.3.2 How much, to whom, and for what?

Between 1992 and 2006, the size and content of developed countries' assistance obligations were closely tied to developing country commitments under the UN Framework Convention. Regarding these questions of assistance, the Convention is specific in some parts but remains rather vague in others. On the one hand, for example, the legal text stipulates that developed countries listed in Annex II are obliged to pay for the costs developing countries incur through commitments such as the preparation of national communications. On the other hand, the UN Framework Convention further specifies that developed countries listed in Annex II should also cover costs developing countries incur for adapting to the adverse effects of climate change (Articles 4.3 and 4.4). On the latter point, however, the wording is not very specific. It could be read as including all adaptation costs which, according to some later estimates of developing country needs, could amount to hundreds of billions of US dollars (TWN 2008: 7). Yet, it could also be read as only covering parts of the costs associated with adaptation in limited circumstances. The same holds for obligations to assist with transfers of technology (Articles 4.3 and 4.5), where both the Convention and subsequent negotiations and agreements left many details open.

The question of who benefits was answered relatively clearly since all developing countries – defined as those non-Annex I countries that claim developing country status – were eligible to receive assistance. Concerning mitigation activities, for example, the Convention invited developing countries to identify projects for which they sought financing in their national communications, including 'an estimate of all incremental costs, of the reductions of emissions and increments of removals of greenhouse gases, as well as an estimate of the consequent benefits' (Article 12.4). Nonetheless, and in line with Articles 4.8 and 4.9 of the UN Framework Convention, some funds put special emphasis on the needs of LDCs and particularly vulnerable developing countries (Dessai 2003). Moreover, towards the end of Phase 1, the GEF began to apply a new 'Resource Allocation Framework' according to which funding was prioritized for countries and projects that exhibited the largest global benefits. This typically meant more funds for relatively strong developing countries including Brazil, China, and India, while smaller and weaker developing countries were allocated a smaller fraction of funds (Ballesteros et al. 2010: 273; Müller 2014).

Overall, moreover, the co-existence of provisions that simultaneously exempted developing countries from obligations *and* asked developed countries to pay for mitigation raised important queries which relate back to the question of sustainable development discussed earlier in the chapter. Correspondingly, climate negotiations and agreements over assistance during Phase 1 were characterized by maximalist requests from developing countries and rather limited promises from developed countries. Parties failed to agree on overarching target amounts of assistance and instead decided to negotiate assistance amounts every four years. The GEF as a major funding channel of assistance in the first phase was equipped with USD (United States dollar) 1 billion during its pilot phase (1991–1994) and then replenished three times with USD 2 billion (1994–1998), USD 2.75 billion (1998–2002), and USD 3 billion (2002–2006). However, since climate change was only one focal area of the GEF, climate finance channelled through the GEF amounted to only about USD 2 billion during Phase 1 as a whole. This amount was used to fund communication commitments of developing countries under the UN Framework Convention plus a limited number of adaptation and mitigation projects (GEF Secretariat 2006; 2018).

3.3.3.3 Which institutional structures should channel and govern assistance?

Finally, developed and developing countries also disagreed about the institutional structures and rules that should channel, govern, and label assistance. Developed countries preferred labelling assistance as official development aid rather than owed due to historical responsibilities or culpability (e.g. ENB 12/123 of 8 November 1999: 9; Rajamani 2006: 83, 107). In line with this position, they consistently favoured using existing channels and institutions over which they held substantial sway, notably the World Bank and the GEF (Horta et al. 2002: 1; Streck 2001: 76). Furthermore, developed countries stressed efficiency as a key principle and sought to establish structures that would channel assistance predominantly to countries and projects with the highest possible global benefits (Coventry 2019: 174). Developing countries, by contrast, preferred the creation of funding institutions that would be directly accountable to the COP, take the local needs of developing countries into account, and put a strong focus on funding for adaptation. Based on their view of assistance as historically owed compensation, they demanded grant-based funding rather than interest-bearing investments even if the latter included concessional lending (Coventry 2019: 159; Bodansky 1993: 468, 538; Goldemberg 1994: 181; Hyder 1994).

In institutional terms, Phase 1 also witnessed two major innovations. First, the CDM of the Kyoto Protocol enabled developed countries to pay for mitigation projects in developing countries and to count the emissions reductions that resulted from such projects towards their own obligations. Funding under this mechanism thus channelled some additional climate finance to developing countries. However, the payments under the CDM do not squarely fit under assistance as a third category of differential treatment because the motivation is different: developed countries invest in them *instead of* investing in emissions reductions at home. Moreover, most funding under the CDM went to 'advanced' developing countries, notably China, Brazil, and India. Finally, funding under the CDM was also ambivalent with a view to the possibility of future mitigation commitments in developing countries because it allowed developed countries to harvest the 'low hanging fruit' and invest in mitigation projects that were particularly cost-efficient.

In 2000 and 2001, the creation of the Adaptation Fund, the Special Climate Change Fund (SCCF), and the LDC Fund marked a major change to the institutional structures for assistance that had initially been created with the adoption of the UN Framework Convention. This expansion of climate finance partly came in response to the demands of developing countries, and the three new funds also led to an increase in funding for adaptation as well as a more pronounced focus on vulnerable countries and LDCs. However, disagreements over the institutional structures for channelling assistance continued to spark much conflict during as well as after this reform period (see Chapter 8 for a more detailed discussion).

3.3.4 A Brief Summary of Developments in Phase 1 (1992–2006)

In sum, four observations about the ways in which the rise of Brazil, China, and India already shaped the contestation and development of differential treatment norms until 2006 are particularly noteworthy. First, with a view to the international legal architecture – the *level of the legal framework* – the Kyoto Protocol that was adopted in 1997 specified many provisions of the UN Framework Convention. Most importantly for our study, the Kyoto Protocol formulated organizing principles for the implementation of the principle of CBDR in relation to climate change mitigation. As an early sign of individualization, Annex I parties were assigned clear numerical targets. In addition, several 'flexible mechanisms' were introduced to allow for efficiency gains, and a compliance procedure was envisaged (though not established until 2005; see Decision 27/CMP.1 of 9–10 December 2005). The implications of the Kyoto Protocol, however, were ambivalent. On the one hand, the system of differential treatment had shown its resilience when the Kyoto Protocol reaffirmed the 'firewall' between developed and developing countries, and exempted the latter from quantified obligations to limit their greenhouse gas emissions. On the other hand, some developed countries continued to reject the general exemption of all developing countries. The reluctance of developing countries to accept either voluntary or binding commitments, combined with the US' refusal to ratify, eventually limited the success of the Kyoto Protocol. Ultimately, international climate negotiations between 1997 and 2005 thus remained largely stalled over the question of developing country commitments.

Second, at a *discursive level*, developed countries regularly sought to overcome the binary distinction between developed and developing countries. Notably, they sought to generate legitimacy for a third category of 'advanced developing countries', 'major economies', or 'major emitters'. With respect to the analytical distinctions of Chapter 1, such calls constituted an attempt to force a fragmentation of the binary system of differentiation. By and large, however, Brazil, China, and India remained firm in their rejection of such language in Phase 1. They continued to insist that they were part of the developing world, and their fellow G-77 members continued to support this view.

Third, important developments occurred at the *institutional level*. Here, the decision to remove Turkey from Annex II signalled that the placement of countries in specific categories was not automatic. Instead, a grey area existed. Moreover, the decision not to add Mexico and South Korea to Annex I and Annex II when they acceded to the OECD set an important precedent with respect to the graduation of countries from the group of those holding special rights (or being exempted from special obligations). In addition, it also added to the impression of 'fuzzy margins' that emanated from the lack of clear classification criteria as well as the large differences between countries that appeared in the same category (Boyte 2010: 88). Furthermore, the Kyoto Protocol introduced individualized differentiation *among* Annex I countries. As all developing countries continued to have the same obligations, this created an asymmetry that added yet another oddity to the international climate regime.

Fourth and finally, the first phase established a strong link between developing country commitments and assistance. For the second phase, this link implied that if developing country commitments were to increase, assistance would likely have to increase as well. Stated differently, the *unmaking of differential treatment* in one area of the international climate would need to be complemented with an *expansion of differential treatment* in the other major area of that regime.

3.4 PROCESSES OF CONTESTATION IN PHASE 2 (2007–2021)

The years from 2007 to 2015 were dominated by the search for a 'post-2012 climate regime'. This search eventually led to the adoption of the Paris Agreement in 2015. Based on the objective to '[hold] the increase in the global average temperature to well below 2°C above pre-industrial levels and [to pursue] efforts to limit the temperature increase to 1.5°C above pre-industrial levels' (Article 2.1[a]), the agreement seeks to 'strengthen the global response to the threat of climate change'.

In terms of differential treatment, the norms and ideas that inform the Paris Agreement are indicative of a reinterpretation regarding at least two of the three areas we discuss in this chapter. First, with respect to the question of how states should be assigned to specific categories of rights-holders and duty-bearers, Article 2.1 stipulates that the agreement 'will be implemented to reflect equity and the principle of common but differentiated responsibilities and respective capabilities'. However, the Paris Agreement neither includes annexes nor takes note of existing ones (see also Honkonen 2009: 263). Instead, Article 4 requires *all parties* to submit 'nationally determined contributions' every five years based on progressive ambition.

Second, with respect to developing country commitments, the Paris Agreement asks states to determine their contributions 'in the light of different national circumstances' (Articles 2.2 and 4.3). On the one hand, this generally implies that developing countries will need to contribute less than developed countries. On the other hand, it means that countries that claim developing country status will no longer be treated homogenously. Because other states will expect more from 'advanced' developing countries than from 'least developed' countries, differentiation becomes more individualized, more gradual, and more informal.

Third and finally, developing country commitments continue to be tied very closely to financial assistance from developed countries. The Paris Agreement thus notes that the agreement aims to achieve its objectives by 'making finance flows consistent with a pathway towards low greenhouse gas emissions and climate-resilient development' (Article 2.1). Moreover, it stipulates that developed country parties 'shall provide financial resources to assist developing country Parties with respect to both mitigation and adaptation in continuation of their existing obligations under the Convention' while 'other parties are encouraged to provide or continue to provide such support voluntarily' (Article 9). We discuss key developments in each of these three areas in further detail below.

3.4.1 Contestation over Country Categories

In terms of differential treatment, COP-13 (2007) in Bali and its major outcomes – the Bali Roadmap and the Bali Action Plan – stand out as a turning point in the history of the international climate regime (Rajamani 2008b). At this conference, discussions on the post-2012 climate regime gained momentum. Negotiators thought it increasingly unlikely that an effective future regime could be built on the Kyoto Protocol's template of targets and timetables for developed countries, combined with an exemption of all developing countries (Bodansky et al. 2017: 110). In a first step, this increased the pressure on rising powers to recognize the difference between themselves and other developing countries. Subsequently, this pressure gave rise to new negotiating coalitions among G-77 members.

3.4.1.1 Growing pressure on Brazil, China, and India

Most importantly, developed countries wanted Brazil, China, and India to accept further central obligations in the climate regime. First, there were continued attempts to distinguish 'least developed countries', 'developed countries', and a new category of 'rapidly developing countries' and to base differentiation on 'objective criteria' (Boyte 2010; Honkonen 2009: 261–262; Rajamani 2008b). Second, developed countries increasingly pressed 'large developing countries' – those seen as competitors in global markets and those seen as necessary parts of a solution to the climate crisis – 'to articulate the conditions under and the forms in which they would undertake climate mitigation commitments' (Dubash and Rajamani 2015: 665).

The EU, for instance, called upon parties to identify solutions that would 'enhance fairness and effectiveness of the climate regime under changing national and international circumstances' (cited in Honkonen 2009: 264) and suggested that 'economically advanced countries must make "fair and effective contributions" to the climate effort' (Rajamani 2012a: 616). Similarly, Japan invoked an 'enlightened sense of solidarity' under which the mitigation targets of states – including those of developing countries – would be tailored more closely to national circumstances (Honkonen 2009: 264; Rajamani 2012a: 616). On other occasions, Japan called upon parties to define the meaning of 'developed' and 'developing' countries more clearly and 'to identify the scope and criteria of those "developing country Parties" required to take actions' (cited in Rajamani 2008a: 48). Australia, Canada, and the US, moreover, insisted on commitments for 'major emitters' (Rajamani 2008a: 48–49; Rajamani 2012a: 616).

Substantively, Annex I parties based this pressure on arguments about the rise in countries' current emissions (see Table 3.1: columns 4 and 5) as well as on improvements in their living standards and levels of development (see Table 3.1: column 1). When they asked Brazil, China, and India to accept commitments, they regularly referred to both aspects (Hallding et al. 2011: 24). The US, moreover, put particular emphasis on the idea that 'the notions of "responsibility" and "capabilities" evolve as the circumstances of countries evolve in the global economy' (Rajamani 2008b: 919).

In addition, rising powers also came under sustained pressure from the global media 'to do more to demonstrate their commitment towards fighting climate change' (Sengupta 2020: 173). This media pressure partly emanated from 'a slew of influential reports' like the Stern Review (commissioned by the government of the UK and published in 2006), the IEA's World Energy Outlook 2007, or the UNDP's Human Development Report for 2007 and 2008 which all 'focused increasing attention on the rising emissions trajectories of India and China in particular' (Sengupta 2020: 173). Moreover, political as well as public debates were fuelled by the Fourth Assessment Report of the Intergovernmental Panel on Climate Change (IPCC). Published in 2007, the report noted that, to reach internationally recognized climate targets, the emissions of developing countries would need to deviate from business-as-usual scenarios, 'even if developed countries make substantial reductions'. The IPCC report added that, 'for the advanced developing countries' – a category that did not exist in international climate law – this deviation would need to occur by 2020 (IPCC 2007: 775; see also 748).

3.4.1.2 The emergence of the BASIC and LMDC coalitions

Politically, attempts to test the unity of developing countries also included the creation of new institutional venues. In the run-up to COP-13 (2007), Germany invited the governments of Brazil, China, and India (along with Mexico and South Africa) to the G8 summit. The purpose of this 'G8+5' was to discuss the future of international climate governance among the largest greenhouse gas emitters. G-20 meetings as well as the Major Economies Forum on Energy and Climate (MEF) later followed up on these discussions (Hallding et al. 2011: 35; Hochstetler 2012: 57).

In response to such efforts, rising powers began to ally more closely. In the run-up to the 2009 Climate Change Conference in Copenhagen, which was widely expected to adopt basic design elements of a 'post-Kyoto' regime, Brazil, China, and India formed a new coalition together with South Africa under the name of BASIC. All four states were important regional leaders and increasingly significant contributors of greenhouse gas emissions (Hochstetler 2012: 56). BASIC meetings primarily served to coordinate positions (Tabau and Lemoine 2012: 201). Within the climate negotiations, however, BASIC kept a relatively low profile, and BASIC members did not set out to challenge the unity nor the negotiating role of the G-77. Instead, BASIC mainly sought to promote 'broader developing world positions' at UN climate talks as well as at informal meetings of the G8, G20, and the MEF (Hallding et al. 2011: 104; Minas 2013: 5).

For the BASIC members, this focus on unity among the G-77 served as a useful cover from emission mitigation expectations (Hallding et al. 2011: 75) or, at least, as a tool to 'buy time' in the process of departing from historical responsibility as the primary justification for differential treatment (Tabau and Lemoine 2012: 204). At the same time, the emphasis on Southern unity also responded to criticism other developing countries had voiced regarding the role the BASIC countries had played at COP-15 (2009) in Copenhagen. There, a group of developing countries had prevented the meeting from adopting the Copenhagen Accord based on substantive as well as procedural grounds (Hochstetler 2012: 58), and several African countries had accused South Africa of having betrayed African interests in agreeing to the Accord (Qi 2011: 309).

In response to the critique, the BASIC countries began to regularly invite members of the G-77, the LDC group, the Arab Group, the African Group, and the AOSIS to its ministerial meetings (Hochstetler 2012: 58–59; see also Hallding et al. 2011). In addition, the language of BASIC statements also sought to emphasize the developing country status of the four members and their common position as G-77 members (Hochstetler and Milkoreit 2015: 219–220). From the perspective of the G-77, in turn, maintaining unity with the BASIC members also held important advantages: their overall negotiating power vis-à-vis developed countries was significantly stronger when they could count regional powerhouses like Brazil, China, India, and South Africa among their ranks. Moreover, substantive agreement persisted in vital areas of the negotiations, most notably on climate finance and technology transfer (Hochstetler 2012: 60–61; Minas 2013: 5). Nonetheless, further ruptures became visible in the proliferation of Southern negotiating coalitions. One such group were the so-called Like-Minded Developing Countries (LMDC) that emerged at COP-17 (2011) in Durban. It included China and India, but also some OPEC countries and members of the Bolivarian Alliance (ALBA). Its membership was held together primarily by strong opposition to more nuanced forms of differentiation, and the coalition was perceived as an 'active blocker' of normative change in international climate negotiations (Dubash and Rajamani 2015: 667, 672).

3.4.1.3 The Paris Agreement and its aftermath

In 2011, COP-17 in Durban formulated a new plan for an agreement to be finalized by 2015. When this date was met at COP-21 in Paris, the new agreement no longer referred to the Convention's annexes, but simply distinguished between 'developed' and 'developing' countries instead. Moreover, while the Paris Agreement was 'guided by the principles of the Convention' including equity and CBDR, it qualified the reference to the latter by adding 'in the light of different national circumstances'. Ultimately, differentiation among parties was thereby transformed from a list-based approach to self-differentiation based on 'nationally determined contributions' (NDCs).

The approach adopted in the Paris Agreement reinterprets the principle of CBDR, but it also generates significant ambivalence. On the one hand, it follows the distinction between developed and developing countries. On the other hand, it leaves open which country falls into which category and thus holds or does not hold a legitimate claim to special rights. Moreover, even if a category can be assigned, the implications are less specific since taking the 'different national circumstances' into account calls for differentiation within each category as well. In a way, the approach created a seeming clarity by requiring *all states* to submit regular and progressive NDCs and by continuing to ask developed countries *to do more* than developing countries. However, this clarity was countered by either subjecting key provisions to national interpretations or postponing their specification to future negotiations.

Overall, informalizing differentiation based on self-selected differentiated commitments reduced the contestation over the placement of states in different categories. Nonetheless, debates continued after 2015. At COP-26

(2021) in Glasgow, for example, Guatemala requested 'that Central America be recognized as a highly vulnerable region', a category that would render the states eligible for special assistance (Gobierno de Guatemala 2021). This indicates that debates over categorization continue to be central for the ability to receive climate finance following Articles 3.2 and 4.4 of the UN Framework Convention. In addition, the Turkish delegation continued to voice its concern with the existing classification of Turkey in order to gain access to climate finance and technology transfer (ENB 12/793 of 16 November 2021: 4; see also ENB 12/747 of 18 December 2018: 19; ENB 12/775 of 18 December 2019: 17). Both episodes illustrate how the problem of 'fuzzy margins' and the related concerns over 'anomalies' still matter in the post-2015 international climate regime.

3.4.2 Contestation over Developing Country Commitments

As pressure on advanced developing countries mounted, the broader question of developing country commitments remained contested as well. Most importantly, the notion of 'long-term cooperative action' under the Convention was understood to entail some form of developing country commitments in the field of climate mitigation. Building on tentative developing country commitments in Phase 1 (e.g. Argentina's 1998 announcement of voluntary commitments), COP-13 (2007) in Bali saw heated debates and, eventually, a new formula for differentiation.

3.4.2.1 Negotiating the Bali Roadmap and Bali Action Plan

A key question at COP-13 (2007) was whether the Kyoto Protocol would continue to serve as a basis for the future or whether states would search for a new 'comprehensive global agreement'. Most developing countries favoured the former option, and when Australia announced that it would ratify the Kyoto Protocol, this added some momentum to the 'Kyoto Protocol track'. Yet, several developed countries as well as AOSIS continued to voice support for a new treaty (TWN 2008: 53; ENB 12/354 of 18 December 2007).

Developing country commitments were central to discussions on both options. In relation to the Kyoto Protocol, for example, the general idea was to aim for a second commitment period that would last until 2020 and seek emissions reductions in the range of 25 to 40 per cent compared to 1990 levels. However, Martin Khor noted at the time, 'the word "architecture" has crept into the discussions' on the mandatory review of the Kyoto Protocol that states would need to undertake in 2008 and, he added, 'some believe the intent is to rewrite the Protocol' (TWN 2008: 19) to include developing county commitments.

A comprehensive proposal to this end was introduced by the Russian delegation (ENB 12/354 of 18 December 2007: 18; TWN 2008: 22–24). It called for an amendment of the Kyoto Protocol that would ask non-Annex I parties to make 'voluntary commitments'. Such commitments, the proposal suggested, could include absolute or relative targets for greenhouse gas emissions, commitments to implement certain policies, and measures or commitments to develop, deploy, or expand low-emissions technologies. Moreover, developing country parties could, according to the Russian proposal, make unconditional commitments or, in line with Article 4.7 of the UN Framework Convention, tie commitments to financial or technology transfers from developed countries.

Australia, Belarus, Canada, Japan, New Zealand, and South Korea supported the proposal. The EU equally stated that 'the proposal should be dealt with seriously' (TWN 2008: 23–24). China and India, by contrast, objected. First, they argued that Article 4.1 of the UN Framework Convention already allowed any developing country to 'take whatever policies and measures it likes to address climate change'. Second, they maintained that there was a procedure in place for countries to voluntarily accede to Annex I for the purposes of the Kyoto Protocol and that, while these rules could be further 'clarified', there was no need to 'simplify' them (TWN 2008: 23).

The Bali Action Plan eventually left open whether the 'Kyoto track' or the 'Convention track' would be prioritized (ENB 12/354 of 18 December 2007: 1–2, 19). By envisaging an 'agreed outcome' and mandating a working group to prepare the latter, however, it signalled that those who favoured a new agreement might hold the better cards (FCCC/CP/2007/6/Add.1 of 14 March 2008: Article 1[b]). Moreover, noting that such an outcome would prescribe 'enhanced national/international action on mitigation of climate change' for developed *and* developing countries, it also set an important marker in terms of differentiation.

While this formulation suggested a move towards greater 'symmetry' – another term that began to appear more frequently in country statements – the specific requirements the Bali Action Plan outlined continued to differ for each group of countries. For developed countries, it envisaged 'measurable, reportable and verifiable nationally appropriate mitigation *commitments or actions, including quantified emission limitation and reduction objectives*'. Article 1(b) on developing country commitments, by contrast, stipulated that the latter would be required to identify and implement 'nationally appropriate mitigation *actions* … in the context of sustainable development, supported and enabled by technology, financing and capacity-building, in a measurable, reportable and verifiable manner' (FCCC/CP/2007/6/Add.1 of 14 March 2008: Article 1(b); italics added).

In sum, the Bali Action Plan thus left serious dents in the 1995 Berlin firewall. It differentiated between developed country *commitments* and developing country *actions*, and it also tied (some of) the latter to financial assistance from developed countries (Rajamani 2012b: 505). In this way, the outcome of COP-13 (2007) '[realigned] the balance of commitments between developed and developing countries' (Rajamani 2008b: 935; see also Jinnah 2017: 294–295). By heeding to one of the core demands of developed countries, this decision opened the path for negotiating a new climate accord in which developing country commitments would figure more prominently.

3.4.2.2 From Bali to Durban

Reacting to heightened pressure, further developing countries began to make concessions regarding their own voluntary commitments. India, for instance, moved away from its backward-looking justification of differential treatment when, in 2007, it announced that its per capita emissions would never exceed those of OECD countries (Ministry of External Affairs – Government of India 2007; see also Rajamani 2009: 346; Gupta 2014: 168). In the run-up to the 2009 Copenhagen Conference, all BASIC members also announced voluntary mitigation commitments and allowed for these targets to be included in the appendix to the Copenhagen Accord (Minas 2013: 2; Sengupta 2020: 186). India declared that it 'will endeavour to reduce the emissions intensity of its GDP by 20–25% by 2020 in comparison to the 2005 level'. Brazil announced nine different mitigation actions that it anticipated to lead 'to an expected reduction of 36.1% to 38.9% of projected emissions of Brazil by 2020'. And China stated that it would 'endeavor to lower its carbon dioxide emissions per unit of GDP by 40–45% by 2020 compared to the 2005 level' (FCCC/KP/CMP/2008/11/Add.2 of 19 March 2009; FCCC/CP/2009/11/Add.1 of 30 March 2010).

Still, views on developing country commitments differed widely. This also became evident in the proposals for a draft agreement which states had submitted before the 2009 Copenhagen Climate Change Conference. The US, Australia, and Japan all proposed draft texts that included mitigation actions from all countries as well as more far-reaching commitments from 'developing country Parties whose national circumstances reflect greater responsibility or capability' (FCCC/CP/2009/3 of 19 May 2009: 20; FCCC/CP/2009/5 of 6 June 2009: 5; FCCC/CP/2009/7 of 6 June 2009: 6). Tuvalu, on behalf of AOSIS, sought a middle ground when it proposed commitments for developed countries and 'other Parties who voluntarily elect to do so' (FCCC/CP/2009/4 of 5 June 2009: 4). Finally, the proposal submitted by Costa Rica represented the contrasting position of developing countries. It highlighted equity and CBDR, explicitly invoked historical responsibility, and asked developed countries 'as a group' to reduce their emissions by at least 25 to 40 per cent from 1990 levels by 2020 and by either 'more than 95 per cent' or 'in the range of 75–85 per cent' by 2050. By contrast, its proposal envisaged developing country commitments to remain dependent on financial and technology transfers (FCCC/CP/2009/6 of 8 June 2009: 6–8).

While states could not agree on any of these proposals at COP-15 (2009), the Copenhagen Accord nonetheless continued to move on the discussion on 'nationally appropriate mitigation actions' (or NAMAs) of developing countries. Notably, it introduced 'the term "supported NAMA" to refer to NAMAs seeking international support for their implementation' and thereby suggested 'that developing countries may also implement NAMAs without support' (Sharma and Desgain 2013: 9). Moreover, the Copenhagen Accord, based on the AOSIS proposal, drove a 'small wedge between Least Developed Countries (LDCs) and Small Island Developing States (SIDS) on the one hand, and all other developing countries on the other' when it suggested that the former 'may' and the latter 'will' implement NAMAs (Jinnah 2017: 295).

Two years later, at COP-17 (2011) in Durban, states managed to agree on key aspects of a second commitment period of the Kyoto Protocol starting in 2013. However, the EU tied its acceptance of a second commitment period to the willingness of parties to work on a new legally binding treaty 'applicable to all parties' (Khor 2020b: 85). On this point, two aspects proved particularly contentious. First, because the EU wanted a legally binding agreement, it sought to amend the reference to a new protocol or another 'legal outcome' in the draft text. Developing countries, by contrast, sought to keep different options open. Second, several developing countries complained that the draft text 'did not even contain the words "equity" or "common but differentiated responsibility"' and noted their unwillingness to 'give up the equity principle' (India's Environment Minister, Jayanthi Natarajan, cited in Khor 2020b: 88). The final decision at COP-13 (2007) allowed for a compromise on the former but not necessarily on the latter aspect: parties agreed to 'launch a process to develop a protocol, another legal instrument or an *agreed outcome with legal force* under the Convention' (FCCC/CP/2011/9/Add.1 of 15 March 2012: 2; italics added) and established a new process called the Ad Hoc Working Group on the Durban Platform for Enhanced Action (ADP) to prepare such an agreement. Yet, the decision only implicitly referred to the principles of equity or CBDR. By qualifying that the agreement would be 'under the Convention', it merely signalled that an 'agreed outcome' would continue to be guided by the principles of Article 3, including the principle of CBDR (Khor 2020b: 89).

3.4.2.3 The Paris Agreement and its aftermath

Following these initial steps, the structure of the new agreement states concluded at COP-21 (2015) in Paris became increasingly visible. As developing countries remained unwilling to accept binding commitments, developed countries opted for 'nationally appropriate' mitigation commitments and actions for all parties. The Paris Agreement codifies this new structure in its requirement for all parties to 'prepare, communicate and maintain successive nationally determined contributions that [they intend] to achieve' and to 'pursue domestic mitigation measures, with the aim of achieving the objectives of such contributions' (Article 4.2).

In terms of differentiated mitigation commitments, the agreement includes five major provisions (see also Pauw et al. 2019). First, a preambular clause reaffirmed that the agreement is concluded to pursue the objective of the UN Framework Convention and 'guided by its principles, including the principle of equity and common but differentiated responsibilities and respective capabilities, in the light of different national circumstances'. Second, the agreement recognized 'that peaking [of greenhouse gas emissions] will take longer for developing country Parties'. Yet, this recognition was also followed by a common commitment 'to achieve a balance between anthropogenic emissions by sources and removals by sinks of greenhouse gases in the second half of this century' (Article 4.1). Even if the latter was meant to be achieved 'on the basis of equity, and in the context of sustainable development and efforts to eradicate poverty', it implied that developing countries would need to adopt net zero targets during the period thus specified as well.

Third, the agreement further recognized that developed country parties 'should continue taking the lead by undertaking economy-wide absolute emission reduction targets'. Developing countries, by contrast, 'should continue their *mitigation efforts*' and were merely '*encouraged to move over time* to economy-wide emission reduction *or limitation* targets' (Articles 4.3 and 4.4; italics added). Fourth, the Paris Agreement reaffirmed that developed countries should provide developing countries with support for the implementation of their mitigation commitments (Article 4.5). Finally, it exempted 'least developed countries and small island developing States' from most commitments and stipulated that these countries '*may prepare and communicate* strategies, plans and actions for low greenhouse gas emissions development reflecting their special circumstances' (Article 4.6; italics added).

In sum, these formulations sealed the envelope for a reinterpretation of the principle of CBDR. In line with the decisions adopted between COP-13 (2007) and COP-17 (2011), the international climate regime moved towards greater 'symmetry' of developed and developing country commitments (Deleuil 2012: 280). Accordingly, developing country observers interpreted the outcome as a 'blurring of the distinctions between developed and developing countries' and therefore a weakening of the CBDR principle (Khor 2020a: 71). In addition, following in the footsteps of the 'nationally appropriate' mitigation commitments and actions of the Bali Action Plan, the 'nationally determined contributions' of the Paris Agreement strengthened the notion of *individualized differentiation* that developed countries had already adopted for themselves in the Kyoto Protocol. Finally, the notion of 'nationally determined' contributions introduced a strong element of self-selected differentiation and hence of *informalized differentiation* (see also Rajamani 2012b: 509–511, 517).

3.4.3 Contestation over Assistance

Like in Phase 1, assistance after 2007 remained closely connected to the question of developing country commitments. As demands for such commitments increased, so did the justifications, extent, goals, and structure of assistance obligations for developed countries. In addition, climate change had increasingly become a reality rather than merely a future prospect to be avoided. One consequence was that, besides funding for adaptation and funding for mitigation, developing countries also demanded compensation for loss and damage.

3.4.3.1 Justifications of assistance

While developed countries sought mitigation commitments from 'all parties', developing countries continued to defend poverty eradication and further social and economic development as their overriding priorities. Focussing on these priorities, they attempted to strengthen the link between commitments on their part and assistance (Thompson 2020: 67). By contrast, arguments based on historical responsibility lost some of their centrality compared to forward-looking arguments related to rising capabilities and emissions in developing countries. As economies developed, moreover, not all claims to assistance were equally persuasive. For example, China, Saudi Arabia, and South Korea had reached higher per capita emissions than the EU average in 2015, and South Korea's GDP per capita had also approximated the EU average in 2015 (see Table 3.1: columns 1, 3, and 5).

At the same time, developed countries had so far fulfilled neither their mitigation nor their assistance obligations. Important large emitters like the US had not ratified the Kyoto Protocol and instead exhibited rising emissions since the 1990s (Gupta 2014: 168). In addition, developing countries described assistance provided through the GEF and the other funds of the climate regime as 'woefully inadequate' and a 'measly sum' (TWN 2009: 10, 16). In this regard, developing countries referred to Article 4.7. of the UN Framework Convention and argued that assistance had to increase substantially to warrant further commitments on their part (Prys-Hansen et al. 2019: 281).

Finally, climate change was no longer just a bleak outlook. Instead, the developing countries that were most vulnerable to global warming started to experience climate-related harm. As a result, loss and damage gained salience as an additional area of assistance during Phase 2 (ENB 12/567 of 11 December 2012: 20; ENB 12/594 of 26 November 2013: 10; TWN 2013: 99–102; 2014: 13–18, 93–97). In this new context, backward-looking arguments of historical responsibility remained central with respect to potential liability and compensation claims related to current and no longer avoidable loss and damage.

3.4.3.2 Amounts and goals

Asked to make new commitments and faced with a more urgent prospect of climate-related harm, developing countries demanded more, and more specific, climate finance. Developed countries, in turn, promised and partially delivered new sums (Bodansky et al. 2017: 111, 113, 147; TWN 2008: 25–26; 2011a: 8; Thompson 2020: 66–68). During Phase 1, the budget of the GEF had been negotiated from replenishment to replenishment. Correspondingly, assistance had been criticized for being unpredictable, unreliable, untransparent, and inadequate (TWN 2010: 6). These issues remained areas of concern in Phase 2. Yet, their severity and extent decreased somewhat. Most notably, the COP-15 (2009) in Copenhagen and COP-16 (2010) in Cancún set overall assistance targets starting in 2010. So called 'Fast-Start-Finance' at a level of USD 30 billion was to support developing countries between 2010 and 2012, and developing countries promised to 'mobilize' USD 100 billion per year starting in 2020 (ENB 12/459 of 22 December 2009: 29; ENB 12/498 of 13 December 2010: 11; Rajamani 2010: 826; 2012a: 611).

Although the kind of assistance flows and the institutional channels that would count towards these targets remained unclear, the fact that climate conferences managed to agree on targets was a novelty. And although developing countries still regarded the sums they were promised as inadequate, climate finance had increased in comparison to the 1990s and early 2000s. In practice, however, developed countries failed to reach the target of USD 100 billion per year by 2020, and they hope to reach this level in 2023. At COP-26 (2021) in Glasgow, some developing countries proposed a record collective goal of at least USD 1.3 trillion per year. On the question of which states would be asked to contribute to this collective goal, the ENB meeting report notes that 'a developed country said parties need to define providers and receivers of the new goal' (ENB 12/793 of 16 November 2021: 21). Who should provide inputs and who should be eligible to benefit from assistance remains contested.

3.4.3.3 Governance structures

Besides contested justifications, amounts, and goals of assistance, the appropriateness of institutional structures for climate finance equally remained controversial in Phase 2. Developing countries continued criticizing the GEF for being overburdened, inadequate, overly bureaucratic, inaccessible, and lacking in transparency (TWN 2010: 25–26). They also did not regard the three new funds created at the turn of the millennium as sufficient to overcome the structural flaws of the GEF (ENB 12/395 of 15 December 2008: 9; TWN 2009: 10).

Developed countries, by contrast, renewed their support for the GEF, arguing that it had effectively responded to developing country needs.

These opposing views clashed at COP-15 (2009) and COP-16 (2010) where the parties took decisions to restructure the institutional landscape of climate finance again (FCCC/CP/2009/11/Add.1 of 30 March 2010; FCCC/CP/2010/7/Add.1 of 15 March 2011; see also Chapter 8). Most importantly, this restructuring included the creation of the Green Climate Fund (GCF), which now operates besides the GEF. The COP decided that a 'significant portion' of assistance should be channelled through the GCF (FCCC/CP/2009/11/Add.1 of 15 March 2011: 7). This is important as the GCF puts a stronger focus on adaptation than the GEF and distributes a relatively larger share of its funds to vulnerable countries.

Finally, COP-19 (2013) also established the Warsaw International Mechanism (WIM) to address the problem of loss and damage associated with climate change impacts (FCCC/CP/2012/8/Add.1 of 28 February 2013: Decision 3/CP.18; FCCC/CP/2013/10/Add.1 of 31 January 2014: Decision 2/CP.19). The question of how parties would respond to loss and damage had gained salience but so far remains unsettled (ENB 12/793 of 16 November 2021: 10–11). The WIM marked a beginning. Its functions, however, remained facilitative, including 'enhancing knowledge', 'strengthening dialogue, coordination, coherence and synergies', and 'enhancing action and support, including finance …, to address loss and damage' (FCCC/CP/2013/10/Add.1 of 31 January 2014: 6–7). In 2015, the Paris Agreement equally '[recognized] the importance of averting, minimizing and addressing loss and damage associated with the adverse effects of climate change' (Article 8). Moreover, COP-25 (2019) set up the Santiago Network to 'catalyse the technical assistance of relevant organizations, bodies, networks and experts, for the implementation of relevant approaches at the local, national and regional level, in developing countries that are particularly vulnerable to the adverse effects of climate change' (FCCC/PA/CMA/2019/L.7 of 15 December 2019). Finally, contestation over loss and damage resurged at COP-26 (2021) and COP-27 (2022). At COP-27 in Sharm El-Sheik, parties also decided to establish a new funding arrangement to help states in dealing with loss and damage, with details to be negotiated in subsequent meetings (ENB 12/818 of 23 November 2022: 9).

Overall, the 2015 Paris Agreement included provisions on all major areas of assistance. It created a successor mechanism to the Kyoto Protocol's CDM (Article 6), recognized the continued importance of adaptation (Article 7), loss and damage (Article 8), technology transfer (Article 10), and capacity-building (Article 11). Most importantly, however, developing countries were partially successful in arguing that the new amounts and goals of assistance for adaptation and mitigation also required a new financing institution which was recognized in the Paris Agreement (Article 9). In this sense, assistance became one of the rare areas *in which differential treatment can be said to have expanded*, as more climate finance has become available. At the same time, the ties between developing country commitments and climate finance have been further institutionalized, and the contestation over who should contribute and be eligible for access to international climate finance continues.

3.5 CONCLUSION

Comparing the developments in Phase 1 and Phase 2, we can see that the understanding of differential treatment in the international climate regime has changed over time. First, the notion that developing countries should be exempt from commitments to limit their greenhouse gas emissions has been replaced by greater 'symmetry' between the commitments of developed and developing countries. Second, and following that decision, the annex-based list approach has been replaced by a system of self-selected differentiation. All countries are now asked to submit their NDCs every five years and formulate their ambition 'in the light of national circumstances'. Third, the binary distinction between developed and developing countries may have lost some of its relevance. However, it continues to guide the access to and provision of assistance. Fourth, the earlier focus on historical responsibility has given way to a much stronger focus on current and prospective emissions as well as on capabilities. Taken together, we can classify these shifts as an individualization and an informalization of the established system of differential treatment. Finally, however, we can also observe an expansion of differential treatment in the field of assistance.

On balance, these changes reveal an unmaking of the system of differential treatment as we used to know it. Compared to the initial version, the revised interpretation not only puts a stronger emphasis on the 'common' element, it also operationalizes the 'differentiated' element in a way that is more nuanced, more informal, more voluntary, more individualized, and more forward-looking. In a nutshell, one could say that the old interpretation highlighted the idea that states had different responsibilities because their historical contributions to the global problem of climate change differed vastly. By contrast, the new interpretation stresses that states have a common responsibility to address the problem, while acknowledging that different states have differentiated responsibilities based on their current emissions and development levels.

How do the observations we make in this chapter compare to those in Chapters 2 and 4? Here, three observations seem particularly noteworthy. First, like in the international trade regime, we observe that an established system of differential treatment is unmade and remade as the distribution of global economic power shifts. However, the form of the unmaking is different: while we observe fragmentation in the trade regime (cf. Chapter 2), individualization is key in the climate regime. Second, the expanding scope of differential treatment regarding climate finance shares some similarities with the resilience of differential treatment in health financing. A main difference is, however, that, in the climate regime, this resilience applies only to one regime area and is part of a package deal that includes the unmaking of differential treatment norms in another regime area. A more interesting similarity might thus lie in the third observation: the increasing reliance on voluntary commitments that is characteristic not only of the Paris Agreement and its NDCs but also of World Health Organization (WHO) financing and its reliance on voluntary contributions (cf. Chapter 4).

Looking at the *dynamics of normative change* in the climate case, the rise of Brazil, China, and India strongly contributes to the changes of differential treatment norms in the international climate regime. It is difficult to imagine that many of these changes would have happened in the absence of major shifts in global power, economic capabilities, and emissions. The analysis of international climate negotiations provides numerous traces of such links (Gupta 2014; Thompson 2020). And our comparison of the two phases 'before' and 'after' the rise of Brazil, China, and India also shows how the contestation over country categories, developing country commitments, and assistance intensified in Phase 2.

In terms of the specific *causes of normative change* we discuss in Chapter 1, moreover, we find evidence for the rationalist, constructivist, and institutional explanation. Thus, coalition unity among developing countries was strong in Phase 1 but weakened in Phase 2 as developing countries that were particularly vulnerable to climate change demanded commitments from rising powers. By contrast, developed countries were often split in two coalitions in Phase 1, but managed to unite around the demand for developing country commitments in Phase 2. Regarding legitimation, the discursive emphasis developed countries placed on contemporary and future emissions and the language of 'major emitters', 'advanced developing countries', and the like eventually paid off and contributed to a relative decline of justification based on historical responsibility. Finally, institutional structures mattered in the form of the limited temporal scope of agreements like the Kyoto Protocol but also in the legal and normative foundations which the UN Framework Convention and the Kyoto Protocol had set for individualized and informalized differentiation.

In Chapters 7 and 8, we zero in on specific conflicts to assess the causal mechanisms that made the reinterpretation of the CBDR principle possible more systematically. Chapter 7 addresses two conflicts over the specific meaning of the norm that developed countries ought to 'take the lead' in reducing their emissions. Chapter 8 complements this account with a reconstruction of two further conflicts over the structures for climate finance that helps us to disentangle the dynamics of both the unmaking and resilience of differential treatment norms in the international climate regime.

NOTES

1. We cite the meeting reports issued by the *Earth Negotiations Bulletin* (ENB) according to their volume (where volume 12 covers international climate negotiations under the UNFCCC) and running number. The reports are available at https://enb.iisd.org/enb/vol12/ (last accessed 11 July 2023).
2. The discussion in this sub-section draws on arguments developed in Dingwerth (2023).
3. We cite official documents related to the UNFCCC process according to their UN document number. While documents published or adopted until 1994 are cited as General Assembly documents (A/…), documents from 1995 onwards are cited as UNFCCC documents (FCCC/…).
4. Depledge (2009: 281) further notes: 'The COP formally recognized the "special circumstances … which place Turkey … in a situation different from that of other Parties included in Annex I". Indicating its satisfaction with this outcome, Turkey acceded to the Convention in 2004. Applying the "special circumstances" clause, Turkey received funding from the GEF for the preparation of its first national communication.'
5. So far, Annex I has only been amended twice: in 1997, COP-3 (1997) reviewed the list of countries in line with the view of Article 4.2(f) of the UNFCCC and included Liechtenstein and Monaco. Czechoslovakia was removed and replaced by the Czech Republic and Slovakia; Croatia and Slovenia were also added. The 17th COP (Durban, 2011) adopted a decision to add Cyprus, a European Union (EU) member state since 2004. By contrast, Kazakhstan sought but was denied inclusion in Annex I. It eventually became 'an Annex I Party for the purposes of the [Kyoto] Protocol' but remained a non-Annex I Party under the Convention (see also Depledge 2009: 279–280).
6. South Korea only 'expressed its intention to take on an emissions target for 2020' in 2008 (Depledge 2009: 277).
7. Sebastian Oberthür and Hermann Ott (2000: 293) note that Organization of the Petroleum Exporting Countries (OPEC) members supported Brazil, China, and India on this point because they assumed that a Kyoto Protocol with voluntary commitments would have had a much higher chance to become ratified in the US Senate – a step the OPEC members sought to prevent.

4. Capacity, willingness, and need in the health regime

Julian Eckl

4.1 INTRODUCTION

Differential treatment plays a key role in global health. However, unlike in the case of trade (Chapter 2) and climate (Chapter 3), differential treatment and the underlying norms are not systematically foregrounded and comprehensively conceptualized in scholarly analyses of global health; this applies even to those scholars who highlight the conflictual relations between developed and developing countries in this regime (e.g. Chorev 2012). Among practitioners, there is similarly no tradition of explicitly referring to the notion of differential treatment; while they discuss certain aspects thereof, they do not talk about it as an overarching phenomenon. A fundamental contribution of the present chapter will consequently be to conceptualize differential treatment in global health and to link dispersed aspects to one another. This will cast a new light on known phenomena and it will reconstruct global health in a manner that makes it more readily comparable to established accounts of differential treatment in trade and climate.

From the perspective of differential treatment, financing is the most important area in global health. This applies not only since health financing is central to global health but also because the link to differential treatment is remarkably strong in the case of financing that is channelled through the World Health Organization (WHO). While not labelled as such, differential treatment has been an integral part of WHO-channelled health financing from the outset and in the wake of decolonization it was shaped by the demands of developing countries in particular. Most importantly, assessed contributions to the budget of the WHO constitute a *legally binding case of differential treatment* while there are generally very few binding international agreements in the health regime, which usually works with various non-binding instruments and is predominated by informal norms (Kates and Katz 2011; Hein and Moon 2013; Morin and Blouin 2019). Furthermore, key aspects of differential treatment in health financing have reached a high level of formalization and operationalization. As a result, the underlying norms of differential treatment have been articulated much more explicitly than in other areas of global health. In sum, WHO-channelled health financing constitutes that area of global health in which differential treatment has been most clearly institutionalized and, as a consequence, it is suited best for analysing changes in differential treatment.

Since both practitioners and analysts of global health tend to look at various aspects of differential treatment individually, there is no established terminology that accounts for the specific form that differential treatment has taken here. This chapter will show that differential treatment in health financing can be conceptualized as capacity, willingness, and need (CWN). In contrast to international norms of differential treatment in the trade and climate regime, CWN is not self-contained within the health regime. Rather, it links health to the wider United Nations (UN) system where key decisions are taken. This requires a research design that is slightly different from the approach taken in the previous chapters on trade and climate. In particular, differential treatment in health financing can only be analysed if developments both at the UN level and at the WHO level are taken into consideration.

While conceptualizing differential treatment in health financing as CWN and accounting for CWN's development across institutional settings are contributions in their own right, the ultimate goal of this regime-level chapter (in conjunction with Chapter 9) is to speak to the overarching discussions of this book. Focussing on the question of how CWN has been contested in view of the rise of Brazil, China, and India and on the question of how it has been adjusted in response, this chapter will show the following. There have been repeated contestations that ranged from attempted unmaking to attempted expanding of CWN. Against the background of these contestations, CWN has been subject to adjustments, but these have often contributed to a preservation of the *status quo ante* and hence to resilience. In particular, attenuated and partial graduation has increasingly been accepted while it was initially heavily contested. These developments have, however, been accompanied by an informalization that has ambivalent consequences and suggests a weakening of differential treatment in a manner that was not anticipated in our initial conceptualization of change (Chapter 1). In essence, it makes differential treatment increasingly voluntary, discretionary, and (non)contributor-exposed.

The analysis that is contained in this chapter spans over five sections. The next section will discuss the relevance of WHO-channelled health financing and it will contextualize the present research in the existing literature. The subsequent section will introduce CWN as the specific form that differential treatment took in WHO-channelled health financing. Focussing on the input side of financing, the two following sections will analyse how and when CWN was contested and adapted during two main phases in the past quarter of a century: first, the phase that covers the aftermath of the Cold War and the early signs of a rise of Brazil, China, and India (mid-1990s up to the financial crisis that began in 2007); second, the phase that covers the time after the 'Western' financial crisis and the obvious rise of Brazil, China, and India (from 2008 to 2020). The final section will conclude. The case studies in Chapter 9 will complement the findings of this chapter with additional details and a discussion of the question of why contestation and adaptation occurred.

Both this chapter and its companion (Chapter 9) are primarily based on a software-assisted qualitative analysis of over 500 primary documents of the relevant UN and WHO decision-making bodies. In the following, these primary sources will be referred to by their official identifier and the year in which an event took place or in which the document was published. Moreover, the analysis was complemented with secondary sources and benefited from the insights gained in an ethnographic long-term study of global health governance (e.g. Eckl 2021).

4.2 ANALYSING WHO AS THE KEY FINANCING CHANNEL FROM THE PERSPECTIVE OF DIFFERENTIAL TREATMENT

Over the past two decades, global health has witnessed a massive increase in financial resources (e.g. IHME 2011; 2020). Although there are more financial resources for global health than ever before, there is also historical continuity in that the rules and norms around financing and its channels remain contested. From the perspective of international norms of differential treatment, not all financing channels are equally important. Leaving aside those forms of purely private financing where neither the source nor the channel involves public players, there are four main groups of financing channels: WHO-channelled financing (channel 1), other kinds of multi- and polylateral financing (channel 2), bilateral financing (channel 3), and domestic financing (channel 4).

Only the norms that underlie channels 1 and 2 are truly *international* norms in the sense that they are negotiated and practised within international society (Bull 1977). As indicated by the term 'polylateral financing',[1] this implies neither that membership is necessarily universal nor that private actors are excluded. The key point that determines relevance for the present purpose is that there are multiple states who govern the relations amongst each other. While this explains the relevance of both channel 1 and 2, it has already been shown in the introduction that WHO-channelled financing (channel 1) constitutes the institutional core of these two channels since it includes legally binding differential treatment. At the same time, non-binding differential treatment, which predominates channel 2, plays a role in the WHO context as well. As will be discussed below, this is a consequence of voluntary contributions to the budget. In other words, by studying WHO-channelled financing (channel 1) one can analyse *both* takes on differential treatment in a nutshell which reinforces the observation made in the introduction that this channel is the obvious starting point for an examination of changes in differential treatment.

Channel 1 – sometimes in conjuncture with channel 2 – has been studied extensively in the literature (e.g. Patz and Goetz 2019: 180–196; Reddy et al. 2018; People's Health Movement et al. 2017: 245–262; Browne 2017; Clinton and Sridhar 2017; Goetz and Patz 2017; Graham 2017a; Sridhar and Woods 2013). Recurrent themes in this literature are the increasing relevance of voluntary financing and the concomitant challenges. While the focus has been on the problematic role that major donors – both public and private – can play in this context, this literature did not systematically analyse how both mandatory and voluntary funding relate to broader questions of differential treatment. The present chapter – together with Chapter 9 – will fill this gap and thereby contribute both to the literature on financing and to the literature on differential treatment.

Regarding the latter (e.g. Rajamani 2006; 2012a), the analysis will provide a reconstruction and conceptualization of differential treatment in an area that has previously been overlooked. This allows for a fresh perspective on known phenomena, including the possibility to trace contestations of CWN over time and across different fora; to account for change, including the degree to which CWN was adjusted to the rise of Brazil, China, and India; and to compare CWN to differential treatment in trade and climate. The analysis will also address somewhat paradoxical observations that question a clear-cut distinction between *contributors* to and *beneficiaries* of differential treatment.

Regarding the former – existing research on WHO financing (channel 1) – the fundamental contribution will be to analyse this issue as a case of differential treatment in the first place and to conceptualize it as CWN. A related theoretical contribution will be to highlight the relevance of norms in financing debates. Based on this conceptual and theoretical shift it becomes possible to analyse the historical development of financing norms, the conflicts around them, their practical consequences, and the positions that Brazil, China, and India have taken towards them over time. The latter will also expand our knowledge on the role of rising powers in WHO financing and reform while the focus has traditionally been on the classic contributors.[2] Moreover, in the existing literature there is a tendency to remain at the WHO level and to treat the UN level as a black box. By contrast, the present analysis will link discussions at the WHO level more systematically to discussions at the UN level than is usually the case.[3] As a consequence, it will be able to unpack the norms that underlie mandatory payments (assessed contributions). A further contribution of the present chapter will be to cast a new light on voluntary contributions and to explain why not only the classic contributors to differential treatment but also the classic beneficiaries, rising powers in particular, value this type of funding.

Finally, the detailed analysis questions established empirical assumptions on financing. For example, accounts of the manner in which assessed contributions are calculated (scale of assessments) are often rather superficial and state that assessments are based on 'gross national product and population' (Lee 2009: 38),[4] but this overlooks the complexity of the methodology according to which the scale is calculated. For example, it gives the wrong impression that populous countries pay more while they are actually likely to pay less than countries with small populations. India and China, in particular, benefit from this effect. Similarly, the findings will cast some doubt on established assumptions regarding WHO and its budget, including the claim that WHO would have adhered to a policy of zero nominal growth since 1993 (e.g. Lee 2009: 39; Chorev 2012: 144; People's Health Movement et al. 2017: 247–248), or the assertion that financing conflicts are mainly conflicts between developed and developing countries (e.g. Chorev 2012). The next section will deepen the discussion of central characteristics of CWN before the two following sections turn to changes over time.

4.3 NORMS OF DIFFERENTIAL TREATMENT IN WHO-CHANNELLED FINANCING

Practitioners do not talk about differential treatment as an overarching phenomenon, but they refer to the underlying norms when they discuss issues such as the scale of assessments, the budget, or strategic budget space allocation. In more abstract terms, one could say that differential treatment in the form of CWN matters in each dimension of financing (input, channels, and output). While individual norms can affect more than one dimension, the following discussion of CWN will link each of the three norms to the contexts in which they are typically addressed.

4.3.1 Legally Binding Input and Capacity to Pay (C2P)

It is a *central obligation* of *all* WHO member states to contribute to the WHO budget – and a failure to meet this financial obligation can be sanctioned through a suspension of the 'voting privileges and services to which a Member is entitled' (WHO Constitution: Article 7; cf. WHO 2020: 4). The Constitution of WHO determines furthermore that the expenses of the organization shall be apportioned among the member states 'in accordance with a scale to be fixed by the Health Assembly' (Article 56). In practice and in line with the understanding expressed when the WHO Constitution was drafted (WHO 1948: 25), this scale is derived from the scale that the UN General Assembly sets for UN contributions. As a consequence, there is a tradition of linking the UN level to the WHO level, but this link has at times been contested.

While differences in WHO and UN membership are among the reasons for which the UN scale cannot be applied directly by WHO, the UN provisions on financing are analogical to the ones for WHO: 'The expenses of the Organization shall be borne by the Members as apportioned by the General Assembly' (UN Charter: Article 17[2]). In other words, both foundational documents determine the institutional process through which the scale of assessments is to be set but neither specifies the methodology through which the contributions of individual member states are to be determined. Crucially, they do not state that each member state would be obliged to contribute an 'equal share'; rather they define financing as a common but differentiated responsibility and the norm, or principle, according to which each member state is assessed has become known as capacity to pay (C2P). In essence, C2P demands that *all member states have to make a payment to the budget according to their relative capacity to pay*. Since C2P relates to a central obligation, it falls into the first category of differential treatment (cf. Chapter 1; Rajamani 2006: 93–118).

In practice, C2P has been operationalized through the methodology that calculates the scale of assessments; the scale of assessments in turn states the relative financial share that each member state has to bear. As it relies on operational definitions, this formula approach can be interpreted as a special case of the definition method for the categorization of parties to international treaties that is discussed by Rajamani (2006: 164–173). While the scale methodology has undergone some historical changes, there are three main steps that express the manner in which C2P has been interpreted.

First, the national income of each country is calculated as a share of world income. Second, relief measures are applied in order to further decrease the relative share of disadvantaged countries while the relative share of most other countries is increased. In this context, indebted countries that are not high-income countries and countries with a low per capita income receive relief. Third, three so-called limits to the scale are applied that, like the relief measures, have redistributive consequences. The limits serve the following purposes: all countries shall make a minimum contribution, Least Developed Countries shall not pay more than the ceiling that has been set for them, and no country shall pay more than the maximum ceiling. Further details of the three steps will be discussed in the empirical section on Phase 1 (1995–2007) to provide the necessary background to the contestations and changes that will be reconstructed there (see section 4.4).

In order to contextualize C2P and its operationalization through the scale methodology, three points should be added. First, the UN scale of assessments is not only applied to the UN budget and – after membership adjustments – to the WHO budget. Further international organizations that apply a membership-adjusted version of the UN scale would be the United Nations Educational, Scientific and Cultural Organization (UNESCO), the Food and Agriculture Organization (FAO), and the United Nations Industrial Development Organization (UNIDO). Second, *equal share* is not only a theoretical alternative to C2P but actually used, for example, by the Association of Southeast Asian Nations (ASEAN), the Organization of the Petroleum Exporting Countries (OPEC), and the Central Commission for the Navigation of the Rhine (CCNR). Third, in addition to equal share, there are *further alternatives* to C2P. A noteworthy example is the scale of assessments of the International Maritime Organization (IMO) that is strongly influenced by its members' gross registered tonnage. For example, this makes Panama, Liberia, and the Marshall Islands the top three contributors in 2017 (A/73/460 [2018]).[5]

While the central role of C2P for the input dimension of WHO-channelled financing is in general not disputed, the disagreements regarding the interpretation and operationalization of this norm are notorious. The visible consequence of these disagreements are the recurrent conflicts over the scale of assessments and the underlying methodology that will be discussed in the empirical sections below and in the case studies in Chapter 9.

4.3.2 Budget Size, Budget Composition, and Willingness to Contribute (W2C)

In addition to conflicts on the fine-tuning of C2P, there have been recurrent debates on the total amount that was to be financed through contributions that were assessed in this manner. These discussions on the size of the regular budget of WHO are consequently a second context in which C2P has been promoted and contested. Not least as a consequence of demands by 'newly independent states', the regular budget increased continuously and considerably in the course of the first decades of WHO's existence (Jacobson 1973) but there were also repeated attempts to keep the budget increases to a minimum (e.g. WHA31.23 [1978]). Over the years, the debates additionally paid attention to the voluntary contributions to the budget that became ever more important and that are subject to willingness to contribute (W2C) as a second norm of differential treatment. This section will first look into the link between C2P and the budget decisions before it analyses the particularities of W2C.

While all member states have an equal vote in budgeting decisions, the financial consequences are differentiated as determined by C2P. This has often led to conflicts between the numerous countries with relatively low assessment rates and the countries at the top of the scale of assessments. Although conflicts over the size of the budget did not disappear, the eventual – but not legally binding – agreement to shift from majoritarian to consensual decision-making can be seen as an attempt to strike a balance between the two groups and their respective sources of power. However, the agreement gave countries with high assessment rates a leverage over the decision-making process that they would not have had otherwise: they could proactively contest and block budgetary decisions that were in the making instead of retrospectively contesting and undermining them by withholding payments. This paved the way towards repeated budget freezes – either with or without inflation adjustments. While there were also some small budget increases, the overall development can be interpreted as the emergence of 'budget moderation' as an accompanying and contested norm. The size of the regular budget is key from the perspective of differential treatment as it determines the volume that is subject to C2P. By the same token, it influences the relative weight of WHO's regular budget in comparison to alternative financing channels.

The WHO Constitution distinguishes between two sources of income (Articles 56 and 57, cf. WHO 2020: 14–15). As the previous discussion has indicated, these two sources are presently referred to as assessed contributions, which are subject to C2P, and as voluntary contributions, which are subject to W2C. This distinction between two sources of income can be seen either as a description of *two distinct financial streams* under the auspices of WHO, or as a description of *two alternative types of input* into a *common financial pool*. The difference between the two interpretations is that the former accepts the idea that those who make voluntary contributions should have a privileged position in determining their use, while the latter asserts that the member states should collectively determine what both the assessed and the voluntary contributions are spent on.

As the empirical sections will show, the actors have repeatedly re-negotiated the boundary between these two sources of income, but a general tendency has been to consider them less and less as two separate financial streams but as two alternative types of input into a common financial pool. As a consequence, there has been a raising of awareness for the normative particularities of W2C and that there are important differences between its enabling and its expectational dimension. With a view to its enabling dimension, W2C is a legal/formal norm in the sense that there are legal provisions that allow for voluntary contributions in the first place (Article 57).[6] With a view to its expectational dimension, W2C is also a social/informal norm in the sense that various details regarding, for example, the terms of the provision of voluntary contributions are continuously debated but not formally regulated. This implies that the tension between legal rules and social expectations is particularly important in the case of W2C.

At the outset, W2C asserts that *member states and other actors are allowed to contribute to the budget according to their willingness to do so*. Building on this foundation, there have been contestations that attempted to clarify – if not reinterpret – the norm in three regards: Is there a responsibility rather than a permission to make voluntary contributions, on what terms should they be made, and who should feel subject to these social expectations (or, eventually, to these formalized obligations)?

In order to understand the contestations around W2C it should be noted that voluntary contributions are ambivalent. On the one hand, they increase the available financial resources *without* increasing the individual contributions of all member states. In other words, W2C has the potential to provide the foundation for a more radical form of differential treatment than C2P since it does not entail obligations for all member states. This applies, in particular, if they meet a collectively formulated financial demand. On the other hand, voluntary contributions are less reliable than assessed contributions since they are, as the term indicates, voluntary and pledges are not necessarily honoured. Moreover, they can serve as a means to informally govern the policies of WHO by setting priorities through earmarking. In this case, member states collectively have less control over it and financial flows might be driven by the concerns of the contributors rather than the needs of the beneficiaries.[7] Thus, W2C can in principle be a stronger form of differential treatment than C2P but its informal character leaves various questions open and an assessment of its implications for differential treatment can only be made in light of the actual practices that have emerged. Consequently, we will come back to this question in the conclusion of this chapter.

4.3.3 Output Dimension and Need for Support (N4S)

N4S is key for the output dimension. In essence, N4S demands that *financial resources have to be allocated according to the need for support*. While practitioners discuss the output dimension under various headings ('regular budget space allocations to regions', 'strategic resource allocation', or 'strategic budget space allocation'), they analyse it primarily in geographical terms. This approach works along two axes.

The first axis is concerned with the relationship between the different layers of WHO. A classic demand of 'newly independent states' and later of 'developing countries' has been that a substantive share of WHO's (regular) budget should be spent on *assistance* in and for countries. As a consequence of WHO's three-layered structure, this inter-layer axis of the output dimension materialized often as a conflict over the relative budget share for, on the one hand, WHO's headquarters in Geneva (first layer) and for, on the other hand, its six regional offices (second layer) that are also responsible for WHO's country offices and their budget (third layer).[8] A landmark decision in this regard was taken when the G-77 (Group of 77) successfully pushed for a minimum level of 60 per cent of the regular budget that had to be spent on 'technical cooperation' (WHA29.48 [1976]), which had by then become the preferred term for 'technical assistance'.

This first axis highlights an important particularity of WHO-channelled health financing: it is difficult to make a clear distinction between *central obligations* (first type of differential treatment) and *assistance* (third type of differential treatment) as they are understood in the literature (Rajamani 2006). While states are obliged to contribute to the WHO budget, the purpose of the budget is determined separately in debates on budgeting and output. From the perspective of differential treatment, it is particularly noteworthy that one part of the budget is used for common endeavours and another part of the budget is used for assistance. In more abstract terms, one could say that the funds are spent on a mix of public and private goods.

This gets us to the second axis, which is concerned with the relationship among units that are part of the same organizational layer. As just mentioned, WHO's regional offices are responsible for the country offices and their budget. While it is ultimately countries that need support, WHO's organizational structure has the practical consequence that the second axis addresses the question of how the relative financial share should be determined that is distributed to each of the six WHO regions. It is in these discussions in particular where N4S, as well as the related principles of 'equity' and 'greatest need', have explicitly been articulated. Importantly, there is the clear ambition that N4S should apply to all sources of funding which can be seen as an attempt to gain some control over the voluntary sources by determining where they will be spent in geographical terms. This reinforces the aforementioned point that the boundary between different sources of funding is repeatedly re-negotiated and shows that W2C and N4S conflict with each other.

N4S is in principle an important element of differential treatment in WHO-channelled health financing. However, neither the first nor the second axis allocates resources to individual countries which makes it less relevant for the purpose of the present study. As a consequence, its contestation and adaptation will not be analysed in the empirical sections below. Instead, some key aspects will be briefly summarized here. Even at this less granular level, the changes regarding N4S can be interpreted as a mere reconfiguration at the heart of which is resilience – in combination with some steps towards graduation.

Resolution WHA51.31 (1998) can be seen as the starting point of repeated attempts to distribute resources more systematically to regions and – indirectly – to countries. N4S has been a recurrent theme on WHO's agenda ever since (A57/24 [2004]; A57/INF.DOC./4 [2004]; WHA57[10] [2004]; EB118/7 [2006]; WHA66[9] [2013]; A69/47 [2016]; WHA69[16] [2016]). In the context of these developments, there are five aspects that matter for the present purpose. First, as indicated at the outset of this section, a striking particularity of N4S remains. The need of individual countries is used in order to calculate the resources for the regions of which they are a part. So far, N4S has not resulted in a methodology that secures resources for individual countries and an evaluation of WHO's presence in countries highlighted in 2016 that there is 'no explicit methodology for matching resources to countries on the basis of need' (WHO Evaluation Office 2016: 2). Second, while the initial model provided only rough guidance, N4S relied more and more on a formula approach and on objectively measurable criteria. Although all iterations of the model retained a certain degree of flexibility and left some discretion to the WHO secretariat, N4S has still developed in the direction of C2P's formula approach. This constitutes a stark difference to W2C that has, as we will see later in the chapter, retained its informal character. Third, differential treatment remains central in the sense that there is continuous pressure to spend money not just in headquarters but also in regions and countries, i.e. on assistance (third type of differential treatment). While not all countries receive direct support, the additional provision of public goods secures that no country is excluded from the benefits of WHO's work. Fourth, while the rules of the methodology were continuously refined, equity and greatest need remained central principles for determining the allocation of resources. Fifth, the efforts to collectively determine resource allocation on the basis of N4S can be seen as one way to counter-balance the tendency that earmarked voluntary contributions flow according to the priorities set by contributors.

4.3.4 Comparison to Differential Treatment in Other Regimes and Outlook

Concluding this discussion on CWN, some of its noteworthy characteristics can be made visible by comparing it to the corresponding bundle of norms in trade (SDT)[9] and climate (CBDR-RC or CBDR).[10] First of all, at their inception SDT and CBDR-RC identified obligations for one group of countries and rights for another. Under CWN, by contrast, *no country is exempt from obligations* and *no country is excluded from benefits*, although CWN leads to considerable differences in financial obligations and benefits. C2P is based on the assumption that every country can contribute at least something, and consequently all countries are legally obliged to do so. Similarly, WHO's budget finances both public and private goods, which implies that all countries can benefit at least to some degree while N4S demands a certain share for private goods that are claimed by individual countries and sets priorities among regions. However, W2C allows countries and other actors to refuse financial responsibility as well as to circumscribe the potential beneficiaries by earmarking contributions for specific purposes.

Secondly, CWN is to a large extent based on a formula approach to differential treatment. C2P, in particular, has been operationalized on the basis of an elaborate methodology. Over the years, N4S has also been increasingly operationalized in such a manner. The long-standing relevance of formulas sets CWN clearly apart from both SDT and CBDR-RC even though no formula has been introduced in the case of W2C yet. Moreover, both in cases with (C2P and N4S) and in cases without a formula approach (W2C), it is in principle possible to conduct a fine-grained differentiation among both contributors and beneficiaries while SDT and CBDR-RC started off with a clear-cut distinction between these two groups as just mentioned.

After this concluding comparison of CWN to SDT and CBDR-RC, we can now address the question of how differential treatment in WHO-channelled health financing has changed over time, i.e. during Phase 1 and Phase 2, respectively. In the health regime, the year 2007 as the onset of the international financial crisis provides a useful endpoint for Phase 1 that was marked by discussions on the anticipated and incrementally visible rise of Brazil, China, and India. The year 2008 as the climax of the crisis serves consequently as the starting point for Phase 2. The time after the financial crisis was characterized by the ever-stronger recognition that a rise had actually taken place and that China in particular had become one of the leading economies in the world. The following discussion will account for general developments in the course of each phase while the case studies in Chapter 9 will zoom in on a crucial conflictual moment of each phase.

4.4 PHASE 1: THE AFTERMATH OF THE COLD WAR AND EARLY SIGNS FOR THE RISE OF NEW POWERS

Phase 1 (1995–2007) covers a time period that was characterized by the aftershocks of the collapse of the Soviet Union which led to the creation of various new states that faced financial challenges. Moreover, it was shaped by neoliberalism and it saw strong economic growth beyond the developed countries which led to the creation of the term 'BRICs' (Brazil, Russia, India, and China) in 2001. In other words, it was a phase during which the USA had her unipolar moment but it was also a phase during which the early signs of a slowly emerging world political transformation could be observed and first reactions to these signs took place.

4.4.1 Legally Binding Input and Capacity to Pay (C2P)

While C2P as such was widely supported during Phase 1, its operationalization and the practical consequences of updated data were highly contested. The most central of these conflicts culminated at the UN level in 2000 and spilled to the WHO level in 2001 where it had repercussions over several years. While the first case study in Chapter 9 zooms in on this specific conflict, accounts for the demands of key countries, and comes up with explanations for the results, this section will foreground two, more general, aspects and developments during Phase 1. First, it will analyse formalized rules: the shape of the scale methodology, the contestations to which the scale methodology became subject, and the results of these contestations, which were mainly resilience but also a further lowering of the maximum ceiling for individual contributions. Second, it will analyse the practical consequences of these rules: the scale methodology led to some graduation during Phase 1 but in comparison to Phase 2 it was still marginal. For the sake of clarity, it is best to discuss shape, contestation, and results for each of the three main steps of the scale methodology individually. Thereafter, we will turn to the practical consequences of the methodology as a whole.

4.4.1.1 Step 1: calculation of national income

The first element of the methodology is the calculation of national income as a percentage share of world income. Some states see it primarily as a first approximation to C2P while others consider it as the best measure for C2P and criticize the subsequent elements as a distortion. There were various disagreements regarding the proper calculation of national income, but the conflicts on the statistical base periods were particularly prominent. In essence, these conflicts were sparked by the practice of calculating national income in a backward-looking manner and based on official statistics, which raised the question of how far back the statistical base periods should reach when countries' average income was calculated.

Against the background of these conflicts, the base periods were adjusted several times, but the overall development was that they were shorter at the end of Phase 1 than at its beginning. Initially, the average of two base periods (seven and eight years) was used for the scale period 1995–1997. Thereafter, a single and shorter base period (six years) was used for 1998–2000. Finally, the average of two base periods (three and six years) has been used ever since 2001–2003 (A73/11 [2018]). The consequence was that the time lag between statistically measured changes in national income and their influence on the UN scale was reduced.[11] Roughly speaking, this change in methodology was supported by countries with a stagnating or declining economy while countries with quickly growing economies such as Brazil, China, and India tended to prefer long statistical base periods that reduced the visibility of their growth.

4.4.1.2 Step 2: application of relief measures

The first relief measure is 'debt relief'. It acknowledges the fact that indebted countries have only a reduced amount of their national income at their disposal (A42/11 [1987]: 7). While debt relief was first introduced in 1985 and originally devised in an ad hoc manner, it was assumed from the outset that developed countries should not be eligible for it (A40/11 [1985]: 6). During Phase 1, eligibility was clearly defined by a per capita income threshold. The threshold, which is in principle still used today (A73/11 [2018]: 57), distinguished between non-eligible *high income* and all other countries.[12]

The exact calculation of debt burden was controversial during Phase 1. Some countries wanted to include only actual debt repayments ('debt-flow method') while others wanted to take theoretically necessary debt repayments into account ('debt-stock method'). Moreover, certain measurements of national income that are used for the first step already take debt-related payments into account; some countries argued consequently that the methodology would be double counting debt and that debt relief could be dropped. In these conflicts, the debtor-friendly debt-stock method prevailed eventually and is still used at the time of writing. Eligible countries who are indebted according to this method have their relative share reduced while it is increased for all other countries.

The second relief measure is 'low per capita income adjustment'. Ever since the 1995–1997 scale, which was used at the beginning of Phase 1, the world average per capita income has served as the threshold and only countries below it are eligible. The degree to which the individual scale of eligible countries is reduced is a function of two elements: first, the relative gap between the threshold and the country's per capita income; second, a gradient that is multiplied with this gap. While a higher gradient means a higher reduction, the gradient had stepwise risen from 40 per cent in 1948 to 85 per cent by 1983. Starting with the 1998–2000 scale, it was reduced to 80 per cent where it has remained ever since (A73/11 [2018]: 54–55). The percentage points that are reduced from the share of the beneficiaries of this relief measure are redistributed to member states above the threshold only (A73/11 [2018]: 54–55, see also 58–59). This limits the burden sharing regarding this relief measure to the non-eligible countries. Also of note, the low per capita income adjustment is calculated on the basis of the debt-adjusted national income, which has at times been criticized since it implies that the effects of one relief measure are further reinforced by a second one.

With a view to this relief measure, there have been controversies regarding both the threshold and the gradient. At an even more fundamental level, low per capita income adjustment has been criticized for primarily benefiting countries with a large population some of which receive a considerable reduction. This applies to China and India in particular. While the reduction of the threshold to 80 per cent can be seen as a step to accommodate some of the criticism raised during Phase 1, low per capita income as such as well as the eligibility of large 'emerging economies' were successfully defended.

4.4.1.3 Step 3: application of limits to the scale

The first limit to the scale is referred to as 'floor (rate)'. It defines the minimum contribution that each member state has to make to the budget. While the rates of countries below the floor will be increased, they are decreased for all others. However, the redistributive consequences of this element are usually small in comparison to the others. The floor was initially set at 0.04 per cent in 1946 and had reached 0.01 per cent by the 1978–1979 scale. For the 1998–2000 scale it was further lowered to 0.001 per cent (A73/11 [2018]: 54–55). This repeated lowering of the floor can be seen as an affirmation of differential treatment but the very existence of the floor can be interpreted as a restraint on C2P since affected countries have to make a payment above their calculated capacity.

While the floor defines a minimum rate, the two so-called ceilings define a maximum rate. First, there is the 'Least Developed Countries ceiling' that has been at 0.010 per cent since 1992 (A73/11 [2018]: 25). While this ceiling reduces the relative shares of affected countries, they are increased for all others – except for those affected by the floor (A73/11 [2018]: 59). The broader implication is essentially that the scale for the Least Developed Countries (as defined by the UN)[13] remains within a range of between 0.001 per cent (floor) and 0.010 per cent (ceiling).[14] This can be seen as a clear commitment to *differential treatment* since the equal share alternative would have been 0.52 per cent for all countries. This requires a brief elaboration.

The obvious *non-differential treatment* alternative to C2P would be the principle of 'equal share' that is used by some international organizations as has been discussed earlier in this chapter. In this case, the pro ratio share would be the same for each country and it would be calculated by dividing 100 per cent by the number of member states. By the end of Phase 1, there were 192 UN member states, which would have resulted in an equal share rate of around 0.52 per cent for each country. This threshold is important since it provides a first approach for identifying *beneficiaries* of and *contributors* to differential treatment.

Much more controversial than the ceiling for Least Developed Countries is the maximum ceiling for individual contributions, which is criticized for constituting a restraint on C2P. While the USA is the only country that has ever reached this ceiling, it would in principle apply to any country. A maximum ceiling has been part of the scale methodology since its inception but its level has declined considerably. At the beginning of Phase 1 it was at 25 per cent. It became a central aspect of the conflict that was mentioned at the outset of this chapter and will be studied in detail in the first case study in Chapter 9. A central consequence of the conflict was that the maximum ceiling was lowered to 22 per cent which constitutes a case of further increase of an existing restraint.

The maximum ceiling has not only had the effect that the USA has constantly been assessed at a rate below her part of world income. It has also implied that the USA did not share any of the burden that results from the redistributive consequences of the other limits to the scale or from the redistributive consequences of the relief measures, both of which have been discussed in the preceding paragraphs (see also A73/11 [2018]: 25–26, 57–59). By contrast, other developed countries are commonly assessed at a rate that is higher than their share of world income since the relief measures *and* the limits to the scale (including the maximum ceiling) result in additional percentage points for these countries. Such an assessment rate above the income share provides a second approach to identifying contributors to differential treatment that complements the equal share threshold of 0.52 per cent. Actually, some practitioners refer to it in conflicts over the scale of assessments.

The focus has so far been on the shape of the scale methodology as well as on contestations and their results. It is, however, important to reiterate that changes in the individual assessment rate of each country are not only the consequence of changes in formalized rules, or modifications to the methodology. Rather, they can also be a consequence of updated data that is applied to the methodology. By the same token, C2P can be adjusted to global economic shifts through each of these factors (or a combination thereof). The next sub-section will address the general practical consequences of both factors during Phase 1.

4.4.1.4 Practical consequences

Figure 4.1 below displays how the scale of assessments developed at the WHO level. The main differences between the WHO level and the UN level are adjustments for membership and a time lag of one year if changes at the UN level are taken into consideration at the WHO level in the subsequent year. Data is provided for six countries that serve as focus countries. In addition to Brazil, China, and India, these are (also in alphabetical order) the traditional major contributors: Germany, Japan, and the USA.[15]

Figure 4.1 shows that during Phase 1 two noteworthy changes occurred among the traditional major contributors. First of all, the reduction of the maximum ceiling from 25 per cent to 22 per cent is clearly visible in the case of the USA. Secondly, Japan's growing economy as well as the effects of burden sharing led to a steep increase that got it close to the reduced scale of the USA. With a view to Brazil, China, and India, Figure 4.1 shows that during Phase 1 the assessment rates of the three countries were considerably smaller than

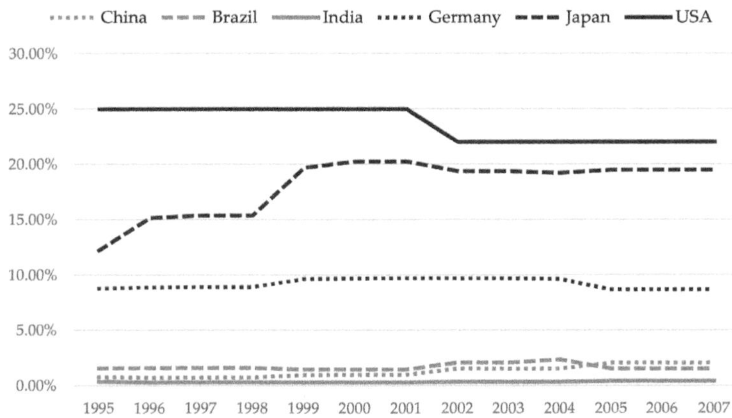

Figure 4.1 *WHO scale of assessments (1995–2007)*

those of the three traditional major contributors. Although the rising powers' assessment rates increased slightly in the course of Phase 1, this constitutes only a marginal graduation – in particular in comparison to Phase 2 as we will see later. This persistent gap between the rising powers and the traditional major contributors is a first indication to the fact that Brazil, China, and India were at the outset clear beneficiaries of differential treatment. An important change among the rising powers was that, towards the end of Phase 1, China's scale surpassed Brazil's.

Complementing the longitudinal data in Figure 4.1, Figure 4.2 illustrates the implications of the individual elements of the methodology for the same countries at a specific point in time.[16]

Figure 4.2 shows that, at the end of Phase 1, Brazil, China, and India all remained beneficiaries of differential treatment also in the specific sense that they contributed less than their share of world income. Moreover, the low per capita income adjustment led to the most substantive reduction for them. India can even be considered a strong beneficiary of differential treatment since she contributed less than the equal share rate of 0.52 per cent. The figure shows furthermore that the maximum ceiling does not only lower the assessment rate for the USA below her world income share, rather it additionally exempts the USA from burden sharing which would have lifted her assessment rate to 33.907 per cent.

By contrast, due to burden sharing, Germany and Japan contribute more than their part of world income and, in this sense, they make a strong contribution

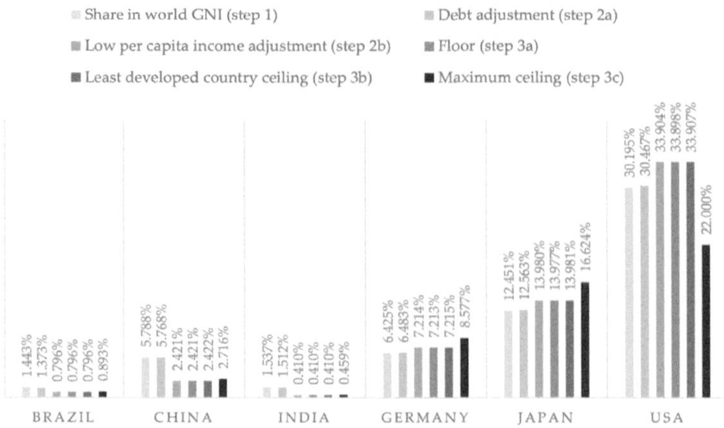

Figure 4.2 *Impact of each element of the methodology on the 2007–2009 assessment rates of the six focus countries*

to differential treatment. While this shows that the status of being a contributor to or a beneficiary of differential treatment is a question of degree, countries that are above the equal share threshold of 0.52 per cent but below the national income threshold can be considered as both contributors (they pay more than the equal share) and beneficiaries (they get a reduction). At the end of Phase 1, this applied to Brazil and China while the reduction for the USA rested on a different rationale. Finally it is important to recall that regardless of whether countries benefit from differential treatment or contribute to it, no country is exempt from the obligation to pay a share of the budget.

4.4.2 Budget Size, Budget Composition, and Willingness to Contribute (W2C)

While budgeting discussions provide insights into the role of willingness to contribute (W2C) as the second norm of differential treatment, they matter also from the perspective of capacity to pay (C2P). In particular, the financial volume to which each of the norms applies has to be determined by member states. This section will take a closer look at general budgeting developments and concomitant normative clarifications during Phase 1. It will thereby foreground three aspects. First, the financial obligations of member states on the basis of C2P underwent fluctuations that have been overlooked in the literature. Second, the relative weight of W2C vis-à-vis C2P increased constantly and, as a consequence, the thinking of member states concerning W2C evolved. Third, differential treatment proved resilient although W2C's informal side has some ambivalent implications, as will become even more obvious during Phase 2.

WHO works with a biennial programme budget, i.e. the budget is agreed upon every two years. While the exact budgeting process has changed over time and while one important change has been that the regional offices have increasingly been consulted, the budget is in principle proposed by WHO's Director-General, considered by the Executive Board, and approved by the World Health Assembly who passes a budgeting resolution every two years (WHO Constitution: Articles 18[f], 34, 55–56; cf. WHO 2020: 6, 10, 14). During Phase 1, these budgeting resolutions were referred to as 'appropriation resolutions'. While budgetary decisions can be amended in the course of a biennium, the biennial appropriation resolutions represent the key decision regarding the size of the budget and its composition. The biennial budget cycle also has an impact on the revision of the scale of assessments, which is updated simultaneously (and whenever a new UN scale becomes available).

During Phase 1, budgeting was particularly complex and quite different from the approach that emerged later. Moreover, the terminology for the budget elements and the manner in which each of them is presented in the appropriation resolutions have changed over time. Even during individual budget discussions, the terminology was not always used in a uniform way. To avoid the ensuing confusion, the present chapter proposes a terminology that can be used consistently. This requires a brief elaboration.

While C2P and W2C play a role in the budgeting process, each of them is closely related to specific elements of the budget. C2P applies to the budget share that will be referred to as 'actual assessment' on member states. The precise amount of this key element of the budget is often only implicitly stated in the appropriation resolutions but it can be arrived at in the following two steps.

First, the 'regular budget' is reduced by 'reimbursement of programme support costs' and by 'non-assessed income'. This step decreases the assessments on all member states and leads thereby to the 'net assessment on member states'. Second, the latter is then further reduced by 'implementation flexibilities' and by the 'financial incentive scheme'. This step decreases the assessed contributions of eligible member states individually and leads thereby to the 'actual assessment'.

This calculation path is insightful in the sense that it exemplifies the specific manner in which the C2P-related part of the budget was interpreted at the outset of Phase 1: the financial obligations of member states were not seen as fixed but as a function of collective reductions through other sources of income (first step) and of individual reductions (second step).[17] Consequently, the actual assessment could even fall below the level of previous biennia but this aspect has been overlooked in the literature that limits itself to an analysis of the regular budget.

The calculation of actual assessment is in no way affected by the resources that were initially called extrabudgetary funds and were eventually referred to as 'voluntary budget' or 'voluntary contributions'. While these resources are subject to W2C, they were long not included into the budgeting process. At the outset, they were not even mentioned in the appropriation resolutions and once they were mentioned, it was initially not specified what they would be spent on. This changed only incrementally as voluntary contributions became ever more relevant and as member states tried to gain at least some control over them. Paying tribute to these altered perceptions of practitioners, the subsequent reconstruction of changes in budget size will trace voluntary contributions only from the moment when they started to appear in the appropriation resolutions. As soon as they are traced, their ever-increasing volume will show that the weight of W2C vis-à-vis C2P increased constantly.

In light of these general considerations and clarifications, it is now possible to take the first budget of Phase 1 as a starting point and to look at the individual budget elements in more detail before the development of key budget elements is investigated over time. The regular budget for the biennium 1994–1995 amounted to USD (United States dollar) 822 101 000 (WHA46.34 [1993]). This sum was financed by multiple elements. Reimbursement of programme support costs by the United Nations Development Programme (UNDP) contributed USD 3 600 000, non-assessed income contributed USD 388 000, and the financial incentive scheme[18] contributed USD 12 741 000, which resulted in an actual assessment on member states of USD 805 372 000.[19] The voluntary budget was not mentioned.

Table 4.1 shows how central budget elements developed during Phase 1. Figures in bold print were directly taken from the appropriation resolutions. The other figures were calculated for the present purpose and – to the extent possible – confirmed with the financial reports of WHO. If there is more than one figure in a cell, it means that there are different interpretations of the available data. In order to reduce the number of columns, 'reimbursements' and 'non-assessed income' were summarized as 'other sources of income'.[20]

As displayed in Table 4.1, from the biennium 1994–1995 to the biennium 1996–1997, both the regular budget and the actual assessment increased (WHA48.32 [1995]). The resolution also approved the use of non-assessed income, 'if available, up to the amount of US$ 10 000 000 in each of the years 1996–1997 for expenditure on priority country programmes'.[21] For the two subsequently following biennia (1998–1999 and 2000–2001), the regular budget *was frozen* at the level of zero nominal growth. However, the actual assessment *fell slightly* for the biennium 1998–1999 and increased visibly for the biennium 2000–2001; this potentially surprising disconnect between

Table 4.1 *Evolution of different elements of the WHO budget (in USD) from 1994 to 2009*

Biennium	Total budget	Voluntary budget	Regular budget	Other sources of income	Implementation flexibilities	Financial incentive scheme	Actual assessment
1994–1995			**822 101 000**	3 988 000		**12 741 000**	805 372 000
1996–1997			**842 654 000**	11 194 300		**3 352 700**	828 107 000
1998–1999			**842 654 000**	5 522 980		**9 994 020**	827 137 000
2000–2001			**842 654 000**	1 700 000		**5 555 567**	835 398 433 (decided 1999) 835 373 210 (adjust. 2001)
2002–2003	**2 235 654 000**	**1 380 000 000**	**842 654 000** (subtotal) **855 654 000** (incl. items financed by add. non-assessed inc.)	500 000	36 153 035	13 474 829 (original) 22 695 215 (added later)	792 526 136 (decided 2001) 769 830 921 (adjust. 2002)
2004–2005	**2 704 611 000**	**1 824 500 000**	**880 111 000**	21 636 000	**12 364 000**	1 574 000	844 537 000
2006–2007	**3 313 441 000**	**2 398 126 000**	**915 315 000**	22 200 000	**8 655 000**	4 051 000	880 409 000
2008–2009	**4 227 480 000**	**3 268 640 000**	**958 840 000**	30 000 000			**928 840 000**

Source: For details on the sources used, see the discussions in the text.

a regular budget that remained at the level of zero nominal growth and a changing level of the actual assessment illustrates the importance of keeping the two separate and can be explained with the fluctuations in the other sources of income as displayed in Table 4.1 (cf. WHA50.25 [1997] and WHA52.20 [1999]).[22] The resolution for the latter of the two biennia also decided to apply from non-assessed income 'US$ 15 000 000 to high-priority programmes'.

As will be discussed in more detail in the first case study in Chapter 9, the subsequent budget for the biennium 2002–2003 was a particular case. It deviated from the usual practice due to the complex package deal reached, due to exceptional expenses, and due to a change in the financial regulations. Depending on how one wants to interpret this situation, one could either state that, formally, the regular budget increased to USD 855 654 000 or one could say that, practically, it remained at the previous level of USD 842 654 000. While the latter interpretation is supported by the statements of the delegates who debated it as a zero nominal growth budget,[23] Table 4.1 above contains both figures in order to account for both interpretations.

Also, in the case of the actual assessment, the situation was unusual. As a matter of fact, it fell considerably to USD 792 526 136, which was the lowest level during Phase 1 until this point.[24] This was a consequence of the combined effect of the usual reductions and of the implementation flexibilities (referred to as 'relief measures') that the Director-General had successfully proposed in order to find a compromise in the negotiations on the scale of assessments and hence regarding the contestations of the operationalization of C2P.[25] While the first case study in Chapter 9 will analyse these events in more detail, it is important to highlight that both a further increase of an existing restraint and graduation (although still marginal if compared to Phase 2) were part of the contestations and that the implementation flexibilities were a reaction to the demands by developing countries in particular. Moreover, the implementation flexibilities were financed by non-assessed income which had inter alia the consequence that no priority programmes could be financed in this biennium. Reducing the actual assessment considerably and sacrificing priority programmes, the contestations of the operationalization of C2P had an even stronger, albeit time-limited, effect on the relative weight of C2P than the budget moderation that led at a maximum to a budget freeze.

A final particularity of the 2002–2003 budget was that 'sources other than the regular budget' (i.e. voluntary contributions) were explicitly mentioned for the first time in the appropriation resolution. Contributing to the unusual characteristics of the biennium, the actual assessment was reduced even further when the Assembly decided one year later (WHA55.7 [2002]) that additional funding would be made available for the financial incentive scheme which resulted in an adjusted actual assessment of USD 769 830 921.[26]

In the three biennia that cover the rest of Phase 1, both the regular budget and the actual assessment increased (WHA56.32 [2003]; WHA58.4 [2005]; WHA60.12 [2007]).[27] However, a particularity of the biennia 2004–2005 and 2006–2007 was that implementation flexibilities (now referred to as 'adjustment mechanism') continued to play a role as demanded by developing countries in particular. This was one of the reasons for which the actual assessment remained considerably below the regular budget.

Also of note, the appropriation resolution for the biennium 2006–2007 was the first one that used the term 'voluntary contributions'. Moreover, it was the last one that allocated resources to the financial incentive scheme (WHA58.4 [2005]).[28] Finally, the appropriation resolution for the biennium 2008–2009 (WHA60.12 [2007]), which was decided in 2007 as the final year of Phase 1, accounted for the activities on which the voluntary contributions were going to be spent by mapping them on the appropriation sections of the regular budget. While the format of the budgeting resolutions would continue to change during Phase 2, this was an important step since it illustrated the efforts to make the voluntary part of the budget more transparent and accountable.

In light of the complexity of the budget conflicts, a few concluding remarks concerning differential treatment during Phase 1 are in order. As the relative weight of W2C vis-à-vis C2P increased, the thinking of member states concerning W2C evolved. Initially, W2C was, in the main, an enabling norm that led to the mobilization of additional funds. There was no systematic discussion on the social expectations towards the voluntary contributors but two developments indicated increasing attention in this regard: the inclusion of voluntary contributions into the budgeting resolutions and the eventual mapping of voluntary contributions on the appropriation sections of the regular budget. In this context, various member states expressed their concern over the increasing imbalance between the regular budget and the voluntary contributions. However, no strong counter-measures were seriously considered; rather, there was a sense of relief to see WHO's *total* budget expand while the assessment on member states was not affected.

This brings us to the observation that the financial obligations of member states on the basis of C2P underwent fluctuations that have been overlooked in the literature. First, the actual assessment was often disconnected from the regular budget and saw even *falling levels*. In the biennium 2002–2003, the actual assessment fell considerably which was to a large degree the consequence of the implementation flexibilities that developing countries had demanded. Regarding the regular budget on which the literature tends to focus, only the decisions in 1997, 1999, and 2001 constituted obvious budget freezes (zero nominal growth); the decisions in 1995, 2003, 2005, and 2007 led to moderate increases of the regular budget that can, at a minimum, be interpreted as adjustments for inflation and for other rising costs (zero real growth). These findings are much more nuanced than the assertion in the literature that WHO had had a policy of zero nominal growth ever since 1993 (e.g. Lee 2009: 39; Chorev 2012: 144; People's Health Movement et al. 2017: 247–248).

Even in the zero nominal growth phase, the conflict over the size of the regular budget was not necessarily a conflict between developed and developing countries. Unlike in the discussions on the scale of assessments, developing countries did not speak as the G-77 and China; moreover, among Brazil, China, and India, Brazil in particular opposed budget increases repeatedly.[29] In other words, the institutional separation of discussions on the scale methodology from discussions on the budget allowed for divergent conflict dynamics although C2P mattered in both cases.

The complex developments during Phase 1 are evidence for the challenges and contestations that differential treatment faced. Nevertheless, it remained overall resilient and graduation was still marginal in comparison to Phase 2.

4.5 PHASE 2: AFTER THE 'WESTERN' FINANCIAL CRISIS AND ITS GLOBAL REPERCUSSIONS

The financial crisis of 2007 and 2008 had an important impact on world politics since it hit the 'Western countries' in particular and led to a reshuffling of actual and perceived relations between 'established' and 'rising powers'. More specifically, the time after the crisis was characterized by the ever-stronger recognition that a rise of Brazil, China, and India had actually taken place and that China, in particular, had become one of the leading economies in the world.

4.5.1 Legally Binding Input and Capacity to Pay (C2P)

Also during Phase 2 (2008–2020), C2P as such was widely supported while the scale of assessments proved repeatedly to be a controversial issue – in particular at the UN level. For the most part, the divergent demands regarding changes to the scale methodology led essentially to a deadlock at the level of formalized rules. Only towards the end of Phase 2 did a new momentum for changes to the methodology emerge. The second case study in Chapter 9 will look into the details of these developments as they manifested in 2018 (UN level) and 2019 (WHO level). While the case study will account for the demands of key countries and will come up with explanations for the results, this section will foreground the following, more general, aspects and developments.

First, it will portray what elements of the methodology proved particularly controversial and which ones were strongly supported (by specific countries and coalitions). Second, this section will show that in spite of the impasse regarding the scale methodology (a case of resilience), its application had much clearer practical consequences than during Phase 1. It led to a visible increase in the assessment rates of Brazil, China, and India on the one hand, and to a decline of the assessment rates of some traditional main contributors on the other hand. While this implies that graduation was much stronger during Phase 2 than during Phase 1, it will be a task of the detailed case study in Chapter 9 to show that Brazil, China, and India simultaneously remained beneficiaries of differential treatment which suggests a case of attenuated graduation.

Regarding contestations of the scale methodology, the relief measures and the maximum ceiling were at the centre of attention. Criticism regarding the former was most clearly articulated by the European Union (EU). For example, with a view to the low per capita income adjustment the EU pointed out that it had the unintended consequence 'to restrict relief to a handful of Member States with a significant share of world GNI, while providing little benefit for the least developed countries'. Moreover, the EU emphasized that, collectively, they were the largest contributor and criticized that its scale was higher than its share of world income while 'some major emerging economies had seen substantial growth in the past decade and should assume a larger share of the Organization's expenses'.[30]

Criticism regarding the maximum ceiling was most vocally expressed by the G-77 and China. They highlighted continuously that the maximum ceiling should be reviewed but otherwise took the position that the methodology should not be revised. They repeatedly affirmed that 'the core elements of the current scale methodology were non-negotiable and must be kept intact', which implies that they clearly opposed the demand to make adjustments to the relief measures. They also pointed out that, as a consequence of the triennial updates of the data, even an unchanged methodology would lead to increased assessments on developing countries.[31] Unsurprisingly, the USA focussed on defending the present level of the maximum ceiling.[32] Overall one could argue that it was not only the divergent calls for change that led to a deadlock but also the fact that the G-77 and China as well as the USA valued contested aspects of the status quo.

While the methodology remained intact during Phase 2, its practical consequences changed considerably and led to continuous graduation of Brazil, China, and India. Figure 4.3 displays the trajectory of the individual assessment rates for the six focus countries on the basis of data for the WHO scale of assessments. For comparative purposes, Figure 4.3 comprises Phase 2 and the end of Phase 1.[33]

Figure 4.3 makes the dynamics among Brazil, China, and India strikingly obvious. While China had already surpassed Brazil by the end of Phase 1, her assessment rate became subsequently clearly dominant among these countries.

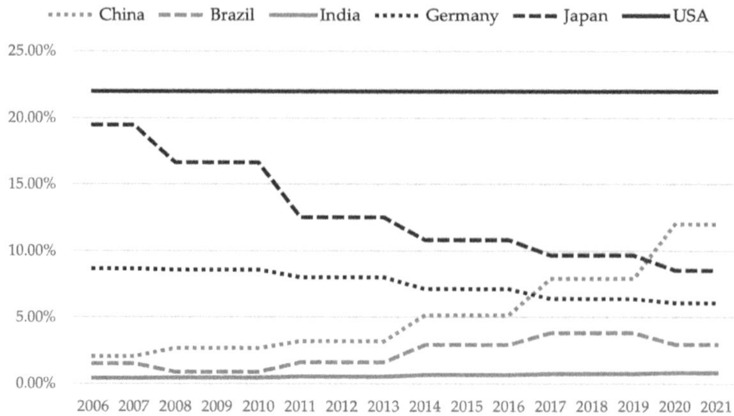

Figure 4.3 *WHO scale of assessments (2006–2021)*

The rate of Brazil declined temporarily before it rose again and went even beyond its original level at the end of Phase 1. The rate of India increased moderately and continuously but at a low level. Moreover, while the rates of Brazil, China, and India had initially been insignificant if compared to the ones of the three traditional major contributors, the picture changed radically in Phase 2. China surpassed Germany in 2017 and Japan in 2020. Only the assessment rate of the USA remained above China's. While these developments clearly show that the practical consequences of the scale methodology led to continuous graduation of Brazil, China, and India, the second case study (Chapter 9) will put these findings in perspective. As mentioned before, it will show that Brazil, China, and India have simultaneously remained beneficiaries of differential treatment which suggests a case of attenuated graduation. At the same time, C2P, as operationalized in the scale methodology, proved resilient.

4.5.2 Budget Size, Budget Composition, and Willingness to Contribute (W2C)

Also during Phase 2, budget-related issues remained contentious. Assessments on member states (and hence C2P) as well as voluntary contributions (and hence W2C) played a key role in these debates. This section will not only account for quantitative changes in financial volumes but also analyse the changes to the budgeting practices that emerged during Phase 2 and that are evidence for a new understanding of WHO's sources of income. Moreover, this section will look into the attempts to clarify the social expectations regarding voluntary contributions and W2C. This will inter alia foreground persistent differences between C2P and W2C. While both have proven resilient, W2C continues to be characterized by informal aspects and by self-determined 'obligations'. As a consequence, Brazil, China, and India could avoid graduation in the case of W2C.

Table 4.2 reproduces budgeting data for Phase 2[34] – and includes the last two biennia of Phase 1 for comparative purposes (cf. Table 4.1 above). Figures in bold print were directly taken from the appropriation resolutions. The other figures were calculated for the present purpose and – to the extent possible – confirmed with the financial reports of WHO. The table clearly shows that, in spite of fluctuations, the voluntary budget remained essential. It continued to increase at the beginning of Phase 2 but fell temporarily before it reached an all-time high at the end of Phase 2.

Regarding budgeting practices, it is first of all noteworthy that neither the financial incentive scheme nor the implementation flexibilities were reintroduced during Phase 2, while they had played an important role during much of Phase 1. Moreover, non-assessed income was no longer budgeted from 2013 onwards.[35] As a consequence, many of the elements that had made the calculation of the actual assessment on member states rather complex during Phase 1 disappeared from the budgeting process. During Phase 2, it became common to discuss the budget in terms of a triad: total budget, assessed contributions, and voluntary contributions. This reduced complexity went hand in hand with a shifting attention.

Many of the discussions during Phase 1 had addressed the question of how member states could get *reductions* on their initial assessment (e.g. through implementation flexibilities as a form of differential treatment). As a consequence of theses varying reduction efforts, the volume of the actual assessment was characterized by fluctuations. During Phase 2, by contrast, the assessed contributions quoted in the budgeting resolutions became synonymous with actual assessment, and member states' financial obligations (based on C2P) provided a more stable financial foundation on top of which *additional* resources were sought (based on W2C). In other words, assessed contributions came to be seen as a legally required minimum contribution of member states to the total budget whilst it was also clear that this type of funding would not be sufficient, which changed the perspective on voluntary contributions.

This new thinking was most clearly expressed by the introduction of an integrated budget in 2013. From then on, it was no longer the assessed contributions that were appropriated to budget sections; rather a *total amount*, which could be financed by assessed *or* by voluntary contributions, was allocated to a more limited number of budget elements; this made it possible to adopt the programme budget in its entirety and to subsequently use assessed contribu-

Table 4.2 Evolution of different elements of the WHO budget (in USD) from 2006 to 2021

Biennium	Total budget	Voluntary budget	Regular budget	Other sources of income	Implementation flexibilities	Financial incentive scheme	Actual assessment
2006–2007	**3 313 441 000**	**2 398 126 000**	**915 315 000**	22 200 000	**8 655 000**	4 051 000	880 409 000
2008–2009	**4 227 480 000**	**3 268 640 000**	**958 840 000**	30 000 000			**928 840 000**
2010–2011	**4 539 914 000**	**3 596 074 000**	**943 840 000**	15 000 000			**928 840 000**
2012–2013	**3 958 979 000**	**3 015 139 000**	**943 840 000**	15 000 000			**928 840 000**
2014–2015	**3 977 000 000**	**3 048 000 000**					**929 000 000**
2016–2017	**4 385 000 000**	**3 456 000 000**					**929 000 000**
2018–2019	**4 421 500 000**	**3 464 600 000**					**956 900 000**
2020–2021	**5 840 400 000**	**4 883 500 000**					**956 900 000**

tions in order to fill funding gaps. In other words, the budget was discussed in terms of the total budget and the secretariat enjoyed an increased flexibility in using the assessed contributions. The implication of this change was, however, that WHO was no longer imagined as a basic structure whose central operations, including key technical programmes, would be financed by assessed contributions while it could perform further tasks if voluntary contributions were available. Rather, assessed contributions became simply one of two alternative funding sources – albeit a preferred one. Constituting legal obligations of member states, assessed contributions were considered more reliable than voluntary contributions and they were valued for having become even more flexible through this decision, while voluntary contributions would commonly be earmarked for specific purposes.[36]

The scope of these changes becomes particularly obvious if the new budgeting practices are compared to the ones at the beginning of Phase 1. While the appropriation resolutions up until 1999 did not even quote the sum that was expected in terms of voluntary contributions, it became more and more common to include voluntary contributions into the planning process – but on the basis of anticipations and aspirations. As a consequence, WHO and its member states became increasingly concerned with the question of whether voluntary contributions would be made available as anticipated and aspired. While delayed, partial, and conditional payment can be a concern even in the case of assessed contributions, WHO and its governance bodies now faced the additional challenge of securing indispensable but uncertain voluntary contributions.

The new approach to budgeting was also reflected in new terminology. In particular, the budgeting resolutions were no longer referred to as appropriation resolutions,[37] which had pointed at the previous practice to appropriate an overall regular budget to specific sections; instead, they became known as resolutions on the programme budget,[38] which would approve both the programme of work and the 'total effective working budget under all sources of funds' as well as allocate the latter to fewer 'categories' (more recently reconceptualized to yet fewer 'strategic priorities') and 'other areas'.

The more recent budgeting resolutions are also proof of a rethinking of the expenditure elements of the budget. This applies to the budget for outbreaks, crises, and emergencies in particular, to which WHO has been paying increasing attention. A closer look at the last budgeting resolution of Phase 2 illustrates this point and the related expectations regarding voluntary contributions. In the budgeting resolution for 2020–2021 (WHA72.1 [2019]), there are two 'other areas', which are governed by additional budgeting rules. One of them comprises emergency operations and appeals. The budgeting resolution highlights that due to 'the event-driven nature of the activities concerned', this would be 'an estimated budget requirement'. By the same token, the resolution authorizes 'the Director-General, where necessary, to incur additional expenditures in [this] area, subject to availability of resources'.

The flexibility that is given to this area highlights two points. First, in the case of emergencies there are particularly high expectations regarding voluntary contributions. Second, only in this case, future necessity and availability of resources determine the volume of voluntary contributions that is acceptable. In the case of *other* expenditure elements, integrated budgeting determines both a funding *target* and an *upper limit*, i.e. the Director-General is authorized to 'finance the budget as allocated …, *up to the amounts approved*' (WHA72.1 [2019]; italics added) while limited transfers can be made among some of the expenditure elements. This partial lid on voluntary contributions is evidence for the general effort to clarify the rules around W2C.[39]

The changing budgeting practices as well as the increasing attention to voluntary contributions were accompanied by an institutional innovation. So-called financing dialogues were introduced (WHA66[8] [2013]), which were not foreseen as formal governance bodies in the WHO Constitution but served the purpose of facilitating a dialogue between the various contributors to the WHO's total budget, including non-state actors. During Phase 2, four financing dialogues (June 2013, October 2013, November 2015, and October 2016) and a so-called partners' forum (April 2019) were held. While each of these meetings aimed at securing funding for a specific time period, they also aimed at clarifying and promoting the principles on which WHO budgeting and financing should be based. For the present purpose, some of these principles are particularly noteworthy since they indicate the increasingly articulated social expectations that come with W2C.

To begin with, there is the principle of reducing the vulnerability of WHO's funding that also encompassed the principle of broadening the contributor (or donor) base. The principle has two meanings: first, it calls for more voluntary contributions to be made by member states beyond the existing major contributors; second, it calls for non-state actors, including private actors, to become new or larger voluntary contributors to the budget. The first meaning was aimed at middle-income countries or rising powers in particular, but, interestingly, no specific countries were called upon to contribute more. The second meaning relates to non-state actors and shows that W2C has a broader scope than more traditional norms of differential treatment such as C2P that are limited to states.

Another relevant principle that was promoted through the financing dialogues is flexibility. Voluntary contributors are increasingly expected to make flexible rather than earmarked voluntary contributions. In particular if flexibility is combined with predictability (a further principle of the financing dialogues), the difference between assessed contributions and voluntary contributions becomes actually quite fuzzy and consequently terms such as 'core voluntary contributions' or 'voluntary assessed contributions' have been suggested to describe this cherished type of voluntary contribution.[40] If voluntary contributions were to be freed from the strings that are usually attached to them, W2C could actually give rise to a more radical form of differential treatment than C2P. The reason for this is that, unlike C2P, W2C does not apply to all member states which implies that some are exempt from obligations altogether. The hopes for flexible and predictable voluntary contributions were, however, not being fulfilled during Phase 2 and W2C therefore remains ambivalent as will be discussed in the conclusion of this chapter.[41]

That predictability emerged as a key principle in the context of the financing dialogues was no coincidence. One of the reasons for the introduction of financing dialogues was the meanwhile recognized unreliability of voluntary contributions. While even assessed contributions had not always proven reliable, WHO faced a massive financing crisis when, in the aftermath of the Western financial crisis that had begun in 2007, a wide gap between projected and actual voluntary contributions emerged for the biennia 2008–2009 and 2010–2011 that was further exacerbated by currency turbulences and led to the dismissal of large numbers of WHO staff. The financial crisis at WHO peaked in 2011 and led eventually to a reform process that went beyond WHO financing as such.[42]

In line with the aforementioned principle to broaden the contributor base, great hopes were initially put on increasing contributions from Brazil, China, India, and other rising powers but they did neither become major voluntary contributors nor were they strong supporters of an increase in assessed contributions. Regarding the first point, Brazil, China, and India did not really feel subject to W2C. Their voluntary contributions remained at a low level even when their graduation became obvious in the context of assessed contributions. This shows that Brazil, China, and India could avoid graduation in the case of W2C. Actually, the voluntary contributions of Brazil and India were commonly so small that a figure displaying the data for all six focus countries separately would be difficult to read. As a consequence, Figure 4.4 displays the aggregate assessment rate and the aggregate voluntary rate for each of the two groups. The share of the voluntary contributions is calculated as the relative share among member states and does not include other actors since our focus is on differential treatment among states.[43]

Figure 4.4 starts in 2016 which was the year before China's assessment rate surpassed Germany's and became the third largest. China's graduation in the case of the assessment rate (C2P) becomes also visible in the figure where there is a clear increase in the aggregate rate for Brazil, China, and India from 2016 to 2017 and from 2019 to 2020. By contrast, rising powers' voluntary rate (W2C) is characterized by fluctuations and an absence of graduation. This applies, in particular, since their voluntary rate is well below their assessment

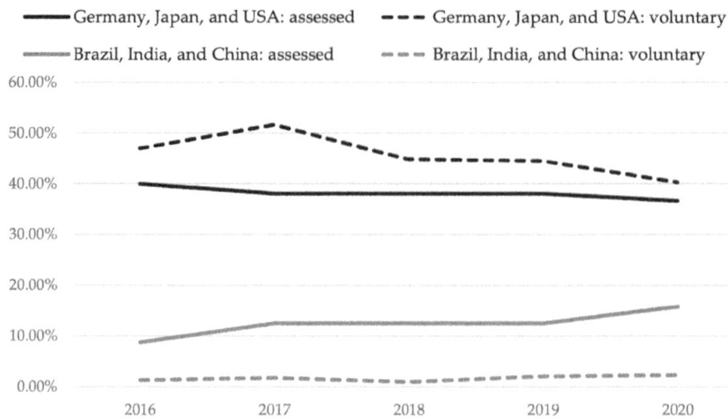

Figure 4.4 *Comparison between developments in assessment rates (C2P) and in voluntary rates (W2C)*

rate and remains marginal. As mentioned before, it is clear that they do not really feel subject to W2C. By contrast, the voluntary rate of the traditional major contributors is clearly above their assessment rate.

This brings us to the question of the support of Brazil, China, and India for an increase in assessed contributions as the second point. Assessed contributions were debated at various meetings but the financing dialogue in 2016 is particularly instructive since a 10 per cent increase was considered at the time, which was much more controversial than the 3 per cent increase that was subsequently proposed and eventually accepted (WHA70.5 [2017]; see also A70/7 [2017]: 12).[44] While Brazil was particularly clear in its opposition to a 10 per cent increase, China and India responded with questions and concerns but did not explicitly reject it. In other words, also in Phase 2 Brazil, China, and India supported differential treatment on the basis of C2P strongly in one context and less so in another: support was strong when the scale of assessments was discussed and this included acceptance of their own incremental graduation (see previous sub-section 4.5.1); however, in budgeting debates rising powers proved sceptical towards increasing the assessed contributions as the actual financial expression of C2P (this sub-section).

Also of note, among the three traditional major contributors, it was primarily Germany that strongly supported even a 10 per cent increase in assessed contributions. The USA and Japan by contrast remained more sceptical. While the dividing line between the supporters and the opponents of a 10 per cent increase in assessed contributions did not follow a division between developed and developing countries, WHO's African Region (AFRO) could be considered as a coalition of developing countries that expressed clear and consistent support for an increase.

Regarding Phase 2, a few key points can be summarized. This phase was characterized by changing budgeting practices that turned the assessments on member states into a minimum contribution that all countries had to make on the basis of C2P. Apart from one increase, the assessed contributions and hence the C2P-related part of the budget stagnated during Phase 2 (zero nominal growth). However, member states no longer received any reductions either and the terms 'regular budget', 'actual assessment', and 'assessed contributions' became synonyms. Voluntary contributions continued to increase and, after a temporary fall, tilted the balance even more in favour of differential treatment in the form of W2C. At the same time, attempts were made to clarify the social expectations regarding W2C which implies that it was no longer perceived as merely an enabling norm. As part of this process, 'core voluntary contributions' were promoted as a solution to much of WHO's funding problems. Of note, these changing expectations focussed on improving the 'quality' of voluntary contributions and therefore addressed mainly those countries and non-state actors who contributed already on a voluntary basis, while Brazil, China, and India could not be convinced that they should make considerable voluntary contributions. This foregrounds that W2C is not based on a formula approach, that it relies on informal rules, and that it leads to self-determined 'obligations' only. As a consequence, there was no graduation of Brazil, China, and India in the context of W2C. Moreover, these countries promoted budget moderation and proved reluctant to support an increase of the C2P-related part of the budget while they had supported C2P in other settings.

4.6 CONCLUSION

WHO-channelled financing can be seen as that part of global health financing that has the clearest and most binding rules regarding differential treatment. In spite of recurrent contestations, CWN has largely proven resilient. As an important adjustment, graduation has taken place, but it came in an attenuated and partial form. However, CWN has also become more informal which has ambivalent consequences and suggests that resilience has been less clear-cut than an analysis of formal rules would suggest. Finally, there has been a further increase of a previously existing restraint. These overall trends for CWN can be further specified by looking at each of the three underlying bundles of norms individually.

In spite of continuous conflicts in the case of C2P, there have been no major changes in the rules of the methodology (i.e. there has been resilience) ever since the decision in 2000 to lower the maximum ceiling to 22 per cent (which was a case of a further increase of a previously existing restraint). Nevertheless, considerable adjustments have occurred due to the practical consequences that followed from updated data that reflected, among other things, the global economic shift. This implies that there has been graduation but it came in an attenuated form – as will be elaborated on further in Chapter 9.

While C2P has in the main proven resilient, the relative share of assessed contributions vis-à-vis voluntary contributions has been shrinking. Moreover, the share of WHO-channelled financing is becoming smaller vis-à-vis other channels in global health. As a consequence of this layering, one could argue that the obligation to contribute financially is increasingly accompanied by an encouragement to do so, i.e. C2P is accompanied by W2C while differential treatment as a whole has become more informal and thereby more voluntary and more discretionary. The answer to the question of whether this informalization represents an expansion, preservation, or unmaking of differential treatment requires a brief elaboration since informalization was not anticipated in our initial conceptualization of change (Chapter 1). As the brief elaboration will show, the answer depends on the social practice that is established in the informal context. While informal differential treatment on the basis of W2C could in theory be an expansion, the current practice is a very specific form of weakening since it allows for informal influence and is generally exposed to the vagaries of (non)contributors. If we want to situate this weakening along the continuum displayed in Figure 1.1 in Chapter 1, it could be placed between resilience and unmaking as it is grounded in the rebalancing of previous existing norms (C2P and W2C).

As discussed at the outset of this chapter, informal arrangements on the basis of W2C have in principle the potential to expand differential treatment for the following reason: even for countries with a low assessment rate, an increase in voluntary contributions can be a better deal than an increase in assessed contributions since C2P implies higher payments *for all* member states (even though in a differentiated manner), while W2C comes without any monetary obligations. In other words, C2P defines the financial responsibilities of member states as common and differentiated while W2C drops the 'common' part and makes responsibilities more diffuse by basing them on an (ad hoc) self-declaration approach. The problem is, however, that it is exposed to the vagaries of non-contributors who can deny any financial responsibility and to the vagaries of contributors who can earmark their contributions and thereby exert informal governance.

From this perspective, one could say that voluntary contributions and W2C can represent a strong case of differential treatment if the funding meets the expectations and is unconditional (i.e. not earmarked); in this case, it adds to the common financial pool without increasing the burden on other countries, in particular the burden on countries with low assessment rates. Thus, the increasing call for more 'core voluntary contributions' by existing contributors can be seen as one avenue that W2C could take (thereby expanding differential treatment). At present, there is, however, a further increase in 'earmarked voluntary contributions' which is problematic but not a case of unmaking of differential treatment. It weakens differential treatment in a very peculiar way. Moreover, the non-contributors contribute their part to this situation.

In this context, it is noteworthy that Brazil, China, and India so far do not really feel subject to W2C – and even less so to the recent specification that voluntary contributions should not be earmarked. In the past years, their voluntary contributions were marginal in light of the overall volume, and they have made no 'core voluntary contributions'. In other words, there was no real graduation of Brazil, China, and India in this case which makes their overall graduation not only attenuated (due to the scale methodology) but also partial. W2C does not work with a formula approach but on the basis of self-determined 'obligations' that leaves graduation at the discretion of the countries concerned. While China seems to accept the fact that existing rules for C2P are giving her a new status as a 'major contributor', she, Brazil, and India are reluctant to provide voluntary funds through multi- and polylateral channels. They prefer to provide support to other countries bilaterally (cf. Huang 2020). This implies also that these rising powers did not take any steps to alleviate the problematic side of the current practices around voluntary contributions. This reinforces the conclusion that in spite of the theoretical potential to expand differential treatment, voluntary contributions based on W2C remain problematic.

The problematic side of current financing that is channelled through WHO has also been noted by the actors themselves and against the background of their discussions, there seem to be three lines along which differential treatment could develop in this area in the near future. First, current trends could continue and there might be 'more earmarked voluntary contributions' (which is an ambivalent if not problematic development from the perspective of differential treatment). Second, there could be 'more core voluntary contributions' (which could reinforce differential treatment.) Both options may or may not include Brazil, China, and India as contributors. Third, there could be a massive increase in assessed contributions that would re-emphasize differential treatment based on C2P. But also in this case, Brazil, China, and India seem to be reluctant to support differential treatment by taking on more financial responsibilities. In particular, they have not been strong promoters of the idea to considerably increase assessed contributions when WHO governance bodies have decided to pursue this option in a stepwise approach (e.g. A75/9 [2022] and WHA76.1 [2023]).

After this extensive discussion of the input side of differential treatment, a few remarks on the output side and N4S are in order. N4S has become more similar to C2P in the sense that it is more and more based on a formula approach. A continuous particularity of this approach is, however, that it uses the need of individual countries to calculate resource allocation at the level of regions while the individual countries are not secured specific amounts of funding. In other words, there are considerable efforts to formalize N4S but this affects only the regional level. Another noteworthy aspect about N4S is that it can be seen as an attempt to regain some control over the question of where voluntary contributions are spent (in geographical terms).

In light of these substantive findings it is important to conclude this chapter by reiterating its central contribution that was the precondition for the analysis. At the outset, this chapter reconstructed and conceptualized differential treatment in WHO-channelled health financing as CWN. Having made CWN visible, it became possible to discern its trajectory and to compare it to differential treatment in other regimes.

NOTES

1. On polylateralism, see Wiseman 2010.
2. For an exception from this tendency, see Gautier et al. 2014.
3. For a text that pays more tribute to this link than most of the literature but deals with it from the perspective of domestic politics in the United States of America (USA), see Mackey and Novotny 2012.
4. For further examples, see Reddy et al. 2018; Clinton and Sridhar 2017: 325; People's Health Movement et al. 2017: 246; Sridhar and Woods 2013: 330.
5. For a general discussion on the (mandatory) financing of international organizations, see Cogan 2016.
6. For an UN-wide perspective with a focus on the enabling dimension of this norm, see Graham 2015; 2017b.
7. Such tensions characterize not only the health regime but the UN system as a whole (Schmid et al. 2021; Goetz and Patz 2017; Graham 2015; 2017a; Mackey and Novotny 2012).
8. On WHO's federal structure and its implications, see Hanrieder 2015 and Graham 2014.
9. Special and differential treatment.
10. Common but differentiated responsibilities (and respective capabilities).
11. A further factor was the phasing out of the scheme of limits at the end of the 1990s. Document A/42/11 (1987) contains a brief review of the scheme of limits as it was introduced in 1985.
12. For the calculation and for the redistribution of shares at beginning of Phase 1, see pages 4 and 5 as well as annexes IIB and IIIB of A/49/11 (1994). For the present situation, see page 57 of A73/11 (2018).
13. The list of Least Developed Countries is reviewed every three years by the Committee for Development Policy (CDP).
14. Before the introduction of this range, other measures were taken to control the rates of Least Developed Countries (see, for example, A46/11 [1991]: 9, and A73/11 [2018]: 54–55, 59).

15. Data is taken from WHA46.15 (1993); WHA48.20 (1995); WHA50.33 (1997); WHA51.21 (1998); WHA52.17 (1999); WHA54.17 (2001); WHA56.33 (2003); WHA57.15 (2004); WHA58.19 (2005).
16. Data is taken from the final UN scale that was adopted during Phase 1 (A61/11 [2006]).
17. In this context, 'non-assessed income' (also known as 'casual income', 'miscellaneous income', or 'other income') calls for a brief elaboration. It covers, for example, interests earned, arrears from previous years, assessments on new members, rentals from WHO's underground parking, as well as income from the sale of equipment and material. It can be appropriated to reduce the assessments on member states unconditionally and collectively (first step) or conditionally and individually (second step). Moreover, non-assessed income has been used to finance priority programmes directly and outside of the 'regular budget'.
18. At the beginning of Phase 1, the rules of the financial incentive scheme applied as established by resolution WHA41.12 (1988).
19. See also A49/7 (1996): 22.
20. To add further to the legibility of the table, the starkly divergent original estimates for the financial incentive scheme are not displayed for the biennia 2002–2003, 2004–2005, and 2006–2007, which had been 3 000 000, 1 000 000, and 1 000 000 respectively.
21. See also EB97/1996/REC/2: 213.
22. For the biennium 1998–1999, see also A53/17 (2000): 12, 52. For the biennium 2000–2001, see also A55/25 (2002): 12, 50; and WHA54.9 (2001).
23. See also PB/2004–2005 (2003): 5.
24. See also A57/20 (2004): 12, 46. This is the amount that countries would have been legally obliged to pay. In the end, it was slightly higher since some member states decided to not avail themselves of the relief measures which resulted in an additional income of USD 5 477 239 (see pages 12–13, 14–15, 55 of the same document).
25. Due to rounding issues, different amounts have been quoted for the relief measures (cf. A54/INF.DOC./10 [2001]: 9, 14; WHA54.17 [2001]; A57/20 [2004]: 54). For consistency, Table 4.1 uses USD 36 153 035.
26. See also A57/20 (2004): 12, 37.
27. For the biennium 2004–2005, see also A59/28 (2006): 14. For the biennium 2006–2007, see also A61/20 (2008): 14.
28. See also A61/20 (2008): 14–15, 56. While the rules of the financial incentive scheme had undergone some change in the course of Phase 1, it was terminated by resolution WHA60.9 (2007), which observed that the scheme 'has failed to encourage prompt payment of Member States' assessments'.
29. E.g. WHA54/2001/REC/3: 22 and WHA56/2003/REC/3: 40; but see also WHA56/2005/REC/3: 71, when Brazil supported the proposed increase by 4 per cent.
30. For an illustrative statement by the EU, from which the quotes have been taken, see A/C.5/64/SR.2 (2009): 4.
31. For an illustrative statement by G-77 and China, from which the quote has been taken, see A/C.5/64/SR.2 (2009): 2–3.
32. For an illustrative statement by the USA, see A/C.5/64/SR.2 (2009): 5.
33. Data is taken from WHA58.19 (2005); WHA60.5 (2007); WHA62.5 (2009); WHA63.5 (2010); WHA64.21 (2011); WHA66.15 (2013); WHA68.12 (2015); WHA69.14 (2016); WHA70.9 (2017); WHA72.12 (2019).

34. Data for Phase 2 is taken from the following budgeting resolutions: WHA62.9 (2009); WHA64.3 (2011); WHA66.2 (2013); WHA68.1 (2015); WHA70.5 (2017); WHA72.1 (2019).
35. See A66/7 (2013): 12.
36. On the introduction of an integrated budget, see WHA66.2 (2013) and WHA66.3 (2013). For an example of a retrospective account, see A70/7 (2017): 11–12.
37. E.g. 'WHA50.25 Appropriation Resolution for the Financial Period 1998–1999'.
38. E.g. 'WHA66.2 (2013), Programme Budget 2014–2015'.
39. The dual function of budget allocation is easily overlooked since scholarly discussions focus mainly on the challenge of reaching the funding target (e.g. Patz and Goetz 2019: 180–196).
40. On the terms 'core voluntary contributions', 'voluntary contributions – core', and 'voluntary contributions – specified', see, for example, A71/INF./2 (2018): 2 (note 1).
41. Being informal meetings, the financing dialogues and the partners forum are not documented through official records. However, background material and reports can (or could) be found at the following URLs: https://www.who.int/about/finances-accountability/funding/financing-dialogue/en/ (no longer available but documented by the Internet Archive at https://web.archive.org/web/20230000000000*/https://www.who.int/about/finances-accountability/funding/financing-dialogue/en/, last accessed 20 October 2023) and https://www.who.int/news-room/events/inaugural-partners-forum, last accessed 14 October 2023.
42. For key documents from 2011, see A64/4 (2011); A64/INF.DOC./5 (2011); A64/29 (2011) as well as EB128/21 (2011); EB128/INF.DOC./2 (2011); EB128/INF.DOC./3 (2011); and https://www.who.int/dg/future_financing/en/ (no longer available but documented by the Internet Archive at https://web.archive.org/web/20230000000000*/https://www.who.int/dg/future_financing/en/, which was last accessed 20 October 2023).
43. Data for the assessment rate is taken from the same documents as in Figure 4.3. Data for the voluntary rate refers to payments to the General Fund and is calculated on the basis of the following documents: A70/INF./4 Corr.1 (2019); A71/INF./2 Corr.1 (2019); A72/INF./5 (2019); A73/INF./3 (2020); A74/INF./4 (2021).
44. The webcast for the fourth edition of the financing dialogue (2016) was available online at https://www.who.int/about/finances-accountability/funding/financing-dialogue/streaming/en/ (it is partially documented by the Internet Archive at https://web.archive.org/web/20230000000000*/http://www.who.int/about/finances-accountability/funding/financing-dialogue/streaming/en/, last accessed 20 October 2023).

PART II

Conflict case studies

5. Conflicts over special and differential treatment in agriculture

Till Schöfer and Clara Weinhardt

5.1 INTRODUCTION

Agriculture is a key area of global trade for developing countries. Not only is agricultural production central in most developing economies, but large proportions of their population – often the poorest segments of society – are also employed in the sector. Developing countries have thus traditionally paid particular attention to the rules of the world trade regime in this realm. When the World Trade Organisation (WTO) was created in 1995, the special situation of developing countries was acknowledged in two main ways: first, the WTO's Agreement on Agriculture (AoA) (1994) contains several provisions that grant greater flexibilities and exemptions to developing countries as compared to developed country members. These provisions fall under the WTO's constitutional principle of special and differential treatment (SDT) for developing countries: differential rights and obligations are reserved for 'weaker' and 'stronger' regime members respectively. Despite this differential treatment, developing countries were disappointed after the end of the Uruguay Round negotiations (1986–1994) when major demands regarding agriculture were not heard. As a result, second, the Doha Development Round launched in 2001 explicitly promised to deliver on agriculture as a key concern for developing countries.

This chapter assesses how conflict dynamics over differentiated rights and obligations for developing and developed countries have changed in agricultural negotiations in response to the rise of Brazil, China, and India. Our premise is that greater heterogeneity among the group of developing countries leads to pressure to adapt a system of differential treatment that relies on the binary distinction between 'developed' and 'developing' countries. Such adaptation is not automatic and can unfold in different ways (cf. Chapter 1). Against this background, this chapter unpacks how and why the global power shift away from Western towards rising powers has shaped the evolution of SDT in the case of agricultural negotiations.

We develop two main arguments: first, we show that the global power shift has led to a loss of Southern coalition unity in agricultural negotiations over time. This, in turn, contributed to the unmaking of the status quo of differential treatment for developing countries as a group. Such unmaking became visible by a shift in the negotiation agenda (despite persistent deadlock) – from a focus on expanding differential treatment for developing countries towards curtailing some of the special rights that already exist. Second, we show how the global power shift contributed to this partial unmaking. The emergence of China and India as major subsidizers in agriculture in the 2010s has dissolved both the legitimacy conceptions and the constellations of interests that were crucial to Southern unity – and their defence of differential treatment.

These findings speak to the larger theme of the book by shedding light on how the global power shift contributes to the partial unmaking of special rights in the world trade regime. The larger overall trend is resilience at the level of the legal framework, i.e. preservation of the legal foundation of differential treatment, and partial unmaking at the level of trade negotiations. In ongoing WTO negotiations, such rights are rarely granted to developing countries as a group anymore. Instead, they remain increasingly reserved for the limited group of Least Developed Countries (LDCs) (cf. chapter 2). While differential treatment for LDCs is less central to agricultural negotiations, developing countries as a group have become more marginalized in their demands to expand their special rights in new agreements and decisions. Against this background, this chapter unpacks not only how, but also why, this pattern emerges.

We show that – amidst a lack of reform at the level of the legal framework – the global power shift has affected the evolution of SDT in agricultural negotiations in two main ways. First, changing interest coalitions across Brazil, China, India, and developing countries have undermined Southern unity in coalitions. Notably, the interests of Brazil as a liberal, export-oriented player in agriculture have diverged too far from the defensive positions of India and China to maintain the developing country G-20 (Group of 20) coalition. While political economy dynamics thus contributed to this decay of Southern unity, we show that economic structures alone are insufficient to explain changing coalition patterns. Second, the emergence of China and India as major subsidizers in agriculture in the 2010s has undermined the legitimacy of the existing system of differential treatment. Their reluctance to give up special rights they hold as developing country members has thus made it more difficult to negotiate an expansion of the status quo on SDT. This, in turn, has undermined Southern coalition unity. In particular, Brazil's decision to abandon the developing country G-20 coalition in the 2010s was, in part, driven by the recognition that the coalition had lost its normative ring in light of India and China's new roles as major subsidizers in agriculture. In addition, the institutionalization of differential treatment in the WTO context shapes how both dynamics – changing interests and legitimacy conceptions – played out.

These findings speak to existing debates on global power shifts and trade multilateralism. They shed light on how the rise of Brazil, China, India, and other rising powers not only shapes the evolution of *liberal* order (Sinha 2021; Weinhardt and ten Brink 2020), but also affects norms and principles that shape North–South relations in the WTO (cf. Zelicovich 2022; Weinhardt and Schöfer 2022). Moreover, they show that the global power shift has gone hand in hand with differences in interests *across* Brazil, China, and India, indicating that patterns of unity of Brazil, China, and India – and Southern unity more generally (Johnson and Urpelainen 2020) – are issue-specific. Lastly, they illustrate that pluralistic research approaches that integrate the analysis of (material) interests with legitimacy conceptions and institutional structures help us to fully understand the complexity of normative change in light of global power shifts.

This chapter relies on a comparative case study approach. We trace the effects of global power shifts on conflict dynamics regarding differential treatment for developing countries by zooming in on two central conflict moments in agricultural negotiations that culminated in 2003 (Cancún Ministerial Conference) and 2017 (Buenos Aires Ministerial Conference). While the former captures a time period 'before' the rise of Brazil, China, and India, the latter conflict moment takes place 'after' their rise (cf. Chapter 1). Regarding the conflict dynamics, our conceptual focus is twofold: first, we trace Southern coalition unity over time, based on the assumption that greater heterogeneity of the Global South may undermine unity concerning SDT. As Brazil, China, and India gain in power, they may lose an interest in defending or expanding differential treatment for 'weak' regime members. This, second, is linked to our assessment of the specific outcomes in both conflict moments. We expect that negotiation outcomes could either indicate resilience or unmaking of the status quo of differential treatment for developing countries. Lastly, the comparison over time helps us to uncover how global power shifts are shaping potential changes or continuities. We seek to explain the patterns we find in light of the explanatory factors that are central to our conceptual framework: political economic dynamics, legitimacy conceptions, and institutional structures (cf. Chapter 1). In terms of sources, we make use of official WTO documents, in particular minutes of meetings from the Committee on Agriculture (CoA) and statements and submissions related to Ministerial Conferences, as well as eight interviews with trade diplomats and experts involved in agricultural negotiations.[1]

In the following sections, this chapter outlines the status quo of differential treatment of developing countries in agriculture before the global power shift. We then trace the effects of the global power shift on conflict dynamics related to special rights for developing countries in agricultural negotiations around 2003 and 2017, before turning to explanations of the observed outcomes.

5.2 SPECIAL AND DIFFERENTIAL TREATMENT IN AGRICULTURE

This section outlines the status quo of differential treatment in the realm of agriculture before the rise of Brazil, China, and India. It shows that many different kinds of differential treatment for developing countries were incorporated during the founding of the WTO in 1995. Despite these provisions however, at the time of the WTO's establishment existing rules were commonly understood as biased in favour of developed countries. Some even label existing rules on agriculture as 'reverse SDT' for developed countries.

5.2.1 Legal Context: The Status Quo in 1995

The WTO's foundational legal framework codified SDT in agriculture. SDT provisions fall into three categories or – negotiation 'pillars' – comprising *market access*, *domestic support*, and *export competition* (cf. Table 5.1). This framing in turn stems from the AoA (1994), which established an international liberalization road map for agricultural products at the end of the Uruguay Round (1986–1994).

Market access discussions revolve around the issue of import restrictions – mainly tariffs and tariff quotas. In this area, SDT becomes apparent because developing countries face both lower average tariff reductions and longer implementation periods. While a developed WTO member had to reduce tariffs by 36 per cent on average by 2001 – including a minimum of 15 per cent for any product – developing countries had until 2004 to reduce tariffs by a 24 per cent average, with a 10 per cent minimum. Moreover, LDCs were completely exempt from tariff reductions, although they were required to bind tariffs at existing levels (cf. Table 5.1).

On domestic support – which covers the provision of subsidies to domestic producers – the AoA introduced a 'box' system: trade-distortive support is marked as belonging to the 'Amber Box', while support with minimal influence on trade flows – such as agricultural research funding – is included in a 'Green Box'. Moreover, a 'Blue Box' is reserved for support that is trade distortive, but also entails limiting production. While the Green and Blue Boxes do not prescribe limits for support, Amber Box measures are required to be reduced to prescribed levels, referred to as *de minimis*. At the conclusion of the Uruguay Round, this reduction requirement was quantified via the single indicator Total Aggregate Measure of Support (AMS).

Domestic support regulation incorporates SDT, first via *de minimis* levels in the Amber Box. While a developed country like France could subsidize its agricultural goods at 5 per cent of the value of production, a developing country like Indonesia could devote up to 10 per cent of a good's production value to domestic support. In relative terms, developing countries thus have a ceiling for their subsidy allowances that is twice as high as those of developed countries. Here again, LDCs obtain complete exemptions from such ceiling obligations. Second, an additional category of 'SDT Box' subsidies (AoA 1994: Article 6.2) is reserved only for developing country members and not subject to limitations. These subsidies contain measures of assistance geared towards encouraging agricultural and rural development in developing countries. Third, when it comes to reducing Amber Box subsidies, those developing countries affected only had to reduce their support by 13 per cent over ten years, as opposed to the 20 per cent over six years required for developed countries. Notably, developing countries that joined the WTO later – such as China in 2001 – often only attained partial access to these SDT measures as a result of their accession negotiations. In the case of China, *de minimis* levels are set between the regular and the SDT level at 8.5 per cent. Moreover, Chinese policy-makers have no access to the 'SDT Box'.

The final pillar of the AoA – export competition – targets subsidies that are specifically designed to increase the competitiveness of agricultural products on the international market. Some SDT measures were included on this issue: while developed WTO members had to decrease their export subsidies by 21 per cent in volume over six years, developing countries had ten years to achieve reductions of only 14 per cent. LDCs were in turn exempted from reductions altogether.

5.2.2 Critique of the Status Quo

While SDT provisions feature across all three pillars in the AoA, they have been widely criticized as insufficient to address the needs of developing countries. Two main points of critique are voiced: first, existing rules of the AoA also contain implicit differential treatment in favour of developed countries, which some have referred to as 'reversed' SDT (WT/GC/W/765/Rev.2 of 4 March 2019). Second, the limited fiscal capacities of developing countries de facto outweigh the special rights they are entitled to, since they are not able to match the subsidy levels of developed countries.

With regard to market access regulations, the issue of 'reverse' SDT becomes apparent on special safeguards: safeguards comprise *legal* tariffs that countries can raise to counter import surges and sudden price fluctuations. In the WTO system, only a limited set of 33 members have access to these tools – labelled the Special Safeguard (SSG) in Article 5 of the AoA – namely

Table 5.1 *SDT provisions in the Agreement on Agriculture (1994) from 1993 to 2007*

Market Access	Domestic Support	Export Competition
• Art. 4.1: Lower average tariff reductions for developing countries (26 per cent with 10 per cent minimum) versus developed ones (36 per cent average with 15 per cent minimum) • Art. 4.1: Longer implementation periods for tariff cuts for developing countries (ten years) compared to general membership (six years) • LDCs required to bind tariff levels at given level but did not have to reduce further	• Art. 6.4: Higher *de minimis* ceilings for developing countries (10 per cent) than for developed ones (5 per cent). *De minimis* for China (8.5 per cent). LDCs exempt from reductions • Art. 6.2: 'SDT Box' allows classification of support measures to be exempt from reductions. Reserved for developing countries only. China exempted • Lower and slower reduction commitments for developing countries with Amber Box measures. These were schedule-specific	• Art. 15.2: Longer timeframe (ten years) for implementation of export subsidy reductions versus general membership (six years) • Art. 2.9(biv): Lower relative reductions of export subsidies from 1986–1990 baseline • LDCs exempted from reduction commitments

those that 'tarrified'[2] their product lists in the 1990s. While rights-holders include Australia, Canada, Japan, the European Union (EU), and the United States (US), the majority of the WTO's developing country members cannot avail themselves of safeguards when needed. A Special Safeguard Mechanism (SSM), which functions similarly to the SSG but is only available to developing countries, has consequently been tabled multiple times during the Doha Round.

With regard to domestic support, policy space for developed states to maintain their subsidies creates a structural imbalance against developing countries. Concerning AMS allowances, all countries committed to binding their domestic support levels at 1986–1988 levels. Many developing countries, however, had no AMS support in this base period, and thus de facto committed themselves not to introduce such support in the future. In these ways, AoA rules favour countries with a high AMS entitlement during the base period – primarily developed countries. Amongst Brazil, China, and India, for instance, only Brazil has an entitlement to AMS. This allowance, however, remains below the level of the EU and the US, resulting in a situation where some rules differentiate in favour of developed countries (AMS), while others favour developing countries (*de minimis*, SDT Box subsidies) (cf. Table 5.2).

Table 5.2 Overview of differential treatment on domestic support in agriculture

	Amber Box subsidies		Blue Box subsidies	'SDT' Box subsidies (Art. 6.2)	Green Box subsidies
	AMS subsidies (in million USD)	*De minimis* subsidies (% of value of production)*			
India	0	10%	Without limit	Without limit	Without limit
Brazil	912	10%	Without limit	Without limit	Without limit
China	0	8.5%	Without limit	No access	Without limit
US	19 103	5%	Without limit	No access	Without limit
EU	72 244	5%	Without limit	No access	Without limit

Note: *Applies for product-specific and non-product-specific support.
Source: Adapted from Sharma and Das 2018: 78.

Moreover, flexibilities in the classification of Green Box subsidies have allowed developed countries to maintain large-scale subsidization programmes against the core AoA aim of reducing such unfair practices. For instance, according to Organisation for Economic Co-operation and Development (OECD) figures, the total support estimate increased on average for all OECD countries from 1986–1988 to 1999–2001 (cited in Pal 2001). Shifting their subsidies out of the reduction-based Amber Box allowed the number of Green Box subsidies in the EU and the US to more than double by the early 2000s (Diakosawas 2001: 24). This effectively enabled the two largest subsidizers of agricultural produce to circumvent support cuts encapsulated in the AoA. While Green Box subsidies are considered as non-trade distorting, the expenditures they entail raise productivity in general. Over time, this unavoidably translates into a trade advantage, simply by virtue of the agrisector increasing output that is available for export (Brink and Orden 2020: 11). This has led some scholars, such as Pritchard (2009: 302) to claim that '[e]lite Northern interests … use[d] the WTO as a tool to preserve their own subsidy regimes, while at the same time enforcing liberalization on the rest of the world'. As Clapp (2006: 565) shows, in the aftermath of the Uruguay Round, 60 per cent of OECD subsidies were exempt from reductions.

Conversely, developing countries were hardly able to make use of the flexibilities that the AoA provided them with. Particularly small developing countries had no capacity to build up large-scale subsidization initiatives of their own in response to similar distortive schemes in OECD countries. While they are, for example, allowed to provide higher levels of trade-distorting subsidies, they simply lack the fiscal means to do so. The Food and Agriculture Organization (FAO) reported in 2000 that most developing countries did not notify any trade-distorting domestic support; if they did so, the reported amount was less than the allowed 10 per cent *de minimis* levels (FAO 2000).[3] This sharply contrasts with developed countries, which often exceeded their *de minimis* levels (ICTSD 2017). From a legal perspective, differential treatment for developing countries consequently does exist on domestic support. In practice, however, major trade distortions in favour of developed countries persist, harming the agricultural sectors of developing countries.

Taken together, these biases in the AoA have led to calls from developing countries to use the WTO's Doha Round – launched in 2001 – to reform agricultural trade. As Maswood (2007: 43) points out, they 'were unambiguous in demands that agricultural liberalization should be the core of any Doha round agreement. They were keen also to recover the lost ground of special and differential treatment, a principle that had been eroded by the Uruguay round agreements'. In the following sections, we examine two conflict moments that were central for agricultural negotiations in the WTO – and the persistent deadlock on most SDT-related demands.

5.3 CANCÚN (2003): UNITY OF SOUTHERN COALITIONS

The 2003 Ministerial Conference in Cancún marked a central conflict moment in agricultural negotiations 'before' the rise of Brazil, China, and India. We show that in this early conflict, Brazil, China, and India stood united with other developing countries. However, Southern unity was far from self-evident and was forged only in the immediate run-up to the Cancún Ministerial Conference. Key demands of this new coalition were the expansion of differential treatment via an SSM and new developed country commitments on reducing domestic support. Conversely, developed countries pushed for better market access for agricultural products in developing country markets. While neither side was able to push through their positions in Cancún, this early conflict signals the resilience of the status quo, coupled with an agenda geared towards expanding differential treatment of developing countries. The resistance of the unified Southern coalition paved the way for an interim agreement in 2004 that took many developing country positions on board. In the following section, the main conflict lines in the negotiations are traced before an assessment of the outcome.

5.3.1 Early 2003: Conflict Lines Cut Across the North–South Division

Prior to the 2003 Ministerial Conference in Cancún, delegations from member states convened in the CoA Special Session. Agricultural reform was high on the negotiation agenda. Brazil, China, and India, and developing countries, however, did not have a uniform negotiation position yet, and conflict lines cut across the North–South division.

In February 2003, prenegotiations on agriculture started to reach a substantial level, as the Special Session Chairman Stuart Harbinson published a draft modalities text that sought to provide the basis for agricultural reform. The draft covered reform proposals for all three pillars – market access, domestic support, and export competition – and set the agenda for the Cancún Ministerial Conference. These reform proposals contained defensive elements, including on domestic support, as well as offensive proposals on market access. While China and India strongly supported and sought to improve the defensive elements of the draft modalities text, Brazil – similar to other agricultural exporters – endorsed and sought to deepen the reform proposals on market access. Developed countries also remained divided. What all sides had in common was that none of them fully endorsed the draft modalities text as a basis for the Cancún Ministerial Conference.

China reacted to the draft modalities text by outlining its approach to agricultural negotiations: regarding export competition and domestic support China proposed to go beyond the tabled reform proposal,[4] signalling a strong support for expanding SDT in agricultural trade. While calling for an ambitious level of tariff reductions regarding market access, these calls were limited to developed countries. A radical Chinese push against developed country subsidies fits well with Indian reactions to the Harbinson draft, which underlined the allegedly imbalanced nature of proposed reforms: the draft modalities text, so India, had a high level of ambition on market access compared to relatively low levels of reformatory zeal on domestic support and export subsidies (TN/AG/R/7 of 24 March 2003: 45–46).

Conversely, Brazil acted as a member of the Cairns Group in these early talks. Consisting of major agricultural exporters, the Cairns Group included both developed and developing countries. As part of this coalition, the Brazilian delegation pursued a strong liberalization agenda in the formal CoA meeting in February, diametrically opposed to India's defensive position on market access: on market access a 'higher level of ambition [was] needed to get rid of trade prohibition under the guise of prohibitive tariffs' (TN/AG/R/7 of 24 March 2003: 1, para. 6). This included the expansion of tariff quotas, a move resisted by several other developing countries. On domestic support, Brazil's position was less opposed to those of China, India, and other developing countries: it demanded substantial and fast reduction of subsidies if the 'chaotic picture' of world agriculture was to be remedied (TN/AG/R/7 of 24 March 2003: 1, para. 6).

In parallel, developed countries also grappled with the question of where to place the emphasis of trade reform. While the US recognized the need to address distortions in all three pillars, it also claimed 'it was only through a substantial result, particularly in market access, that the United States saw meaningful income gains for all Members' (TN/AG/R/7 of 24 March 2003: 2, para. 9). The European Communities (EC) instead called for a 'comprehensive, balanced and therefore doable approach in all areas'. Such a supposedly pragmatic approach stood in contrast to 'over-ambitious calls from a minority of export-oriented Members' (TN/AG/R/7 of 24 March 2003: 9–10, para. 41). Indeed, Honma (2004) finds that while the US insistence on increasing market access can be compared to the negotiation position of Brazil, Canada, and the Cairns Group, the EC and Japan instead focussed on limiting reductions both on tariffs and on domestic support.

With a revised modalities text on the table in March, divergent positions of Brazil, China, and India continued to dominate negotiations. In a statement with Australia, Brazil criticized proposed tariff reductions as too limited (TN/AG/R/8 of 18 July 2003: 25) and characterized market access as the foundation of the WTO and the 'cornerstone of the Doha Agenda' (TN/AG/R/8 of 18 July 2003: 12, para. 77). India regarded the revised draft as a slight improvement and hardened its support for two specific defensive elements of the text: lists of Special Products (SPs),[5] and a SSM reserved for developing countries to counter import surges with market access restrictions. The Indian delegation promoted both as conditions for any further consideration of the proposals (TN/AG/R/8 of 18 July 2003: 36). Support for SPs and the SSM should in turn be seen as an explicit attempt to expand the differential treatment of developing countries beyond the AoA status quo.

US approaches to the revised text pushed for more substantial reform across the board, but with a particular focus on market access. While this included proposals on reducing domestic support, it also meant 'orienting S&D treatment towards facilitating market-oriented reform, not circumventing trade liberalization' (TN/AG/R/8 of 18 July 2003: 10, para. 65). Here, we consequently see an explicit conflict line emerging between China, India, and other developing countries – who sought market access exemptions and flexibilities via SPs and an SSM – and a US/Cairns Group emphasis on all-encompassing agricultural trade liberalization.

5.3.2 Nascent Southern Coalition Unity in Mid-2003

The tables begin to turn around mid-2003, as an increasingly unified developing country position becomes apparent in a flurry of statements by Brazil, China, and India both at formal and informal CoA sessions in June and July. The strongest proof for the emergence of a developing country bloc comes with the establishment of the Alliance for SP and SSM in mid-2003 – a group that became known as the G-33. Consisting of India, Indonesia, Nigeria, Pakistan, and a number of smaller developing countries, the Alliance authored a strongly worded manifesto against inequities in the existing system of agricultural trade (TN/AG/R/10 of 9 September 2003: 46–48): domestic markets were 'deluged' by products that relied on subsidies from developed countries. SDT had in turn been unable to stop the erosion of the 'only available instrument of defence and protection: tariffs' (TN/AG/R/10 of 9 September 2003: 46). The group declared that no agreement in the agricultural negotiations could be viable without inclusion of SPs and the SSM, elaborated to such an extent that they provided operationally effective SDT.

While Brazil did not join the G-33 coalition, Brazil, China, and India's positions started to come closer together. Brazil's core reform aim – 'to integrate all countries into the world trading system' (TN/AG/R/10 of 9 September 2003: 15, para. 81) – continued to sit uneasily with Indian and Chinese approaches to market access that sought to carve out special rights and stagger full liberalization. In a coalescence of the positions of Brazil, China, and India, however, the Brazilian delegation used its final pre-Ministerial statement to underline that any outcome on market access was contingent on an outcome on subsidies and that adjustment in this latter area claimed precedence: 'How can developing countries – counting only with border measures for their protection – feel confident to undertake further tariff reductions unless they have clear indications that their markets and vulnerable farmers will not be affected by subsidized imports?' (TN/AG/R/10 of 9 September 2003: 36).

August 2003 also saw the emergence of a common US–EC draft text on agricultural reform (JOB[03]/157 of 13 August 2003). The proposal indicated a hardening of their positions as several issues of concern for developing countries were left out. While the European position had been more nuanced before, this draft text seemingly suggested a push towards the unmaking of SDT in agricultural trade. The clearest omission is the absence of SPs from the text, despite their inclusion in all drafts of the modalities text under discussion in the CoA and their central position in developing countries' statements. The SSM, while mentioned, is included on a severely limited basis, with the language used suggesting that it could only be triggered for a certain group of products. Moreover, Khor (2004) notes that the proposal maintains the existing special safeguards included in the AoA, which disproportionately protect developed country markets. Vague formulations of domestic support regimes – excluding the Green Box subsidies and only partially addressing existing export subsidies – in turn provide ample room for the EC domestic aid programmes, as well as the Bush administration's USD (United States dollar) 180 billion farm subsidies.

5.3.3 The Cancún Ministerial Conference: A Polarized North–South Conflict

The position of the EC and the US allowed for a strong backlash – and stronger Southern unity – to emerge during the Ministerial Conference in Cancún (10–14 September 2003). In particular, the G-33 was soon accompanied by other newly formed Southern coalitions, most notably the G-20. This political grouping, led by the Brazilian and Indian delegations, consisted of Brazil, China, and India, as well as several other large developing countries. Indeed, several Cairns Group countries that had previously been sympathetic to a US-centred market access push were now counted amongst the G-20. The most notable example is Brazil, which underwent a shift from trade liberalization promotion in the Cairns Group to founding and leading the G-20. Moreover, the G-90 coalition emerged during the Conference, representing a common platform for the African Group, the LDC Group and the African, Caribbean, and Pacific Group. In response to the low level of development-oriented provisions in the US–EC text, both new groupings submitted their own proposals at the Conference. Nuances between individual country positions remained, however targeting of developed countries provided common ground between them.

The G-20's push for SDT expansion, supported by a newly unified coalition of Brazil, China, and India, represented a major game-changer, particularly as Brazil converged its position with those of other developing country members. The G-20 proposal contained a range of SDT measures focussed on limiting the impact of market access changes on the economies of developing countries (JOB[03]/162 of 20 August 2003; WT/MIN[03]/W/6 of 4 September 2003). These included smaller tariff reductions and longer implementation periods for developing countries, the establishment of SP lists and an SSM, and no commitments on tariff quota expansion or reductions of quota tariff rates. Moreover, the SSM was to be made available solely to developing countries. The proposal further sought to maintain *de minimis* levels for developing countries and to extend the 'SDT Box' subsidies for targeted programmes of low-income producers in developing countries. The G-90 proposal shared a focus on market access protections, albeit with further provisions specifically for LDCs (WT/MIN[03]/W/17 of 12 September 2003). The overlap with the G-20 proposal in turn underlines how developing countries of different sizes converged around certain common negotiation areas in early 2000s' agriculture discussions.

Coordinated opposition to the US–EC document signalled a growing negotiation impasse and increased division among the WTO membership over agriculture. For its part, the EC responded to the Southern coalitions with a dismissal of the proposed expansion of differential treatment for developing countries:

> But let us recall that the goal remains: The integration of developing countries into the world economy. In years to come, they will not thank us if we only manage to create a two tier membership in the WTO. So let us continue down this path of integration and avoid the creation of a group of Members who have second-class responsibilities, but also only second-class rights. (WT/MIN[03]/ST/5 of 10 September 2003: 1)

Brazil, China, and India in turn all put the onus on developed countries to move on domestic support, export subsidies, and development issues before expecting commensurate measures to be taken by developing countries (WT/MIN[03]/ST/7 of 10 September 2003; WT/MIN[03]/ST/12 of 10 September 2003; WT/MIN[03]/ST/28 of 11 September 2003). The unified opposition of the G-20 to the US–EC proposal was decisive for the resulting deadlock and ultimate breakdown of the Conference. The 2003 Cancún Ministerial was thus seen as a turning point, given that the G-20 coalition managed for the first time to effectively block proposals by established powers (Heldt 2017; Maswood 2007) with the G-20's position on domestic support being instrumental in this regard (Hopewell 2016: 80–82).

5.3.4 Assessment of the Outcome: Resilience of the Status Quo

Some scholars perceive the failure of the 2003 Cancún Ministerial Conference as a victory for developing countries (Narlikar and Tussie 2004; Srivastava 2008; Efstathopoulos 2012). Others emphasize that the failure of the Ministerial Conference harms the legitimacy of the WTO (Kurtz 2004; Narlikar and Wilkinson 2004) and global economic development (Sharma 2004). With regard to SDT, the breakdown of negotiations in Cancún meant the resilience of the status quo: no new rules were negotiated, and the AoA remained unchanged. At the same time, however, the breakdown shaped the negotiation agenda in ways that can be seen as a cautious step towards the expansion of differential treatment for developing countries. It paved the way towards a revised negotiation text in 2004 – the July Framework Agreement – that was seen as favourable for developing countries (Maswood 2007: 56). The agreement contained several refinements of the previous state of play in agricultural negotiations, including cuts in domestic support across all three boxes. This signals not only that existing differential treatment remained resilient, but that addressing the AoA's 'reverse SDT' on domestic support was seen as a legitimate undertaking. Southern coalitions thus hoped that an expansion of their differential treatment could soon be negotiated. While Cancún did not lead to concrete outcomes, the deadlock thus signalled resilience – and a possible future expansion – of SDT rather than its unmaking.

5.4 BUENOS AIRES (2017): THE END OF SOUTHERN COALITION UNITY

By the 2010s, the global power shift towards rising powers in the Global South had become much more apparent. This section examines if and how the resulting greater heterogeneity among developing country WTO members affected conflict dynamics in agricultural negotiations.

Negotiation standstill in the 2000s had rested on a strict fault-line between a group of developing countries – including Brazil, China, and India – and developed members, in particular the US and Europe. We find that by the mid-2010s this conflict line had shifted. This became apparent at the 2017 WTO Ministerial Conference in Buenos Aires at which agriculture played a central role, as well as during the years prior to the Conference (2015–2017). Two trends stand out: first, the G-20 – counting Brazil, China, and India amongst its membership – disappeared from the negotiation scene. Instead, new constellations emerged. They not only cut across previous North–South division, but also drove a wedge between Brazil on the one hand, and China and India on the other. The economic rise of Brazil, China, and India played a key role here, as China and India had become major subsidizers of agricultural products by the 2010s. Trade distortions caused by domestic support regimes thus no longer fell along North–South lines in this second conflict moment. Second, the move towards domestic support discussions rather than broader reform proposals allowed for a more direct juxtaposition and entrenchment of opposing positions, as fewer compromise packages were on the table.

While the deadlock of the early 2000s is thus largely repeated, we find a notable shift: these new conflict dynamics signal a partial unmaking of differential treatment in the sense that negotiations on differential treatment for the developing country group become increasingly deadlocked – and marginalized. In contrast to the 2000s, it was increasingly deemed impossible to reach a comprehensive agreement on agriculture that addressed developing country concerns.

5.4.1 Conflict Lines in the Mid-2010s: The Nairobi Ministerial Conference (2015) and its Aftermath

The 2015 Nairobi Ministerial Conference stands out due to the strong push, both in the run-up to and during the December Conference itself, for the establishment of an SSM. The G-33 coalition, including India and China, was clearly the most active actor in this regard (see JOB/AG/29 of 17 July

2014; IP/C/M/78/Add.1 of 4 May 2015; IP/C/M/80/Add.1 of 22 February 2016; IP/C/W/605 of 23 February 2015). A rebalancing of international agricultural law was to be based on the proposed SSM and SP lists, to protect developing countries from import surges and price swings (TN/AG/GEN/36 of 28 July 2015: para. 5). These designs for SDT expansion were allegedly being defended against a more dismissive attitude permeating the WTO in the mid-2010s. Efforts aimed at ‘simplification’, ‘recalibration’, and ‘lowering of ambition’ were thus resisted by the G-33 (TN/AG/GEN/36 of 28 July 2015: paras. 7–8). Moreover, one G-33 proposal sought to prohibit safeguard use against products originating from LDCs and certain developing countries (JOB/AG/65 and WT/MIN[15]/W/34 of 9 December 2015: para. 10).

However, hesitance by the wider membership to adopt the G-33 proposal led to the passing of superficial decisions on an SSM at Nairobi. These decisions respectively imbued the CoA with a negotiation mandate for the SSM (WT/L/978 and WT/MIN[15]/43 of 21 December 2015) and a dedicated session on public stockholding (WT/L/979 and WT/MIN[15]/44 of 21 December 2015). The inability to move forward on the central issues of market access and domestic support is problematized in a December report by the Chairman of the CoA: not only had there been ‘no convergence on domestic support or market access’ in the negotiations (TN/AG/32 of 8 December 2015: para. 5) in general, but the particular standstill on an SSM rested on members’ ‘opposition to the idea of an outcome on SSM at MC10 [Ministerial Conference 10] in the absence of a broader outcome on agriculture market access’ (TN/AG/32 of 8 December 2015: para. 15). Nonetheless, the 2015 Ministerial Conference does mark the conclusion of discussions on export competition, as a third agricultural decision required developed countries to immediately remove export credits and granted a longer implementation period for developing countries (WT/MIN[15]/45 and WT/L/980 of 21 December 2015).

Furthermore, in September 2016, the US initiated a complaint against China’s domestic support subsidies for wheat, rice, and corn that allegedly exceeded China’s commitments under the AoA in the time period of 2012 to 2015 (Brink and Orden 2017: 1–2). In particular, the US questioned whether Chinese measures remained within its 8.5 per cent *de minimis* level. While the US itself was not an active participant in the Buenos Aires Ministerial Conference and its preparatory sessions (see the next section), its opposition to rising Chinese domestic support measures contributed to the deadlock (Hopewell 2019). A US back-seat role in Buenos Aires was more attributable to the 2017 change of administration, and the bureaucratic process of setting up a new trade team, rather than a lack of interest in the negotiation issues.[6]

5.4.2 Conflict Lines Before and at the Ministerial Conference in Buenos Aires (2017)

The 2015 Nairobi Ministerial Conference reveals the entrenched standstill on market access issues. From this point onwards, increasingly polarized discussions over domestic support take centre stage. According to a summary report on the preparatory talks by CoA Chair Stephen Ndün'gü, the membership was bifurcated: some members devoted their energies towards the creation of an overall limit on domestic support – either fixed or floating. Other members called for the elimination of AMS entitlements, primarily reserved for developed country members, as a prerequisite for further reform (JOB/AG/107 of 25 July 2017: para. 2.7).

The 2017 agricultural fault-line at Buenos Aires is exemplified by two opposing proposals (cf. Table 5.3) which cut across the North–South division and mark the end of the unity of Brazil, China, and India that had helped to forge the G-20 coalition. One of the proposals involved a submission by the EU and Brazil that sought to introduce a universal cap to domestic support regimes (JOB/AG/99 of 17 July 2017). An India–China counterproposal in turn took aim at the AMS in order to refocus reform on distortions in developed countries (JOB/AG/102 of 18 July 2017).

The EU–Brazil draft text submitted in July 2017 can, overall, be read as an attempt to curtail the differential treatment of developing countries in agriculture. Implicitly, it targets India and China, both of which had become major providers of subsidies by that time. At the technical level, the proposal contains two different designs for domestic support: on the one hand, a fixed cap, based on a member's agricultural value of production and a reference year to be negotiated would permanently lock in a ceiling for subsidies (JOB/AG/99 of 17 July 2017: para. 1A). Alternatively, the proposal suggested simply lowering the existing floating caps on support and linking them to a fixed value of production (JOB/AG/99 of 17 July 2017: para. 1B). SDT is built into the proposed mechanism in the form of a 2 per cent higher subsidy allowance for developing countries. However, cementing upper boundaries in this way effectively dismantles the existing *de minimis* ceilings – as well as their SDT elements – by decoupling from production value in the calculation of support allowances. As Sharma and Das (2018: 85) point out, the differential treatment of developing countries would be curtailed, given that the 2 per cent difference between the *de minimis* of developed and developing countries is a significant reduction from the current 10 per cent difference in the *de minimis* allowances for developed and developing countries.[7] They conclude that the EU–Brazil proposal 'would … make developing countries worse off as compared to the developed countries' (Sharma and Das 2018: 85). This assessment applies in particular to India, China, and other emerging powers, who are among the few developing country members in a position to make full use of their *de minimis* subsidy allowances.

The counterproposal submitted in July 2017 by China and India is marked by a more direct, confrontational tone, and seeks to not only defend but also expand existing SDT. While the EU–Brazil document sought to construct a common system of support caps for all WTO members (with some SDT included), the India–China text targets the existing privileges reserved for countries under the AMS scheme (JOB/AG/102 of 18 July 2017: para. 1). AMS entitlements, 90 per cent of which accrue to developed states, provide certain members with the ability to support their agricultural sectors beyond *de minimis* levels. Neither India nor China hold AMS entitlements, which in turn implies that their own domestic support schemes would remain exempt from these proposed reductions. Further domestic support reform was made contingent upon the elimination of ‘the AMS entitlements of developed Members’ (JOB/AG/102 of 18 July 2017: para. 21).

The four-step AMS elimination plan contained in the India–China proposal solely addresses reductions of product-specific AMS in developed country members (JOB/AG/137 of 22 June 2018: para. 3a–d). The developing country members that have access to these mechanisms are treated more abstractly, with a proposal for a separate set of disciplines that contained SDT (JOB/AG/137 of 22 June 2018: para. 3e). The majority of the proposal consists of a long list of product-by-product subsidies employed under AMS by the US (JOB/AG/102 of 18 July 2017: paras. 4–9), the European Union (JOB/AG/102 of 18 July 2017: paras. 10–16), and Canada (JOB/AG/102 of 18 July 2017: paras. 17–20). Reducing these levels, or even instituting a fixed cap on support, would in turn widen the de facto margin between the subsidy allowances of developed and developing countries, and thus expand the differential treatment of developing countries.

By October 2017, the Chair of the CoA reported that the membership remained broadly divided between ‘those that favour an overall limit on trade-distorting support, whether based on a percentage of the value of production or on a monetary ceiling; and those that consider that the AMS should be eliminated – notably because it allows for product-specific subsidy concentration’ (JOB/AG/117 of 24 October 2017: para. 2.3). Divisions further existed on Article 6.2 ‘SDT Box’ subsidies reserved for developing countries and the need for reform of the existing system of AMS and *de minimis* provisions (JOB/AG/117 of 24 October 2017: paras, 2.4–2.5). In particular, whether or not the SDT support granted to developing countries in Article 6.2 subsidies should be counted as part of a country’s capped allowance has proven to be a controversial question (ICTSD 2017: 4–5). Such changes to the WTO’s domestic support regime consequently risk curtailing and further unmaking SDT, a concern that was reflected in the following November 2017 summary

Table 5.3 Central difference in the EU–Brazil and India–China proposals

	AMS subsidy allowances	*De minimis* subsidy allowances	Assessment in terms of SDT
EU–Brazil proposal	Cap domestic support – AMS and *de minimis* combined – either via different caps or lowering existing floating caps		Curtailment: Differential treatment continues, but the differences become more marginal (difference in *de minimis* reduced from 10 per cent to 2 per cent*)
India–China proposal	Dismantle AMS allowances of developed country members	No reform	Expansion: Differential treatment continues (*de minimis*), but differences become more pronounced because AMS is abolished for developed countries

Notes:
*Assessment based on Sharma and Das (2018).
It remained unclear whether 'SDT Box' subsidies would be included in the cap as well. If they were, differential policy space would be further curtailed.

statement on the progress of agricultural negotiations: 'Some Members reiterated their sensitivities regarding Article 6.2 and de minimis entitlements, and made clear their opposition to any attempts *to curtail these entitlements*' (WT/GC/M/169 of 17 November 2017: 24; italics added).

New conflict lines became increasingly complex, as other developing and developed country members contested both the EU–Brazil and the India–China proposal in Buenos Aires. A Ministerial Declaration submitted by the LDC Group, for instance, honed in on domestic support from a different angle: as distortive measures that supposedly excluded LDC producers from the international market, AMS and product-specific *de minimis* supports were to be eliminated completely and Green Box criteria reviewed. LDCs would not be required to commit to any reductions (WT/MIN[17]/40 of 11 December 2017: paras. 1.1–1.2). These positions differed both from the EU–Brazilian and the India–China proposals, underlining the disunity of negotiation frames amongst developing countries. Conversely, for the Cairns Group, the key to domestic support reform lay in the reduction of existing 'massive entitlements', which allowed nine members to enact over USD 625 billion in distortive support. The Cairns Group used data on both AMS and *de minimis* entitlements for a mixed group of actors[8] to arrive at this quantification of trade-distortive support (JOB/AG/91 of 19 May 2017: para. 7 and fn. 2). Both proposals reflect common criticisms of biases in WTO rules on agriculture; it is primarily large economies that are able to distort agricultural markets by means of domestic support, regardless of their status as developed or developing countries.

Amidst increasingly polarized debates, and the flurry of more compartmentalized negotiation coalitions, no agreement on domestic support was reached at the Ministerial Conference in December 2017 (MC11). Instead, differences between a more 'defensive' category of actors – most prominently India and China – seeking to limit domestic support reform to AMS allowances, and a more 'offensive' set of states – including Brazil and the EU – aiming to tackle general support levels spilled over into the post-MC11 period. While the US took a back-seat role in Buenos Aires, it was implicitly clear that any future agreement would also need to accommodate the US–China conflict over Chinese domestic support measures that played out in the WTO's Dispute Settlement Body (Hopewell 2019).

5.4.3 Assessment on the Conflict Outcome in Buenos Aires (2017)

In Cancún (2003), deadlock was seen at least as a partial success for developing countries. By the mid-2010s it had turned into a sign that WTO members had lost their faith in the possibility of comprehensive agricultural reform. Already in October 2017 a General Council meeting noted that 'a substantive outcome does not seem to be within reach for MC11' (WT/GC/M/169 of 17 November 2017: 26). The failure to reach an agreement in Buenos Aires was entangled with the wider crisis of the WTO, triggered by the refusal of the US 'to reaffirm the "centrality of the multilateral trading system" and the need to support "development" – both in the run-up to the meeting and during its final hours' (Hannah et al. 2018: 2584).

Buenos Aires also shows that Southern coalition unity could not be maintained anymore: there was a diminishing willingness of developing countries to negotiate together in large coalitions or groups. This signals a growing interest both among developing countries themselves, but also developed countries, to further differentiate between developing countries (Zhuawu and Soobramanien 2017: 2–4). The repeated deadlock further signalled a shift from a (hopeful) push for expansion of differential treatment by the G-20 towards a defensive approach on SDT. Most prominently, the EU–Brazil proposal was geared towards the curtailment of the special rights of developing countries in agriculture. Conversely, the India–China proposal sought to avoid the curtailment of existing differential treatment for developing countries. While the SDT expansion pushed for in the early 2000s – via an SSM – by Brazil, China, India, and the G-20 was still pursued in this latter period by the G-33, it became more marginal (and less realistic) than previously. In these ways, the 2017 deadlock signifies a shift towards the unmaking of the status quo of differential treatment for developing countries: it becomes increasingly marginalized in negotiations of new agreements and decisions.

5.5 HOW THE GLOBAL POWER SHIFT SHAPES THE EVOLUTION OF DIFFERENTIAL TREATMENT

While the conflict in 2003 was characterized by Southern unity, 2017 saw the rise of disunity across Brazil, China, and India, and between them and developing countries. This disunity is central for understanding how the global power shift towards Brazil, China, and India has shaped the evolution of SDT for developing countries. First, the emergence of India and China as major subsidizers in agriculture undermined Southern unity in coalitions. Second, India and China's reluctance to give up special rights – even when criticized from both developed and developing countries – contributed to the loss of legitimacy – and hence unmaking – of the status quo. Lastly, in line with our expectations (cf. Chapter 1), we find that institutional factors mediated the effects of both changing interest constellations and legitimacy conceptions.

In the following sub-section, changing coalition dynamics and their effects on differential treatment are unpacked across the two conflict moments by combining rationalist, constructivist, and institutionalist explanatory lenses.

5.5.1 Interest Constellations: Domestic Support as a Game-changer

Rationalist approaches expect that norms of differential treatment for developing countries will be unmade if coalitions of states that challenge the existing system of special rights become stronger and/or more united relative to the coalitions that support the status quo (cf. Chapters 1 and 4). We find that the loss of Southern unity reflects changing interest constellations: developed countries become unwilling to grant concessions to rising powers as they become major agricultural players, and hence competitors. Moreover, other (smaller) developing countries increasingly cease to back claims of rising powers to differential treatment in agriculture. The rise of China and India as major providers of subsidies for agricultural products in the 2010s thus obfuscates traditional North–South conflict lines. However, the effect of these changing incentive structures on coalition unity is not as straightforward as expected: instead of Brazil, China, and India cumulatively receiving increased pressure from 'below' (developing countries) and 'above' (developed countries), rising powers are not cohesive as a group. Brazil, China, and India held diverging interests in agriculture from the start; what changes as they gain in power is that these pre-existing differences become more pronounced. From a rationalist perspective, the initial Southern unity in Cancún was thus more surprising than the disunity that characterized Buenos Aires.

5.5.1.1 The interests of Brazil, China, and India in agriculture: different starting points

Brazil comprised the third biggest agri-exporter worldwide, both in 2003 and the mid-2010s. At the time of writing, it also remains the world's biggest supplier of sugar, orange juice, coffee, poultry meat, and soya beans (WTO 2017: 95; WT/TPR/S/140 of 1 November 2004: 113). This carves out a special position for Brazil in agricultural negotiations: its agricultural goods have consistently been highly competitive on the international market with little to no recourse to subsidies. This leads to an offensive stance in agricultural negotiations and explains why Brazil is in favour of the reduction of domestic support programmes.

Chinese interests in the agricultural regime provide a counterpoint to the export-oriented Brazilian economy. The low relative comparative advantage (RCA) of Chinese agricultural products underlines the continued problems China faces when competing on the international agrimarket. Indeed, China's RCA dropped between 2003 and 2017, indicating a decline in competitiveness. At the same time, the Chinese economy underwent vast changes that allowed it to decrease the share of agriculture in its GDP from 12.4 to 7.5 per cent. Similar patterns can be observed with regard to its share of the labour force employed in agriculture. Despite a radical decrease however – from 49.1 to 26.98 per cent – a large share of China's work force is still employed in agriculture (World Bank 2022). Diversification of the economy, while successful, has consequently not yet completed a large-scale shift of workers out of the agricultural sector. Compounding this need to protect and or manage change in domestic agriculture, China has consistently been a net importer of foodstuffs over the past two decades. Moreover, since the 2008 world food price crisis, protection of domestic markets has become a priority for Chinese policy-makers amidst food security concerns. Together, these features in China's trade profile have led to a persistently defensive stance since its WTO accession in 2001.

India's interests in agriculture are shaped by the continued prevalence of large-scale subsistence farming in its economy, i.e. of small, peasant-based production for domestic, rather than international, markets. The need to safeguard rural employment and the livelihoods of peasant farmers has consequently led to defensive interests in agricultural trade. The sector continues to be dominant in the Indian labour market: in 2017, 43.93 per cent of the Indian labour force was employed in agriculture. Moreover, in the early 2000s and late 2010s, India was a net food exporter, with large surpluses vis-à-vis the EU and the US (World Bank 2022). Akin to Chinese negotiation priorities, India consequently benefits from targeting domestic support regimes in developed countries and promoting defensive measures on market access. Moreover, an internal focus on food security and labour market stability helps to explain

India's prominent use of subsidies under the AoA's 'SDT Box' – the only one amongst Brazil, China, and India.

Divergent interest constellations initially led to divergent positions in agricultural negotiations: Brazil, a strong agricultural exporter, submitted joint statements with the Cairns Group; India underlined the needs of large subsistence farming populations; and China stressed its accession requirements and the need for reform to be targeted at developed countries. The ability for these states to come together in a strong developing country coalition such as the G-20 is not immediately apparent from these pre-Cancún positions. So what changed?

5.5.1.2 Political economy dynamics and the demise of the G-20

What made the G-20 – and particularly Brazil and India – come together in 2003 was joint opposition to the US–EC proposal. While their interests continued to diverge in many regards, this proposal changed the strategic context of the negotiations. As a large exporter, Brazil held a key interest in demanding a reduction of domestic support measures provided by developed countries. At the same time, India was adamant in opposing US–EU demands to further liberalize market access in agriculture, given developmental concerns. Interests of both actors were thus at stake when the EU and the US tabled their proposal for Cancún. As a former Brazilian diplomat recalled, the Brazilian trade negotiator at the time, Flávio Damico, and the Indian agricultural negotiator, Rajesh Aggarwal, 'saw the mistakes in this joint proposal by [the] US and EU'. They realized that 'Brazil is not going to have the market access we need in Europe and the US, and the market access in agriculture is going to be given by poor countries like India, China'. The representative added that 'this is really the point of departure of the G-20, Brazil and India found a way; "Okay, I cover your back, you cover mine"'.[9]

This convergence of positions, however, reflected a strategic choice rather than a clear-cut convergence of economic interests. It was possible because Brazil decided not to pursue its market access interests vis-à-vis India, China, and other developing countries:[10]

> [What w]e had in mind was basically to sweep under the carpet our offensive interests in terms of the Indian and Chinese market … So, what we did was dampen our ambitions in terms of our requests for taxing farmers in India and China, and then basically starting on domestic subsidies.

This newfound common ground between India and Brazil was further extended to a larger group of 20 developing countries, including the so-called 'Group of 5' comprising India, Brazil, China, South Africa, and Argentina.[11]

By the mid-2010s, however, this common strategic ground between Brazil, China, India, and other developing countries had disappeared. This change was driven, at least in part, by the strengthening of large-scale subsidy regimes in rising powers. As Hopewell (2019: 211) shows, while domestic support in developed countries has significantly decreased since the early 2000s, emerging economies like India and Indonesia have coupled their economic rise with an expansion of their subsidization programmes – with China overtaking the OECD average support in 2013.

Broader alliances of developing countries, including the G-20 and the G-90, have thus become too costly to persist, as Brazil, China, and India have become part of the problem for net-exporting developing countries (Hopewell 2022). The African Group, for instance, demanded a reduction of *all* subsidies in Buenos Aires, while India and China only focussed on those that are prevalent in developed countries.

The attention of developing countries seeking domestic support reform further shifted from subsidies in developed states to Chinese subsidies. By the time of the Nairobi Ministerial Conference (2015), China had become a major global agricultural producer. The composition of subsidies in 2016 (cf. Figure 5.1) shows that China by this point had not only become the primary provider of subsidies across the board, but also with regard to product-specific Amber Box subsidies. Moreover, in 2016, China was also the largest provider of Green Box subsidies in nominal terms (cf. Figure 5.1). In parallel, the US and Europe were increasingly replaced by China as the primary export market for Brazil's agricultural goods.

An increase in Chinese and Indian subsidies also reinforced divergent economic interests across Brazil, China, and India. This divergence in turn allowed for a fracturing of previous coalitions on agriculture. In particular, it led Brazil to re-evaluate the extent to which a shared coalition with China and India, such as in the G-20, continued to serve its interests. As a Brazilian trade diplomat recalled:[12]

> It is when China … really becomes the big China as we know it, and the agricultural characteristics of India started to change. India started with … some subsidies, some sort of domestic support … And I think the nature of the alliance started then to change … The partnership is starting to really be changing from the inside, and this is really the beginning of the end, if you wish, of this strong alliance.

Brazilian priorities consequently shifted from targeting EU markets in the early 2000s to a greater focus on domestic subsidy regimes in China, and even India as well. This led to a change in perceptions as 'at some point, the G-20 started to be used by China and India as a sort of insurance policy that Brazil would be defending their policy options the same way that we had

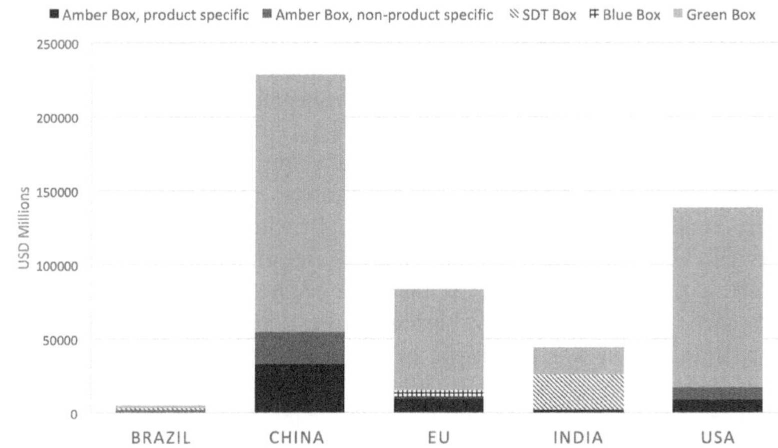

Note: 2016, in USD millions.
Source: Based on WTO notification data.

Figure 5.1 *Composition of domestic support measures by selected countries*

been defending at the beginning of the Doha Round'.[13] The rise of China thus implied that it was becoming a main market for other agricultural exporters in the developing world. This in turn facilitated the erosion of the G-20 by the time of the Nairobi Ministerial Conference as initial common ground on domestic support disappeared.

5.5.2 Legitimacy Conceptions: The Lost 'Normative Punch' of Developing Country Coalitions

While rationalist explanations convincingly point at the increasing heterogeneity of economic interests across Brazil, China, India, and other developing countries in the 2010s, they cannot fully account for Southern unity in the early 2000s. The case of agricultural negotiations illustrates how the rise of Brazil, China, and India has gone hand in hand with a loss of normative support for the developing country coalitions that seek to expand, or just defend, their special rights. It has, first, undermined the legitimacy of existing systems of differential treatment, and the claims of rising powers to these rights. Conversely, in the early 2000s, this legitimacy was central to Brazil's decision to join India and China, rather than the established powers, in agricultural negotiations. Second, the rise of Brazil, China, and India has led to ambiguity in the identity conceptions of rising powers themselves, which has further unmade the social cohesion of their coalitions.

5.5.2.1 From narratives on North–South imbalances to geopolitical deadlock

The rise of Brazil, China, and India has had a significant effect on legitimacy conceptions: it has reduced the perceived moral high ground of developing country coalitions, as systems of differential treatment increasingly become contested. How did this happen? Initially, legitimacy conceptions helped to unify a Southern coalition. At the time of the 2003 Cancún Ministerial Conference, a central narrative bridging the divergent economic interests of Brazil and India was the theme of an unjust, or imbalanced, agricultural system along North–South lines: while developed countries have the capacity to provide high levels of (trade-distorting) subsidies, developing countries need to protect poor farmers and address food security concerns. WTO rules thus needed to expand on their notion of SDT by reducing the allowed levels of domestic support in the developed world, while increasing flexibilities for developing countries.

In the run-up to the Cancún Ministerial Conference, Brazil, China, and India used this narrative of an unjust agricultural system – biased in favour of the developed world – to support their demands for expanding the differential treatment of developing countries. India prominently stated in 2003 (TN/AG/R/6 of 21 February 2003; italics added):

> The significance of, and the need for, special and differential treatment for developing countries in the agriculture sector rests on two pillars. The first pillar is the elimination of distortions in the agricultural sector through heavy subsidization of domestic production and exports *by many developed countries* which, by every analysis, adversely affects developing countries' opportunities for development. The second pillar is the need to enable *developing countries* to effectively address food and livelihood security and rural development interests through appropriate flexibility in domestic policy for agriculture.

This North–South framing of the conflict was further reinforced when it was pointed out that developing countries such as India were not even able to provide meaningful subsidies themselves: 'Whilst large agricultural exporters were trying to move towards a purely mercantilist approach, India did not have the resources to use subsidies nor did it have income generation opportunities outside agriculture for its 650 million poor farmers' (TN/AG/R/9 of 25 August 2003).

The narrative that WTO rules favoured the developed world further aided the perceived righteousness of the claims of developing country coalitions. A Brazilian trade diplomat recalled 'the outcome of the Uruguay round … had not delivered anything really concrete and substantial for developing countries'.[14] The Doha Round, launched in 2001, had the explicit mandate to address such unfinished business after the Uruguay Round, in particular on agriculture.

A narrative of past imbalances in trade legislation bound together a diverse group of net-exporting and net-importing developing countries to push for SDT expansion and the dismantling of protections and subsidies in developed country markets. The lacking coverage of these elements in the 2003 US–EC proposal allowed for common notions of fairness and justice to emerge that bridged the Doha Development Agenda's mandate with the tackling of food security and rural poverty concerns, as well as the promotion of an inclusive multilateral trading system. Together, these varied arguments for the rebalancing of international trade provided the ideational underpinnings for an unprecedentedly strong set of developing country coalitions in the early 2000s that managed to bring negotiations at the WTO to a standstill over agriculture.

These narratives, however, were undermined by the rise of Brazil, China, and India. That China, and to a lesser extent also India, continued to claim differential treatment for developing countries – despite their new role as major subsidizers in agriculture – challenged the narrative of correcting historical imbalances that favoured developed countries. By the mid-2010s, demands to reduce domestic support ceased to be solely a developing country issue. As a trade diplomat put it: 'The divide that united developing countries in the past as claiming reforms and as claiming new rules that would affect agriculture systematically is not there anymore because developing countries are now also part of this distortive picture of agricultural trade'.[15]

Against this background, the EU–Brazil proposal tabled at Buenos Aires proposed to change existing rules: it implicitly sought to curtail the special rights of India and China as major subsidizers among developing country members. The legitimacy of states like China pushing for SDT expansion was increasingly contested. Other governments thus noted that 'if you see the big picture, it's a developed country' and maintained that it became increasingly difficult for China to claim that 'me and Burundi, we need special and differential treatment'.[16] While Cancún was about improving differential treatment of developing countries in agriculture, at Buenos Aires the status quo of these special rights thus became subject to contestation.

With the global agricultural system being less clearly imbalanced along North–South lines, China and India shifted their strategy and tried to appeal to the imbalances in existing rules on AMS entitlements. The joint China–India proposal on domestic support reform tabled at the Buenos Aires Ministerial Conference in 2017 states along these lines (JOB/AG/137 of 22 June 2018):

> Any meaningful attempt at reforms in agriculture subsidies must address the asymmetry between the developed Members on the one hand and most of the developing Members on the other hand in their respective entitlements to AMS [Aggregate Measurement of Support] beyond de minimis and the flexibility to provide high product-specific support.

Yet, the Southern coalition lost part of its 'punch' as legitimacy conceptions concerning the justification of different sides' claims became more complex. This, in turn, made it less attractive for Brazil to join a developing country coalition at Buenos Aires. Instead, for the first time it teamed up with the EU.

Moreover, the global power shift towards Brazil, China, India, and others meant that negotiations over differential treatment for developing countries became caught up in the geopolitical contest between established and rising powers. Particularly during the Trump administration, discussions at the WTO moved towards explicit US–China conflict and away from EU–US discussions (Hopewell 2020). The issue of differential treatment for developing countries was drawn into this conflict as well. As a former trade diplomat claims:[17]

> Countries like India or the other developing countries are seeing that wherever they go to, they become the unintended victim of this. Because the US has to come up with some criteria on S&D [SDT] that they want to capture China with but then the other five also are getting captured in that sense.[18]

5.5.2.2 Status ascriptions and the binary developed/developing country distinction

In the early 2000s, Brazil, China, India, and other developing countries were also united by the fact that the binary developed/developing country distinction was still considered meaningful and remained relatively uncontested. By the 2010s, these conceptions had changed substantively; not only did the sense of solidarity across an increasingly heterogeneous group of developing countries fade away, but Brazil, China, and India themselves adopted divergent approaches on their own status. The resulting difficulties in maintaining a shared identity further diminished the grounds for Southern coalition unity in the 2010s.

During the Cancún Ministerial Conference there was a shared developing country identity, as a Brazilian trade delegate recalls:[19]

> The developing world is perhaps one of the largest of these coalitions somehow, but with a sense of identity that you are part of the developing world and that you need a sort of coalition: a coalition that is predicated on different elements of the

developing world. That is what a large significant part of a generation of diplomats and others think about.

The statement reflects that one element of this shared developing country identity is the perceived weakness of developing countries, which, in turn, creates the need for building coalitions. This sense was reinforced by the perceived threat emanating from the US–EC proposal:[20]

In Cancun, when the EU and the US came together, you can imagine that if that agreement had gone forward, my government would have fallen overnight. So, there was no way that the Indian government could sign on that thing. It was just a question that whether you had been alone and say no, or you form a coalition, and this is what we did.

Similarly, the way in which the G-20 presented itself as a 'countervailing force to the US and the EU' was instrumental at that time for China, who was trying to establish itself as an economic power.[21] Brazil similarly did not want to lose India as a partner, which facilitated the G-20 after the EU and the US came together.[22]

The sense of a shared developing country identity dissipated in the 2010s. The question of whether or not Brazil, China, and India could legitimately claim to be developing country members, given their economic rise, began to challenge the binary developed/developing country distinction (Weinhardt and Schöfer 2022). Notably, Brazil, China, and India themselves started to interpret their own status as developing country members of the WTO differently: India has strongly reinforced its developing country identity in agricultural negotiations, which is also unlikely to change in the foreseeable future. China instead has adopted a comparatively flexible approach: while formally defending its status as a developing country, it has not always defended the special rights this status comes with. Brazil has adopted a middle ground position between developed and developing countries; while maintaining its self-declared status as a developing country member of the WTO, it has become less interested in using this status to negotiate differential treatment. In 2019, the Brazilian government officially announced that it would forego the use of its developing country status to claim SDT in ongoing negotiations (Mano 2019). These three different interpretations of developing country status are summarized in the following statement:[23]

If you see the three of us, India, China, Brazil, we are moving in three different directions. So to have a common position, it's becoming more and more and more complicated. So you have Brazil, who has this internal dilemma, one foot is on the one side, one foot is on the other side. You have India, going that direction of 'still a developing country' … You have China becoming a powerhouse in every domain. And we label ourselves BRICS and developing world. This is not working.

Brazil's new self-ascribed position was, however, hardly compatible with the Indian and Chinese proposal on agriculture tabled in Buenos Aires which continued to emphasize their need for flexibilities as developing country members. Increasingly divergent status ascriptions across Brazil, China, and India have thus further contributed to the disunity of Southern coalitions, and hence the unmaking of special rights for developing countries as a group.

5.5.3 The Institutionalization of Differential Treatment and Regime Complexity

The rise of Brazil, China, and India has affected both interest constellations and legitimacy conceptions in ways that make it difficult to maintain Southern coalition unity. The resulting unmaking of special rights, however, needs to be contextualized to allow for a better understanding of why specific conflict issues in both time periods became pertinent. This section shows how the institutionalization of differential treatment and obligations in the world trade regime have contributed to specific conflict dynamics in agriculture. In particular, it shows how the perceived loss of legitimacy of existing systems of differential treatment is inherently linked to the absence of clear rules for graduation. Moreover, we discuss the lack of forum shopping opportunities concerning agriculture.

5.5.3.1 The institutionalization of differential treatment and path dependencies

WTO rules do not contain a clear definition of who counts as a developing country. Instead, members can self-declare the status they hold. This auto-election approach (cf. Chapter 1) provides the background for changes in legitimacy conceptions as Brazil, China, and India gained in power. The perceived loss of moral high ground for developing country coalitions was partly driven by increased contestation concerning Chinese and Indian subsidy flexibilities. Article 6.4b of the AoA (1994) prominently specifies that '[f]or developing country Members, the de minimis percentage under this paragraph shall be 10 per cent' – as compared to 5 per cent for other members. The AoA itself, however, does not specify who counts as a developing country member and relies on the general principle of self-declaration. Moreover, there exists no sunset clause that stipulates that the terms of the agreement need to be re-negotiated after a specific period of time.

This institutionalization, in turn, has made it possible for rising powers such as China or India to continue to claim developing country status. Since there are no criteria for graduation, they can access flexibilities for as long as they see fit. These claims, however, lost some of their legitimacy in the eyes of other WTO members, given that China and India had become major subsidizers in agriculture. The resulting politicization in agricultural negotiations has arguably further contributed to the hardening of deadlock. Conversely, if clear criteria to delineate developing country status had existed, they would have either confirmed or disproven the claims of China and India. While criteria can become subject to contestation themselves, the way in which they facilitate graduation is likely to reduce politicization and contestation (cf. the case of public health financing, Chapter 9).

The case of differential treatment for developing countries in agriculture is, moreover, peculiar in the sense that even existing provisions have come under fire with the EU–Brazil proposal in Buenos Aires. The particular way in which differential *de minimis* limits are applied as a *relative* measure to the value of production in a specific year explains why even existing special rights became controversial: the higher limits granted to developing countries became contested as soon as the values of production of Brazil, China, and India skyrocketed. Not only did India reach roughly equal production levels by 2017 compared with the EU and the US, but China's absolute production level exceeded the combined output of other states by more than six times in volume. Regarding the agricultural sector overall, China seems to be compliant with total support allowances (Glauber et al. 2020: 9). Against this background, existing rules became part of the conflict in Buenos Aires. If a different institutionalization of differential treatment had been chosen, the bone of contention that the EU–Brazil proposal sought to address may not have been there in the first place.

5.5.3.2 The absence of 'contested multilateralism' and negotiation deadlock

The larger institutional context also acts as a mediating factor. The issue of domestic support, which has proven central to WTO negotiations, is only negotiated at the multilateral level. If no agreement on major contested issues in agriculture can be found at the WTO level, there exist no real possibilities for forum shifting to increase pressure at the multilateral level. A trade expert commenting on the agricultural strategy of African countries alluded to this lack of alternatives: 'There is recognition that you will not have global agricultural reform and that you have to find a new strategy or investment that will drive agricultural productivity … You are not going to change the trade distorting subsidies.'[24]

The lack of forum shifting opportunities also helps to explain why deadlock at the WTO has been persistent: members who are dissatisfied with the status quo simply lack the means and fora to increase pressure on WTO members that blocks progress in negotiations on domestic support – and agriculture more generally.

In bilateral trade negotiations involving major subsidizers – notably the EU, the US, China, and India – the question of domestic support is not commonly tabled. This is because the zero-sum nature of negotiations over agricultural subsidies leaves few incentives to make them part of bilateral or regional free trade negotiations. Moreover, power asymmetries are amplified in these settings and many (developing) countries that seek subsidy reductions are smaller markets. For instance, African countries intended to make European domestic support measures in agriculture part of their negotiations of Economic Partnership Agreements (EPA) with the EU. The EU, however, simply refused to make binding commitments on the elimination of domestic subsidies part of the EPA texts, which merely contain 'commitment to transparency on domestic support for the farming sector' (European Commission 2018a).

Both the specific institutionalization of differential treatment and the absence of forum shopping opportunities concerning agricultural negotiations thus facilitated the marginalization of differential treatment for developing countries.

5.6 CONCLUSION

In the case of agriculture, we have seen the hardening of negotiation deadlock over time. When it comes to differential treatment, this entrenched standstill has had two effects: on the one hand, the inability to find consensus has kept existing rights resilient against curtailment initiatives. Flexibilities have nevertheless become more contested, as some of their beneficiaries have become major subsidizers. On the other hand, particularly on market access, developing country proposals for SDT expansion have failed to bear fruit. While in the 2000s there was still hope that such an expansion could happen, this hope dissipated in the 2010s (and beyond). This arguably facilitates an unmaking of special rights for the developing country group akin to the one we observe in WTO politics generally (cf. Chapter 2).

Brazil, China, and India play a central role in negotiation deadlock and the unmaking of special rights. In the case of agriculture, we see a clear unity of Brazil, China, India, and other developing countries at the 2003 Cancún Ministerial Conference. This newfound unity contrasts sharply with the disunity across Brazil, China, and India – most prominently on domestic support – at the Buenos Aires Ministerial Conference in 2017. While in the first phase, coalition unity allowed for resilience against US–EU reform designs and even optimism for SDT expansion, in the second conflict moment disunity contributed to the unmaking of SDT.

How do we explain the effect the rise of Brazil, China, and India has had on the evolution of SDT? A rationalist perspective goes a long way in explaining the floundering of the G-20 coalition – founded in Cancún – and its eventual disappearance in the 2010s. It helps us to see how the rise of Brazil, China, and India has added a further decisive layer of divergence in economic interests: the G-20 was held together by a trade-off between Brazil and India, fusing their interests in fending off market opening (India) and the reduction of market-distorting subsidies in the developed world (Brazil). By the mid-2010s, the terms of this 'grand bargain' ceased to be meaningful. India, and even more so China, had become major subsidizers in agriculture – as well as major export markets for Brazil – which made Southern unity too costly. Instead, Brazil sided for the first time with the European Union.

What a rationalist perspective does not fully capture is why the G-20 emerged in 2003, despite the divergent economic interests of Brazil, China, and India. While Brazil and India did manage to find common ground leading the G-20, this outcome was far from obvious, considering Brazil is a highly competitive export-oriented agricultural player, while India is much more protectionist and characterized by subsistence farming. Legitimacy conceptions are insightful here: precisely because both Brazil and India perceived that joining forces and framing their demands in terms of differential treatment for developing countries could make them more forceful, bridging the differences in their economic interests became possible. Southern unity in Cancún was thus inextricably linked to what Narlikar (2020: 1) refers to as the paradox that powerlessness may serve as a 'formidable weapon' in international negotiations: 'effective and persuasive narratives about poverty are bringing about a fundamental transformation of powerlessness itself into a source of power'. The perceived moral high ground of the G-20, however, was undermined by the way in which the economic rise of Brazil, China, and India turned the tables; trade-distorting subsidies ceased to be a 'problem' of the developed world that a united developing country front could oppose.

The rise of Brazil, China, and India has, on the one hand, increased the weight they can put behind demands to expand differential treatment for developing countries, but, simultaneously, it has made it more difficult to maintain Southern unity and the moral high ground. It seems that while the Southern coalition was not economically strong enough in 2003, it lost its 'normative punch' and common ground once Brazil, China, and India were strong enough to push their demands through. Instead of an unmaking of differential treatment rules as such, it is rather the unmaking of the legitimacy of the system that contributes to normative curtailment. This delegitimization rests on two factors: the emergence of China and India as major agricultural subsidizers and the juxtaposition of a India–China negotiation strategy – which targets existing privileges for developed countries – and a Brazilian approach seeking to negotiate new rules. Disunity *across* Brazil, China, and India, and not only between Brazil, China and India, and other developing countries (Hopewell 2022), also contradicts scholarly assessments that continue to emphasize Southern unity in WTO negotiations (Johnson and Urpelainen 2020).

Lastly, institutionalist perspectives remind us that neither outcome was 'natural' in the sense that neither the power equilibrium nor the lost moral high ground simply followed from interests and prevailing legitimacy conceptions. Both were in large part shaped by the particular institutionalization of differential treatment in the world trade regime and the path dependencies it facilitated.

NOTES

1. Interviews were conducted between June and October 2021 via telephone. Six of the interviewees were (former) trade diplomats. Interviewees included (former) representatives from Brazil (3) and India (1); for China's position, we rely on primary sources.
2. Tariffication describes the conversion of non-tariff market access protections into tariffs. This simplifies the picture of trade distortions as protectionist measures are converted into clear-cut, easily quantifiable tariff levels.
3. Note that the failure to notify domestic support can be the result of capacity constraints, rather than the absence of domestic support as such.
4. China demanded a substantial reduction of developed country export subsidies and AMS subsidies by 50 per cent in the first year of implementation and the elimination of the rest in the following year (TN/AG/R/7 of 24 March 2003: 25–26).
5. SP lists allow for some room for manoeuvre regarding tariff cuts based on food security and rural development concerns, and are hence primarily of interest to developing countries.
6. Brazilian Trade Delegate Interview, 30 August 2021.
7. Note that this 10 per cent difference is comprised of a 5 per cent difference for both product- and non-product-specific support.
8. Australia, Brazil, Canada, China, the EU, India, Indonesia, Japan, and the US.
9. Brazilian Trade Delegate Interview, 9 June 2021.
10. Brazilian Trade Delegate Interview, 20 July 2021.
11. Former Indian Trade Delegate Interview, 14 June 2021.
12. Brazilian Trade Delegate Interview, 9 June 2021.
13. Brazilian Trade Delegate Interview, 30 August 2021.
14. Brazilian Trade Delegate Interview, 20 July 2021.
15. Brazilian Trade Delegate Interview, 30 August 2021.
16. Brazilian Trade Delegate Interview, 30 August 2021.
17. Former Indian Trade Delegate Interview, 14 June 2021.
18. This sentiment was echoed in several interviews (Brazilian Trade Delegate Interview, 20 July 2021; Trade Expert Interview, 8 October 2021; Brazilian Trade Delegate Interview, 30 August 2021).
19. Brazilian Trade Delegate Interview, 30 August 2021.
20. Former Indian Trade Delegate Interview, 14 June 2021.
21. Brazilian Trade Delegate Interview, 20 July 2021.
22. Former Indian Trade Delegate Interview, 14 June 2021.
23. Brazilian Trade Delegate Interview, 9 June 2021.
24. Trade Expert Interview, 8 October 2021.

6. Conflicts over transition periods for developing countries in intellectual property rights

Till Schöfer

6.1 INTRODUCTION

Intellectual property rights (IPR) have often been an issue of North–South conflict in the World Trade Organization (WTO). Traditionally, the Global North seeks 'maximal' protection of patents and trademarks to increase the gains from the innovations they create while the Global South prefers 'minimalist' protection to allow for technology transfer, reliance on generic brands, and lower prices (Morin et al. 2018). The structurally different positions that the Global South and the Global North hold in the international knowledge economy have underpinned these conflicting interests, with the majority of patents and trademarks originating in industrialized countries. This makes IPR prone to debates about whether and to what extent developing and developed country WTO members should hold differential rights and obligations to take account of development concerns. Recent demands to waive core provisions of the Agreement on Trade-Related Aspects of Intellectual Property Rights (TRIPS) in order to facilitate vaccine production in response to the COVID-19 pandemic echo these concerns.[1]

However, the rise of Brazil, China, and India holds the potential to change established conflict lines as they are caught between old 'minimalist' positions and new imperatives for 'maximalist' protection. As their position in the global knowledge economy is shifting, they may begin to increasingly side with the Global North. China became the top filer of international patents in 2019, surpassing the United States (US) (WIPO 2020). The number of domestic patent applications from India has grown significantly and Brazil has managed to establish itself as a competitive player in knowledge-intensive industries such as aerospace and automobiles (Morin et al. 2018: 266–267). The literature so far sees 'mixed' positions of Brazil, China, and India on IPR, with a combination of 'maximalist' and 'minimalist' positions (Morin et al. 2018; Serrano

2016). These mixed positions thus elevate Brazil, China, and India to a special position: if they side with other developing countries (unity of Southern coalitions), this could lead to resilience; conversely, if they side primarily with developed countries (disunity of Southern coalitions), we expect that unmaking of special rights for developing countries becomes more likely. At the same time, we assume that the bargaining strength of these coalitions is mediated by the role of legitimacy concerns[2] and institutional opportunity structures (Alter and Meunier 2009; Gehring and Oberthür 2009; Morse and Keohane 2014; Raustiala and Victor 2004).

To trace the effect of the global power shift on the evolution of differential treatment, this chapter zooms in on existing provisions of special and differential treatment (SDT) in the TRIPS Agreement. To assess changes over time, we focus on two conflict moments – one in the early 2000s and one in the early 2010s. Transition periods were chosen as cases of differential treatment in the intellectual property (IP) regime of the WTO, as they represent the primary format of SDT in the TRIPS Agreement. Only WTO developing country members and those members defined by the United Nations (UN) as Least Developed Countries (LDCs) are allowed to delay TRIPS implementation. However, this seemingly uncontroversial operationalization of the SDT norm has led to conflicts over three main issues: i) the question of who should benefit – all developing countries or only LDCs?; ii) the adequate lengths of transition periods; and iii) should it be possible to renew transition periods, and how should this be done?

We find that transition periods, over time, become restricted to LDCs: by the 2010s, the re-negotiation of transition schedules focusses solely on the sub-group of LDCs as transition periods of larger developing countries elapse without successful extension. While LDCs attempted to extend these narrower rights, such demands were only partially successful, and their rights remain largely unchanged as they are (re)negotiated over time. The unmaking of special rights for the group of developing countries thus goes hand in hand with resilience of these rights for the narrow sub-group of LDCs.

We show that high levels of Southern unity make the resilience of differential treatment for LDCs possible. Both in the 2000s and early 2010s, Brazil, China, and India sided with developing countries – or the LDC sub-group – in their demands to make differential treatment more substantive by expanding transition periods – either by making them automatic or permanent, or by negotiating an extension that was not foreseen in the original codification of the norm. In the second conflict, moreover, this support occurred despite the fact that Brazil, China, and India lost their direct stake in transition schedule extensions. Unity amongst developing countries, however, only leads to a very limited norm expansion, as legitimacy concerns and institutional opportunity structures mediate the bargaining power of Southern coalitions: LDCs do not get the permanent exemptions they strive for. The developmental benefits of providing transition periods in IP remain so contested that granting more extensive differential rights, even for the economically marginal group of LDCs, was not considered a legitimate demand. Regime complexity also contributed to entrenchment of this conflict along North–South lines.

These findings speak to the broader theme of the volume by zooming in on the conflict dynamics that shape the trend of fragmentation. In our trade overview chapter (cf. Chapter 2), we described a process of resilience of differential treatment – at the level of the legal framework – and a tripartite unmaking in day-to-day negotiations via processes of fragmentation, individualization, and informalization. In the field of IPR, only the first of these unmaking processes takes place, as debates over differential rights narrow to concentrate solely on LDCs. Zooming in on the conflict dynamics that shape this fragmentation allows us to unpack the role of Brazil, China, and India in shaping the evolution of differential treatment. Our findings show, first, that the effect of the global power shift on differential treatment can vary within different regime areas. In agricultural negotiations, the interests of Brazil, China, and India increasingly diverge from those of other developing countries (cf. Chapter 5), which contributes to the unmaking of special rights. Conversely, with regard to negotiations on IPR transition periods, the continuous support of Brazil, China, and India for LDC demands is crucial for maintaining coalition unity. While they are unable to achieve significant norm expansion, their support for the LDC proposal arguably prevents further norm erosion. Second, we show that maintaining Southern coalition unity remains more feasible if the direct interests of Brazil, China, and India are not at stake. In such situations, they tend to side with Southern coalitions, partly because of historical South–South ties and the contested relationship between IP protection and development. Third, and perhaps surprisingly, the reluctance of developed countries to extend the differential treatment of the economically marginalized group of LDCs illustrates that the effectiveness of differential treatment as such remains highly contested in the trade regime (regardless of the global power shift).

Lastly, this chapter contributes to the existing literature on IPR in the WTO by uncovering the conflict lines associated with transitional scheduling – an issue, that has largely been overlooked as uncontroversial (Moon 2011). In contrast to existing narratives that find that conflict lines on IPR increasingly blur North–South lines (Morin et al. 2018), conflict lines remain stable on the issue of transition periods for LDCs.

The following section provides a brief historical and legal overview of the IP regime and introduces the issue of transition scheduling. Thereafter, the chapter examines conflict lines over transition periods in two timeframes (2001–2003 and 2011–2015). Lastly, the chapter assesses the factors that help explain the role of Brazil, China, and India in these outcomes, with a focus on state interests and coalition-building, as well as the ways in which legitimacy concerns and institutional opportunity structures act as mediating factors of bargaining strength (cf. Chapter 1). In this assessment, we focus on the role of Brazil, China, and India in shaping the negotiation outcomes. Empirically, the chapter relies on eight interviews with former trade negotiators,[3] minutes of TRIPS Council debates,[4] proposals submitted to the WTO, and secondary literature.

6.2 SPECIAL AND DIFFERENTIAL TREATMENT IN TRIPS

6.2.1 IP Protection and Development

IPR play an important role in discussions on international development (Correa and Seuba 2019). The widening of the 'knowledge gap' between developing and industrialized countries and the simultaneous shift towards a global knowledge economy have added salience to these debates. Two interlinked questions emerge: on the one hand, fears of an overregulated 'thicket of patents' engendering a needlessly litigious domestic market raise the issue of finding an appropriate level of IP protection to secure economic growth without stifling innovation (Baker et al. 2017). On the other hand, the need for developing countries to undergo 'catch-up growth' before being able to seriously compete with industries in industrialized economies problematizes a 'one-size-fits-all' approach to international IP regulation (Odagiri et al. 2010).

How a strong domestic IP regime spills over into economic growth is a puzzle both for economic theorists and those studying the question empirically. Particularly as pertains to patents, IPR contain the double promise of providing incentives for a sustained level of high innovation and limiting the use of existing knowledge.[5] Such a 'removal of knowledge' from a domestic or international commons in turn makes the 'artificial scarcity' (Hindley 1971) of IP problematic for economists who recognize the importance of education and knowledge dissemination to the development of poorer economies (Baker et al. 2017). Moreover, while some analysts find a strong empirical link between increased patent protection and levels of foreign direct investment and technology transfer to poorer states (Park and Lippoldt 2008; Robbins 2009), others argue that imbalances in the global knowledge economy demote IP protection in developing countries to a vehicle for the obtainment of rents by corporations from developed economies (Baker et al. 2017).

6.2.2 The 1995 TRIPS Regime and North–South Conflict Lines

The IP regime that emerged from the Uruguay Round was fundamentally different to international IP regulation pre-1995. While minimum IP standards on issues such as patents, copyright, and trademarks had previously been administered across various fora – notably the World Intellectual Property Organization (WIPO), the Paris Convention, and the Berne Convention – the TRIPS Agreement marked a more one-track approach within the auspices of the WTO. Envisioned as an international minimum level of IP protection, the provisions of TRIPS were far stronger than those of its predecessors. Moreover, TRIPS significantly expanded the areas of protection covered by international IP law, allowing previously neglected regulation on industrial designs, sound recordings, and integrated circuits to be incorporated (Dreyfuss 2009). Importantly, for the first time, TRIPS introduced solid enforcement mechanisms (Serrano 2016: 354). This move towards the WTO in the 1990s was in turn facilitated by industrialized country frustration with the lack of IPR progress and enforcement mechanisms in WIPO and the Convention on Biological Diversity (CBD). The US, the EU, and Japan thus fronted a push for a stronger – and broader – international IP regime that culminated in the articulation of an IP minimum in international trade law (Sell 2011).

The TRIPS Agreement represented a Global North initiative that met with resistance from developing countries (Groombridge 1999). Yet, this resistance did not prevent the conclusion of TRIPS. One hampering factor was that negotiations were characterized by a general lack of knowledge concerning the content and consequences of a trade-and-IP agreement amongst developing country delegates.[6] The legal sophistication of the proposed text submitted by Global North actors consequently could not be matched by an alternative proposal stemming from developing countries.[7] Instead, the Indian delegation, with the support of other larger developing states, negotiated the inclusion of development-oriented clauses in the final agreement.[8]

The TRIPS Agreement is thus regarded as ‘a milestone in the concerted efforts by industrialised countries to strengthen IP protection for patents, copyrights, and trademarks’ (Serrano 2016: 345). Conversely, the terms of TRIPS for smaller economies have long been criticized, as they are often perceived as a bitter pill swallowed by developing countries in a 1990s’ trade-off for agreements on agriculture and textiles (Moschini 2003: 29–30). The dominance of industrialized countries as patent-holders at the time made IP regulation an issue disproportionately favourable to the ‘Quad’ negotiating group, comprising the US, Canada, the European Union (EU), and Japan.

Attempts to increase IP protection standards are often portrayed as welfare-enhancing liberalization (‘maximalist’ agenda); while low standards or the lack of harmonized standards (‘minimalist’ agenda) are regarded as obstacles to trade liberalization – a view that many developing countries contest. The latter fear that stronger IP protection limits technology transfer and increases retail prices, which may prevent access to innovations.

To address some of the concerns of developing countries, TRIPS includes a number of SDT provisions, meant to offset their disadvantaged position in the knowledge economy. These provisions take the form of more generous transition schedules for developing countries and LDCs (TRIPS Articles 65, 66.1) and promises for technical assistance and technology transfer (TRIPS Articles 66.1, 67). Further flexibility could in turn be achieved by exploiting wide discretion for implementation regarding the clauses of the TRIPS Agreement on compulsory licensing, government use of patents, parallel imports, protection of undisclosed data, and 'limited exceptions' to the granting of exclusive rights (Musungu and Oh 2006). Careful formulation of domestic patent laws could consequently ensure conformity with TRIPS while simultaneously guaranteeing developing countries some limited policy space to achieve their developmental goals. Note, however, that these latter TRIPS flexibilities are not explicitly framed in terms of differential treatment and can, theoretically, be employed by all WTO members.

6.2.3 Transition Periods as Part of the 'TRIPS Flexibilities'

There are three types of transition periods built into TRIPS for developing countries: while all WTO members could avail themselves of a one-year grace period before full implementation of the TRIPS Agreement (Article 65.1), this transitional period was extended to five years for developing countries (TRIPS Article 65.2) (transition period 1995–2000). Notably, TRIPS includes a separate set of arrangements for LDCs. These poorest WTO members are given ten years to 'create a viable technological base' and to combat economic, financial, and administrative constraints (TRIPS Article 66.1) (transition period 1995–2005). If these vaguely defined conditions were not met, individual LDCs could submit requests for further extensions to the TRIPS Council – a right not explicitly granted to developing countries as a whole. Lastly, there is an additional transition period pertaining to 'areas of technology not so protectable in [developing country] territory' that shapes debates about access to medicines (TRIPS Article 65.4). It provided an additional period of five years for countries that did not have any patent protection of pharmaceutical or agrochemicals at the entry of force of the Agreement in 1995.

6.3 CONFLICTS OVER TRANSITION SCHEDULES

The potential for IPR to either hinder or promote economic development allowed transitional grace periods to become important conflict issues in the

WTO discussions on IP. On the one hand, granting flexibility to developing countries was meant to allow countries to build up stronger capacities before liberalization via harmonized standards. On the other, the fairly brief five-year transition allotted to developing countries – and ten years for LDCs – allowed critics to suggest that this form of differential treatment was arbitrary and not development-oriented, but rather aimed at the rapid expansion of TRIPS coverage. This section delineates conflict lines at two crucial conflict moments in the early 2000s and the early 2010s, when previously negotiated transition periods for developing countries and LDCs were supposed to be phased out. Main conflict lines emerged over: i) who should benefit from extended transition periods (LDCs only or all developing countries); ii) how to determine the adequate length of a transition period; and iii) whether and how to allow for the renewal of transition periods.

We show that throughout both conflict moments, negotiating positions develop along North–South conflict lines. In the first conflict period, India and Brazil joined forces with the African Group and other developing countries to demand an extension of transition periods. However, we find that the inability to receive an extension for developing country members in the early 2000s – and subsequent unmaking of special rights via fragmentation – partly followed from the lack of coherence of Southern coalitions when faced with a relatively united Global North: the African Group proposal – supported by Brazil and India – competed with a separate LDC proposal. By the time of the second conflict in the early 2010s, Southern unity had increased – with Brazil, China, India, and other developing countries uniformly supporting the LDC proposal. However, unity of the Global North in opposition to LDC demands remained strong, which meant that unity of Brazil, China, and India with Southern coalitions did not translate into major gains. In the end, transition schedules for LDCs were renewed, but their implementation-related rights were only marginally expanded. This constituted resilience of differential treatment for LDCs amidst heavy contestations.

6.3.1 The Conflict in the Early 2000s (2001–2003)

The first conflict emerged in the late 1990s and early 2000s, when the transition periods originally granted to developing countries in TRIPS were set to expire. The conflict played out clearly along North–South lines, however the South was not unified internally: while Brazil and India sided with the African Group, Global South positions were not well coordinated and the LDCs submitted their own proposal. Ultimately, demands for an all-developing country transition period extension were unsuccessful in light of opposition from a more unified Global North. The finalization of relevant ministerial decisions by 2003, as well as the expiry of prior transition periods, in turn allowed debates over transition schedules to fade away after this point. Only the proposals aimed at the LDCs managed to translate into legislation, resulting in the resilience of the differential treatment of this sub-group.

As early as 1998, three years after the WTO establishment, trade delegates from larger developing economies raised concerns regarding the implementation of differential treatment provisions in TRIPS. A first conflict issue that emerged was the question of the adequate length of (existing) transition periods for developing countries. In a November communication the Indian delegation stressed that favourable treatment for developing countries had to be evaluated and that increases in transition periods offered a potential remedy to ongoing implementation issues (WT/GC/W/108 of 13 November 1998). These general concerns were expanded upon in a statement from Egypt, which argued that the length of transitional periods was chosen 'haphazardly and with no objective basis or linkage to the level of development …' and that they were 'excessively optimistic regarding the pace at which institutional and human capacity can be built in developing countries …' (WT/GC/W/109 of 5 November 1998).

Egypt further argued that while Articles 65–66 consequently did provide some leeway for developing countries, 'many developing countries will still find great difficulties in implementing the TRIPS Agreement due to weak institutional structures, the absence of the required expertise and lack of resources, financial or otherwise' (WT/GC/W/109 of 5 November 1998). Egyptian critiques of transition periods were in turn explicitly supported by India in a later communication, alongside criticisms of the insufficiency of technical assistance in combatting implementation issues (WT/GC/W/114 of 18 November 1998).

The preparatory talks for the 1999 Ministerial Conference were in turn marked by a unified Quad Group response to critiques of TRIPS transition schedules. The European Communities (EC) emphasized that derogations from existing TRIPS provisions were unwelcome: 'There should therefore be no question, in future negotiations, of lowering of standards or granting of further transitional periods' (WT/GC/W/193 of 2 June 1999). A Japanese statement on IPR echoed this stance, accentuating that members should ensure the full implementation of TRIPS – rather than a renewal of transition periods (WT/GC/W/242 of 6 July 1999).

With the commencement of the Doha Round in November 2001, the question of transition scheduling started to gain traction. A drive to clarify the relationship between the TRIPS Agreement and the protection of public health resulted in a Special Session of the TRIPS Council in June 2001, which allowed actors from both the Quad Group and the group of larger developing countries to discuss potential nuances to TRIPS implementation. Most notable is a proposal submitted by Brazil and cosponsored by India, the African Group,

Indonesia, and 14 other developing country actors: declaring that 'nothing in the TRIPS Agreement should prevent Members from taking measures to protect public health' (IP/C/W/296 of 29 June 2001), the proposal included provisions on transitional agreements, suggesting that the TRIPS Council could consider extending the transitional periods for developing countries (Article 65.4) and LDCs (Article 66.1) (ibid.). A counter proposal submitted by the EC in turn did not incorporate extensions, but underlined that 'in the view of the EC and their member States … special transitional arrangements and other provisions give these countries a sufficiently wide margin of discretion in implementing it' (IP/C/W/280 of 12 June 2001).

By October 2001, the group around Brazil, India, and the African Group concretized their demands in a new proposal, circulated both in the TRIPS Council and the General Council. The cautious extension proposal mentioned above was replaced by a strong declaration of further extensions that was justified both in terms of implementation and manufacturing capacities (IP/C/W/312 and WT/GC/W/450 of 4 October 2001):

> In view of the special needs and requirements of developing and least-developed country Members, their economic, financial and administrative constraints, and their need for flexibility to create a viable technological base, the transition period provided for their benefit under Articles 65.4 and 66.1 of the TRIPS Agreement shall be extended for another period of five (5) years from the expiration of the transition periods thereunder … without prejudice to further extensions.

By referring both to developing countries and LDCs, the developing country group also opened a second conflict line: Who should be the rights-holders regarding differential treatment? The strong focus of the proposal on the delayed implementation of TRIPS for developing countries stood in stark contrast to the approach of developed country actors: in October 2001 the US, Canada, Japan, Switzerland, and Australia circulated a document that emphasized the status of the TRIPS Agreement as a necessary basis for international IPR. The needs of developing countries and LDCs are in turn solely addressed in a clause on the importance of technical assistance in helping these states implement their TRIPS obligations (IP/C/W/313 of 4 October 2001).

In a negotiated balance of these different positions (cf. Correa 2002), November 2001 witnessed the adoption of the Declaration on the TRIPS Agreement and Public Health. However, the transition schedule extensions mentioned above were not incorporated. Instead, only LDCs were granted an exemption from the implementation of the patent regulations in TRIPS Sections 5 and 7 until 2016 – and only with regards to pharmaceuticals. Original proposals for across-the-board extensions for developing countries were consequently replaced by LDC-only transition schedules on pharmaceutical products (WT/MIN[01]/DEC/2 of 20 November 2001).

The conflict over *who should benefit* from longer transition periods, and the resulting bifurcation of the developing country group into LDCs and non-LDCs, became even more apparent in the following two years. With the establishment of a Committee on Trade and Development (CTD) in 2001, the African Group re-energized its push for greater incorporation of SDT in existing WTO agreements. In a 2002 Joint Communication, the Group consequently reaffirmed that 'transition periods shall not be arbitrarily set or inadequate … developing and least-developed country members shall always have a right to extend transition periods provided that they shall notify the World Trade Organisation …' (TN/CTD/W/3 of 24 May 2002). A revision of this document the same year contained agreement-specific proposals for SDT implementation. The document proposes 'developing country Members shall be entitled to extensions beyond the additional 5 year period under Article 65.4 relating to other areas of technology required to be protected under the TRIPS Agreement' (TN/CTD/W/3/Rev.2 of 17 July 2002). Statements of support for the African Group proposal in turn came from India, Argentina, and Malaysia (IP/C/M/40 of 22 August 2003: paras. 218, 221, 223).

Southern unity of coalitions, however, was not as strong as it initially seemed. This is because at the same time the LDC Group submitted its own proposal to the CTD. This step was notable in the sense that it clearly emphasized the SDT needs of LDCs – regardless of the concerns of other developing countries pertaining to transition schedules. The proposal suggested an expansion of differential treatment regarding the procedures on the renewal of existing transition periods in TRIPS, and thus added a third (only LDC-related) line of conflict to the negotiations: the proposed amendment was to automatically grant extensions to any LDCs who had not established a viable technological base by the end of their transition period (TN/CTD/W/4/Add.1 of 1 July 2002). According to TRIPS Article 66.1, LDC members have to officially request an extension before the TRIPS Council. This alternative proposal, however, sought to rule out the requirement of consent from TRIPS Council members and placed the burden of proof on those who opposed the extension. Support for the LDC proposal came from the delegations of Kenya, Egypt, Argentina, and Cuba (IP/C/M/40 of 22 August 2003: paras. 209, 210, 213) – but not from India or Brazil who supported the African Group proposal.

Both proposals were simultaneously submitted to the TRIPS Council in May 2002 and faced uniform opposition from a united Global North. In response to the LDC request for automatic extensions, the US reiterated that the current agreement was already flexible enough on LDC extensions, as exemplified by the 2001 decision on public health (IP/C/M/40 of 22 August 2003: para. 204). The Canadian delegation mirrored this approach in its dismissal of the LDC proposal, stating that Article 66.1 was already sufficient as a mechanism for requesting extensions (IP/C/M/40 of 22 August 2003: para.

206). Representatives from Switzerland and Japan joined in this hesitation to support the LDC text, arguing that 'an open-ended extension of the transition period under Article 66.1 could lead to the loss of momentum to prepare the implementation within the prescribed period' (IP/C/M/40 of 22 August 2003: para. 212).

Quad Group actors adopted a similar opposition to transition period extensions for developing countries as a whole. The US emphasized that the existing transition period was a 'more than adequate period of time for developing country Members to implement product patent protection for those areas of technology that were not protected when TRIPS came into force' (IP/C/M/40 of 22 August 2003: para. 215). A counterproposal authored by the US and discussed at an informal meeting with the African Group (IP/C/M/40 of 22 August 2003) in turn failed to develop into proper TRIPS legislation. By 2004 a TRIPS Council Secretariat document summarizing progress on the two proposals made no reference to the transition extension for developing countries as a whole (JOB[04]/164 of 19 November 2004). While the LDC proposal was not adopted as such, it is of note that in 2005 LDCs *collectively* received an extension until 2013 (IP/C/40 of 30 November 2005).

In short, base differences between actors from the Quad Group on the one hand and Brazil, India, and other developing countries on the other allowed transition periods to become a node of conflict in early 2000s IPR debates (for an overview, cf. Table 6.1). Opposing positions were ultimately built on different opinions on who should benefit from extended transition periods, how to determine their adequate length, and what procedures should guide their potential renewals. The conflict ran strictly along North–South lines, with Brazil and India supporting the African Group proposal.

A division between developing countries and LDCs became apparent, however, when the LDCs submitted their own proposal on transition periods. This fragmentation of Southern coalitions arguably limited their chances of success, given the Global North remained relatively united in their opposition to both proposals. As a result, transition schedules for developing countries were not extended, and the support of India and Brazil for the African Group proposal did not translate into meaningful negotiation outcomes. This resulted in an unmaking of special rights for the developing country group. Instead, only LDCs were able to lock in further differential treatment, keeping their differential treatment resilient. Parallel attempts to reform the transition schedules in the TRIPS Agreement for developing countries and to go beyond the individualized procedures of the LDCs for extension requests could thus only yield success for the latter initiative.

6.3.2 The Conflict in the Mid-2010s (2011–2015)

Unable to secure an extension, by the 2010s, non-LDC developing countries had to implement the TRIPS Agreement. It is of note, however, that this did not decrease the salience of the North–South conflict over the issue of transition schedules. Both with regards to pharmaceuticals and TRIPS enforcement in general, 2013–2015 witnessed considerable debate over the granting of further extensions to the LDC sub-group. Despite losing their direct stake in this debate, larger developing countries actively participated in these discussions, defending the differential treatment of LDCs. This stronger unity of Southern coalitions in the 2010s signals a continued divide between members of the Quad Group on the one hand and Brazil, China, India, and smaller developing countries on the other over the developmental benefits of IP protection. Contention continued to centre on the adequate length of transition periods and the procedures for their renewal. By the 2015 Ministerial Conference, requests for LDC transition period extensions could claim success, albeit in a watered-down state compared with the original proposals. These extensions comprise the resilience of differential treatment for LDCs, made possible via Southern unity.

The general transition period granted to LDCs in 2005 had allowed these marginal economies a further eight years to build up a viable technological base (IP/C/40 of 30 November 2005). The 2002 Declaration on Public Health was slightly more generous, with an extra 13.5 years given to LDCs in the pharmaceutical sector (IP/C/25 of 1 July 2002). With enforcement deadlines approaching in 2013 and 2016 respectively, LDCs thus launched proposals for further extensions in 2011. A November 2011 Elements Paper circulated by Bangladesh on behalf of the LDC Group stressed the continued relevance of extensions, as the conditions of LDCs had not changed over the previous eight years. Recalling that industrialized countries had committed to providing enhanced technical assistance, the paper went on to stress the need for a further extension (IP/C/W/566 of 11 November 2011).

In the TRIPS Council such an extension was further defended as a necessary tool in these countries' fight against the after-effects of the global financial crisis (IP/C/M/67 of 15 February 2012: para. 338). Already in this initial phase, without a draft text on the table, the Quad Group signalled their position: in November 2011, the US stated that while an extension for LDCs was a 'matter of great importance', its support of the 2005 extension had been 'premised on the importance of promoting IP protection and enforcement, particularly as a significant driver of the development goals of LDCs'. From the outset, a 'maximalist' logic was consequently pursued by the US, implying that any derogations from TRIPS enforcement were to be limited and temporary in nature. The delegations of Japan, Canada, Australia, and Switzerland joined in this consensus (IP/C/M/68 of 14 February 2012: paras. 8, 9, 10, 11).

Continued calls for greater technical assistance and transition flexibility culminated in November 2012 with an official extension request under Article 66.1. Pointing to the high rates of poverty, low human capital, and inadequate infrastructure in their countries, LDCs questioned their ability to benefit from TRIPS implementation. A waiver was subsequently sought in order to secure the 'policy space' needed to access technology and educational resources that could aid the development of LDCs. This marked a novelty when compared to previous extension requests, as it suggested making exemptions permanent (IP/C/W/583 of 5 November 2012):

> In view of the impossibility of determining when individual LDCs will be able to overcome the constraints that prevent them from creating a viable technological base, the transition period should remain in force while the Member is considered a least developed country in the WTO.

Debates over the exemption of LDCs from TRIPS implementation came to a head in 2013. Members of the LDC Group used TRIPS Council meetings to stress their lacking financial, educational, and human capacity to implement TRIPS and promoted the concept of 'policy space' as a means of developing the tools necessary to overcome developmental challenges (compare IP/C/M/72 of 13 May 2013: paras. 11.12, 11.22, 11.30, 11.52). Rwanda for instance argued that '[t]he negotiated period in the last extension of seven and a half years was absolutely inadequate and of limited practical value to LDCs for dealing with development challenges and developing a viable and sound technological base. An indefinite duration would give LDCs certainty and predictability' (ibid.: para. 11.56).

Strong support for the LDC proposal came from Brazil, China, and India. The Brazilian delegation anchored its backing of an unconditional LDC exemption in the importance of SDT more generally (ibid.: para. 11.20). China also backed the LDC initiative, highlighting that these developing countries continued to face serious economic, financial, and administrative constraints and that they were thus justified in requesting 'maximum flexibility' (ibid.: para. 11.29). India also supported the LDC request, pointing to the marginal role of these economies in world trade, their vulnerability, and their limited infrastructure. The Indian delegation further honed in on the separate provisions for LDCs in the TRIPS Agreement, including a right to request individual extensions: the framers of the TRIPS Agreement thus 'duly recognized their need for exemption from the obligations under the Agreement …' (ibid.: para. 11.38). The ability of LDCs to request individual extensions was thus reimagined as recognition of the need for LDCs to remain exempt from TRIPS implementation. Support for the exemption-based proposal also came from South Africa, the African Group, the African, Caribbean and Pacific Countries (ACP) Group, and Association of Southeast Asian Nations (ASEAN) (ibid.: paras. 11.33, 11.19, 11.26, 11.34), illustrating greater Southern unity of coalitions than in the 2000s.

The approaches of industrialised states to LDC transitions were markedly different. While the Canadian delegation was quick to welcome efforts by LDCs to implement TRIPS and indicated its openness to addressing their difficulties, it hastened to add that any solution should help them better integrate into the international trading system. In terms of a permanent exemption, the message was clear: 'Canada therefore believed there was a need to find an appropriate timeframe to build upon the infrastructure and human capital in LDCs' (ibid.: para. 11.45). A similar approach was adopted by Australia, which supported an extension in principle but focussed on the timeframe and parameters for extension rather than engaging with the request for an 'unlimited' transition period (ibid.: para. 11.51). The US in turn reiterated its conviction that a permanent waiver would not be beneficial for LDCs (ibid.: paras. 11.64–66). Portrayals of IP protection and innovation as cornerstones of development also made up statements by the EU and Japan (ibid.: paras. 11.69–76 and 11.77), and underlined the uniform, 'maximalist' positions the Quad Group nations took against the LDC proposal. The EU delegation further criticized the use of LDC status as a threshold as opposed to a distinct timeframe for the transition (ibid.: para. 11.71). The Swiss delegation went so far as to remind members that the LDC Group was not actually proposing a further extension, but indefinite non-application of TRIPS provisions (ibid.: para. 11.60).

By 2013 the issue of granting a transition period extension to an economically marginal sub-group of developing countries had consequently been transformed into a North–South conflict over the implementation of TRIPS. The unconditional support LDCs received from Brazil, China, and India in their push for an indefinite extension contrasts sharply with the focus on timeframes, hitherto LDC progress, and defences of IP protection that constitute developed country statements.

At a 2013 TRIPS Council meeting, the Indian delegation stressed that 'any artificial deadline would not help in creating a sound and viable technological base …' (New 2013). Despite this clear support for the original LDC proposal, unified opposition from developed country actors, led by the US and the EU, made the success of this initiative unlikely (Saez 2013). Instead, in June 2013 the TRIPS Council approved an eight-year collective extension for LDCs (IP/C/64 of 12 June 2013). Some analysts still saw this as a success, particularly as the decision did not include a 'no-rollback' clause as in 2005 (Syam 2014). Others, however, took issue with this denial of permanent exemptions.

At an October TRIPS Council Meeting on public health, India highlighted the North–South conflict lines over LDC demands (IP/C/M/74/Add.1 of 28 November 2013: para. 75):

> We found strong resistance from the developed country Members to provide an indefinite extension till the LDCs graduated … the permanent exemption from the provisions of the TRIPS Agreement to all countries while they are classified as LDCs continues to be the most significant exception to ensure access to low-cost generic medicines in LDCs …

The conflict over TRIPS implementation in LDCs continued in March 2015, as LDCs pushed for a separate extension for pharmaceuticals. Quoting a Joint United Nations Programme on HIV/AIDS UNAIDS report that stressed the need for an extended transition, the LDC Group submitted a proposal that claimed it was 'imperative for LDCs to retain maximum policy space to enable them to confront their health burdens'. On pharmaceuticals LDCs again requested an extension for as long as a member remained an LDC (IP/C/W/605 of 23 February 2015; IP/C/M/78/Add.1 of 4 May 2015: paras. 497–503). Cognizant of the controversial nature of an indefinite extension, the representative of the LDC Group devoted an entire section of their June statement before the TRIPS Council to '[t]he issue of duration for as long as we are LDCs'. In it, the delegation declared 'it would be unconscionable for WTO Members to grant LDCs … a time limited transition period …' as this would create an 'uncertain environment' for producers of affordable medicines. Here again, the ability of LDCs to apply for individual extensions under Article 66.1 was interpreted as a recognition of the constraints LDCs faced. The statement went on to claim that the socio-economic situation of LDCs had deteriorated and the health need in these nations had increased (IP/C/M/79/Add.1 of 2 September 2015: paras. 378–380). The LDC submission was in turn supported by Brazil, China, and India (IP/C/M/78/Add.1 of 4 May 2015: paras. 508, 510–511, 512).

Full support for the unconditional, graduation-linked transition period came from South Africa, the African Group, as well as Brazil, China, and India at the subsequent June 2015 TRIPS Council meeting, again illustrating Southern unity of coalitions in this time period (IP/C/M/79/Add.1 of 2 September 2015: paras. 386–387, 382–385, 412, 426–428, 438). Referencing the 2013 meetings on the general waiver, the Indian delegation stressed the continued relevance of its position then and its consistent support for the extension request of LDCs 'without any conditionalities' (ibid.: para. 412). China, on the other hand, rooted its support for the LDC request in the 'economic, financial and administrative constraints of LDC Members, as well as the close relation between the access to certain pharmaceutical products and human life' (ibid.: para. 438). Turning to developed countries, the Chinese delegation further urged industrialized economies to provide more incentives and encourage technology transfer to LDCs (ibid.: para. 438). The Brazilian delegation used the June meeting to again support LDCs and to push for a producers-users balance in international IP protection. Brazil even took the floor twice during the same meeting to stress to members that the discussion at hand was about pharmaceuticals and not the general transition period discussed two years earlier (ibid.: paras. 426–428, 483–485).

However, opposition from the Global North also remained strong. The Japanese delegation remained cautious and stressed that LDCs could still make use of the general transition period (ibid.: paras. 440–443). This echoes the Australian opposition to permanent exemptions for LDCs (ibid.: paras. 472–473). The EU, on the other hand, simply stated its willingness to resolve any legal uncertainty and 'ensure LDCs flexibility' (ibid.: para. 458). Informal meetings held by the US with the representatives of the LDC Group in turn ensured that the negotiation outcome again fell short of the original goals of LDCs.

US disagreement with the indefinite timeframe, combined with its insistence that individual LDCs could use Article 66.1 to request an extension whenever needed, yielded a decision to extend the LDC transition on pharmaceuticals until 2033 (Saez 2015). Reactions to this watering down of the original request again fall along North–South conflict lines: the delegations of the US, Japan, Switzerland, and the EU (IP/C/M/80/Add.1 of 22 February 2016: paras. 344, 379, 381–382, 374–375) voiced their support for the decision in a November 2015 meeting. While Brazil, China, and India (ibid.: paras. 388, 376, 371–373) also supported the consensus they nevertheless voiced critiques. The Brazilian delegation for one pointed out that the solution fell short of the objective of LDCs, but would be supported, as it was a compromise the LDC Group agreed with (ibid.: para. 388). India, on the other hand, claimed that the freedom of extension encapsulated in Article 66.1 should be interpreted as mandatory, i.e. that the TRIPS Council could not deny requests for extension or impose further conditionalities on LDCs: 'Despite the overwhelming support for the LDC request from all developing countries and many developed countries, a developed country has negotiated an outcome with the LDCs which is a derogation from the provisions of Art. 66.1' (ibid.: para. 372).

Evidently, in the 2010s developed–developing country conflicts remained strong. This is surprising, as we would expect the interest of larger developing countries in transition schedules to decrease as their direct stake in the negotiations vanished. While discussions over implementation issues in the early 2000s could consequently rely on the parallel attempts of LDCs and developing countries to secure extensions, by the 2010s only the issue of transition periods for LDCs was on the table. While there was general agreement over the need for transition periods for LDCs as part of SDT in the world trade regime,

Table 6.1 *Overview of attempted norm expansion and negotiation outcomes*

First Conflict Moment (2001–2003)	
June 2001 Proposal (Brazil, India, African Group, Indonesia, and others)	Transition period extensions for developing countries and LDCs
October 2001 Proposal (Brazil, India, African Group, and others)	Transition period extension of five years for developing countries (Art. 65.4) and LDCs (Art. 66.1)
Outcome: November 2001 Declaration on the TRIPS Agreement and Public Health	**LDCs exempt from implementing TRIPS Arts. 5 and 7 for pharmaceuticals until 2016**
May 2002 Proposal (African Group)	Transition period extensions for developing countries (Art. 65.4)
May 2002 Proposal (LDC Group)	Transition period extensions for LDCs should be granted automatically
Outcome: November 2005 Decision on LDC Transition Period Extension	**Transition period extension for LDCs until 2013 'No roll-back clause' ensures existing IP in LDCs is protected**
Second Conflict Moment (2011–2015)	
November 2011 Elements Paper (LDC Group)	Transition period extension for LDCs
November 2012 Proposal (LDC Group)	TRIPS waiver for LDCs
Outcome: June 2013 Decision on LDC Transition Period Extension	**Transition period extension for LDCs until 2021**
February 2015 Proposal (LDC Group)	TRIPS waiver for LDCs on pharmaceuticals
Outcome: November 2015 Decision to Extend Pharmaceuticals Transition Period for LDCs	**Transition period extension until 2033**

it remained highly contested how to operationalize it. The Global North remained united in its opposition to making transition periods permanent for LDCs and instead sought to promote domestic IP enforcement as a guarantor of economic development. In the end, LDCs only made marginal gains by securing an extension of transition schedules – but without making them permanent. Unity of Southern coalitions – including Brazil, China, and India – in this second conflict moment thus translated into the resilience of differential treatment for LDCs.

6.4 HOW THE RISE OF BRAZIL, CHINA, AND INDIA SHAPED THE NEGOTIATION OUTCOMES ON TRANSITION SCHEDULES

Conflicts over TRIPS transition schedules fell along North–South lines. However, Southern unity was less strong in the 2000s as compared to the

2010s, while Northern unity remained relatively high throughout both conflict moments. Brazil, China, and India were not able to get an additional expansion of transition schedules for developing countries, including themselves, nor did their backing of the LDC demands to make the extension renewal automatic or permanent lead to an expansion of differential treatment. Arguably, norm expansion was only successful at the margins, with LDCs surpassing the individualized, application-based procedures for extension requests in the TRIPS Agreement by obtaining collective extensions. Against this background, this section unpacks the state preferences at stake that shaped coalition patterns and analyses legitimacy concerns and institutional opportunity structures as mediating factors of bargaining strength. Together, these factors provide a better understanding of why we observe resilience concerning the differential treatment of LDCs.

Despite the rise of Brazil, China, and India within the global knowledge economy, they continue to hold a shared interest in 'TRIPS flexibilities' similar to LDCs and other developing countries. This facilitated Southern coalitional unity, especially in the 2010s. The meagre success their coalition had, however, can be partly explained by the way in which the contested ideological nature of the link between IP protection and development delegitimized LDC demands. The belief in the developmental benefits of 'maximalist' IP protection explains why opposition from the Global North remained so strong, given the marginal economic role that LDCs play in the world economy. Lastly, ample forum shopping opportunities reinforced the North–South stalemate in the WTO.

6.4.1 State Interests and Coalition-building: Unity of Brazil, China, and India with the Global South

In the first conflict moment, India and Brazil sided with the African Group and other developing countries. This can be partly explained by converging interests in maintaining longer transition periods. By the 2000s, most of the 73 developing countries that were WTO members at the time and many LDCs had already put in place some form of patent legislation in line with TRIPS obligations (Musungu and Oh 2006: 7). This meant that transition schedules were not necessary for some of them – even though it is important to mention that in half of these cases the laws for TRIPS implementation pended approval in domestic legislatures (Deere Birkbeck 2009: 13). Moreover, enforcement mechanisms in developing countries often remained weak (Deere Birkbeck 2009: 14). India, and to some extent Brazil, however, belonged to the group of developing country members that made active use of transition schedules in the early 2000s.

Regarding the pharmaceutical sector in particular, India used the ability to delay stronger patent protection. The transition period granted in TRIPS Article 65.4 allowed India to become a global producer of generic drugs. For example, India became the leading producer of antiretroviral therapy for HIV patients, rising to 80 per cent of the annual global supply (UNAIDS 2011: 32). Next to India, only 12 other WTO members made use of this specific transition period for the pharmaceutical sector – including Brazil (Musungu and Oh 2006: 7). While the generic industry of Brazil is less dominant compared to the one of India, Brazil at the time had a very high number of people dependent on HIV medication (UNAIDS 2011: 22). This meant that India, and to some extent Brazil, had a shared interest in supporting the proposal of the African Group for an extension of the transition schedule for developing countries. Moreover, both countries have some interest in lax enforcement of pharmaceutical patents in LDCs; historically, poorer developing country markets have been reliant on generic producers in rising powers like Brazil and India (Atal 2016). On the specific issue of pharmaceuticals, the economic interests of Brazil, China, and India thus align with LDC demands for exemptions or transition extensions.

More generally, Brazil, China, and India were primarily importers rather than exporters of innovation in the early 2000s, and thus faced more costs than benefits from immediate TRIPS implementation. This is because stronger patent protection raises the costs of products and potentially endangers employment in production sectors that rely on imitation (Deere Birkbeck 2009: 10). According to a World Bank study cited by Deere Birkbeck (2009: 10), the costs from TRIPS implementation remained high:

> In 2002, the World Bank estimated that TRIPS implementation would generate annual net losses for Brazil of US$530 million, for China of US$5.1 billion, for India of US$903 million.

The willingness of Brazil and India to push back against the implementation of TRIPS not only reflects these interests, but also represents a change in positions in the early 2000s as compared to the 1990s. Developing country attitudes to IP had sharpened during the late 1990s, both as a consequence of piecemeal TRIPS implementation and as part of a larger globalization backlash.[9] For example, Brazil and other Latin American countries had initially sought quick implementation of TRIPS in the 1990s. According to one former delegate, this was the result of international pressure by private companies and industrialized economies to refrain from flexibility use, as well as domestic initiatives to attract foreign investment.[10] In the early 2000s, on the other hand, a more development-oriented approach to IPR emerged in Brazil, South Africa, and several Latin American states, encompassing more assertive positions on patent rights and TRIPS application domestically, constitutional court cases regarding licensing disputes, as well as a more combative tone regarding natural resources, biodiversity, and the development dimension.[11]

In particular, developing countries focussed on a larger effort related to full implementation of the flexibilities and SDT provisions in *all* the Uruguay Round Agreements.[12] Centring debates on IPR around the fulfilment of already negotiated obligations consequently allowed Brazil and South Africa to join India in a more defensive stance against an increasingly stringent IPR regime.

However, this learning process also meant that in the early 2000s, Southern positions on IP were often still relatively uncoordinated. Highly uneven levels of TRIPS implementation across the Global South (Deere Birkbeck 2009: 12–14) arguably made it difficult to find a coherent position on transition schedules across the different coalitions. As a result, many commentators lamented the lack of coordination between developing country states in the early 2000s (Geiger 2012; Abdel-Latif 2005).

By the end of the decade, however, common IP policy-making initiatives and a more self-assertive tone characterized the behaviour of developing nations. However, this did not inevitably translate into support of Brazil, China, and India for LDC proposals. By the early 2010s, Brazil, China, and India, in particular China, had developed significant technological capabilities. In contrast to the early 2000s, when the costs of TRIPS implementation remained high for Brazil, China, and India, their increasing role as knowledge producers went hand in hand with rising benefits from stronger IP protection. This suggests that they could have held an interest in joining the Global North in their opposition to the waiver demands of LDCs.

However, a closer look at the economic interests of Brazil, China, and India shows that their economic rise did not translate into a clear-cut shift from a 'minimalist' to a 'maximalist' position on IP protection. While domestic IP protection did increase across Brazil, China, and India, benefits from patents or trademarks are often still passed on to foreign companies. In India and Brazil, for instance, the majority of national patent applications still belong to foreign entities (Muzaka 2019: 360–362) – a trend that is different for China (Cheng 2019: 147). Nevertheless, according to World Bank estimates, in 2015 88 per cent of IP benefits still went to entities in the US, the EU, and Japan (Muzaka 2019: 352–353). This signals that despite their economic rise, Brazil, China, and India still hold an interest both in 'maximalist' and 'minimalist' positions.

This ambiguous position is replicated at the level of TRIPS implementation, where Brazil, China, and India at times go beyond their obligations in some areas of IP (so-called TRIPS-plus commitments), whilst at the same time making use of TRIPS flexibilities elsewhere. In China, for instance, some domestic forces push for stronger IP protection at the national level, while at the same time it ranks among the main patent infringers at the local level (Morin et al. 2018: 264; Serrano 2016: 359). Similarly, Brazil emerged as a strong force against a 'maximalist' IP agenda in the world trade regime, even though it had adopted strong patent legislation at the domestic level that went beyond TRIPS requirements (Morin et al. 2018: 268). Out of Brazil, China, and India, India is clearest in its opposition to a 'maximalist' IP regime, even though this seems only partly interests-based, and partly a reflection of strong ideological beliefs in the importance of technology transfer and weak IP protection for development (Serrano 2016: 356). Yet, both India (2005) and China (2008) articulated domestic patent laws that made full use of the flexibilities in the TRIPS Agreement, particularly on compulsory licensing (De Menezes 2018). These ambiguities in the economic interests of Brazil, China, and India thus partly explain why it was conceivable for them to side with LDCs.

In general, the first half of the 2010s is characterized by a more proactive and organized group of developing countries. Their aims were to minimize the fallout of TRIPS-plus provisions in the trade agreements of the Quad Group, to advocate for continued TRIPS flexibilities, to formulate common foreign policy priorities, and to integrate their interests in new pieces of international IP legislation. With the rise of Brazil, China, and India this has in turn allowed these countries to emerge as leaders of a broader coalition of developing economies and to vocally counter the erosion of implementation flexibilities.

Support of Brazil, China, and India for LDC proposals thus forms part of a larger North–South conflict over IP protection. A trade official underlined that proposals on transition scheduling needed to be seen as part of a larger platform that emerged in the 2000s on implementation-related issues. The 2003 proposal of the African Group for developing country extensions must consequently be seen as just one element of an agenda that tackled up to 110 issues in the WTO agreements flagged by developing countries. Misgivings about the developmental impact of the Uruguay Round Agreements were in turn amplified by resistance to the notion that 'SDT was to be only transitory', targeted at ensuring full participation in the multilateral trading system.[13]

Notions of political solidarity and South–South ties were also important in facilitating Southern unity of coalitions in the second conflict moment. Recalling debates over LDC extensions, one former trade negotiator emphasized the strong support that these marginal traders received from Brazil, India, and Egypt and the consultations that some of these delegations entered into with the LDC Group.[14] Sympathy both for extension requests and for permanent exemptions were in turn linked by several interviewees to wider political notions of solidarity between developing country members at the WTO.[15] An LDC insistence on pushing for exemptions rather than extensions was in turn partly explained as a result of NGO consulting.[16] Increased bilateral ties between Brazil, China, and India on the one hand and individual LDCs on the other exemplified new coalition-building initiatives.[17] One official explained developing country support for LDC proposals as follows:

> It's largely political. These countries ultimately are our allies on many issues as well. There are many alliances at work in the WTO. And often times a country will support another even if they don't have such a large stake in the issue.[18]

The coalescence of developing county actors in this manner in turn mirrors the parallel formation of the BRICS Group (Brazil, Russia, India, China, and South Africa). Properly founded in 2011, the BRICS Group promoted both a continued balance of rights and responsibilities in the WTO and the development mandate of the Doha Round (BRICS 2011). It is of particular note that the 2012 New Delhi Summit underlined the adverse effects of trade protectionism in the economies of the Quad members, particularly on LDCs (BRICS 2012). Here, consequently a group of rising powers frame their interests in a way that includes the poorest members of the developing country group. This type of alliance building also took place more specifically on IPR.[19]

In short, the rise of Brazil, China, and India has not yet translated into a clear-cut shift from a 'minimalist' to a 'maximalist' agenda on IP protection. This made it possible for Brazil, China, and India to unanimously support the LDC proposal in the 2010s and to secure the resilience of differential treatment for LDCs. Growing Southern coalition unity in the early 2010s did not, however, translate into norm expansion. While the Global South increasingly united, the Global North – led by the US – was also united in its opposition to LDC proposals.

6.4.2 Legitimacy: Contestation of the IP-development Nexus

To understand the outcomes described above, it is important to consider the normative environment that helped to shape the legitimacy of competing negotiating positions. In contrast to agriculture negotiations (cf. Chapter 5), the status of Brazil, China, and India as rights-holders regarding differential treatment did not play a major role in IPR debates. The shift to granting transition periods solely to LDCs already occurred in the early 2000s. However, legitimacy conceptions nonetheless influenced the negotiation dynamics regarding transition schedules. In particular, divides between 'minimalist' and 'maximalist' approaches to IP protection and development underpinned opposing demands. They explain both the inclination of Brazil, China, and India to support later LDC proposals, as well as the stubborn resistance of the Global North to give in to the demands of these peripheral traders. From the perspective of the Global North, LDC demands for permanent exemptions would undermine, rather than facilitate, development. The question to what extent implementation of the TRIPS Agreement serves to further development policy thus adds an ideological dimension to the drive to extend transition schedules.

In terms of explaining the positions of Brazil, China, and India on IPR, it is important to consider divides over integration into the multilateral trading system. Describing WTO politics in the early 2000s, one former trade delegate accentuated the presence of 'combative developing country delegates, talking about the development dimension' with a focus on sovereign rights over natural resources and biodiversity.[20] This sovereigntist approach in turn contrasts heavily with the integrative thrust emanating from developed countries over the past 20 years:

> The developed countries are consistently trying to undermine the special rights of developing countries and they follow a strategy of graduation. And not just in the international trade regime, everywhere.[21]

These ideological differences reinforced the opposing positions of Global North and Global South coalitions. In October 2001, the US, Canada, Japan, Switzerland, and Australia circulated a document that defended their reluctance to renew transition schedules for pharmaceutical products with reference to the 'maximalist' ideological position that linked stronger IP protection to developmental gains. Framed as a potential preamble, the proposal declared that WTO members 'recognize that strong, effective and balanced protection for intellectual property is a necessary incentive for research and development of life-saving drugs and, therefore, recognize that intellectual property contributes to public health objectives globally' (IP/C/W/313 of 4 October 2001). This is extended even further in the requirement for members to reaffirm their 'commitment to the TRIPS Agreement and its implementation' due to its contribution to making medicines more available. An earlier Japanese statement on IPR also reflected this 'maximalist' stance, accentuating that members should first ensure the full implementation of the TRIPS Agreement and that harmonization of IPR systems of different jurisdictions would actually promote the further economic development of developing countries (WT/GC/W/242 of 6 July 1999).

The US representative emphasized in the June 2003 TRIPS Council meeting that (IP/C/M/40 of 22 August 2003: para. 215):

> [H]is delegation believed that a prolonged transition period under Article 65.4 would discourage those developing country Members that had not yet done so from implementing product patent protection in certain important technologies. This could have the effect of impeding the growth of these innovative industries in those Members and undermine economic development.

Aside from the economic benefits of full implementation, the statement by the US addressed the fundamental question of the purpose of the WTO: 'Extended transition periods would also run contrary to the objectives of the multilateral trading system, which was to remove barriers to trade, including non-tariff barriers such as the lack of adequate and effective intellectual property protection' (IP/C/M/40 of 22 August 2003: para. 215).

This 'maximalist' ideological perspective on the link between IP protection and development was strongly opposed by Brazil, China, India, and other developing countries. The Venezuelan delegation – akin to India – attacked the structural limitations in the trade profiles of developing countries, stating that development goals are 'not automatically reached by trade liberalization, nor are they helped by just allowing transitional periods' (WT/GC/W/279 of 29 July 1999; WT/GC/W/282 of 6 August 1999). Instead, officials from the Global South emphasized that it would be necessary for developing countries to be able to actively create their own patentable subject matter before implementing stronger IP protection. The African Group proposal emphasized that all provisions in the TRIPS Agreement should be read in light of its objectives, including the need 'to promote the development of manufacturing capacities of pharmaceuticals'. This statement echoed a 'minimalist' ideological perspective on IP protection based on the need to become competitive in the knowledge economy before enforcing stronger protection regimes. A 'minimalist' perspective was also echoed by India: 'Excessive protection of IPRs may end [a] virtuous cycle of knowledge transmission and regeneration in the developing world' (WT/GC/W/114 of 18 November 1998).

Paying attention to these ideological divides also allows us to understand why the Global North was so reluctant to accept an automatic or permanent exemption for LDCs. In 2003, the US stated that automatic extensions risked permanent derogation from TRIPS implementation, which would in turn be counterproductive as IP protection formed the basis for further development (IP/C/M/40 of 22 August 2003: para. 205). The Canadian delegation mirrored this approach in its dismissal of the LDC proposal: implementation of a minimum level of IPR was fundamental to attracting investment and improving the economies of LDCs. Development was thus based – at least in part – on the implementation of TRIPS obligations by a specific deadline (IP/C/M/40 of 22 August 2003: para. 206).

This 'maximalist' perspective was reiterated in 2013, when Canada encouraged LDCs to adopt 'measures that would help create an enabling environment for development through a transparent and rules-based regulatory framework' (IP/C/M/72 of 13 May 2013: para. 11.44). The US in turn reiterated its conviction that 'IPR protection and enforcement provided critical incentives for creation and innovation that would promote economic growth and create jobs'

(IP/C/M/72 of 13 May 2013: paras. 11.64–66). Similarly, the delegate from Switzerland (IP/C/M/72 of 13 May 2013: para. 11.62)

> wondered, whether from a long-term perspective, a decision of the Council to declare TRIPS provisions inapplicable to LDCs for good would actually be the most beneficial decision to promote the objective of establishing economic development and competitiveness of LDCs in the world trade system. LDCs had also to gain for their own IP assets as they implemented the Agreement and put in place an IP protection system.

In contrast, permanent exemptions for LDCs were supported by non-LDC developing countries with a strong and regular emphasis on the 'policy space' that the development and infrastructure deficits of these nations necessitated. The Brazilian delegation anchored its backing of an unconditional LDC exemption in three arguments: Firstly, SDT was an important systemic component in the WTO and TRIPS ensuring that international trade was an effective motor of international development. Secondly, Brazil was invariably supportive of policy space in the domestic implementation of international IP legislation – again, to secure developmental potential. Lastly, the integration of developing countries into an international knowledge economy was presented as a daunting challenge, the 'complexity of which could not be properly assessed when the Uruguay Round was completed' (IP/C/M/72 of 13 May 2013: para. 11.20). An early 2000s' integrative thrust regarding TRIPS was subsequently seen as a miscalculation that should not be repeated for the poorest economies.

The support of China for the LDC proposal in the 2010s reflects a similar ideological perspective on the IP protection-development nexus: only once a viable technological base was built up with the given flexibility could WTO members count on more effective participation of LDCs in the global trading system (IP/C/M/72 of 13 May 2013: para. 11.29). The support of India for the LDC proposal was, moreover, justified with reference to the need to 'support … all initiatives that promote access to medicines at affordable costs to the people living in the poorest countries of the world' (IP/C/M/78/Add.1 of 4 May 2015: para. 511).

This larger conflict over development and IPR thus helps to explain both the strong support that Brazil, China, and India gave to an LDC proposal that they had no direct stake in, as well as the strong opposition of major developed countries from the Global North to granting LDCs automatic or permanent exemptions from TRIPS implementation.

That being said, the implementation of the TRIPS Agreement and 20 years of economic development have also allowed for changes in this strong North–South polarization over IP implementation. As one trade negotiator and long-term IP expert put it, while in the 1990s the developing country appreciation of TRIPS was not positive, by 2020 many Latin American and Asian countries had accepted IP as part of their development. Most of Asia and parts of Africa, however, still remained convinced that international IP regulation was primarily 'for the developed world'. The same official noted that while previously Brazil, India, South Africa, and Nigeria – amongst others – were clearly positioned to limit the consequences of IP, this has been changing in the latter half of the 2010s. As a result, some actors, most notably Brazil, have become less vocal on the supposedly negative impact of IP enforcement in developing countries.[22]

At the same time, the recent global COVID-19 pandemic has engendered renewed pushes for policy space and limits to TRIPS implementation: in October 2020, the delegations of India and South Africa submitted a draft decision to the TRIPS Council concerning waivers from the implementation of Sections 1, 4, 5, and 7 of the TRIPS Agreement. While this call for derogations from TRIPS implementation is noteworthy in itself, it further stresses that the right of LDCs to request transition schedule extensions under Article 66.1 shall not be impeded (IP/C/W/669 of 2 October 2020). The need to secure the policy space of WTO members on IP matters during a health crisis – and of LDCs in particular – has consequently survived over the past two decades and provides an ideological backdrop to conflicts over transition scheduling. While divides over the IP-development nexus have, on the one hand, stopped LDCs from achieving exemptions, they have also enabled a Southern unity that has left differential treatment for LDCs resilient.

6.4.3 Institutional Opportunity Structures: Forum Shopping Reinforces Stalemate

Differing institutional opportunity structures can affect the influence of Brazil, China, and India, as the ability to forum shop can either support or undermine the demands of these larger traders. Arguably, opportunities for forum shopping have further entrenched the North–South conflict lines within the WTO. As a result, support of Brazil, China, and India for LDC transition schedule proposals in the 2010s – and the resilience of their differential treatment – can be seen as part of a larger attempt to push back against 'TRIPS-plus' obligations that go beyond TRIPS in bilateral or plurilateral initiatives outside the WTO.

Prior to the finalization of the Uruguay Round in 1995, WIPO provided the main stage for IP regulation (Sell 2011). Thereafter, the passing of the TRIPS Agreement shifted the centre of gravity of the IPR regime to the newly formed WTO. The vital issue of access to medicines in turn allowed the World Health Organization (WHO) to play a strong forum role, while attempts by developing countries to marry biodiversity concerns with TRIPS gave prominence to the CBD. These multilateral fora were accompanied by a flurry of bi- and plurilateral trade agreements (PTAs), which have increasingly incorporated IP-related provisions. This latter development was mainly a result of deadlock between members of the Quad Group and Brazil, China, and India regarding TRIPS reform. Industrialized economies thus transferred their attempts to gain deeper commitments on IP protection to the bilateral level while developing countries used the TRIPS Council and other multilateral forums to defend their interests.

Parallel negotiation aims in turn resulted in different policy-making trajectories in the 2000s. While developing countries paired with NGOs (non-governmental organizations) to promote the formulation of further flexibilities regarding TRIPS and public health, the US attempted to restart talks on a Substantive Patent Law Treaty (SPLT) and an Internet Copyright Convention in WIPO (Sell 2011). These early 2000s' initiatives had differing levels of success. The anthrax attacks of 2001 allowed industrialized economies to recognize the utility of exemptions from strong patent protection for pharmaceuticals (Lee 2015; Kumar 2018). This backdrop, paired with a drive by NGOs to tackle the HIV/AIDS crisis in developing countries, consequently allowed for the signing of the 2001 Doha Declaration on TRIPS and Public Health. The 2002 attempt by the US to restart the SPLT in turn did not bear fruit.

Vertical forum shifting in the form of a flurry of plurilateral trade agreements (PTAs), bilateral investment treaties (BITs), and European Partnership Agreements (EPAs) allowed actors from the Quad Group to incorporate TRIPS-plus provisions in individual treaties with developing countries (Sell 2011). In doing so, they avoided the type of universal consensus and coalition-building required by the WTO. As one former official claimed, it had become apparent that it was impossible to go beyond the TRIPS Agreement in the WTO, thus necessitating a shift of the TRIPS-plus push to the bilateral level.[23] In essence, this bifurcated international IPR politics as developing countries continued to push for the conservation of TRIPS flexibilities and developed countries attempted to strengthen international IP legislation in bilateral policy-making.

Developing countries, supported in their endeavours to secure TRIPS flexibilities by various international organizations (De Menezes 2018), also attempted to expand the TRIPS Agreement. The protection of traditional knowledge, folklore, and biodiversity was thus pursued by these countries in the TRIPS Council, along with initiatives by some developing countries for an expansion of the geographic indicator protections available for wines and spirits (Dreyfuss 2009). Such initiatives were echoed in WIPO, where the adoption of a Development Agenda in 2007 entailed the creation of a Committee on Development and Intellectual Property (CDIP) and the formation of a Development Agenda Group (DAG) (May 2007; Deere Birkbeck 2016). The replacement of the heavily technical outlook of the WIPO by a development-oriented approach was led by Brazil, India, and Argentina.[24] Several interviewees stressed the conversion of WIPO from an institution focussing on the harmonization of technical standards to a development-conscious body as a significant forum change.[25]

Accompanying these efforts to incorporate developmental priorities in multilateral trade fora, the late 2000s witnessed attempts by the Quad Group to expand IP regulation plurilaterally. Most notably, in 2007 negotiations amongst the Quad Group, Australia, New Zealand, South Korea, Switzerland, Mexico, and Morocco would yield the Anti-Counterfeiting Trade Agreement (ACTA). This Quad-led initiative was widely considered an affront to established multilateral avenues of IP policy-making. While ACTA also accentuated divisions within the developed country group – the European Parliament notably rejected the agreement in 2012 – it is still of note that the remaining negotiators signed the agreement. The proliferation of TRIPS-plus provisions, such as those on the ACTA negotiating table, in turn led analysts to declare that the TRIPS flexibilities that were meant to ensure policy space were at risk of losing their relevance (Sell 2011).

Developing countries took to the TRIPS Council in the early 2010s to sharply criticize the growing trend of TRIPS-plus provisions as embodied by the ACTA draft text. Lengthy contributions by China and India consequently honed in on the 'even more phenomenal and strong' (IP/C/M/63 of 4 October 2010: para. 250) trend of legislating below the multilateral level, the 'systemic concerns' (IP/C/M/63 of 4 October 2010: paras. 255, 257) this trend engendered, and the fact that '[a]greements such as ACTA had the potential to completely upset the balance of rights and obligations of the TRIPS Agreement' (IP/C/M/63 of 4 October 2010: para. 273). The Brazilian delegation summarized the fears of developing countries as follows (IP/C/M/63 of 4 October 2010: para. 318):

> Brazil shared the main thrust of the statements by China and India, emphasizing two points of particular concern. The first one was the ACTA negotiating process, which lacked the legitimacy of initiatives conducted in multilateral organizations and had been conducted in a non-transparent atmosphere of secrecy that was not conducive to trust. The second one was that ACTA might, in addition to being TRIPS-plus, end up being TRIPS-minus to the extent that it contributed to narrowing down the scope for flexibilities.

Indeed, a rejected proposal by China attempted to protect countries from the adverse effects of such extra-WTO trade legislation, arguing that provisions of FTAs should be mandated to conform with the TRIPS Agreement, should not 'create distortive effects', and should not restrain a member's 'autonomy for utilizing its public enforcement resources' (IP/C/M/63 of 4 October 2010: para. 259).

While developed country actors continued to pursue mega-regionals such as the Trans-Pacific Partnership, rising powers also created new legislative initiatives: 2012 witnessed the commencement of negotiations on the Regional Comprehensive Economic Partnership (RCEP) under the leadership of China. Similarly, negotiations in WIPO led by developing countries allowed for the signing of two major IP agreements on protections for audio-visual performances – the 2012 Beijing Treaty – and on access to knowledge for the visually impaired – the 2016 Marrakesh Treaty. Within the WTO, the 2010s witnessed a continued push for amendments to the TRIPS Agreement that would use disclosure of origin provisions to protect the biological diversity, traditional knowledge, and folklore that disproportionately made up the IP interests of developing countries (Yu in press).

In short, the expansion of bilateral IP regulation – at the behest of developed countries – has included TRIPS-plus provisions, which stand in contrast to attempts of Brazil, China, and India to preserve policy space for development purposes. Fears of erosion in non-multilateral fora consequently drive the push by developing countries to keep existing flexibilities intact in the WTO. This broader context helps us to understand why the unity of Brazil, China, and India with the Global South in terms of coalitions only yielded resilience and was not sufficient to facilitate a significant expansion of differential treatment for LDCs in the 2010s, given the issue became entangled in the firmly entrenched North–South conflict over IP in the broader regime complex.

6.5 CONCLUSION

The relationship between IP protection and economic development remains contested. This allows IPR to become a prime centre of North–South conflict in the trade regime. Quad states have pushed for the full and universal implementation of the TRIPS Agreement as well as an expansion of the existing IPR regime via TRIPS-plus provisions, while larger developing countries have jealously guarded flexibilities available to them to secure their policy space.

These underlying forces erupt in full conflict when developing countries – or even a marginal sub-group – propose extensions for their TRIPS transition schedules or call for permanent exemptions. Such derogations stand in diametric opposition both to attempts of industrialized economies to move the legislative frontier beyond the TRIPS minimum, as well as the 'maximalist' logic they promote in general: integration into the global trading system is promoted as a motor for economic growth and a key poverty alleviation tool for developing country members. Differing appraisals of the value of such integration for development in turn make this 'maximalist' logic clash with the 'minimalist' emphasis of Brazil, China, and India on policy space. The strong rejection of extensions for developing countries and the watering down of LDC proposals underline an ongoing process of contestation regarding the differential treatment of developing countries.

Debates over transition scheduling in the TRIPS Agreement further underline a strong Southern unity that promotes norm expansion and enables the resilience of differential treatment for LDCs. This runs counter to expectations that the rise of Brazil, China, and India would blur North–South divides. The proposals reviewed above push for expansion of the normative frontier in three ways. Firstly, the push for extensions for the developing country group as a whole goes beyond the assumption that the 1995 schedules were to be the final say on transition flexibilities. Secondly, the LDC proposals for a collective extension run counter to the individual, application-based procedure envisaged in TRIPS. Lastly, the promotion of permanent exemptions for LDCs marks a significant attempt at expanding existing SDT rights. The latter strategy holds particular currency as LDCs recently (at the time of writing) submitted a request for a further transition schedule extension encompassing the duration of their status as an LDC, as well as a further 12 years following graduation from the LDC Group (IP/C/W/668 of 1 October 2020). In keeping with the legislative trends described above however, in June 2021 LDCs were not granted exemptions but instead gained a transition period extension until 2034 (IP/C/88 of 29 June 2021).

Cumulatively, these proposals accentuate a process of resilience concerning the rights of the LDC sub-group. On the one hand, the narrowing of the group of rights-holders to LDCs marks a fragmentation of differential treatment. On the other hand, proposals by Global South actors aimed at norm expansion clash with efforts by developed states to achieve norm erosion. Together, these trends result in severely limited norm expansion as LDCs only manage to get transition schedule extensions, albeit at a collective instead of an individual level. The continued validity of the differential treatment norm, as evidenced in these extensions, thus signals an overall trend of resilience amidst heavy contestations.

While during the first conflict moment lacking coordination between developing countries allowed for the adoption of TRIPS-plus provisions in a flurry of trade agreements, the more self-assertive tone from developing countries thereafter balances out the international stage. This deadlock between developing country states trying to promote flexibilities and Quad Group states trying to promote TRIPS-plus provisions in turn limits potential negotiation areas between the two blocs.

In a nutshell, the use of non-multilateral fora to engender a TRIPS-plus push, as well as stronger coordination between Brazil, China, and India from the mid-2000s onwards has driven a vocal defence of implementation flexibilities by larger traders. We thus find that in the case of the TRIPS regime, the economic rise of Brazil, China, and India does not necessarily undermine their unity with the Global South – in contrast to negotiations on agriculture (cf. Chapter 5).

Continued divides over the utility of IP protection for development purposes provide the main ideological backdrop to the alignment of Brazil, China, and India with Southern coalitions. As we have seen in the second conflict moment, the rights of LDCs can evolve into a significant arena of conflict as the small issue of transition schedules for LDCs has become a proxy issue for larger divides on IPR, development, and integration into the world trading system.

This chapter also sheds light on the role of Brazil, China, and India in global governance. The case of transition periods shows that they are willing to support a key norm for developing countries – SDT – even when its applicability is limited to LDCs. Their willingness to side with Southern coalitions helped to renew transition periods for LDCs in the 2010s on TRIPS. However, this unity – driven by shared interests in maintaining 'TRIPS flexibilities' as well as political South–South ties – did not necessarily tip the balance of power at the negotiation table towards SDT expansion because major developed countries were also relatively united in their opposition. On the flipside, the support of Brazil, China, and India for the LDC proposal arguably prevented further norm erosion. The fact that, so far, LDCs have been successful in getting extensions to their transition schedules shows that differential treatment for this sub-group of developing countries remains resilient over time. It remains to be seen, however, whether IPR conflicts will continue to fall along North–South lines.

NOTES

1. In March 2022 the United States (US), European Union (EU), India, and South Africa agreed upon a draft waiver text. In practice, this would give all developing countries accounting for less than 10 per cent of global COVID-19 vaccine exports permission to manufacture vaccines for three–five years without consent from patent-holders (Shalal and Farge 2022).
2. These could include perceptions of fairness (Narlikar 2006) or other legitimacy concerns (Weinhardt 2020).
3. Interviews were conducted via telephone in October 2020.
4. Statements were chosen that stemmed from Brazil, China, India and the Quad Group, however other actors that were particularly vocal in the debates, such as the delegates of Egypt, Switzerland, the African Group, or the LDC Group were also included.
5. Compare Arrow's 'Information Paradox' in Arrow (1962).
6. Former Trade Delegate Interview, 5 October 2020; Former Trade Delegate Interview, 6 October 2020; Former Trade Delegate Interview, 6 October 2020 (b).

7. Former Trade Delegate Interview, 5 October 2020.
8. Former Trade Delegate Interview, 5 October 2020.
9. Former Trade Delegate Interview, 9 October 2020.
10. Former Trade Delegate Interview, 9 October 2020; Former Trade Delegate Interview, 14 October 2020.
11. Former Trade Delegate Interview, 9 October 2020.
12. Former Trade Delegate Interview, 14 October 2020.
13. Former Trade Delegate Interview, 14 October 2020.
14. Former Trade Delegate Interview, 6 October 2020 (b).
15. Former Trade Delegate Interview, 6 October 2020; Former Trade Delegate Interview, 6 October 2020 (b).
16. Former Trade Delegate Interview, 5 October 2020.
17. Former Trade Delegate Interview, 6 October 2020 (b).
18. Former Trade Delegate Interview, 9 October 2020.
19. The 2016 New Delhi Trade Ministers' Meeting stressed 'the importance of cooperation on intellectual property rights (IPR) towards the development of a BRICS perspective that will be informed by national priorities'. The formation of a 2010–2014 Joint Action Plan between Brazil and China, including a Working Group on Intellectual Property, fits in with this new cohesion. (BRICS 2016; De Menezes 2018).
20. Former Trade Delegate Interview, 9 October 2020.
21. Former Trade Delegate Interview, 9 October 2020.
22. Former Trade Delegate Interview, 6 October 2020.
23. Former Trade Delegate Interview, 6 October 2020.
24. Former Trade Delegate Interview, 6 October 2020.
25. Former Trade Delegate Interview, 5 October 2020; Former Trade Delegate Interview, 6 October 2020; Former Trade Delegate Interview, 6 October 2020 (b); Former Trade Delegate Interview, 9 October 2020; Former Trade Delegate Interview, 14 October 2020.

7. Conflicts over climate mitigation commitments

Klaus Dingwerth

7.1 INTRODUCTION

At their first annual conference in 1995, parties to the UN Framework Convention on Climate Change (UNFCCC) agreed to exempt developing countries from commitments to limit their greenhouse gas (GHG) emissions. The conference is known as COP-1 (Conference of the Parties). As it took place in Berlin, the decision countries took at COP-1 was named the 'Berlin Mandate'. Sixteen years later, the same parties – plus a few new additions – convened for COP-17 (2011) in Durban. This time, they put an end to the exemption they had agreed upon in Berlin. Instead, they launched negotiations for creating a new legal instrument that would be 'applicable to all parties'.

In this chapter, we ask two questions: What characterizes and distinguishes the decisions taken in Berlin and Durban? And what made each decision possible? Additional questions follow from this starting point: Which confluence of factors contributed to the decision to exempt developing countries from new commitments in future efforts to negotiate a protocol to the 1992 UN Framework Convention? How did those factors change over time to force an unmaking of that distinction? And, above all, which role did the perception and reality of the rise of Brazil, China, and India – and possibly other 'major emitters' – play in this context?

For our purpose, the Berlin Mandate is a useful conflict case study for the early years of regime formation. The decision to launch negotiations on a protocol to the UN Framework Convention in which developing countries would incur 'no new commitments' further solidified the distinction the UN Framework Convention had drawn between Annex I and non-Annex I parties (cf. Chapter 3). Although it did not fully determine the subsequent decisions, the decision set the terms of international climate law and politics for at least the following decade. It set the regime on a specific institutional path and provided the immediate backdrop for the adoption of the Kyoto Protocol in 1997. Moreover, the decision is a particularly strong example of the unconditional leadership norm that characterized the climate regime during the early years of international climate governance. According to this norm, the notion that developed countries should 'take the lead' implied that they, and they alone, should accept legally binding targets and timetables (Gupta 2014: 70–72). Finally, the exemption of developing countries from new commitments in the Berlin Mandate is of interest because the United States (US) as well as other developed countries had signalled their preference for a different solution. This not only turned developing country commitments into a major bone of contention at the Berlin conference (Grubb et al. 1999: 46), it also rendered the outcome of COP-1 (1995) puzzling.

At COP-17 (2011) in Durban, states again made a decision to begin negotiations on a new climate treaty. More precisely, parties agreed to 'launch a process to develop a protocol, another legal instrument or an agreed outcome with legal force under the Convention applicable to all Parties'. To conduct the new negotiations, parties established a new subsidiary body of the UN Framework Convention. Known as the Ad Hoc Working Group on the Durban Platform for Enhanced Action (ADP), this body was to complete its work 'as early as possible but no later than 2015'. Substantively, the work was to be informed by science – notably the latest Intergovernmental Panel on Climate Change (IPCC) report – and parties were specifically requested 'to explore options for a range of actions that can close the ambition gap with a view to ensuring the highest possible mitigation efforts by all Parties' (FCCC/CP/2011/9/Add.1 of 15 March 2012: Decision 1/CP.17, Arts. 2, 4–8; see also ENB 12/534 of 13 December 2011: 28).[1]

The Berlin Mandate and the Durban decision to establish the ADP lend themselves for a comparison because they are functionally equivalent: both served to launch negotiations on a new legal agreement that marked a turning point in the history of international climate governance. At the same time, the decisions differ in two major ways. First, while the Berlin Mandate launched a process aimed at 'strengthening of the commitments of the Parties *included in Annex I*', the decision to establish the ADP referred to a legal outcome '*applicable to all parties*' (italics added).

Second, the Berlin Mandate makes ample reference to equity, to the principle of common but differentiated responsibilities (CBDR), to the 'specific needs and concerns of developing country Parties', to the right to development, to 'the fact that the largest share of historical and current global emissions of greenhouse gases has originated in developed countries', and to prevailing differences in per capita emissions (FCCC/CP/1995/7/Add.1 of 6 June 1995: Decision 1/CP.1, para. 1[a]–[f]). By contrast, the decision on establishing the ADP does *none of that*. It recognizes that 'climate change represents an urgent and potentially irreversible threat to human societies and the planet' and that it therefore 'requires to be urgently addressed by all Parties'. It '[notes] with grave concern' the 'significant gap' between emission pledges and known pathways to remain below two degrees of global warming. And it concludes that 'fulfilling the ultimate objective of the Convention will require strengthening of the multilateral, rule-based regime under the Convention'. The latter phrase – 'under the Convention' – remains the only hint that principles such as equity and CBDR shall continue to guide the development of the new legal agreement (Maguire 2013: 265–267). In this way, the balance shifts from differentiation based on the principle of CBDR to 'symmetry' signalled through a new emphasis on the efforts of 'all Parties'. In the terminology we have introduced in Chapter 1 of this book, both differences signal a clear unmaking of differential treatment norms for developing countries as a group – first in the way special rights and obligations are institutionalized, and second in the emphasis placed or not placed on the principle of CBDR.

In the remainder of this chapter, we trace the processes that made these opposing outcomes possible. We start with a reconstruction of the negotiations that led to the two decisions in 1995 and 2011, respectively. A further section then examines how the strength and unity of bargaining coalitions, the specific dynamics of normative contestation, and the opportunities offered by the institutional structures at the time enabled or constrained certain choices. For our analysis of the first conflict, we rely on the official UNFCCC documentation of COP-1 (Berlin, 28 March to 7 April 1995) as well as of the two preceding sessions of the International Negotiating Committee (INC-10, 22 August to 2 September 1994 and INC-11, New York, 6–17 February), on the meeting reports offered by Hermann Ott (1994) for INC-10 and by the IISD's *Earth Negotiations Bulletin* (ENB) for INC-11 and COP-1, and on the accounts participants and other observers provide in the secondary literature.[2] For COP-17 (2011), our sources include the official UNFCCC documentation of the climate meetings in Bangkok, Bonn, Panama, and Durban (all in 2011), the ENB reports as well as the 'Climate Updates' the Third World Network (TWN) provided for these meetings. Where appropriate, we complement our analysis with accounts of the meetings provided in the secondary literature and in media reports about the negotiations.

In sum, our analysis adds to the existing literature in two important ways. First, rather than comparing negotiations on the Kyoto Protocol with negotiations on the Paris Agreement, we put the spotlight on two conflict moments that gave rise to the respective mandates for the negotiations of these major treaties. For a reconstruction of the historical development of special rights and obligations in the international climate regime, these mandates are particularly relevant. Second, the results of our analysis highlight how the interplay of institutions, ideas, and interests made both the Berlin Mandate and its dismantling in Durban possible. In brief, prior institutional decisions were a strong background force in both conflicts. They defined the rules of the game, prestructured the terrain of possible outcomes, and shaped the strategies different actors chose to pursue their ends. In the foreground, the members of the Umbrella Group – among them notably Australia, Canada, Japan, New Zealand, and the US – pursued a two-fold strategy. First, they delayed meaningful climate action to a date after 2012. Second, they embarked on a strong and continuous effort to delegitimize the CBDR principle and its implementation in the international climate regime. As our reconstruction in this chapter reveals, this strategy paid off in the long run and it contributed significantly to the unmaking of differential treatment as we used to know it in Bali (2007), Copenhagen (2009), Durban (2011), and eventually Paris (2015).

7.2 NEGOTIATING THE BERLIN MANDATE

In this as well as in the following section, we reconstruct the key dynamics that characterized the negotiation processes leading up to two decisions on the same issue: a new mandate for climate negotiations. The first of these decisions occurred in 1995, the second in 2011. Since the rise of Brazil, China, and India falls squarely between these dates, reconstructing the two conflicts can serve as a basis for examining how global power shifts affected the conflict dynamics.

7.2.1 The Run-up to the Berlin Mandate: INC-10 and INC-11

The full title of the first decision of the first Conference of the Parties to the UN Framework Convention reads 'The Berlin Mandate: Review of the adequacy of Article 4, paragraph 2(a) and (b), of the Convention, including proposals related to a protocol and decisions on follow-up' (FCCC/CP/1995/7/Add.1 of 6 June 1995: Decision 1/CP.1). Because the subparagraphs listed in the title of the decision deal with the specific commitments of 'developed country Parties and other Parties included in Annex I', the climate change negotiations listed this item under the heading of the 'adequacy of commitments'. The need to discuss this item followed directly from the text of the 1992 UN Framework Convention. In Article 4, paragraph 2(d), the Convention requires that the Conference of the Parties 'shall, at its first session, review the adequacy of subparagraphs (a) and (b) above', that its review should be based on best available science, and that 'based on this review, the Conference of the Parties shall take appropriate action', including the possibility of adopting 'amendments to the commitments in subparagraphs (a) and (b) above'.

In principle, the review of the adequacy of commitments thus had a fixed deadline, but an open outcome (A/AC.237/47 of 16 December 1993: 7–10; A/AC.237/65 of 25 July 1994: 6–8). A first option for parties to the Convention was to decide that the commitments were adequate. In this case, no further action was required, and COP-1 (1995) would simply time the second review – scheduled by the Convention to take place 'no later than 31 December 1998' (Article 4, para. 2[d]) – or leave such a decision to future meetings. A second option was to conclude that evidence was still insufficient to allow for a proper conclusion on the adequacy of commitments. Finally, the review could, as it eventually did, conclude that commitments were inadequate. In this case, states once more faced several options: to amend the Convention, to adopt a protocol, or to adopt a legally nonbinding resolution that would 'clarify or interpret the relevant text' of the Convention (A/AC.237/47 of 16 December 1993: 10).

Regarding these outcomes, the constellation of interests had barely changed since the adoption of the UN Framework Convention in 1992. Roughly speaking, both the developed world and the developing world each fell into three camps. Among developed countries, the European Communities (EC) – with 12 members in 1992 and 15 members in 1995 – included several countries that were technological leaders, that had 'called for action on climate change ever since the issue emerged politically', and that had already adopted 'indicative targets' for limiting their GHG emissions at the national level (Grubb et al. 1999: 30; see also Paterson 1996: 39–42). As a negotiation block, the EC thus 'tried to demonstrate a leadership role since the beginning' (Gupta 2014: 156). It favoured a climate regime based on the precautionary principle, aimed at minimizing the negative effects of climate change through a stabilization of GHG emissions in industrialized countries, and called for increased energy efficiency in developing countries.

The US was more reluctant to seek strong international action, in part because of its 'low-price energy culture' (Grubb et al. 1999: 31) and the related fear that ambitious emission reduction targets would be costly. Together with Australia, Canada, Japan, and New Zealand, the US formed the so-called JUSCANZ coalition.[3] Facing 'greater difficulty than the EU in reducing emissions below 1990 levels' (Grubb et al. 1999: 34), the members of this coalition acted as a counterweight to the EC position, notably on the question of quantified reduction targets. Finally, the Russian Federation and other central and eastern European countries primarily fought for the recognition of their interests through the creation of a category of countries with economies in transition (CEITs) (Bodansky 1994; Grubb et al. 1999: 27–35; Gupta 2014: 154–161; Oberthür 1993: 38–41, 126–132; Oberthür and Ott 2000: 40–49; Paterson 1996: 49–71).

Among developing countries, the members of the Alliance of Small Island States (AOSIS) pushed for early and meaningful internationally coordinated mitigation action as well as for funding for adaptation. This interest distinguished the AOSIS members from the bulk of the G-77 (Group of 77) and China whose main emphasis was on the 'ecological debt' of industrialized countries, on development concerns, and on the need to combine climate-related commitments with financial and technology transfer from industrialized countries (see also Chapter 3). Finally, the Organization of the Petroleum Exporting Countries (OPEC) countries had a strong interest in preventing ambitious international climate action. In the negotiations, they emphasized scientific uncertainty and stressed that solutions would need to consider the special situation of developing countries whose economies depended on the exports of fossil fuels (Grubb et al. 1999: 35–36; Gupta 2014: 161–169; Oberthür 1993: 41–44, 122–124; Oberthür and Ott 2000: 52–58).

Against this background, the terms of the review of the adequacy of commitments were agreed at the Ninth Session of the INC (INC-9 in 1994). In their discussions on the adequacy of commitments, delegations also considered 'the need for broader action beyond the year 2000 … based on the understanding that the provisions of [Article 4 of the 1992 UN Framework Convention] refer to the present decade' (ENB 12/1 of 6 February 1995: 1). Subsequently, the issue was discussed at three further meetings: INC-10 in August and September 1994, INC-11 in February 1995, and COP-1 in March and April 1995.

In the run-up to INC-10, the interim Secretariat prepared a compilation of positions parties had taken on the review of the adequacy of commitments. On the tensions around developing country commitments, the Secretariat note informs that (A/AC.237/65 of 25 July 1994: 16):

> Many countries felt that since the commitments of Article 4.2(a) and (b) apply to Annex I Parties only, any additional commitments should be restricted to this group of Parties. However, it was concluded by several countries that in the light of the objective of the Convention and the need for a global approach, all countries would have to contribute to the further elaboration of the Convention, with developed countries continuing to take the lead. Consequently, it was considered that non-Annex I Parties would also have to be engaged somehow in additional commitments and/or should be encouraged to play a greater role in combating climate change. Suggestions in this regard included more detailed communication requirements, joint implementation activities and limitation of emission growth for certain more industrialized developing countries.

In the two weeks of negotiations at INC-10, parties made little progress. Germany introduced a position paper that outlined elements of a future protocol. Together with a stabilization target and a call for reductions, the paper included 'a long list of measures in the field of energy, transport and tax reform' (Ott 1994). Yet, only few delegations lent their support and the overall response to the German proposal has been described as 'reserved' (Ott 1994; see also Paterson 1996: 68).

The G-77 and China, moreover, were strongly opposed. First, they stressed 'the need to focus on the implementation of existing commitments of Annex

I Parties' (A/AC.237/76 of 10 October 1994: 15). Second, the G-77 and China responded specifically to the demand that 'certain more advanced developing countries' should accept limitations in emission growth. This demand had received strong support from members of the JUSCANZ group, and it now also figured in the 'German Elements Paper' (A/AC.237/L.23/Add.1 of 27 September 1994). The G-77 and China noted that 'any suggestions relating to further commitments for non-Annex I Parties were not acceptable'. Some countries added that 'any consideration of commitments by non-Annex I Parties must necessarily wait for the effective demonstration of leadership by Annex I countries as called for in the Convention, by means of real reduction of their emissions of greenhouse gases' (A/AC.237/76 of 10 October 1994: 15; see also Ott 1994).

After INC-10, the interim Secretariat provided a synthesis of the national submissions it had received from state parties to the 1992 UN Framework Convention thus far. Of the 15 countries reporting, nine 'projected an increase to the year 2000 in the absence of additional measures' (A/AC.237/81 of 7 December 1994: 7). Summarizing information available in early 1995, Paterson (1996: 69) argues that 'of the major ten emitters of CO_2, only the UK, Germany and Russia … were likely to meet their stabilization commitment, with the emissions of France, Japan, the US, Canada and Italy all likely to rise, as were those of the EU as a whole'. These numbers lent support to an emerging consensus among Organisation for Economic Co-operation and Development (OECD) countries that the existing commitments were insufficient to meet the objectives of the UN Framework Convention. Nonetheless, the US rejected the call for a protocol with 'targets and timetables' and instead proposed a vaguely formulated 'formal process for considering next steps', aimed at 'establishing a "new aim"' (Krägenow 1995: 57; Oberthür and Ott 1995: 145–146; Ott 1994).

Based on these reservations, governments gathering at INC-11 could not yet agree that current commitments for Annex I parties were inadequate. While a draft decision had included such language (A/AC.237/WG.I/L.28 of 16 February 1995: 50–51), that conclusion was omitted from the final decision. Instead, the latter merely '[recognized] that Article 4.2 (a) and (b) is only a first step' towards the objective of the Convention and that it would be reviewed at COP-1 (A/AC.237/91/Add.1 of 8 March 1995; see also ENB 12/11 of 20 February 1995; Oberthür and Ott 1995: 146). Moreover, the meeting also considered a proposal for a protocol which Trinidad and Tobago had submitted for COP-1 (1995) on behalf of AOSIS. This document, known as the AOSIS Protocol, represented the strongest support for a targets and timetables approach thus far. In line with non-governmental organization (NGO) proposals made at INC-10, it required each Annex I party to 'reduce its 1990 level of anthropogenic emissions of carbon dioxide by at least 20 percent by the year

2005'. On the particularly tricky question of developing country commitments, it further proposed that (A/AC.237/L.23 of 27 September 1994: Article 3.3),

> any Party not included in Annex I of the Convention that has expressed its intention to be bound by Article 4.2(a) and (b) of the Convention in accordance with Article 4.2(g) of the Convention, may in its instrument of ratification, acceptance, approval or accession to this Protocol, or at any time thereafter, notify the Depositary that it intends to be bound by Articles 3 to 5 of this Protocol.

This formulation opened the door for voluntary commitments from developing countries without openly challenging the unity among the G-77 and China. Yet, as Russia and the OPEC countries opposed negotiations on further commitments and as there was 'little movement on either side', agreement emerged neither on the adequacy of commitments in general, nor on the specific proposals submitted by AOSIS and by Germany (ENB 12/11 of 20 February 1995: 9; Oberthür and Ott 1995: 146).

7.2.2 The Berlin Mandate

Seven weeks later, governments eventually reached such an agreement at COP-1 (1995), though only at the last minute (ENB 12/21 of 10 April 1995: 2; Oberthür and Ott 1995). In its opening sentence, the Berlin Mandate thus informs that,

> '*the Conference of the Parties*, at its first session, *having reviewed* Article 4, paragraph 2(a) and (b), of the 1992 UN Framework Convention on Climate Change, and *having concluded* that these subparagraphs are not adequate, *agrees* to begin a process to enable it to take appropriate action for the period beyond 2000' (FCCC/CP/1995/7/Add.1 of 6 June 1995: Decision 1/CP.1, preambular clause; italics in original).

The remainder of the decision then spells out which principles will guide that process (para. 1), what the process will aim for (para. 2), and how it will be organized (paras. 3–6).

In terms of the principles that would guide negotiations, the Berlin Mandate reaffirmed the specific needs and concerns of developing countries, their 'legitimate needs … for the achievement of sustained economic growth and the eradication of poverty' as well as their right to sustainable development. Moreover, it stresses the historical responsibility of developed countries as well as the 'still relatively low' per capita emissions of developing countries, while noting that 'the share of global emissions originating in developing countries will grow to meet their social and development needs' (FCCC/CP/1995/7/Add.1 of 6 June 1995: Decision 1/CP.1, para. 1[a]–1[d]). On the way forward, three aspects of the Berlin Mandate are of interest for the purpose of our study. They include the following provisions:

- that the process will aim at strengthening the commitments for 'developed countries/other Parties included in Annex I' not only in relation to policies and measures, but also through setting 'quantified limitation and reduction objectives within specified time-frames, such as 2005, 2010 and 2020, for their anthropogenic emissions by sources and removals by sinks of greenhouse gases not controlled by the Montreal Protocol' (para. 2[a]);
- that, in setting such targets, the process would '[take] into account the differences in starting points and approaches, economic structures and resource bases, the need to maintain strong and sustainable economic growth, available technologies and other individual circumstances, as well as the need for equitable and appropriate contributions by each of these Parties to the global effort' (para. 2[a]);
- and that the process would '*not introduce any new commitments for Parties not included in Annex I*, but reaffirm existing commitments in Article 4.1 and continue to advance the implementation of these commitments in order to achieve sustainable development, taking into account Article 4.3, 4.5 and 4.7' (para. 2[b]; italics added).

The final part of the Berlin Mandate then stipulates that the so-called AOSIS Protocol would continue to be 'included for consideration in the process' along with other proposals for discussion. Moreover, the Berlin Mandate established a new working group for the negotiation process and asked the group 'to ensure completion of the work as early as possible in 1997, with a view to adopting the results at the third session of the Conference of the Parties' (FCCC/CP/1995/7/Add.1 of 6 June 1995: Decision 1/CP.1, paras. 5–6).

As the preceding account has already shown, the decision to start negotiations without new commitments for developing countries was not straightforward. Only a few months earlier, for example, the official report of INC-10 (1994) had noted that 'some … countries were of the opinion that action by Annex I Parties alone would be insufficient in the light of the objective of the Convention and therefore raised the question how global action could be promoted' (A/AC.237/76 of 10 October 1994: 16; see also Oberthür and Ott 1995: 145). Among those countries, the US had taken the position that 'any new commitments for industrialized states would have to be accompanied by commitments for some more developed G 77-States' (Ott 1994; see also Oberthür and Ott 1995: 145). Similarly, Australia had called for a 'gradual, greater involvement of developing countries in commitments and action to reduce emissions' (A/AC.237/MISC.43 of 7 December 1994: 5), while Austria had commented that 'the future development of the Convention will also need the contribution by at least some of the more advanced developing countries' and that 'the considerations for the future negotiating process should take this necessity into account' (A/AC.237/MISC.43 of 7 December 1994: 7). Between INC-10 (1994) and INC-11 (1995), Germany had, in its 'German Elements Paper', acknowledged that developed countries would need to take the lead. Yet, the German government had also seen a need 'to work towards balanced commitments on the part of industrialized and developing countries' (A/AC.237/L.23/Add.1 of 27 September 1994: 3), and its position had been echoed by other European Union (EU) member states (Greece, A/AC.237/MISC.36 and Add.1 of 3 June 1994: 48; The Netherlands, A/AC.237/MISC.36 and Add.1 of 3 June 1994: 54). Finally, Russia had joined the group of sceptics when it suggested that 'even the best efforts leading to reduction of GHG emissions by Annex I Parties, might not achieve the ultimate goal of the Convention' because 'some Parties to the Convention do not take commitments to limit or stabilize the level of their GHG emission' (A/AC.237/MISC.43/Add.1 of 6 February 1995: 3).

If opposition to the exemption of developing countries from new commitments was so widespread in September 1994 and February 1995, how could such an exemption become an integral part of the unconditional leadership norm that emerged in the Berlin Mandate negotiated only two months later? As we will see later in this chapter, two shifts in position were central. First, the EU's concession to exempt developing countries from new commitments allowed the G-77 and China to support negotiations on stronger mitigation commitments. Second, US acceptance of such an agreement added pressure on the remaining JUSCANZ members, on Russia, and on the OPEC members. As a result, any attempt to answer what made the Berlin Mandate possible will need to account for the shifts in the positions of the EU, the G-77, and China, and of the US as well as other parties who had fought hard against stronger commitments, let alone ones that fell exclusively to developed countries. We will examine these shifts in more detail once we have compared the decision on the Berlin Mandate with the decision to dismantle the 'Berlin firewall' taken at COP-17 (2011) in Durban.

7.3 DISMANTLING THE BERLIN MANDATE

Like the previous section, this section first recollects the main steps in the decision-making process leading up to the decision to establish the ADP. Subsequently, we focus on those aspects of the decision that relate most directly to differential treatment norms and discuss which specific steps in the decision-making process require further analysis.

7.3.1 From Bali to Durban: The Lead-up to the Negotiations

As we have outlined in Chapter 3, the stage for the decision to launch negotiations for a new legal agreement that would apply to 'all parties' had already been set at COP-13 (2007) in Bali, COP-15 (2009) in Copenhagen, and COP-16 (2010) in Cancún. With the formal establishment of the Ad Hoc Working Group on Long-Term Cooperative Action under the Convention (AWG-LCA), the Bali Action Plan had initiated a 'Convention track' in parallel to ongoing negotiations over a second commitment period for the Kyoto Protocol. Moreover, the Bali Action Plan had dropped references to Annex I and non-Annex I countries and instead merely distinguished between 'developed' and 'developing countries'. Finally, it had introduced the notion of 'nationally appropriate mitigation actions' (NAMAs) for developing country parties (FCCC/CP/2007/6/Add.1 of 14 March 2008: Decision 1/CP.13, para. 1[b]). At COP-15 (2009), states had subsequently defined a simple format for communicating such mitigation commitments and actions in two appendices to the Copenhagen Accord (FCCC/CP/2009/11/Add.1 of 30 March 2010: Decision 2/CP.15). These formats reintroduced the distinction between Annex I and non-Annex I parties when they envisaged quantified economy-wide emissions targets for 2020 for the former and a listing of mitigation actions for the latter.

Finally, at COP-16 (2010), states formally took note of the pledges each government had submitted. These pledges were summarized in two documents. The first was a 'Compilation of economy-wide emission reduction targets to be implemented by Parties included in Annex I to the Convention' (FCCC/SB/2011/INF.1/Rev.1 of 7 June 2011). Here, developed countries committed to cutting their emissions by between 5 and 40 per cent in relation to individually selected base years until 2020. In many pledges, however, the more ambitious targets were conditional on developing country commitments or action. Australia, for instance, was willing to commit to 20–25 per cent reductions 'if the world agrees to an ambitious global deal capable of stabilizing levels of GHG in the atmosphere at 450 ppm carbon dioxide equivalent (CO2 eq) or lower'. If such agreement was not forthcoming, Australia's unconditional target remained limited to a 5 per cent emissions cut. Similarly, the EU was willing to reduce emissions by 30 per cent compared with 1990 levels 'provided that other developed countries commit themselves to comparable emission reductions *and that developing countries contribute adequately according to their responsibilities and respective capabilities*'. Echoing this signal to the likes of Brazil, China, and India, Japan likewise announced a 25 per cent target 'premised on the establishment of a fair and effective international framework *in which all major economies participate and on agreement by those economies on ambitious targets*' (FCCC/SB/2011/INF.1/Rev.1 of 7 June 2011: paras. 5, 9, 14; italics added).

The second document was a 'Compilation of information on nationally appropriate mitigation actions to be implemented by Parties not included in Annex I to the Convention' (FCCC/AWGLCA/2011/INF.1 of 18 March 2011). In this counterpart to the first document, developing countries communicated their voluntary ambitions. As one of the 'major emitters' sought out by developed countries, Brazil listed a total of 11 actions which it anticipated 'to lead to an expected emissions reduction of between 36.1 per cent and 38.9 per cent *below its projected emissions* in 2020' (ibid. para. 30; italics added). China announced three objectives. First, it aimed 'to lower its CO2 emissions *per unit of GDP* by 40–45 per cent by 2020 compared with the 2005 level'. Second, it sought 'to increase the *share of non-fossil fuels* in primary energy consumption to around 15 per cent by 2020'; and third, it envisaged 'to increase forest coverage by 40 million ha and forest stock volume by 1.3 billion m3 by 2020 compared with the 2005 levels' (ibid. para. 43; italics added). India announced that it would 'endeavour to reduce the *emissions intensity of its GDP* by 20–25 per cent by 2020 compared with the 2005 level' (ibid. para. 71, italics added) while Indonesia (ibid. para. 72) and South Africa (ibid. para. 155) communicated that their voluntary mitigation actions would aim to reduce their respective GHG emissions by between 26 and 34 per cent compared to business-as-usual scenarios. Finally, Mexico and South Korea as the two OECD members that were not Annex I parties announced a 30 per cent reduction compared with business-as-usual (Mexico: ibid. para. 94; Republic of Korea: ibid. para. 150).

7.3.2 Bangkok, Bonn, and Panama: The Immediate Run-up to COP-17 (2011)

The set-up we have sketched indicates the general direction the negotiations on 'long-term cooperative action' had taken by 2011. Yet, three key questions remained open. First, would states be able to agree to a second commitment period under the Kyoto Protocol – and if so, what would commitments look like? Second, how would differentiation be organized in a new global agreement? And third, which specific contributions would be expected from 'advanced developing countries', 'major economies', or 'major emitters'? In 2011, answers to these questions were sought in a series of international negotiations.

At the Bangkok Climate Change Talks (3–8 April 2011), the linkage between the two negotiation tracks was at the centre of debate. In the Ad Hoc Working Group on Further Commitments for Annex I Parties under the Kyoto Protocol (AWG-KP), several developing countries, including Brazil, China, and India, put pressure on developed countries to accept a second commitment period under the Kyoto Protocol. Speaking on behalf of the G-77 and China, Argentina emphasized 'that a second commitment period is necessary for a successful outcome in Durban'. Similarly, China called the failure to secure a second commitment period 'unacceptable' and asked Annex I parties not to 'come up with any conditionalities'. This position was echoed by the Arab Group for which Egypt noted that 'continuity of the Kyoto Protocol is a condition for any agreement under the AWG-LCA' (ENB 12/499 of 11 April 2011: 9, 12).

Developed countries focussed on the ultimate objective of the UN Framework Convention instead. The EU, for instance, argued that 'the starting point of discussions should be logical consequences of maintaining environmental integrity'. Because exemptions for some countries were known to cause carbon leakage, the EU maintained that 'discussions should not only consider Annex I party commitments but provide clarity on actions by non-Annex I parties'. As a result, it sought to continue negotiations on both tracks in parallel. This was a clear indication that the EU would not accept a second commitment period under the Kyoto Protocol lightly, but instead tie its acceptance to progress on a new 'global, ambitious and binding post-2012 regime'. Other countries were even more reluctant to take on new commitments under the Kyoto Protocol after 2012. Notably, Japan and Russia announced at the end of the Bangkok meeting that they would not take part in a second commitment period (ENB 12/499 of 11 April 2011: 9–12; TWN 2011b). Finally, the position of AOSIS members was aligned with the G-77 and China on most issues. However, AOSIS members viewed the attempt to link both tracks to obtain mitigation commitments from 'major emitters' more positively (ENB 12/499 of 11 April 2011: 13).

At the subsequent UN Climate Change Conference in Bonn (6–17 June 2011) and the Panama City Climate Change Conference (1–7 October 2011), both sides continued to make progress in one track conditional on progress in the other. Yet, actual progress remained limited. Instead, Canada joined Japan and Russia in clarifying its intention not to commit to a second commitment period under the Kyoto Protocol. As a result, any prospective deal in this track was now limited to legally binding commitments for European countries plus possibly Australia and New Zealand.

In discussions under the 'Convention track', moreover, developed countries sought a new terminology that might allow for broader agreement. Arguing that a new agreement should be 'adaptable to evolving circumstances' (ENB 12/521 of 10 October 2011: 11), they challenged the interpretation of the CBDR principle as applying to a fixed set of states listed in Annex I and Annex II. The US position was particularly clear in this regard. In Bonn, it proposed a legally binding protocol in which developed countries as well as developing countries 'with greater responsibility' would accept mitigation targets in a '2020 timeframe', and it further suggested that mitigation commitments would not be stagnant but '[reflect] changing circumstances of developing countries' (TWN 2011c: 1). In Panama, the US reaffirmed this position. Arguing that four of the ten top emitters were non-Annex I parties, it held that the UN Framework Convention needed a revision to 'reflect today's and tomorrow's economic realities, and not that of 1992' (TWN 2011d: 32–37). Its preference was therefore either to let some parties graduate or to replace the rigid annexes with a more continuous scale of differentiation. In its statements, moreover, the US emphasized that the legal quality of future commitments would need to be 'symmetrical', although the content could distinguish, for instance, between economy-wide commitments for developed countries and more specific commitments for developing countries (TWN 2011d: 36). Further proposals mentioned the possibility of agreeing on 'different peaking years' for developed and developing countries (ENB 12/513 of 20 June 2011: 22) or the standardization of developing countries' NAMAs (ENB 12/521 of 10 October 2011: 8). Developing countries, however, rejected these proposals.

7.3.3 The Negotiations in Durban

For COP-17 (2011) in Durban, Russia had submitted a proposal for amending Article 4.2 of the 1992 UN Framework Convention. The proposal envisaged that the list of countries in Annex I and Annex II would be reviewed periodically. It was motivated by the observation of 'changes in economic and technological development that have taken place since the adoption of the Convention in 1992 and are continuing to do so'. As a result, the letter accompanying the proposed amendment suggested, 'a periodic review of Annexes I and II to the Convention in the light of the most up-to-date scientific information, objectively reflecting the dynamics and reality of the current socio-economic development of the Parties to the Convention' was necessary (TWN 2012: 57). Delegations fought over the proposed amendment mid-way through COP-17 (2011) on 6 December. When discussions signalled a stalemate, the Russian delegation suggested that, because all means for forging a consensus on the proposed amendment had been exhausted, a vote should be held in the plenary meeting of COP-17 (2011). In line with the UN Framework Convention, this would have allowed parties to accept the amendment based on a three-quarters majority. In the heated debate that followed, however, developing countries remained clear in their view that the means for reaching a consensus had not been exhausted (TWN 2012: 57–60). Eventually, parties agreed to take up the issue at future conferences and to 'include the item on the provisional agenda for COP 18' (ENB 12/534 of 13 December 2011: 4).

The conflict over the Russian proposal sent two important signals. First, it showed that the way differentiation was organized under the 1992 UN Framework Convention was contested not merely by the US but by many other states who held commitments under Article 4.2 as well. Second, it confirmed the impression that the way Annex I and Annex II had been set up by the UN Framework Convention precluded meaningful adjustment. Because it demonstrated the impossibility of amending the Annexes, the episode thus lent further support to those who called for a general overhaul of the differentiation regime.

Despite these reservations, a key aspect of the Durban Conference remained the continuation of the Kyoto Protocol through a second commitment period. China, speaking on behalf of the BASIC countries – Brazil, South Africa, India, and China – stated that 'defining a second commitment period should be the main priority for Durban'. Arguing that 'it is hardly conceivable that a country would leave the Kyoto Protocol to do more', it also criticized Canada, Japan, Russia, and the US for their failure to take the lead and thereby fulfil their commitments under the UN Framework Convention (ENB 12/534 of 13 December 2011: 11; TWN 2012: 43–44). The general thrust of China's argument was echoed by other developing countries. The representative for the G-77 and China, for instance, stressed that the Kyoto Protocol was the 'cornerstone of the multilateral climate change regime' and, as such, 'must be preserved and strengthened'. Similarly, the African Group considered a second commitment period 'absolutely crucial', and AOSIS, the LDC Group, and the Arab Group all stressed that the credibility of the negotiation process depended on a second commitment period (TWN 2012: 12–13, 26–29).

This heavy emphasis on securing a second commitment period put the EU in a difficult position in the negotiations at COP-17 (2011). The US had never ratified the Kyoto Protocol. Japan, Russia, and Canada were unwilling to sign up for a second commitment period. And Australia and New Zealand left their options open. As a result, the EU was the single party that committed to renewing the Kyoto Protocol for another five- or eight-year period (Bauchmüller 2011). In its communications before Durban, it had announced a 30 per cent reduction target contingent on a new and 'inclusive' legally binding agreement. Procedurally, its exceptional position allowed the EU to play a leading role at COP-17 (2011): if developing countries wanted to save the Kyoto Protocol, the EU could define at least some conditions. Substantially, this condition was acceptance of negotiations on a new agreement 'applicable to all countries' under the Convention track (Hedegaard 2011; *Agence France Press* 2011; Dunmore 2011). As one observer noted (Clark 2011),

> The EU … went to Durban with a new negotiating position: almost alone among wealthy countries, it said it would agree to a second round of pledges under Kyoto

> when the first expired at the end of 2012. But it insisted it would do so only if the rest of the world agreed to start talks on a 'road map' towards a new pact legally binding on all.

Getting other states to accept that position was not straightforward. But eventually, the EU managed to bring the AOSIS and the LDC Group on board based on the interest all three groups shared in increasing ambition. Together with other developed countries, the EU also accepted a linkage between mitigation and funding. While calling 'for a process to deliver a new global, comprehensive and legally-binding framework to be completed by 2015', the EU thus simultaneously 'reaffirmed [its] commitment to jointly mobilize USD 100 billion annually by 2020' and agreed to a COP decision that rendered the Green Climate Fund (GCF) operational (ENB 12/534 of 13 December 2011: 14; see also Chapter 8). Finally, it reassured China and India that they would 'simply be expected to turn their earlier Cancun pledges into new legal arrangements' (ENB 12/534 of 13 December 2011: 30).

However, conflicts remained. In negotiations in the AWG-LCA track, they centred on differences over a 'shared vision for long-term cooperation', on differentiated reporting and monitoring requirements for developed and developing countries, and on enhanced action on adaptation. As negotiations moved into the second week, none of the three 'amalgamation documents' Working Group Co-Chair Daniel Reifsnyder presented on 3 December, 7 December, and 10 December helped to forge a consensus on a broad range of issues (ENB 12/529 of 5 December 2011: 3; ENB 12/532 of 8 December 2011; ENB 12/534 of 13 December: 26–27). The conflict was eventually resolved through an extension of the AWG-LCA mandate for another year and through Reifsnyder's decision to present a draft outcome document to the COP plenary for adoption as 'draft conclusions proposed by the Chair' rather than as a consensus document from the working group (FCCC/AWGLCA/2011/L.4 of 9 December 2011; see also ENB 12/534 of 13 December 2011: 26; TWN 2012: 49–53). This decision drew strong criticism from developing countries. Several parties expressed their view that the text failed to reflect the CBDR principle, did not mention historical emissions, and 'blurred the distinction between developed and developing country obligations' (TWN 2012: 83–88).

A second conflict proved even harder to resolve. Here, parties debated whether a future agreement should be developed by the AWG-LCA or by a new body, and which legal form such an agreement would take (ENB 12/534 of 13 December 2011: 22–23; TWN 2012: 40–42). On the latter point, the EU had made particularly clear that it wanted a legally binding instrument. In this, it received support from the US – which insisted on 'legal parallelism' for all significant emitters – as well as from other developed countries. This time, however, developed countries were not alone. Instead, members of AOSIS and of the LDC Group also signalled a preference for a legally binding agreement. In the words of one observer, these parties considered anything less than a legally binding agreement to 'be an affront to their grave existentialist crisis' (Rajamani 2013: 163). In a press conference on 5 December, China signalled a possibility that it might accept a legally binding post-2020 agreement, based on certain conditions Moreover, Brazil also sent a similar signal that it was willing to accept a 'robust, legally-binding instrument' (ENB 12/530 of 6 December 2011: 2). The main opposition to such language came from India. Arguing that the legal form should not be prejudged, the Indian delegation insisted that this question could only be settled once the actual content of the agreement was known. As these differences could not be resolved and the Conference was already running more than a day over time, the final hours of COP-17 (2011) saw intense fighting over the wording of the mandate for negotiating a future agreement.

The draft decision introduced by COP President Maite Nkoana-Mashabane stipulated that 'the Conference of the Parties ... decides to launch a process to develop a protocol, another legal instrument *or a legal outcome under the Convention* applicable to all Parties' (FCCC/CP/2011/L.10 of 10 December 2011: para. 2; italics added). In a plenary meeting on 11 December, however, the EU clarified that it sought a protocol or another legally binding instrument and could not accept the less specific option of 'a legal outcome' that had been added at the last minute and entailed the possibility of legally nonbinding COP decisions as well (Clark 2011; ENB 12/534 of 13 December 2011: 27; Rajamani 2013: 164).

As disagreement persisted, COP President Nkoana-Mashabane called a break and requested that the EU and India settle their differences (Goswami 2011). The 'nearly 40 frantic minutes' that followed have been called 'the huddle that made history' (Clark 2011). Connie Hedegaard, the EU Commissioner for Climate Action, and Jayanthi Natarajan, the Indian Minister of Forests and Environment, who had just defended her country's position in a powerful and emotional speech, confronted each other with their teams. COP President Nkoana-Mashabane and UNFCCC Executive Director Christiana Figueres joined them and were 'flanked by Todd Stern of the United States, China's Su Wei, [the] Brazilian Ambassador and other ministers' (Goswami 2011). In the discussions, Natarajan reaffirmed that India 'would not sign on to a legally binding deal at this time', while COP President Nkoana-Mashabane sought to reassure her that the deal was '[not] for now [but] for later'. One suggestion was to introduce wording on equity as a concession to the Indian position, but the US signalled its objection, stipulating that 'there should be parity, no equity' (Goswami 2011). Eventually, someone – different sources credit either US legal adviser Susan Biniaz or Brazil's lead negotiator Luiz Alberto Figueiredo – proposed the wording that both parties would eventually agree on: an 'agreed outcome with legal force' (Clark 2011; Patel 2011). One report of the event notes that Natarajan 'would have liked a little more time to consult and contemplate' but that 'the South African presidency didn't have the luxury of time' because the Conference was running over time and ministers had their flights 'booked and rebooked' (Goswami 2011).

7.3.4 The Durban Package

The decisions adopted at COP-17 (2011) were comprehensive. With regard to the reinterpretation of the 'lead-taking' norm, three decisions were central: the outcome of the work of the AWG-KP (Decision 1/CMP.7), the establishment of an ADP (Decision 1/CP.17), and the outcome of the work of the AWG-LCA (Decision 2/CP.17).

Decision 1/CMP.7 sets the stage for a second commitment period under the Kyoto Protocol. More specifically, it sets out to 'ensure that aggregate emissions of greenhouse gases by Parties included in Annex I are reduced by at least 25–40 per cent below 1990 levels by 2020'. On the duration of the second commitment period, it lists two options – until the end of 2017 or 2020 – and requests the AWG-KP to make a final decision at a subsequent meeting. Finally, like the Kyoto Protocol itself, Decision 1/CMP.7 includes a table in which parties that sign up for a second commitment period will list their numerical targets. This table included information on currently envisaged targets but still needed to be finalized before a second commitment period could begin. The indicative figures list 20 to 30 per cent reductions for the EU and Switzerland, 30 to 40 per cent reductions for Norway, and the document further informs that Australia and New Zealand were 'prepared to consider submitting information on [their quantified emission limitation and reduction objectives]' contingent on certain conditions (Decision 1/CMP.7, Annex 1, notes a and l).

Decision 1/CP.17 establishes the ADP as a new subsidiary body under the UN Framework Convention and assigns to this body the task of '[developing] a protocol, another legal instrument or an agreed outcome with legal force under the Convention applicable to all Parties' (para. 2). The fact that the mandate fell to a new body meant that the development of the new agreement was no longer formally guided – and constrained – by prior decisions taken at COP-13 (2007) and COP-16 (2010), which had informed the mandate of the AWG-LCA. Paragraphs 3 and 4 of the decision further specify that the group 'shall start its work as a matter of urgency in the first half of 2012' and 'complete its work as early as possible but no later than 2015' so that any new agreement it would come up with could come into force by 2020. Finally, the decision is also noteworthy for what it does not say: it neither contains a reference to CBDR, nor to equity. Instead, the preambular clauses refer to the urgency of the challenge that is required to be addressed 'by all Parties', notes the global nature of climate change which 'calls for the widest possible cooperation by all countries and their participation in an effective and appropriate international response', and notes 'aggregate emission pathways consistent with having a likely chance of holding the increase in global average temperature below 2°C or 1.5°C above pre-industrial levels' as a goal.

Finally, Decision 2/CP.17 is a 52-page document that covers a diverse range of 'outcomes' of the AWG-LCA work. From the perspective of differentiation, its emphasis on 'equitable access to sustainable development' is noteworthy. This formulation, which originates from an earlier decision taken at COP-16 (2010) in Cancún, is specifically used in connection to the task of 'identifying a time frame for the global peaking of greenhouse gas emissions' (para. 2), and the AWG-LCA is explicitly requested to consider it 'through a workshop at its next session' (para. 4). In addition, Decision 2/CP.17 also refers to the modalities of reporting and reviewing nationally appropriate mitigation commitments or actions of developed countries (paras. 5–31 and Annexes I–II) as well as of the reporting and consultation process related to developing countries' NAMAs (paras. 32–62 and Annexes III –IV). In principle, the document maintains the distinction earlier conferences had drawn between a more rigorous 'review' of developed countries commitments and actions and a softer 'consultation' related to the mitigation actions of developing countries.

In the aftermath of Durban, some participants and observers noted the historical relevance of the outcomes of COP-17 (2011). Towards the end of the Conference, the Brazilian delegate thus commented that 'we are on the verge of approving the most important result after the Berlin Mandate' (ENB 12/534 of 13 December 2011: 27; see also TWN 2012: 81). EU Commissioner Hedegaard (2011) called Durban a 'breakthrough' and 'the beginning of a new phase in international climate policy'. Other observers interpreted the fact that Brazil, China, and India had accepted (future) legal constraints on their future emissions as 'a shift in old geopolitical certainties that could spell a substantial change in the way global climate talks are conducted' (Clark 2011: 13) or simply noted that in Durban, 'the new world order had its first visible impact' (Dehmer 2011: 1). While some greeted this development as an adjustment to new economic realities, others were more critical. For them, the most significant contribution of COP-17 (2011) was the way in which negotiations had side-lined the principle of CBDR and thereby undermined, if not terminated, differentiation as the climate regime had known it since 1992 (*The Hindu BusinessLine* 2011; Rajamani 2013: 163). If this is a plausible interpretation, the puzzle we are confronted with is the following: How did the members of the G-77 and China come to accept such bold concessions to the EU, to the US and to other Annex I parties, given that they had strongly rejected similar moves at and ever since COP-1 (1995)?

7.4 WHAT MADE CHANGE POSSIBLE?

The comparison of the Berlin Mandate and the decision to establish the ADP reveals a fundamental norm change. In line with our discussion in Chapters 1 and 3, the Durban effort at 'respecting while recasting' (ENB 12/534 of 13 December 2011: 29) the CBDR principle clearly qualifies as an instance of the unmaking of differential treatment norms for developing countries as a group. But what made this unmaking possible? In this section, we zero in on three dynamics around institutional opportunities, around negotiating coalitions, and around normative contestation. Based on our three theoretical models introduced in Chapter 1, on the more general description of broader trends in Chapter 3, and on the detailed reconstruction of the two specific decision-making processes in the preceding two sections, Figure 7.1 provides a first illustration of possible storylines worth probing.

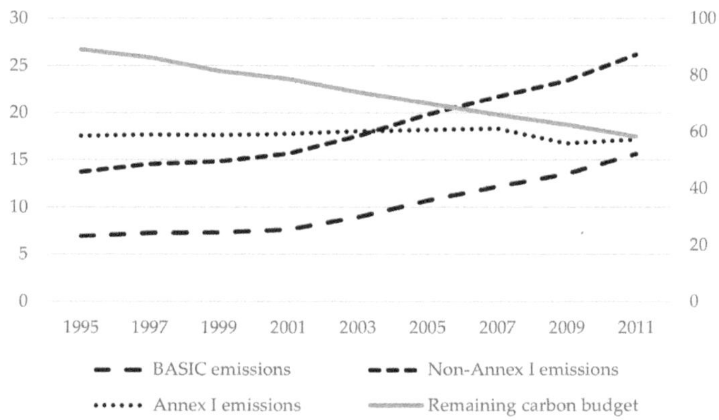

Figure 7.1 *Possible storylines linking conditions and outcomes*

Methodologically, we pursue two avenues to conduct our probe. To answer *if* interests, ideas, and institutions mattered, we check whether the difference we observe in the outcomes of COP-1 (1995) and COP-17 (2011) finds a plausible match in the initial conditions stipulated by each theoretical approach we have developed in Chapter 1. Since the concepts that underlie these approaches are rather broad, this exercise includes asking *which* interests, ideas, and institutional aspects could have made a difference. Moreover, to answer *how* interests, ideas, and institutions mattered, we also search for 'fingerprints' that render a specific dynamic plausible. Here, we seek to identify the traces that the different conditions our three theoretical explanations highlight should have left in the empirical material if they did indeed play the roles our models would expect them to play (Beach and Pedersen 2019; Nullmeier 2021).

7.4.1 Institutional Dynamics

To understand specific decisions taken in international climate negotiations, we need to know the institutional context. Just like the Berlin Mandate builds on the 1992 UN Framework Convention, any effort to make sense of the decisions taken at COP-17 (2011) in Durban must take the specific architecture of the Kyoto Protocol and the content of the Bali Action Plan into account. Three aspects are noteworthy in this regard.

First, prior institutional choices conditioned the choices delegations confronted at COP-1 (1995) and COP-17 (2011). For COP-1 (1995), the UN Framework Convention provides the immediate institutional context. Three institutional choices made in Rio in 1992 prestructured the negotiations in Berlin: the heavy emphasis the Convention put on the principles of CBDR and equity, its institutionalization of differentiation in the form of Annexes I and II, and a specific article that required states to review the adequacy of commitments and take 'appropriate action' based on such a review. The Berlin Mandate responds to this legal requirement, and it sticks to the dividing line of the two annexes not least because states had agreed only three years earlier that this line was a valid realization of the idea of CBDR.

In 2011, by contrast, the institutional context of COP-17 (2011) supported normative change rather than continuity. Here, the most immediate context was not the UN Framework Convention, but instead the end of the first commitment period under the Kyoto Protocol that forced states to devise a 'post-2012' regime. In Durban, many developing countries thus reaffirmed their view that the Kyoto Protocol was the 'cornerstone of the climate regime' (TWN 2012: 13). They also linked the credibility of the claim that developed countries were 'taking the lead' in the fight against global warming to the renewal of the Kyoto Protocol through a second commitment period. For developed countries, by contrast, '2012' represented an opportunity to alter the design of the international climate regime. Both demands are closely linked to the earlier decision to organize the Kyoto Protocol around 'commitment periods' and to select the years from 2008 to 2012 as the first such period. As '2012' was approaching, the demands led to the creation of two parallel negotiation streams, and negotiation in these streams largely structured the process leading up to Durban. Moreover, the institutional choices the two working groups made further shaped the road to Durban. Notably, the NAMAs of the Bali Action Plan implied a slow but important departure from the rigid exemption that had characterized the climate regime ever since the Berlin Mandate (Rajamani 2013). Like the Durban outcome itself, this departure was facilitated by the way in which '2012' loomed over the future of the international climate regime.

Second, domestic institutional structures mattered, notably in relation to the major players in the climate regime. Here, a key difference is that COP-1 (1995) happened before the unanimous passing of the Byrd–Hagel Resolution in the US Senate in July 1997 while COP-17 (2011) took place after that decision. Because the US constitution requires Senate approval for international treaties, the resolution locked in the expectation that the US would not accede to a legally binding agreement that exempted major developing countries (see also Chapter 3). At COP-1 (1995), US accession to such an agreement already seemed unlikely to governments, notably since the mid-term elections in November 1994 – only a few months before COP-1 – had brought a sweeping victory for the Republican Party and led them to control both the Senate and the House of Representatives (Oberthür and Ott 2000: 76–77). Once the Byrd–Hagel Resolution had passed, however, a legally binding agreement based on a neat separation of Annex I and non-Annex I parties was off the table regardless of which party held the US Presidency or a majority in Congress. As a result, any agreement meant to include the US would require a new formula for differentiation. Combined with the first point, this implied that a future unmaking of differentiation had thus become significantly more likely after 1997, that developing countries faced an incentive to make use of their existing exemption until 2012, and that '2012' was therefore the most likely date for a re-negotiation of differential treatment norms.

Finally, alternative institutional options outside the UNFCCC framework played a marginal role in the early climate regime of 1995, and their relevance increased only slightly by 2011. On the one hand, regional organizations like the International Energy Agency (IEA) or the OECD already seemed inadequate in 1995 because of the 'future dependence of the North on the South' in combatting climate change (Sebenius 1994: 288–289). At best, participants noted that they 'could lend valuable support' in developing protocols to the UN Framework Convention to which not all parties would need to accede (Kjellén 1994: 169). On the other hand, UN General Assembly resolutions would have lacked the legal force of a convention.

By 2011, when the 'dependence of the North on the South' was increasingly recognized, regional organizations played an even less significant role. Moreover, the activities of issue-specific international organizations remained limited to the regulation of emissions originating from international air and sea travel, which the AGW-LCA discussed under the label of sectoral approaches. Some sources, however, note that after the failure of Copenhagen in 2009, there were concerns that future agreements might be negotiated in smaller forums like the Asia-Pacific Forum, the G8, the G20, or the Major Economies Forum on Energy and Climate (MEF) (Hurrell and Sengupta 2012: 475–476). We do not, however, find strong evidence for such a role in our empirical material. Moreover, at least some rising powers were members of all of these forums, except the G8, so that developed countries faced difficulties using these institutions as alternative venues to exert pressure on the UNFCCC process.

7.4.2 Coalition Dynamics

As we have just seen, the institutional context strongly shaped the negotiation dynamics of COP-1 (1995) and COP-17 (2011). At the same time, it does not solve some of the puzzles we identified earlier in this chapter. In the 1995 review of the adequacy of commitments, for instance, several options were on the table. And in 2011, the nearing end of the first commitment period may have made certain outcomes more likely, but it still remained open whether the G-77 and China would accept future legal commitments. So, how did state interests change between 1995 and 2011, and what did such changes mean for the strength and unity of negotiating coalitions?

Here, our analysis reveals another clear variation in the conditions that marked the negotiations in 1995 and 2011. In 1995, the Southern negotiation coalition was united behind the call for developing country exemptions. The Northern coalition, by contrast, was divided between the EU and JUSCANZ. In 2011, the situation was reversed. Developed countries shared a common interest in a future agreement in which 'all parties' would accept commitments. In comparison, the G-77 and China were divided. Whereas members of AOSIS and the LDC Group were sympathetic to a strong future agreement, BASIC members continued to reject commitments for themselves. These changes in coalition strength and unity can also be linked to differences in outcomes.

The adoption of the Berlin Mandate is frequently described as the result of specific coalition dynamics that characterized the negotiations at COP-1 (1995) (Arts and Rüdig 1995: 486; Krägenow 1995: 73–96; Oberthür and Ott 1995: 145, 154; 2000: 78–79). According to this narrative, the Berlin Mandate originated from a coalition between the EU and 'more progressive' developing countries, notably AOSIS members who had submitted a draft protocol with specific targets and timeframes for emission reductions for COP-1 (1995). In the development of that draft protocol, NGOs – notably the London-based Foundation for International Environmental Law and Development (FIELD) – had already played a central part. As Sebastian Oberthür and Hermann Ott (1995: 145; see also Krägenow 1995: 73–74) recall, these organizations continued to play a role in Berlin: 'In the middle of the first week of COP-1, the NGOs managed to get hold of an informal OECD paper which indicated that the EU was about to give in to the US resistance against a strong mandate'. By making this information public, these well-networked NGOs exercised enough public pressure 'to push the EU towards sticking to its original position' and support an ambitious mandate for targets and timetables.

In response, EU members assured developing countries that they 'would not have to shoulder additional obligations in the next steps' (Oberthür and Ott 1995: 145). One source attributes this assurance to 'several industrial countries – notably the Netherlands' (Oberthür and Ott 1995: 145), another one to 'a joint initiative of Germany and the other EU member states' (Oberthür and Ott 2000: 79), and a third one holds that it was Germany which clarified that its elements paper from September 1994 had been replaced by a European Council decision from March 1995 which no longer treated mitigation commitments for 'certain advanced developing countries' as a requirement (Krägenow 1995: 73–74; see also European Union – The Council 1995: 4). Regardless of its precise origin, the assertion is widely seen as a game-changer. It allowed major developing countries like China and India to support a protocol. This way, a coalition of the EU and larger parts of the G-77 and China could form on this issue (Arts and Rüdig 1995: 485). Led by India, and once more assisted by environmental NGOs, a group of developing countries – with the notable exception of OPEC states – presented the so-called 'Green Paper' as a basis for further negotiations leading up to the Berlin Mandate. Once AOSIS, the EU, and large parts of the G-77 and China had found a common position, however, this allowed environmental groups to put the blame for a prospective failure of the climate talks on the US, its JUSCANZ allies, and the OPEC states. When the US eventually shifted its position, Canada and Australia followed and the Berlin Mandate could be adopted, even though several OPEC members added some reservations after its adoption (Oberthür and Ott 2000: 79; see also Arts and Rüdig 1995: 485; Krägenow 1995: 74; FCCC/CP/1995/7 of 24 May 1995: 23).[4]

Overall, the Southern coalition lost support from the OPEC members but gained cohesion in return. Thus, non-Annex I parties may have come to Berlin with heterogeneous preferences, but they all agreed on 'no new commitments', rendering concessions on this issue particularly powerful. At least on this specific aspect, they got what they wanted because they were united – and because their Northern counterparts were not. Northern disunity meant that the OECD countries were unable to submit a draft proposal for a protocol before COP-1 (1995) themselves. This strengthened the position of the AOSIS Protocol as the most advanced negotiation text available in March 1995. Moreover, the EU was too weak to achieve its preferences on its own. To secure a mandate for negotiations, it needed to build a broader coalition, and to forge a broader coalition it had to offer something to non-Annex I parties.[5]

At COP-17 (2011), the constellation was reversed. Here, a Global North that was united in its call for contributions from 'all parties' faced what observers have varyingly called a 'fractured South' (Death 2012: 982), a 'breakup of developing countries' (Dehmer 2011: 1, our translation), or a shaking up of 'entrenched boundaries and positions' out of which 'critical new alliances were forged' (ENB 12/534 of 13 December 2011: 29; see also Hurrell and Sengupta 2012: 473). The novelty was not that the EU and AOSIS managed to find a common position: that was true of COP-1 (1995), already. What was new was that the common EU and AOSIS position was now shared by members of the LDC Group and the African Group, that it did not face opposition from the US and other developed countries, and that rising powers like China spoke on behalf of their own negotiating coalition, the BASIC coalition. A fingerprint for the causal relevance of this new constellation is that progress in the negotiations coincided with coalition-building dynamics. The report of the ENB for COP-17 (2011) thus notes (ENB 12/534 of 13 December 2011: 30; see also Bäckstrand and Elgström 2013: 1380–1382):

> It took a critical engagement between the EU, AOSIS and LDCs to really inject a sense of direction and pace into the negotiations as the countdown to the end of the Conference began. There was a palpable shift in the atmospherics after EU Commissioner Hedegaard joined with AOSIS and the LDCs in issuing a public statement backing the EU 'roadmap' plan linking the second commitment period to the early launch of new negotiations under the Convention.

Other observers shared the impression that the new alliance had the potential to overcome the gridlock between the US, China, and India (Clark 2011). Moreover, delegates and observers equally noted the significance of China speaking on behalf of BASIC countries during the Conference and 'wondered how a more coordinated position of BASIC countries might influence these negotiations' (ENB 12/525 of 30 November 2011: 3). However, the common BASIC position proved to be rather weak. In fact, it has been noted, 'things began to become difficult for India and China when other rising powers like Brazil and South Africa too were said to be siding with the EU roadmap', thereby putting 'Indian and Chinese negotiators … on the tight spot' (*The Kathmandu Post* 2011).

When we consider the sources of the changes in the constellation of interest between 1995 and 2011, problem pressure, the actual growth of rising powers, and domestic policy responses stand out. In terms of the problem pressure, GHG emissions had risen significantly since between 1995 and 2011 – global emissions had increased from 32.69 Gt per year (1995) to 45.08 Gt per year (2011), and atmospheric concentrations of CO_2 from 363 ppm (1995) to 392 ppm (2011).[6] In addition, the science of global warming made significant progress from the publication of the IPCC's first assessment report (AR1) in

1995 to its fourth report (AR4) in 2007. Looking at both aspects in combination, states not only had a better understanding of their specific vulnerabilities, but those vulnerabilities had also increased significantly since 1995. The emissions of rising powers played a role in this regard: for the four BASIC countries, they had represented 6.93 Gt – and hence slightly above 20 per cent of the global total – in 1995. By 2011, they had more than doubled to 15.64 Gt and now represented around 35 per cent of the global total. The emission profiles of rising powers were thus a concern not only to low-lying island states. They also mattered for other states with a relatively low capacity for adapting to a warmer world.

Finally, domestic policies affected the constellation of interests as well. In 1995, technological leaders like the EU had clear incentives to adopt a protocol with targets and timetables. For economies thriving on cheap energy and lagging in green technology, this was not necessarily the case. And for energy-intensive economies that competed with the rising economies of Asian developing countries, a protocol that exempted the latter from additional costs was not attractive at all – hence the JUSCANZ alliance and hence also the US emphasis on 'symmetry' rather than 'differentiation' (see Grubb et al. 1999: 50). By 2011, these differences had not vanished, but most developed economies had made some adjustments to the expectation of a more carbon-restricted future. Moreover, domestic policies may also have undermined coalition unity among the BASIC countries at COP-17 (2011). The Chinese delegation thus initially criticized the EU demand for a legally binding agreement applicable to 'all parties'. However, some observers note that, 'behind the scenes, ... it was clear China's position had altered'. On the one hand, they maintain, China sought to avoid the blame it received after the failure of COP-15 (2009) in Copenhagen. Instead, it 'went to Durban eager to promote its green credentials' and 'boasted ... China's rising dominance of renewable energy markets, a five-year plan that for the first time includes plans for emissions trading and carbon intensity reduction targets'. Unlike in 1995, this would imply that China had now embarked on a domestic path to reform its development model – a path that made it easier to accept a legally binding agreement to limit its future GHG emissions (Clark 2011: 13).[7]

7.4.3 Ideas Regarding Legitimacy and Identity

So far, we have argued that the institutional context as well as changes in the constellation of interests facilitated a change in the differentiation regime. A full explanation, however, will also take relevant shifts in the discursive environment into account. In Chapter 1, we have thus argued that significant adjustments to systems of special rights and obligations will only take place if the binary distinction between developed and developing countries is successfully challenged, if the major justifications for differential treatment norms (or for their application to rising powers) lose legitimacy, or if rising powers actively seek a new status in the international order and therefore no longer claim special rights.

In relation to the first and second aspect, there are clear differences between 1995 and 2011. Contestation of the binary distinction between developed and developing countries increased markedly, not least because of the increasing GHG emissions and economic capabilities of some non-Annex I parties. In addition, justifications based on historical responsibility were challenged in a context in which the emissions of non-Annex I parties had come to surpass those of Annex I parties and the remaining carbon budget was decreasing rapidly (cf. Figure 7.1). But how exactly did climate policy discourses support the Berlin Mandate? And how exactly did such discourses change to make the dismantling of the 'Berlin firewall' between developed and developing countries possible?

In relation to COP-1 (1995), three aspects are central: the framing of developing countries in negotiations on the UN Framework Convention, the specific interpretation of the lead-taking norm in international climate governance, and the self-conception of the EU as a 'normative power'.

The framing of developing countries in the run-up to the 1992 UN Framework Convention highlighted three aspects. First, developing countries had not contributed to the problem. Second, they had a right to development. Third, they were needy. On the first point, India had proposed in 1991 that a preamble of the UN Framework Convention should '[note] the fact that the largest part of the current emissions of pollutants into the environment originates in developed countries, and [recognize] therefore that these countries have the main responsibility for combating such pollution' (A/AC.237/Misc.1/Add.3 of 18 June 1991: 3; see also Dasgupta 1994: 133–136). Similarly, China had emphasized that the principle of equity called for a balanced distribution of burdens in accordance with historical responsibility, with Brazil noting 'that policies to counter climate change should recognize the "polluter pays principle"' (A/AC.237/Misc.1/Add.4/Rev.1 of 23 July 1991: 3–4; A/AC.237/Misc.1/Add.14 of 17 September 1991: 3; see also the Philippines on behalf of the G-77 and China, in ENB 12/15 of 31 March 1995). According to this logic, *equal* contributions could only be demanded once the historical emissions of developed countries matched those of developing countries. Yet, achieving the ultimate objective of the Convention ruled out this possibility: there were simply not enough emissions left to reach parity *and* prevent dangerous anthropogenic climate change. As a result, the historical contributions alone provided sufficient reason for developing countries to justify a long-term differentiation in commitments. What this argument left open, however, was at which level developed countries could reasonably demand *any* contribution from developing countries.

On this question, developing countries invoked their right to development as a further ground for justification (see also Hyder 1994: 212–213). The UN General Assembly had prominently recognized this right in its 1986 Declaration on the Right to Development (UN General Assembly Resolution 41/128), and the 1993 World Conference on Human Rights in Vienna had further stressed its status as a fundamental human right. In the context of the climate negotiations, India's position was that the Convention needed to (A/AC.237/Misc.1/Add.3 of 18 June 1991: 3):

> [recognize] that developing countries have as their main priority the eradication of poverty and the achievement of economic and social development and that their emissions must grow to accommodate their development needs, reflecting the equal right of all peoples in matters relating to living standards.

China, in turn, proposed that 'an appropriate level of economic development is the prerequisite for adopting concrete control measures to address climate change, and all the peoples in the world are entitled to an appropriate standard of living' (A/AC.237/Misc.1/Add.4/Rev.1 of 23 July 1991: 4–5). In the context of COP-1 (1995), these frames remained relevant. Brazil and Colombia, for instance, argued that asking developing countries to take on new commitments would 'compromise' or 'jeopardize' their right to development (ENB 12/14 of 30 March 1995: 1–2).

In their own contributions, developed countries commonly emphasized developing country needs as a reason for differentiation. At the same time, they avoided references to a right to development or to historical emissions. The US, for example, saw a need for 'technical and financial assistance, to facilitate the fulfilment by the developing countries of their obligations' (A/AC.237/Misc.1/Add.1 of 22 May 1991: 92). Similarly, the EC indicated that it was 'fully aware that not every country is able to take the necessary measures by itself alone' and hence called upon developed countries to 'declare their readiness to grant the necessary, adequate support' (A/AC.237/Misc.1/Add.1 of 22 May 1991: 16). This emphasis turned 'neediness' into the special feature that distinguished the two groups. As Joyeeta Gupta (2014: 54) has noted, this frame ascribed a more positive identity to developed countries. Instead of designating them as 'polluters', it allowed developed countries to 'grant support' to those countries who needed assistance.[8] This way, the EC recognized that developing countries were in a 'special situation' because they had to 'make the development necessary due to their economic and social circumstances compatible with measures for the protection of the environment and the climate' (A/AC.237/Misc.1/Add.1 of 22 May 1991: 16).

In the negotiations of the Berlin Mandate, major challenges to the discursive frame the 1992 UN Framework Convention had established came from Australia and Russia. Australia thus spoke of 'industrialising developing countries' and held that, as the economies of these countries grew, 'there will be an increasing contribution of greenhouse gases by them to atmospheric concentrations'. Accordingly, the Australian government saw 'increasing evidence that it will simply not be enough for developed countries to take action alone if we are to achieve the objective of the Convention' (A/AC.237/MISC.43 of 7 December 1994: 5). Along the same lines, Russia argued that 'even the best efforts leading to reduction of GHG emissions by Annex I Parties might not achieve the ultimate goal of the Convention'. Even though its statements frequently stressed the uncertainties associated with climate science, Russia further pointed out that, 'as is shown by recent IPCC results, emissions of a large group of Parties to the Convention, not included in Annex I, are dramatically increasing' (A/AC.237/MISC.43/Add.1 of 6 February 1995: 3). This statement primarily served to support a call for reviewing the adequacy of commitments of *all* parties. But it also revealed that Annex I parties expected developing country emissions to rise steadily, eventually equalling the emissions of developed countries by around 2020 (see also Germany, A/AC.237/MISC.36 and Add.1 of 3 June 1994: 39; Oberthür and Ott 2000: 56, 287, 299).

The existing lead-taking norm helped the G-77 and China to fend off such challenges. In Article 3.1 of the 1992 UN Framework Convention, states had thus agreed that 'the developed country Parties should take the lead in combatting climate change and the adverse effects thereof'. This general norm was further specified in three ways. First, the UN Framework Convention stated that the policies and measures developed countries would adopt 'will demonstrate that developed countries are taking the lead in modifying longer-term trends in anthropogenic emissions consistent with the objective of the Convention'. Second, states agreed that 'the return by the end of the present decade to earlier levels of anthropogenic emissions of carbon dioxide and other greenhouse gases not controlled by the Montreal Protocol would contribute to such modification' (Article 4.2[a]). Moreover, lead-taking also included efforts to 'make space for growth in developing countries' and to help the latter in their efforts to mitigate and adapt to global warming (Gupta 2014: 69–72; see also Chapters 3 and 8).

In practice, however, the review of the adequacy of commitments showed that most OECD countries had neither proven able to return their emissions to 1990 levels, nor to 'modify longer-term trends in anthropogenic emissions'. At COP-1 (1995), they were thus in a poor position to claim that they had already demonstrated leadership and to therefore call on developing countries to follow their lead. The formulations of the UN Framework Convention provided an important background for developing countries' rejection of commitments unless effective leadership had taken place (ENB 12/11 of 20 February 1995: 9). At INC-11 and COP-1 (1995), they held 'that repair for damage to the environment should be borne by those principally responsible for the damage', that it was 'inappropriate for developing country Parties to undertake new commitments' (Philippines on behalf of G-77 and China, ENB 12/14 of 30 March 1995: 2), and that 'any attempt to reassign responsibilities could be interpreted as transferring the burden to the victims rather than the perpetrators of climate change' (Philippines, ENB 12/4 of 9 February 1995: 2). They stated that it was 'urgent that Annex I Parties live up to their commitments', reminded developed countries that these commitments also included the provision of financial resources (China, ENB 12/20 of 7 April 1995: 1), and argued that amendments should be negotiated 'only when present commitments are fulfilled' (Philippines, ENB 12/5 of 10 February 1995: 1; see also ENB 12/4 of 9 February 1995: 2). Additionally, they pointed out that Annex I parties had failed not only to reduce their emissions, but also to propose specific targets and timetables for the future even though many Annex I parties had themselves acknowledged the inadequacy of commitments (Malaysia, ENB 12/4 of 9 February 1995: 2; Uganda, ENB 12/15 of 31 March 1995: 1; see also Grubb et al. 1999: 47).

By the time COP-17 (2011) took place, climate policy discourses had changed significantly. First, developing countries were no longer described as a homogeneous category. Second, historical emissions had become less accepted as a reason for differentiation, and developing countries sought to recast CBDR as a 'dynamic' principle. Third, and most importantly, climate change itself was no longer imagined primarily as a 'North-South challenge' but rather as a 'global collective action problem' (Bäckstrand and Lövbrand 2019: 523). This shift put the 'ultimate objective' of the 1992 UN Framework Convention centre stage: the Convention was there to 'prevent dangerous anthropogenic climate change', and without contributions from 'major developing countries', the numbers 'simply' did not add up!

On the first point, the categories of 'developed' and 'developing' continued to figure prominently in negotiations at COP-17 (2011). At the same time, however, the language of 'large emitters', 'major emitters', 'major developing countries' had become pervasive. This was part of broader discursive shift in which rising powers had become depicted as the 'great irresponsibles' even though their historical emissions remained low and even though they had strengthened their domestic climate policies (Hurrell and Sengupta 2011: 467).

At COP-17 (2011), several delegations stressed the growing emissions of rising powers as a key challenge for mitigating global warming. Australia was particularly clear in this regard. In the early days of the Conference, it stated that 'rapid industrialization in large developing countries had lifted many out of poverty' and 'had also raised emissions in these countries' (TWN

2012: 13). As a result, Australia argued, a new agreement that went beyond Annex I parties had become both feasible and necessary. At a later stage, the Australian delegation thus noted that 'the emission reduction pledges by (developed and developing) countries cover 80% of global emissions' in comparison to the 13 to 17 per cent covered by a second commitment period under the Kyoto Protocol: 'The Kyoto Protocol', Australia maintained, 'cannot of itself deliver emission reductions required for keeping temperature increase to 2 degrees Celsius, without legally binding mitigation targets by all major economies' (TWN 2012: 27).

Here, too, the nearing end of the first commitment period was important. However, observers also note that 'the invocation of planetary boundaries, tipping points and thresholds has given climate governance a renewed sense of urgency' around the time of the Durban Conference (Bäckstrand and Lövbrand 2019: 523). As the remaining carbon budget decreased and problem pressure increased, arguments based on historical emissions could now more easily be portrayed as 'backward-looking'. Importantly, however, developed countries were not alone in promoting a 'forward-looking approach' for addressing global warming. Speaking for the LDC Group, for example, Bangladesh argued that LDCs must be able to develop, thus effectively claiming a primary right to development for this smaller group (ENB 12/521 of 10 October 2011: 13). Grenada, speaking on behalf of AOSIS, famously declared that 'if they develop we die', a reference that could be understood to include developed countries as well as rising powers (TWN 2012: 81; Hurrell and Sengupta 2012: 473). Moreover, newly established forums such as the Cartagena Dialogue for Progressive Action (established in 2010) or the Climate Vulnerable Forum (established in 2009) promoted discourses around 'shared' rather than 'differentiated' responsibilities as well (Blaxekjær and Nielsen 2014). Some of these groups also advocated a more ambitious temperature goal. Yet, if states disagreed on whether limiting global warming to 2°C could be achieved in the absence of developing country commitments, the 1.5°C temperature goal AOSIS and the LDC Group advocated implied even more clearly that rising powers had to contribute. Based on these tensions, historical emissions as well as an unconditional right to development lost their centrality in the international climate policy discourse. Instead, 'equitable access to sustainable development' gained ground as a new compromise formula (FCCC/CP/2011/9/Add.1 of 15 March 2012: Decision 2/CP.17, para. 2).

7.5 CONCLUSION

The outcome of COP-17 (2011) has been described in stark terms. For Andrew Hurrell and Sandeep Sengupta, Decision 1/CP.17 is 'indicative of the diminishing ability of the developing world, especially emerging powers, to maintain their case for "differential" treatment on the subject of climate change' (Hurrell and Sengupta 2012: 472). Even worse, Lavanya Rajamani has viewed it as 'the final blow to differentiation in the climate regime' (Rajamani 2013: 163). Our comparison of the outcomes of COP-1 (1995) and COP-17 (2011) may be seen as confirming the general impression which underpins these assessments: while the Berlin Mandate helped to *make* special rights for developing countries as a group, the Durban Platform constitutes an important step in *unmaking* the way these rights had initially been institutionalized in the climate regime. At the same time, however, our reconstruction in this chapter adds some nuance. Thus, even though differential treatment as we used to know it may have been unmade in Durban, and even though the new system that replaced it is 'more dynamic' and characterized by a stronger 'parallelism' between developed and developing countries, it still holds a place for differential treatment as such.

How, then, can we account for the very different outcomes of COP-1 (1995) and COP-17 (2011)? In Chapter 1, we have stated three broad theoretical assumptions about what makes an unmaking of special rights possible. The empirical analysis sheds some light on all three assumptions. Notably, it helps us see *which* institutions, *which* interests, and *which* ideas made a difference in Berlin and Durban, and how all three sets of factors combined to generate a specific outcome. Specifically, our discussion suggests a division of labour in which institutions were a powerful force in the background that incentivized and allowed developed countries to adopt a two-fold strategy aimed at building new coalitions and challenging the legitimacy of the CBDR principle.

Regarding the first aspect, prior institutional choices defined the rules of the game in three important ways. They determined the timing of future decisions. They influenced the processes through which such decisions would be reached. And they prestructured the options states would consider. As a result, prior institutional decisions strongly affected the dynamics of contestation. With respect to the first conflict we examined, the institutional context clearly favoured stability because states had just agreed on Annexes I and II three years earlier. In the second conflict, by contrast, prior institutional decisions favoured normative change because they had made 2012 the focal point for re-negotiating the Kyoto Protocol. Finally, at least since 1997, states knew that the next opportunity for changing the rules of the game would arise in or shortly before 2012. As a result, they concentrated their efforts on this date.

In practice, developed countries in general, and the members of the Umbrella Group more specifically, pursued a two-fold strategy. First, they adopted a 'wait and see' approach to the implementation of their own commitments and hence delayed ambitious climate action until after 2012. This inaction spurred a considerable change in the constellation of interests that characterized negotiations in Durban. Notably, problem pressure increased dramatically, leading highly vulnerable countries to develop a keen interest in ensuring ambitious climate targets (and actions) for *all* countries that emitted a significant amount of GHG. As a result, members of AOSIS, of the LDC Group, and of the African Group sided with developed countries in Durban.

Second, developed countries invested in a continuous and powerful effort to delegitimize differential treatment norms and the way in which they had been implemented in the climate regime. They introduced new terms like 'major emitters', 'major economies', or 'larger developing countries'. They argued that the CBDR principle needed to be interpreted in a 'dynamic' manner and that its implementation therefore required 'adjustments' as 'circumstances evolved'. They also demanded 'symmetry' and 'parallelism' in the legal form of commitments for different countries. Here, too, the members of the Umbrella Group led the campaign effort. However, other developed countries, including the EU, readily joined them in their critique of the present system and their demands for a 'more balanced' differentiated regime in the future.

An important aspect of the two-part strategy was that its composite elements mutually supported each other. Thus, developed countries used the alleged lack of legitimacy of the way differential treatment had been institutionalized as an excuse for their inaction: they claimed that being subject to commitments when major developing countries where exempted was unfair. And in return, the 'wait and see' approach discredited the CBDR principle: it suggested that a global collective action problem like climate change could not be solved based on special rights and obligations that some states were unwilling to accept as a basis for cooperation.

As the rapidly decreasing remaining carbon budget took centre stage in the climate policy discourse, this two-tiered strategy eventually paid off. However, two caveats must be noted. First, our discussion does not necessarily imply that developed countries had a clear strategy from the very start. Instead, our discussion in this chapter, as well as in Chapter 3, suggests that they developed such a strategy gradually as '2012' drew closer. In addition, even though the strategies worked, neither the Berlin Mandate nor the Durban outcomes were inevitable. As we have argued in this chapter, the Berlin Mandate had been considered improbable shortly before COP-1 (1995). Moreover, had states made different decisions in Berlin (and then Kyoto), the differentiation regime could indeed have looked very different – with shorter timeframes, more specific triggers for developing country commitments, and the like. Arguably, this would have altered the way states thought about, and contested, the CBDR principle as well. Second, even within the Kyoto framework, we can imagine that the US could have come to see the emergence of a carbon-restricted world not so much as a threat to its fossil fuel-driven energy culture, but rather as an opportunity to hold or expand its role as a global technological leader. If so, COP-17 (2011) could have turned out very differently, too.

In the end, however, our reconstruction of how negotiations in Berlin and Durban *did* unfold suggests that the success of COP-1 (1995) eventually became a pyrrhic victory for developing countries. The Berlin Mandate may have recognized the special rights of the developing world. However, the developed world largely failed to fulfil its own special obligation to 'take the lead', and it later used that failure as an excuse to debunk the special rights clause in the post-2015 regime.

NOTES

1. We cite the meeting reports issued by the *Earth Negotiations Bulletin* (ENB) according to their volume (where volume 12 covers international climate negotiations under the UNFCCC) and running number. The reports are available at https://enb.iisd.org/enb/vol12/ (last accessed 11 July 2023).
2. We cite official documents related to the UNFCCC process according to their official document number and date of publication. While documents published or adopted until 1994 are cited as UN General Assembly documents (A/…), documents from 1995 onwards are cited as UNFCCC documents (FCCC/…).
3. The acronym turned into 'JUSSCANNZ' when Switzerland and Norway joined the group. Group members reorganized as the Umbrella Group in later years. At the beginning of 2022, the Umbrella Group includes Australia, Belarus, Canada, Iceland, Israel, Japan, New Zealand, Kazakhstan, Norway, the Russian Federation, Ukraine, and the US (cf. UNFCCC, 'Party Groupings' at https://unfccc.int/process-and-meetings/parties-non-party-stakeholders/parties/party-groupings, accessed 7 May 2022).
4. A possible challenge to the notion of 'Southern unity' at COP-1 (1995) could point to the fact that, at a crucial moment in the negotiations, the G-77 and China formally broke ranks with its OPEC members to create a 'Green Group'. Does that not contradict our argument about Southern unity? It is certainly true that the G-77 and China were primarily united in their emphasis on historical responsibility as well as their call for financial support and technology transfer (Borione and Ripert 1994: 83–84; see also Dasgupta 1994; Hyder 1994; see also Chapter 8). At the same time, OPEC members not only contributed significantly to global warming through their economic activities, but they also scored relatively high on gross domestic product (GDP) and GDP per capita. As a result, excluding the oil exporters provided the remaining developing country coalition – still a very heterogeneous group – with greater coherence. This coherence, in turn, allowed the group to take a stronger position on future mitigation action, notably once the EU had signalled its support for 'no new commitments' for non-Annex I parties. Moreover, while the new and now more unified Southern coalition lost merely eight members in exchange for gains in internal cohesiveness, the OECD camp remained roughly split in half, with the EU and JUSCANZ members divided on the question of future commitments (Arts and Rüdig 1995: 483).
5. The eventual shift in the US position is more difficult to rationalize. It may be traced to a range of factors: to developing country concessions on the possibility of joint implementation, a key demand of the US delegation; to US awareness of its strong bargaining power in the negotiations that would follow; to the pro-environmental stance of Vice President Al Gore and the country's head of

delegation (Arts and Rüdig 1995: 485–486); or to the more cynical expectation that the deal negotiated in Berlin would serve US interests well because a strong protocol would never pass a Senate in which the Republicans held the upper hand (Oberthür and Ott 2000: 78).

6. Emissions data are based on information found here: https://www.pik-potsdam.de/paris-reality-check/primap-hist/ (last accessed 18 October 2023), which is itself based on the PRIMAP-hist dataset (Gütschow et al. 2016; 2021). Data on atmospheric concentration is based on Mauna Loa Monthly Averages as published by the US National Oceanic and Atmospheric Administration's Global Monitoring Laboratory; cf. https://gml.noaa.gov/ccgg/trends/graph.html (last accessed 15 April 2022).
7. Hurrell and Sengupta (2012: 477–478) note, however, that the Indian policy was not so different and that India, too, saw some economic benefits linked to an increasing demand for, for instance, wind energy. Moreover, Brazil had witnessed significant changes in its climate policy since 2007 as well.
8. In later years, the emphasis on this frame would pave the way for singling out Least Developed Countries (LDCs) as the legitimate recipients of differential treatment. In the context leading up to and of COP-1 (1995), however, the LDCs were hardly ever mentioned.

8. Conflicts over the institutional landscape of climate finance

Simon Herr

8.1 INTRODUCTION

Differential treatment in the climate regime most prominently concerns the question of who should reduce emissions, by how much, and when (cf. Chapters 3 and 7). Climate finance enjoys less relative prominence compared to these central emissions reduction obligations. Yet, without climate finance, agreement in the international climate regime would arguably collapse. As a fundamental support structure underlying climate agreements, climate finance aims to redistribute capabilities to weaker countries such that they, too, can contribute to the response to global warming even though they bear relatively little responsibility. As the central manifestation of assistance, climate finance thus aims at and is crucial to increasing the overall effectiveness and equity of the international climate regime.

The importance of assistance as a vital category of differential treatment is widely accepted (Rajamani 2006: 94). But given its potential to differentiate and (re-)distribute benefits and burdens, the specifics of climate finance have always been deeply contested terrain. This chapter zooms in on two major conflicts between developed and developing countries over the institutional landscape of climate finance. Both hold vital insights for understanding and explaining differential treatment dynamics in the climate regime. The first conflict occurred before the rise of Brazil, China, and India. After disputes over climate finance had been building up throughout the 1990s, they culminated in negotiation deadlock between 2000 and 2001. Negotiators eventually found a way out of this impasse in the decision to create three new funds: the Special Climate Change Fund (SCCF), the Least Developed Countries (LDC) Fund, and the Adaptation Fund. The second conflict reached its critical climax after the rise of Brazil, China, and India in 2009 and 2010 and led to the creation of the Green Climate Fund (GCF).

The two conflicts arose out of deep-rooted differences between developed and developing countries regarding the interpretation and institutional

Table 8.1 *Climate finance institutions under the Financial Mechanism of the UN Framework Convention*

Name	Year established	Contributors	Beneficiaries	Governance body	Available volume since creation (USD)
Global Environment Facility (GEF)	1989–1991	40 donor countries (including, Brazil, China, and India)	Developing countries and countries with economies in transition (EITs)	GEF Council	8.3 billion
Special Climate Change Fund (SCCF)	2001	Subset of Annex II countries	'Vulnerable developing countries'*	GEF Council	360 million
Least Developed Countries Fund (LDC Fund)	2001	Annex II+	Least Developed Countries (LDCs)	GEF Council	1.6 billion
Adaptation Fund	2001	2 per cent levy on Certified Emission Reductions under the CDM + voluntary countries	Developing countries that are parties to the Kyoto Protocol	Adaptation Fund Board	1.05 billion
Green Climate Fund (GCF)	2009–2010	Developed and developing countries + further public and private sources	Developing countries	GCF Board	7.2 billion

Note: *Technically, all non-Annex I countries are eligible but the SIDS and 'vulnerable' developing countries in Africa and Asia are prioritized (Heinrich Böll Stiftung and ODI 2019d).
Source: Numbers are based on data from GEF (1994; 2021a); GEF Secretariat (2006: 15; 2018: 160); GEF IEO (2014: 38); Heinrich Böll Stiftung and ODI (2019a; 2019d; 2019b; 2019c); FCCC/CP/2001/13/Add.1 of 21 January 2002: Decisions 7/CP.7, 10/CP.7; FCCC/CP/2009/11/ Add.1 of 30 March 2010: Decision 2/CP.15; FCCC/CP/2010/7/Add.1 of 15 March 2011: Decision 1/CP.16; FCCC/CP/2011/9/Add.1 of 15 March 2012: Annex to Decision 3/CP.17; UNFCCC (2022a; 2022b).

implementation of differential treatment. Three overarching issues between developed and developing countries have refused to disappear over the years and cocreated both major conflicts. First, the 'adequate' volume of climate finance to be channelled from which duty-bearers to which rights-holders for which ultimate goals. Second, the concomitant commitments to be borne by rights-holders in return for funds. And third, the rules that govern the institutional operationalization and implementation of climate finance between duty-bearers and rights-holders. Both conflict outcomes in turn have shaped the institutional landscape of differential treatment in general and climate finance specifically.

We study the two conflicts to investigate how global power shifts relate to three questions. First, do the contestation and conflict dynamics differ before and after the rise? Second, do the respective conflict outcomes differ? And third, can the observed changes to climate finance be regarded as unmaking or resilience of differential treatment norms? Superficially, the new funds born out of both conflicts could be misconstrued as merely neutral additions to the Global Environment Facility (GEF) which had previously served as the only financing channel in the climate regime. Neutrality would mean that the new funds had left differential treatment unchanged. Upon closer inspection, however, both conflicts not only resulted in additional climate financing channels, they also altered the character of differential treatment. To put it briefly, more money is now flowing through an increased number of individual institutions from different duty-bearers to different rights-holders and goals on different terms.

Interpreting these outcomes requires nuance. Developing countries challenged the existing institutional landscape in both conflicts and demanded more assistance in line with a relatively rigorous reading of the United Nations (UN) Framework Convention. They have managed to uphold a relatively united front in climate finance despite the rise of Brazil, China, and India, and used moral pressure as well as their growing material power to argue for institutional change. Developed countries, by contrast, generally regarded existing climate finance institutions (i.e. the GEF) as sufficient and efficient to structure assistance under the climate regime. Despite occasional disunity, they influenced both conflict outcomes by controlling input volumes, diluting contributory responsibility, and demanding efficiency. In sum, all four new additions can be viewed as examples of institutional *layering*. The specific form of layering, however, differed. Creating the SCCF and LDCs Fund meant a better reflection of the diversity in the group of developing countries, but merely added layers *within* the existing structures of the GEF. By contrast, the institutional independences of the new Adaptation Fund and GCF represent instances of *branching out*, meaning that they grew out *besides* the existing institutional structures of the GEF rather than just forming additional layers within it (Harmeling and Kaloga 2011: 25; Horta et al. 2002: 1).

On the one hand, the greater number of institutions as well as higher overall levels of funding thus imply that beneficiaries of differential treatment ended up with a greater variety of channels they could turn to. Developing countries, including Brazil, China, and India, have also generally been able to defend their status as rights-holders, although particularly vulnerable developing countries now receive increased attention. On the other hand, industrialized countries have kept overall levels of climate finance far below the expressed needs of rights-holders (TWN 2010: 6). Furthermore, developed countries succeeded in diffusing their responsibility as contributors since the new institutions are open to inputs from a 'variety of sources' (Rajamani 2010: 827; Vanderheiden 2015: 34). Overall, however, climate finance amounts to a rare case of resilience and even partial expansion of differential treatment. As such, it stands out against the general trend of unmaking special rights we observe in this book.

The chapter proceeds as follows. In the following section, we explore the conflict-laden links between climate finance and differential treatment, briefly discuss relevant funding flows, and lay out the structure of both conflicts. Subsequently, sections 8.3 and 8.4 retrace the negotiations and outcomes of the first and second conflicts respectively. Section 8.5 interprets the observations in terms of our theoretical framework. The final section concludes.

8.2 RECURRING CLIMATE FINANCE ISSUES AND THE STRUCTURE OF BOTH CONFLICTS

Before turning to the conflicts in detail, some preliminary remarks on climate finance flows and the structure and content of both conflicts are helpful to understand the discussion in the following sections. First, the United Nations Framework Convention on Climate Change (UNFCCC) defines climate finance broadly as 'local, national or transnational financing – drawn from public, private and alternative sources of financing – that seeks to support mitigation and adaptation actions' (UNFCCC 2022c). Since our focus is on differential treatment norms, we concentrate exclusively on climate finance flowing through the Financial Mechanism of the 1992 UN Framework Convention. According to Article 11 of the Convention, the GEF as the interim operating entity of the Financial Mechanism would be the only climate finance channel. However, conflicts between developed and developing countries have since arisen over how differentiated climate finance should be organized and implemented. Climate finance conflicts specifically manifested as disagreements over the concepts of adequacy, additionality, transparency and predictability, incremental costs, eligibility and concomitant commitments of rights-holders, accessibility, and governance. Table 8.2. further shows that contestation can be grouped as pertaining predominantly to the *input*, *output*, and institutional *throughput* dimensions of climate finance.

Second, the overall climate finance flows we observe are small compared to other climate-related funding activities (Buchner et al. 2019). Throughout the 30 years of climate negotiations, the budgets of all funds under the Financial Mechanism taken together have amounted to only about USD (United States

Table 8.2 Key conflicts over differential treatment in climate finance

Dimension	Concepts	Conflicts between developing and developed countries
Input	Adequacy	Developed and developing countries fought over how much funding is appropriate both in general, as well as for what goals (e.g. mitigation versus adaptation versus loss and damage).
	Additionality	Beneficiaries criticized that climate finance would crowd out other finance flows and that it is often viewed as aid instead of owed.
	Transparency and predictability	Developed and developing countries criticized each other as well as the GEF for being non-transparent and unreliable. This predominantly concerned inputs but also the output and throughput dimensions.
Output	Incremental versus full-cost funding	Beneficiaries frequently expressed difficulties in obtaining cofinancing and demanded full-cost funding (i.e. baseline plus incremental costs). Developed countries, by contrast, often only agreed to covering incremental costs (i.e. additional costs above baseline to make projects sustainable).
	Eligibility and concomitant commitments	At the project level, developed and developing countries disagreed over which types of projects (e.g. mitigation versus adaptation) are eligible for receiving full or incremental costs funding. Whether all developing countries should be equally eligible and in exchange for what also led to disputes.
Throughput	Accessibility	Beneficiaries have repeatedly criticized climate finance for being slow and bureaucratic and demanded easier and more expedient access to funds.
	Governance	Conflicts over climate finance governance have concerned beneficiaries' representation in decision-making bodies, voting, and decision-making rules, as well as institutions' accountability to the COP and potential outside influences.

dollar) 15 to 20bn (cf. Table 8.1). To put this into perspective, the costs associated with repairing the damages brought on by the disastrous 2021 floods in the German Ahr Valley alone are estimated to be around USD 30bn (DW 2021). Furthermore, of these overall resources dedicated to climate finance, only about one out of every ten dollars was allocated in our first period of investigation (until 2007) while the rest was only granted gradually throughout the second phase and in response to the conflicts we study (GEF 2021a; GEF IEO 2014; Heinrich Böll Stiftung and ODI 2019a; 2019d; 2019c; 2019b; UNFCCC 2022a; 2022b).

Third, the original structure of the Financial Mechanism for the UN Framework Convention centred around the GEF, meaning that the subsequent institutional changes also relate to the prominence of this original institution. The GEF was the oldest climate fund started in 1992 with four focal areas, including climate change. The initial overall budget for its pilot phase amounted to USD 1bn (GEF 2021a; Streck 2001: 73–74). Since then, contributors have replenished the overall budget of the GEF in four-year cycles. Donor countries have been contributing an agreed minimum each, and additional voluntary contributions have helped reach the agreed overall replenishment levels (GEF Trustee 2021). Over time, GEF replenishments for all focal areas taken together have increased from between USD 2bn and USD 3bn before 2010 up to more than USD 4bn after 2010 (GEF 2021a). Out of these overall budgets, about one third has historically been dedicated to the climate change focal area (GEF Secretariat 2006: 15; 2018: 160; GEF IEO 2014: 38). Decisions about how budgets are spent are taken by the major decision-making body of the GEF, the GEF Council. It adopts decisions by a double-weighted majority representing 60 per cent of contributions as well as 60 per cent of participants (GEF 2019: 17).

Fourth, resource allocations under the different climate finance channels differ substantially. The specific needs of developing countries as beneficiaries of climate finance are recognized in several articles of the 1992 UN Framework Convention. Notably, Articles 4.3. and 4.4. specify that 'developed country Parties and other developed Parties included in Annex II shall provide new and additional financial resources to meet the agreed full costs incurred by developing country Parties in complying with their obligations'. Moreover, the same group of contributors 'shall also assist the developing country Parties that are particularly vulnerable to the adverse effects of climate change in meeting costs of adaptation'. In this regard, not just overall funding levels, but also the distribution of funds *among* rights-holders is important. As the discussion below will show, developed countries preferred resources to flow to those rights-holders and projects with relatively advanced capacities since this promised greatest cost-efficiency and 'global benefits'. By contrast, developing countries generally argued for a resource allocation based on local needs.

Comparing the approximate resource allocation of the GEF, Adaptation Fund, and GCF in phase two reveals that – relatively speaking – the GEF has allocated resources in greater accordance with the preferences of developed countries. It has allocated about USD 0.8bn to Brazil, China, and India; USD 0.5bn to LDCs; and USD 0.3bn to Small Island Developing States (SIDS) (GEF 2021a; GEF Secretariat 2006; 2018; GEF Trustee 2021). The Adaptation Fund and GCF, by contrast, have emphasized the provision of resources to vulnerable developing countries. While the Adaptation Fund has only allocated about USD 0.01bn to Brazil, China, and India (and among these only to India), it has allocated USD 0.22bn to the LDCs, and USD 0.12bn to the SIDS (Adaptation Fund n.d.; Heinrich Böll Stiftung and ODI 2019a; UNFCCC 2022a). Similarly, during its initial resource mobilization period, the GCF allocated USD 0.61bn to Brazil, China, and India, and USD 2.53bn and USD 0.96bn respectively to the LDCs and SIDS (GCF n.d.-a; n.d.-b; Heinrich Böll Stiftung and ODI 2019b; UNFCCC 2022b). This rough comparison shows that the new funds created after the respective conflicts allocate significantly more resources (both relatively and absolutely) to the vulnerable LDCs and SIDS than the GEF does.

Fifth, both conflicts exhibit a tripartite dynamic. They begin with a 'prelude' phase during which tension between developed and developing countries built up. They culminate in a respective 'crisis and decision' moment at which these tensions contributed to negotiation deadlock out of which negotiators took a restructuring decision. And eventually, each conflict fades out in an 'implementation' period during which the decisions taken at the respective crisis moment are operationalized. For understanding the negotiation dynamics and outcomes in relation to the rise of Brazil, China, and India, all three phases are equally relevant. During both preludes, for example, developing countries criticized and challenged the existing institutional structures but failed to effect sufficient structural change. And both implementation phases showed that the decisions taken at the crisis moment were practically implemented in a way that eased the previously built-up pressures.

8.3 CONFLICT 1: MORE FUNDS FOR ADAPTATION AND VULNERABLE COUNTRIES

This section turns to the first major climate finance conflict which occurred in our first period of investigation (1992–2007). It retraces the disputes between developed and developing countries that eventually led to the creation of more funds, especially for adaptation and vulnerable countries. The conflict resulted in the addition of new institutional layers within as well as branching alongside the GEF. Arguments of developing countries for more climate finance relied on their moral claim to assistance. These normative arguments were based on historical contributions of developed countries to climate change as well as on the legal provisions contained in the UN Framework Convention. Expecting emissions and capabilities of rising powers to grow, however, developed countries were reluctant to grant further resources without concomitant commitments. Overall, climate finance flows through the Financial Mechanism therefore remained limited, amounting to only about USD 2bn in this first phase.

8.3.1 Prelude: The Initial Establishment and Contestation of the GEF

The first climate finance conflict essentially started with the initial institutional set-up of climate finance under the 1992 UN Framework Convention. Based on previous experiences with multilateral treaties in the 1970s and 1980s (Rajamani 2006: 119–121), Organisation for Economic Co-operation and Development (OECD) countries anticipated that once the UN Framework Convention was adopted, it would require a Financial Mechanism to channel assistance from stronger to weaker members. France, quickly joined by an increasingly environmentally conscious Germany and then other OECD members, suggested creating a funding institution under the new convention and embedded into the existing landscape of international economic institutions, notably the World Bank (Horta et al. 2002: 1; Streck 2001: 76). The World Bank, the United Nations Development Programme (UNDP), and the United Nations Environment Programme (UNEP) then formally established the GEF as a joint endeavour, initially designed for a three-year pilot programme to cofinance incremental costs of sustainability projects in developing countries (Streck 2001: 72–75). While the three organizations served as 'Implementing Agencies' of the GEF, their roles, responsibilities, and powers were distributed asymmetrically. Whereas the World Bank was to house the GEF Secretariat, run GEF investment projects, and administer the GEF Trust Fund, UNDP and UNEP acted as 'junior partners' in charge of providing 'scientific guidance' and 'technical assistance'. This again broadly reflected the preferences of the OECD and contributed to the dismay between duty-bearers and rights-holders (Horta et al. 2002: 5).

So, even though the GEF was formally established 'on the eve of the 1992 Rio Earth Summit' (GEF 2021b) and then started serving the climate regime, it had already been conceived of and outlined before. The question of which institution should channel climate finance was immediately fraught with conflict between developed and developing countries. The group of developing countries preferred creating a new 'green fund' that would be guided by and accountable to the Conference of the Parties (COP). Developed countries, chief among them the US, however, preferred entrusting climate finance to an existing institution. As contributors, they also preferred maintaining strong ties between the World Bank and climate finance (Bodansky 1993: 468, 538; Coventry 2019: 159; Goldemberg 1994: 181; Hyder 1994; Sjöberg 1999).

In this respect and in its earliest form as a special climate programme within the World Bank, the GEF can thus be described as a *pre-emptive* institution inserted into several environmental conventions by an influential sub-group of developed countries (Coventry 2019: 157–159). Developing countries agreed to this initial arrangement provided that the GEF would only become the 'interim' operating entity of the Financial Mechanism and since it was tasked with immediate restructuring (Coventry 2019: 159; Gupta 2014: 60). Still, much of the ensuing distrust in developing countries towards the GEF, but also towards the Financial Mechanism more broadly, can be traced back to this initial attempt at setting the agenda in line with the preferences of contributors (e.g. Horta et al. 2002: 1).

To receive GEF funding, beneficiaries must be members of the respective conventions. In this way, the conventions and the GEF reinforce one another (GEF 2021a; Streck 2001: 90). The 1992 UNFCCC established a general grouping of duty-bearers and rights-holders. It did not determine reliable or specific financing levels, but its provisions were legally binding and thus differed from other, purely voluntary, forms of international assistance. Developing countries have since had not just a normative but also a legal claim on climate finance. In the first phase, they built their calls for more assistance predominantly on this foundation. Among the legal provisions, the promise to cover costs associated with, first, the commitments of developing countries under the Convention and, second, the adaptation to adverse effects are among the most far-reaching operationalizations of differential treatment in the climate regime. Consequently, related debates over what these provisions entail continued to fuel conflicts about climate finance over the years (cf. Verheyen 2005: 91–93).

Responding primarily to initial reservations of developing countries against the GEF, Article 21 of the 1992 UN Framework Convention demanded that the GEF be 'appropriately restructured'. Importantly, it required GEF membership to be made universal (GEF 1994: 5–7; Streck 2001). This call for restructuring shows that although developed countries had held strong influence over decisions on the initial shape of the GEF, developing countries immediately began challenging the institutional landscape of climate finance on normative and practical grounds. Yet, none of the articles of the 1992 UN Framework Convention specified the exact relationship between the GEF and the COP. While this ambiguity appeared necessary at the time to secure agreement on the Convention, it also became a breeding ground for dissatisfaction and institutional contestation (Coventry 2019: 160–161).

Climate conferences in the mid-1990s demonstrated the rising tensions over climate finance between developed and developing countries. In 1995, for example, COP-1 acknowledged the 1994 GEF Report (FCCC/CP/1995/7/Add.1. of 6 June 1995: Decision 9/CP.1) which states that '[t]he restructured GEF is to continue operating ..., thus avoiding the creation of a new institution' (GEF 1994: 8).[1] This formulation shows that soon after it was named the interim operating entity of the Financial Mechanism, the GEF had formed and expressed the will to fulfil this task alone. An early and explicit institutional goal of attempts at reforming the GEF has thus been to remain open to structural change if necessary to avoid fragmenting or expanding the institutional landscape (Coventry 2019: 159; Sjöberg 1999). Developed countries welcomed this development while developing countries accepted it only reluctantly to wait and see how the GEF would perform in practice.

COP-1 (1995) also replenished the GEF and decided on its eligibility criteria. The 1994 GEF report had stated that the GEF 'closely observes' the eligibility criteria as decided by the COP (GEF 1994: 8). However, the provisions operating procedures of the GEF, including its eligibility criteria, were closely aligned with those of its implementing agencies. Such influence of institutions outside the 1992 UN Framework Convention over GEF governance procedures contributed further to the dissatisfaction among developing countries who wished to keep the GEF more directly and exclusively under COP control (e.g. Ballesteros et al. 2010: 269; Coventry 2019: 161–162).

Countries which planned to be contributors to the newly restructured GEF had to renew their corresponding intent. The COP set the target for the first replenishment period of the GEF (1994–1998) at USD 2bn. Contributors not only met but exceeded this goal, and about one third of the funds were programmed for the climate change focal area (GEF 2021a; GEF IEO 2014: 38). Interestingly, Brazil, China, and India had been 'recipient donors' from the start (GEF Trustee 2021: 3). The Conference also explicitly mentioned and welcomed 'cofinancing' which featured prominently in the GEF restructuring (GEF 1994). Unable to reach agreement on the related controversial concept of incremental costs, however, COP-1 (1995) merely acknowledged the complexity and difficulty of the matter and asked that the concept should be applied flexibly and pragmatically on a case-by-case basis (FCCC/CP/1995/7/Add.1 of 7 June 1995: Decision 11/CP.1). Such calls for pragmatic case-by-case evaluations already hinted at a more layered approach to funding but had not yet been fully implemented structurally.

Between 1996 and 1999, the GEF came under renewed fire regarding its input, institutional throughput, and output dimensions. Developing countries demanded that the full incremental costs of implementing measures under the Convention and of adaptation be met, pushing for an essentially *unlimited* interpretation of Article 4.4 of the Convention. At first sight, this dispute appears as a dispute on assistance alone. However, developing countries argued that developed countries were additionally trying to generally shift burdens onto developing countries by altering the operational rules and holding back on funding (ENB 12/38 of 12 July 1996: 4, 12).[2] Subsequent conferences correspondingly expressed concern over the difficulties experienced by developing countries. Developing countries achieved explicit recognition by the COP that these difficulties were linked, among other things, to the GEF's 'operational policies on eligibility criteria, disbursement, project cycle and approval, [and] the application of its concept of incremental costs'. The COP formulated strategies to meet these challenges, such as greater procedural transparency and again a pragmatic case-by-case approach. Lacking an institutional alternative, however, the COP decided that the GEF should continue to be the operating entity of the Financial Mechanism and adopted a Memorandum of

Understanding to further regulate relations between the GEF and the COP (FCCC/CP/1996/15/Add.1 of 29 October 1996: Decisions 11/CP.2, 12/CP.2).

Between 1997 and 1999, climate finance began to also be more explicitly related to conflicts over central obligations and concomitant commitments of assistance rights-holders (cf. Table 8.2). For example, the G-77 (Group of 77) and China stressed that mitigation commitments and assistance were exclusively the obligations of developed countries (ENB 12/76 of 13 December 1997: 4). In addition, the 1997 Kyoto Protocol specified and partially extended the Financial Mechanism of the 1992 UN Framework Convention. Articles 10 and 11 of the Kyoto Protocol thus called for the provision of 'new and additional' finance from developed to developing countries to meet beneficiaries' 'agreed full costs ... of existing commitments under ... the Convention'. Moreover, the Kyoto Protocol repeated previous calls for such finance to be 'adequate and predictable' (ENB 12/76 of 13 December 1997: 10–11). In 1998, the Buenos Aires Plan of Action welcomed the second GEF replenishment (USD 2.75bn) and inter alia specified that the GEF should provide more funding for adaptation in developing countries and further streamline and simplify the availability and accessibility of funds (FCCC/CP/1998/16/Add.1 of 20 January 1999: Decisions 1/CP.4, 2/CP.4, 3/CP.4). Developing countries, however, suggested that the GEF should be more fundamentally 'politically reoriented' to better meet their needs, and reiterated their calls for institutional alternatives to the GEF (Coventry 2019: 164–165; ENB 12/80 of 5 June 1998; ENB 12/90 of 5 November 1998; ENB 12/92 of 9 November 1998).

Despite such ongoing discord between developed and developing countries over the different climate finance dimensions, negotiating parties appeared to have remained hopeful in the 1990s. They tried to make progress on these issues and took decisions to improve the efficiency and effectiveness of the existing structures of international climate finance (e.g. ENB 12/11 of 20 February 1995: 10). Importantly, in its last review prior to the upcoming crisis moment, the COP also decided more generally that the GEF should be an operating entity of the Financial Mechanism. Through this decision, the 'interim' specifier from previous decisions eventually disappeared (FCCC/CP/1998/16/Add.1 of 20 January 1999: Decision 3/CP.4).

8.3.2 Crisis Decision for Layering and Branching Out: Three New Funds under and besides the GEF

After the initially hopeful start of climate finance, the disappointing experiences of developing countries with GEF funding levels, goals, and practices cocreated a negotiation deadlock at the 2000 COP-6 in The Hague. This deadlock and the eventual creation of three new climate finance institutions form the crisis moment and decision part of the first climate finance conflict.

While the disagreement between the European Union (EU) and US on sinks and supplementarity is regarded as the most visible reason for the stalemate at COP-6 (2000), some observers have argued that the dissatisfaction of developing countries with climate finance issues alone would likely have sufficed to capsize this conference (ENB 12/163 of 27 November 2000: 18).

In the run-up to the Conference, conflicts between developed and developing countries that had already become visible during the 1990s reappeared with force (Coventry 2019: 164; with reference to ENB 12/38 of 22 July 1996; ENB 12/40 of 3 March 1997; ENB 12/70 of 4 December 1997; and ENB 12/80 of 5 June 1998). They revolved around input volumes, whether financial assistance should be provided in exchange for concomitant commitments by developing countries, and if so, in exchange for which commitments exactly. Moreover, to what extent the GEF or potential alternative structures should cover funding for adaptation, especially in particularly vulnerable and LDCs, remained contentious among parties going into the Conference (ENB 12/163 of 27 November 2000: 5, 8; ENB 12/151 of 18 September 2000: 15).

Developed and developing countries thus arrived at what eventually became the first of two parts of COP-6 (2000) with fundamentally different, often opposing, demands. Although the GEF had been restructured during the 1990s, the G-77 and China continued to call for more and clearer guidance. Arguing that the GEF had failed to provide adequate funding thus far (ENB 12/110 of 14 June 1999: 7), they also demanded more directly accessible, more transparent, and more predictable funding, especially for adaptation and for vulnerable countries. The restructuring reforms had given developing countries a majority of seats and hence an effective veto over Council decisions. In practice, however, the Council typically takes decisions by consensus based on recommendations by the Chair (Coventry 2019: 162; Horta et al. 2002). On top of these disputes, the G-77 and China voiced procedural objections in relation to climate finance negotiations and so the delegations negotiating financial issues at the beginning of COP-6 (2000) failed to make significant headway (ENB 12/163 of 27 November 2000: 4). Overall, developing country demands expressed the view that climate finance under the GEF had failed to fulfil the moral demands arising out of the historical injustices prevailing in the causes and consequences of climate change.

Developed countries, by contrast, generally regarded the GEF as effective and efficient. The EU, for example, argued that the existing Financial Mechanism had 'responded effectively to developing country needs' (ENB 12/110 of 14 June 1999: 7; ENB 12/123 of 8 November 1999: 4). Views had also clashed on additionality, when the G-77 and China expressed that climate finance should be additional to aid, while Japan argued that such financial additionality was not required (ENB 12/123 of 8 November 1999: 9). Some developed countries (notably Denmark, the United Kingdom, and Canada), however, acknowledged that climate finance should better respond to the needs of LDCs and put a greater focus on adaptation (Coventry 2019: 168). Such instances signalled a certain degree of openness towards change as well as disunity among developed countries.

When ongoing differences over GEF funding could not be settled at COP-6 (2000), negotiations increasingly slid into stalemate. Realizing that agreement on the conflictive climate finance concepts could perhaps not be reached within the GEF alone, delegations from developed as well as developing countries grew increasingly creative in their search for ideas to find a way out of the negotiation impasse. The spectrum of available options for institutional change included suggestions for incrementally or again rigorously reforming the GEF, for fully rebooting climate finance, and for adding either new institutional layers within the GEF or even branching out (cf. section 8.5).

The G-77 and China, supported by the African Group but strongly opposed by the US, Canada, Japan, the Russian Federation, and other developed countries, called for the creation of an 'adaptation fund'. That fund, the coalition argued, should be independently funded by levies on the Kyoto Protocol mechanisms and operate next to the GEF (ENB 12/163 of 27 November 2000: 12). The proposal was not completely new. Saudi Arabia, for example, had already voiced a similar proposal for a new funding institution (Coventry 2019: 164; ENB 12/151 of 18 September 2000: 15–16). It would have represented an instance of branching out as it would have created a new and independent institution besides the GEF.

Such proposals, however, were a direct strike against the GEF and against developed countries supporting its exclusive status. The call for independent inflows into a potential new fund could have severely diminished the influence developed countries held over the institutional landscape of climate finance. Consequently, proposals for new institutions ignited strong reactions among developed countries which further exacerbated the negotiation deadlock (ENB 12/151 of 18 September 2000: 15–16; ENB 12/163 of 27 November 2000: 18). The *Earth Negotiations Bulletin* (ENB) report thus records that 'the US, Canada, Japan, the Russian Federation, Hungary and Australia' opposed the proposal. Japan announced in turn that an Umbrella Group proposal for a new 'funding window' under the GEF, with greater focus inter alia on adaptation and the needs of vulnerable countries, would be tabled. Moreover, the EU presented its own proposal. Yet, even in the informal high-level plenary that assembled in the last week of negotiations, developed and developing countries could not agree on either of the ideas floating around (ENB 12/163 of 27 November 2000: 5, 12).

COP-6 (2000) President Jan Pronk eventually proposed a negotiation text as a way out of the crisis. As 'crunch issues', he identified funding for adaptation and capacity-building under the GEF, modalities and conditionalities of GEF funding, and the question of whether the GEF should remain the sole financing channel under the Financial Mechanism (ENB 12/163 of 27 November 2000: 4–8). Building on this diagnosis, he drafted a formal note on his 'personal responsibility', which formed the basis for the eventual restructuring of the institutional climate finance landscape. The note of the President suggested: 'an Adaptation Fund, a Convention Fund, and a Climate Resources Committee, as well as increasing resources for climate change funding. The Adaptation Fund would be a new fund under the GEF … with special consideration given to the needs of the LDCs and SIDS' (ENB 12/163 of 27 November 2000: 5; FCCC/CP/2000/5/Add.2 of 4 April 2001: 4–5). The proposed Adaptation Fund would be financed by a share of the proceeds from the Clean Development Mechanism (CDM) of the 1997 Kyoto Protocol. The proposed Convention Fund would be a new 'funding window' under the GEF. Both would receive separate guidance and have a stronger focus on funding for adaptation, especially in vulnerable and LDCs. The proposed task of the Climate Resources Committee, in turn, would be to advise climate finance institutions (ENB 12/163 of 27 November 2000: 5).

The proposal of Pronk combined elements of layering and branching out. Deciding in favour of his proposal would thus have meant that new funding institutions would be created and equipped with increased funding volumes, which would have been in general accordance with the demands of developing countries. On the other hand, it would have secured a strong role for the GEF, thereby reflecting the preferences of developed countries. The suggestion of adding new funds that were structurally placed both under *and* besides the GEF, however, was met with a cautious reaction by negotiating parties. Its exact consequences for the levels and operational structures of funding remained vague. In addition, attempts of developed countries to link funding under the Convention to developing country commitments under the 1997 Kyoto Protocol led to strong objections from the G-77 and China. Unable to find agreement during the ultimate weekend of COP-6 (2000), the Conference decided to suspend its Sixth Session and resume negotiations in 2001 (ENB 12/163 of 27 November 2000; FCCC/CP/2000/5/Add.2 of 4 April 2001).

The official meeting report of the resumed COP-6 (2000) supports the argument that disagreements over the Financial Mechanism were a major contributor to the failed negotiations. It recognizes the concerns of the G-77 and China 'about overburdening the GEF', about the communication requirements as a basis of funding, about the specific concerns of LDCs, and about the voluntary or mandatory nature of contribution levels as crucial reasons for the deadlock (ENB 12/176 of 30 July 2001: 4). In the resumed negotiations, though, both developed and developing countries managed to agree on a way out of crisis. Specifically, they established the SCCF and the LDC Fund. Moreover, they agreed on the establishment of the Adaptation Fund under the

1997 Kyoto Protocol 'for financing concrete adaptation projects in developing countries' (ENB 12/176 of 30 July 2001: 5; FCCC/CP/2001/5 of 25 September 2001). To what extent exactly the new funds would be entangled with the GEF remained unsettled, however.

The decisions taken at the crisis moment had been tedious to reach and left many negotiating parties disappointed (ENB 12/176 of 30 July 2001). Although COP-6 (2000) established new institutions with a focus on adaptation and the needs of vulnerable countries, their legal quality and overall levels of funding, governance structures, and operational guidelines remained in flux. And while the Adaptation Fund was indeed to be financed under the CDM of the Kyoto Protocol and further voluntary contributions, the US withdrawal from the Kyoto Protocol struck a significant blow to any hopes of high input levels. Developing countries felt they had traded in their insistence on mandatory and binding levels of funding from developed countries for the establishment of the three new institutions. The ENB report of the meeting thus quotes one developing country delegate as sceptically noting that developed countries 'have shown us the blank checks, now the question is will they actually enter any figures' (ENB 12/176 of 30 July 2001: 13). At the same time, however, developing countries had been able to fend off demands for new central commitments in exchange for climate finance under the new funds. Furthermore, even though the GEF remained the predominant funding institution of the international climate regime, developed countries had failed in their effort to maintain it as the exclusive channel under the Financial Mechanism.

8.3.3 Implementation: Powering Up the New Funds

The 2001 Marrakesh Accords agreed at COP-7 contain the formal decisions that created the new funds (Decision 5/CP.6; FCCC/CP/2001/5 of 25 September 2001: 36; FCCC/CP/2001/13/Add.1 of 21 January 2002: Decisions 7/CP.7, 10/CP.7). Reverting to a less confrontational tone, negotiators formulated a draft decision on guidance to the LDC Fund with simplified procedures to ease access, recognizing that LDC concerns were most pressing (e.g. Dessai 2003: 296). Before further details could be set in agreed writing, however, major developed countries (including the EU and US) suggested postponing further discussion of the new funds (ENB 12/189 of 12 November 2001: 12).

Between 2001 and 2008, negotiating parties operationalized the three new funds. Negotiations focussed first on operationalizing the LDC Fund and the SCCF. The COP postponed further operationalization of the Adaptation Fund to prioritize LDC concerns and because it was to be funded by the proceeds from the CDM under the 1997 Kyoto Protocol which had yet to enter into force (Coventry 2019: 157, 174; Dessai 2003: 296; FCCC/CP/2001/13/Add.1 of 21 January 2002: 32–33).

Negotiations at COP-7 (2001) to COP-12 (2006) appeared calmer. Discontentment of developing countries with the GEF had been partially appeased as the new funds and their respective focal areas held real promise to formulate more nuanced responses to their interests and needs. The LDC Fund and the SCCF were created to specifically take the climate change-related burdens of the most disadvantaged countries into account and fund alleviatory measures (FCCC/CP/2001/13/Add.1 of 21 January 2002: Decision 5/CP.7). Similarly, the creation of the Adaptation Fund meant a greater focus on funding for adaptation. Together, the new institutional structures promised that cost-efficiency and the focus of the GEF on global benefits could be complemented with a stronger concern for the local needs of vulnerable beneficiaries.

Crucially, however, according to the decisions that had created the new institutions, all three new funds were originally to be managed by 'an operating entity of the financial mechanism', which at the time meant the GEF. This would merely have meant adding layers to an otherwise unchanged institutional landscape. In this respect, the implementation phase was characterized by the same recurring disagreements that had characterized negotiations in previous years. Developing countries reiterated their calls for more independent climate finance (both overall and for adaptation and vulnerable countries) and stressed that the GEF continued to inadequately fulfil the needs of developing countries regarding input volumes, institutional structures, and output usability. Developed countries, in turn, continued their support for greater GEF influence but occasionally also joined criticisms of developing countries, again signalling some measure of openness and disunity (Coventry 2019: 170–171).

As these issues threatened to creep from the GEF into the new institutions, too, developing countries attempted to further separate the new funds from the GEF. For example, they tried to secure operational independence, equitable representation, direct COP oversight, as well as direct access (Coventry 2019: 174–176). Furthermore, the G-77 and China voiced concern over the conditionality of GEF funding when, at COP-8 (2002), the GEF expressed its understanding that its operational procedures would also apply to the new funds until further guidance by the COP (e.g. ENB 12/209 of 4 November 2002: 9).

Conversely, developed countries undertook several attempts to closely tie the new funds to the GEF and avoid further institutional fragmentation of the climate finance landscape. For example, underlining initial text from COP-7 (2001), developed countries shared the expectation of the GEF that it would have a prominent and permanent role in governing the Adaptation Fund. At COP-12 in 2006, the EU, Canada, Switzerland, and Norway similarly called for the GEF to be designated as the operating entity for the Adaptation Fund and Japan, Norway, and Switzerland noted 'the GEF is best placed to manage the Fund' (Flåm and Skjærseth, cited in Coventry 2019: 175; see also ENB 12/318 of 20 November 2006: 14).

In the end, inflows into the SCCF and the LDC Fund remained voluntary, and both remained smaller funds managed by and thus structurally similar to the GEF (UNFCCC 2022c; see also Table 8.1). These two new funds typically take unanimous decisions with the GEF and follow guidance of the GEF Council. Since the SCCF and the LDC Fund did not establish independent governance structures, developing countries began to regard them as GEF extensions with an institutional structure that they had been bemoaning for years (Coventry 2019: 173).

Nevertheless, the new funds differ from the GEF in terms of their sources of funding (input dimension), their governance structures, accessibility, transparency, and voting procedures (throughput dimension), as well as their eligibility criteria and goals (output dimension). All new funds have funding for adaptation on their agenda. This was important to developing countries who had previously criticized the GEF for its neglect of that topic (e.g. Dessai 2003: 299). Moreover, the new funds not only complement GEF funding but also compete and overlap with it. While all developing countries are technically eligible to receive funding, the most vulnerable among them now receive substantially more attention while Brazil, China, and India neither contribute nor (substantially) benefit (cf. Table 8.1). The Adaptation Fund is structurally most distinct from the GEF. It is independently governed, directly accountable to the COP, and recipient countries can directly access it through their national implementing entities (Adapation Fund Board 2017; Harmeling and Kaloga 2011: 27). The Adaptation Fund thus ended up representing a case of branching out while the LDC and SCC Funds were institutionally integrated into the GEF.

Overall, the decisions taken at the crisis moment and their eventual implementation represent an expansion of differential treatment. The new institutions move the institutional landscape for international climate finance closer to the preferences of developing countries for adequacy and additionality. At the same time, they exhibit persistent similarities with the GEF on matters of governance, transparency, and predictability.

8.4 CONFLICT 2: MORE FUNDS FOR BOTH MITIGATION AND ADAPTATION IN EXCHANGE FOR CENTRAL OBLIGATIONS

This section retraces a second major climate finance conflict. This conflict started during the implementation phase of the first conflict and culminated in the creation of the GCF, another climate finance institution with operational independence from the GEF. The implementation phase then lasted until at least 2014 when the GCF became operational and had completed its initial resource mobilization (GCF n.d.-b).

Three observations are particularly important to understand the dynamics and outcome of this second climate finance conflict. First, as already described in the previous section, developing countries continued to experience frustration with the GEF and suggested that its maladies had wormed their way into the GEF-governed new funds, too. In this respect, the new Resource Allocation Framework of the GEF, which went into effect in 2005, aggravated concerns of developing countries. Under this framework, GEF resources were concentrated in relatively strong developing countries. Since more advanced developing countries have greater capacities for absorbing, managing, and using inflows, such allocation reflected preferences of developed countries for the highest possible global benefits instead of local needs of developing countries (Ballesteros et al. 2010: 273; Coventry 2019: 174). Second, calls from developed countries for central obligations in developing countries (especially rising powers) were growing louder. Developing countries eventually began offering central obligations but in turn demanded a corresponding increase in climate finance (cf. Chapter 3). And third, even though funding levels had remained below expectations, the experience of setting up the Adaptation Fund had taught developing countries that branching out an institutional alternative to the GEF was possible. Together, these circumstances strengthened the unity among developing countries and encouraged them in challenging the GEF anew.

8.4.1 Prelude: Recurring Issues with the GEF and Renewed Hope for an Institutional Alternative

While the Adaptation Fund was created in 2001, earnest negotiations on its operationalization only began in 2005 when the first conferences under the Kyoto Protocol were held (Coventry 2019: 174; FCCC/CP/2016/10/Add.1 of 31 January 2017). The difference in timing may appear minute but it meant that delegations had had time to experience the SCCF and the LDC Fund in practice. Whether the Adaptation Fund should similarly be operationalized as a further layer under the GEF or take on a more independent institutional form consequently became a central bone of contention.

Like in previous years, developed and developing countries remained divided over the role and influence of the GEF. At COP-11 in 2005, for example, the G-77 and China expressed concern that the newly established Resource Allocation Framework and the cofinancing requirements of the GEF could pose barriers to operationalizing and accessing the Adaptation Fund. If the Adaptation Fund were to be managed by the GEF, allocating its resources among developing countries would likely also follow the logic of the GEF which could run counter to the intended greater focus on adaptation and the needs of vulnerable countries (Müller 2006: 23–24). The G-77 and China thus supported direct COP authority over the Adaptation Fund, a view that was separately underlined by, for example, Alliance of Small Island States (AOSIS) and Namibia (Coventry 2019: 175; with reference to ENB 12/282 of 30 November 2005; ENB 12/289 of 8 December 2005; ENB 12/291 of 12 December 2005). On further GEF replenishments, both developed and developing countries agreed that 'new and additional' and substantially more climate finance was needed to appropriately respond to the mounting threats of climate change. Recognizing these developing country concerns, COP-13 (2007) decided to scale up, enhance, and simplify the needs assessment of the Financial Mechanism, the accessibility and availability of its funds as well as its complementarity with other sources of funding. These measures, once more, sought to further streamline and simplify procedures and access to funding (especially for LDCs and SIDS) and to more systematically integrate lessons learned from previous funding activities (FCCC/CP/2007/6/Add.1 of 14 March 2008: Decisions 6/CP.13, 7/CP.13).

Developed countries initially sought to secure GEF influence over the Adaptation Fund just as they had with the LDC and SCCF (Flåm and Skjærseth 2009: 110). Importantly, however, since it had not ratified the 1997 Kyoto Protocol, the US, as perhaps the most important negotiating party among developed countries, was excluded from crucial negotiations on the Adaptation Fund. Japan, the EU, Canada, and Norway reiterated at different points their position that the GEF should be the operating entity for the Adaptation Fund and the GEF expressed its corresponding willingness to take on this role (Coventry 2019: 175–176; ENB 12/291 of 12 December 2005: 15).

Eventually coming down in favour of the preferences of developing countries, however, Decision 28/CMP.1 contained operational details of the Adaptation Fund – for example on its sources of funding from the CDM and its direct accountability to the parties. Importantly, and against the expressed will of developed countries, the decision only *took note of* the aspiration and proposal of the GEF to also operate this new fund (FCCC/KP/CMP/2005/8/Add.4 of 30 March 2006: 3). The eventual input sources, governance, and one-country-one-vote voting structures, as well as accessibility, were strikingly different from those of the GEF (cf. Table 8.1). Decision 5/CMP.2 then further specified that the envisaged independent Adaptation Fund Board should govern the fund – the Board 'shall be from Parties to the Kyoto Protocol, follow a one-country one-vote rule and have a majority of Parties not included in Annex I to the Convention' (FCCC/KP/CMP/2006/10/Add.1 of 26 January 2007: 28–29). COP-13 (2007) in Bali and COP-14 (2008) in Poznan finalized the operational details of the Adaptation Fund. They, inter alia, established the independent Adaptation Fund Board and ensured direct access to the fund through national implementing agencies. The influence of the GEF over the Adaptation Fund had hence been broken as it was reduced to limited secretariat services. Branching out besides the GEF, the Adaptation Fund could since be regarded the most independent and directly accessible fund of the Financial Mechanism (Grasso 2011: 364; FCCC/KP/CMP/2007/9/Add.1 of 14 March 2008: Decision 1/CMP.3; FCCC/KP/CMP/2008/11/Add.2 of 19 March 2009: Decision 1/CMP.4).

Despite these successes of the G-77 and China in setting up the Adaptation Fund, however, its funding levels did not suffice to close the gap between what the GEF offered and what developing countries argued they needed (cf. Table 8.1; TWN 2010: 6). Against this backdrop, calls for a renewed fundamental institutional revision grew louder and negotiations on the GCF were set in motion.

8.4.2 Crisis Decision for Branching Out: Creating a Second Operating Entity besides the GEF

Despite their initial hopes for the new funds, their practical experiences between 2001 and 2009 had left the G-77 and China disappointed and refuelled their united search for alternative institutional arrangements. The Brazilian government, for example, speaking for the group at COP-15 (2009), criticized the fixed budget of the GEF for not taking the needs of developing countries into due consideration (TWN 2010: 25–26), and it expressed support for a completely new mechanism directly guided by the COP (Brazil, cited in Prys-Hansen et al. 2019: 282–283). This would have amounted to a complete rebooting of climate finance. The G-77 and China further criticized the inadequate overall levels of climate finance, calling instead for new resources amounting to USD 200–400bn annually and preferably flowing through a new institution (TWN 2010: 6). Following similar concerns voiced by other members of the G-77 and China, Barbados compared 'the difficulties of access to having "been given an ATM card without the PIN number"' (ENB 12/427 of 17 August 2009: 9). Moreover, the G-77 and China together with AOSIS opposed applying the Resource Allocation Framework of the GEF to non-Annex I communications, insisting on full-cost funding and making a suggestion to 'go beyond the GEF' if necessary (ENB 12/354 of 18 December 2007: 5; TWN 2008: 25–26). Without substantial institutional alternatives, however, such threats necessarily rang hollow. Rights-holders called for 'fast-track finance' and simplified procedures to access funds, arguing that around USD 200bn were needed by developing countries for emissions reductions and 'hundreds of billions of dollars more for adaptation activities' (TWN 2008: 7).

A further cause of dissonance was the fact that the Adaptation Fund was still not fully operational. The details of procedural coordination between the COP, GEF, Adaptation Fund, and World Bank, as well as the corresponding inability of the Adaptation Fund to take effective project financing decisions, added further dismay (ENB 12/395 of 15 December 2008: 9). Going into COP-15 (2009) in Copenhagen, developing countries still generally regarded the current institutional set-up as 'inadequate', the LDC Fund as 'completely underfunded', and called the USD 172m pledged to it a 'measly sum' (TWN 2009: 10). Funds flowing through the GEF did not receive a much more merciful verdict either when developing countries called them 'woefully inadequate' (TWN 2009: 16).

Developed countries, again, saw things differently. They sought to avoid further institutional fragmentation and wanted to keep the focus on cost-effectiveness, measurability, and output transparency as envisaged in the GEF Resource Allocation Framework. In the newly established Ad Hoc Working Group on Long-Term Cooperative Action (AWG-LCA), which was also charged with negotiating the future of climate finance, developed countries thus repeatedly and emphatically voiced their opposition to new climate finance institutions (Coventry 2019: 180). In relation to attempts at dividing rising powers from the group of developing countries, a notable example occurred at COP-14 (2008) when Japan suggested 'broadening the scope of developed countries and differentiating among developing countries with the possibility of graduation'. Expectably, this and similar proposals to differentiate among non-Annex I parties based on objective (current) criteria was met with firm rejection (e.g. Brazil, speaking for the G-77 and China, ENB 12/395 of 15 December 2008: 13; see also Vanderheiden 2015: 39). However, the issue of differentiated developing country commitments in exchange for an expansion of climate finance had gained traction (see also Chapter 3).

In light of these entrenched views, several proposals for institutional change emerged. In 2008, for example, South Africa had 'proposed streamlining financing mechanisms and reconsidering the institutional framework', while Egypt 'urged new funding mechanisms', the G-77 and China and others 'proposed creating an umbrella multilateral fund under the Convention', and 'Mexico, Indonesia and India suggested creating a multilateral fund under the Convention with foreseeable and scalable contributions by developed countries and a transparent and inclusive governance structure'. According to India, such a potential new institution should be governed by a new Executive Board with an equitable and balanced governance structure. Smaller developing countries, too, called for new institutions, for example when AOSIS 'proposed the establishment of a Convention Adaptation Fund' (cited in Prys-Hansen et al. 2019: 282–283; Coventry 2019: 179; with reference to ENB 12/360 of 3 April 2008; ENB 12/361 of 4 April 2008; ENB 12/365 of 3 June 2008). AOSIS further suggested that new resources should be channelled through the UNFCCC process and recommended 'an insurance mechanism and a technology fund'. India, together with other developing countries and LDCs, even called for 'a

2% levy on all capital transfers in developed countries to support adaptation, stressed that financial flows should be scaled up to 1.5% of the gross domestic product (GDP) of developed countries, and that 70% of funding for adaptation should be earmarked for LDCs, SIDS and African countries' (ENB 12/439 of 12 October 2009: 9). Funding for adaptation should hence again play a central role in the potential new institution (Coventry 2019: 179). With respect to COP oversight, developing countries attempted fully branching out the potential new fund such that it would not only be 'accountable to' or 'guided by' the COP (like the GEF) but be placed under direct and full COP authority (like the Adaptation Fund). This characteristic, however, was eventually excluded (Vanderheiden 2015: 34).

In what would turn out to become a crucial proposal, Mexico 'proposed a world climate change fund, or green fund, on mitigation, adaptation and technology transfer, with participation of all countries and contributions according to greenhouse gas emissions, population and GDP' (ENB 368 of 6 June 2008: 1). Opposing such suggestions of objective criteria that could potentially lead to more than voluntary contributions even by developing countries, China joined the far-reaching proposal of India in stating that 'funding should come from developed countries as a percentage of their GDP, and that financial initiatives outside the UNFCCC should not be counted as fulfilment of developed country commitments' (ENB 12/368 of 6 June 2008: 1). China and India thus initially proposed removing the option on a 'new green fund' or a world climate change fund (ENB 12/439 of 12 October 2009: 10; ENB 12/421 of 15 June 2009: 4). Such positions illustrate how rising powers continued siding with other developing countries, using their increased material power to demand higher levels of finance while at the same time demanding that inputs should be provided by developed countries.

Developed countries noted the general momentum for institutional change and formulated their own counterproposals. Most significant among them was the US suggestion for a new character in the climate finance landscape. According to the US proposal, the GEF would continue serving as the operating entity, but funding priorities and eligibility criteria would be decided by the COP, governance would be balanced between developed and developing countries, and all parties except LDCs would contribute according to their respective capabilities. Instead of branching out, this proposal would have meant an incremental or fundamental restructuring of the GEF. Expectably, the G-77 and China immediately responded that 'the US proposal does not address the problems with the current financial mechanism'. Countering the US proposal, Tanzania suggested 'using the structure in place under the Protocol's Adaptation Fund to address issues of governance and access' (ENB 12/439 of 12 October 2009: 10–11). China stressed that the whole Financial Mechanism, and not just its operating entity, was under review. The main problem, according to China, was the lack of funding from developed countries which had 'not met their financial obligations under the Convention' (TWN 2009: 18).

Eventually, it was the Mexican proposal in combination with the input from the US that built the foundation for the creation of a new funding institution. Apparently, developed countries were willing to accept reduced GEF involvement given new concomitant developing country commitments, so long as the World Bank remained the trustee of the new fund, and so long as the new institution was also open to inputs from a 'variety of sources' (Coventry 2019: 182). A complete decoupling of the GEF from the World Bank, however, remained unacceptable to major developed countries just as it had been in the first conflict (Sharma 1996: 81). Japan supported the establishment of the new fund but reiterated its demands for more transparency in recipient countries when it made its support conditional upon strong measurement, reporting, and verification structures (TWN 2010: 19).

COP-15 (2009) in Copenhagen is often regarded as a 'failure' (cf. Chapter 3). Yet, some of the formulations in the Copenhagen Accord signal real progress on climate finance and planted the seeds of later successes. The Copenhagen Accord eventually contained the formulation that a new and independent institution should be created. The signatories agreed that the new fund 'shall be established as an operating entity of the financial mechanism'. This meant it would work besides rather than under the GEF and represent a further instance of institutional branching out. In response to potentially rising developing country commitments, it would cover both funding for mitigation and adaptation and have a 'governance structure providing for equal representation of developed and developing countries' (ENB 12/459 of 22 December 2009; TWN 2010; FCCC/CP/2009/11/Add.1 of 30 March 2010).

On the one hand, the Copenhagen Accord thus encouraged hopes of developing countries that the new fund could follow the example of the Adaptation Fund. On the other hand, the decision text was – not unlike the decisions taken during the first crisis moment of the conflict – brief and vague enough to leave room for later operationalizations in greater accordance with the interests of developed countries (Coventry 2019: 182). Among the most tangible outcomes was the goal of mobilizing USD 30bn in 'fast start finance' between 2010 and 2012, mobilizing annual climate finance flows of USD 100bn starting in 2020, and scaling up climate finance in between (ENB 12/459 of 22 December 2009). Regarding the throughput dimension, the Copenhagen Accord specified that a 'significant portion' of such funding should flow through the new 'Copenhagen Green Climate Fund' (ENB 12/459 of 22 December 2009; TWN 2010; FCCC/CP/2009/11/Add.1 of 30 March 2010: 7).

8.4.3 Implementation: Powering up the Green Climate Fund

Following the crisis and decision moment, COP-17 (2010) in Cancún formally established the GCF (ENB 12/498 of 13 December 2010: 29). More urgently than during the 2000/2001 crisis, developed countries, especially the US and Japan, voiced demands for greater commitments by developing countries in exchange for the set-up of the new fund (e.g. TWN 2011a: 6, 11, 19). This illustrates once more how developed countries used their control over funding inputs to push developing countries into accepting central obligations. Developing countries, by contrast, renewed their suggestion for a new funding approach based on objective criteria, according to which developed countries should pay 1.5 per cent of their GDP in assistance instead of the USD 100bn annually by 2020 (ENB 12/498 of 13 December 2010: 11). In contrast to the strong focus on normative pressure in the first conflict, such bold proposals demonstrate how developing countries were beginning to trust more in their rising material power to increase inputs from developed countries. While this proposal was rejected, COP-16 (2010) paved the way for a new binding agreement (ENB 12/498 of 13 December 2010: 28). Negotiators also recognized – albeit again only by 'taking note' – the Copenhagen climate finance goals of USD 30bn in fast start finance between 2010–2012 as well as the goal of USD 100bn annually starting in 2020. They agreed that such climate finance for developing countries should be 'scaled-up, new and additional, predictable, and adequate' and flow in significant parts through the GCF (FCCC/CP/2010/7/Add.1 of 15 March 2011: Decision 1/CP.16). In the end, however, no final decision could be reached on which level of funding the GCF should initially be equipped with (TWN 2011a: 75).

The climate conferences between 2011 and 2014 served to fix the institutional structures of the GCF and designate it as another operating entity of the Financial Mechanism besides the GEF (ENB 12/534 of 13 December 2011: 5). As well as '[l]aunching the Green Climate Fund', COP-17 (2011) also adopted a governing instrument for the GCF which specified that the fund should 'make a significant and ambitious contribution to the global efforts' of combatting climate change and be 'guided by' the principles and provisions of the 1992 UN Framework Convention (FCCC/CP/2011/9/Add.1 of 15 March 2012: Decision 3/CP.17). The Governing Instrument thus only indirectly referred to the principle of common but differentiated responsibilities and respective capabilities (CBDR-RC) instead of explicitly incorporating it.

Creating distance between the new GCF and existing differential treatment provisions was a crucial goal of developed countries who tried to tap into further sources of funding besides their own contributions. In this respect, the Governing Instrument states that the fund 'will' receive financial inputs from developed countries and 'may also' receive financial inputs from a variety of other sources, including private sources and voluntary contributions by other countries. Importantly, no formula or other objective criteria were established for regulating the inputs of individual countries into the GCF (Vanderheiden 2015: 35). The GCF, while established under the Financial Mechanism, thus also explicitly channels finance that is not directly pertinent to differential treatment. Its openness to a 'variety of sources' can be regarded as a significant dilution of the responsibilities of developed countries in the area of financial assistance. Consequently, China argued that public funds should form the main part of long-term climate finance to ensure its adequacy and predictability (Prys-Hansen et al. 2019: 284), and, at the time of writing, neither Brazil nor China or India have become contributors to the newly established funds.

On the eligibility criteria for receiving GCF funding, the COP did not decide for change. All developing country parties remained generally eligible to receive resources from the fund with freedom to use such resources for both mitigation and adaptation actions (FCCC/CP/2011/9/Add.1 of 15 March 2012: 63; see also Table 8.1). The GCF Governing Instrument reiterated that funds shall be 'balanced' between adaptation and mitigation while ensuring an 'appropriate' allocation of funds to 'other activities'. Such language, while remaining vague, suggested a reorientation of climate finance with respect to major issues identified in Table 8.2. For example, it put the importance of funding for adaptation on a par with funding for mitigation. In its output dimension, the Instrument also recognizes the special needs of LDCs, SIDS, and African states by proposing 'minimum allocation floors for these countries as appropriate'. Crucially, such finance for most vulnerable countries 'will be tailored to cover the identifiable, additional costs of the investment necessary to make [projects] viable' (FCCC/CP/2011/9/Add.1 of 15 March 2012: 64–66). These GCF characteristics represented important departures from the GEF's way of financing and were also reflected in actual funding flows.

Regarding overall funding levels, the G-77 and China nonetheless continued to voice concerns. China, for example, demanded the establishment of a 'roadmap' for scaling up climate finance to reach the envisaged level of USD 100bn annually by 2020. In response, COP-18 (2012) in Doha 'encouraged' developed countries to provide funds for 2013–2015 at the same levels as during the fast start finance period in 2010–2012. Many participants, especially developing countries, saw this as falling short of what had been envisaged originally at COP-13 (2007) in Bali. Despite the formal establishment of the GCF, the lack of concrete replenishment commitments to the new fund meant that many developing countries still regarded it as an 'empty shell' (ENB 12/567 of 11 December 2012: 28).

Overall, the second conflict was once more resolved by reshaping the institutional climate finance landscape and branching out a new institution that held a promise to take concerns of developing countries more seriously. In practice, however, this addition proved insufficient to settle the climate finance disputes between developed and developing countries (e.g. ENB 12/793 of 16 November 2021).

8.5 INTERPRETING THE CONFLICT DYNAMICS AND OUTCOMES: IDEAS, INTERESTS, AND INSTITUTIONS

In the context of our study, climate finance represents a puzzling policy field: it stands out against the general trend of an unmaking of differential treatment norms we observe in other parts of this book. This section interprets the two conflicts and their implications for differential treatment in terms of our theoretical framework which includes rationalist, constructivist, and institutionalist approaches (cf. Chapter 1).

In the following sub-sections, we argue that *competing normative ideas* about and justifications of climate finance (sub-section 8.5.1) as well as *conflicting interests* regarding amounts and goals (sub-section 8.52) resulted in *conflicted institutions* (sub-section 8.5.3) and so enabled the decisions we have sketched out above. This corresponds to the distinction between differing *justifications*, *amounts and goals*, and *structures* we observe regarding assistance in our overview in Chapter 3. It appears that, overwhelmed by the multiple contradictory demands posed to it, the existing institutional climate finance landscape failed to satisfy its stakeholders' diverse wants and needs in the preludes of both conflicts. The ensuing frustration among rights-holders, as well as the growing contributory expectations placed upon them, strengthened their united contestation of existing institutional structures. The crisis moments that resulted from the contestation in both phases created incentives for negotiating parties to opt for institutional additions. Branching out and layering eventually served as a release valve in both conflicts and proved preferable to profoundly altering pre-existing structures.

Faced with such contestation, negotiating parties had several options of adapting the institutional climate finance landscape to their conflicting interests and competing ideas when talks ran into crisis at The Hague in 2000 and then again at Copenhagen in 2009. Four principal decision options at the respective crises could thus have been:

- Maintaining the status quo: the COP could have kept the GEF as is. This scenario, however, would have required developing countries to give up challenging the existing structures.
- Incremental reform: negotiating parties could have kept the GEF but restructured it in line with a new set of agreed upon requirements in recurring reviews of the Financial Mechanism.

- Rebooting climate finance: a third option could have been for developed and developing countries to reach agreement on more fundamentally dismantling and rebooting the Financial Mechanism.
- Branching out and layering: finally, states had the option of adding new climate finance institutions to the Financial Mechanism, which would either create institutions besides or under the GEF.

As the previous sections have shown, the COP eventually decided for layering and branching out in both crisis moments. In this regard, both conflicts resembled each other. Since developing countries remained united with Brazil, China, and India as GEF challengers favouring an expansion of differential treatment in both conflicts, the first option ('maintaining the status quo') lacked support. Option three ('rebooting climate finance') was also particularly unlikely since developed countries had no interest in a fundamental dismantling of the GEF. Despite their differences over the GEF, parties could thus not agree that abolishing the GEF altogether or increasingly eroding differential treatment in assistance were viable paths (Horta et al. 2002: 2). Still, while the different options outlined above may thus have been associated with different likelihoods and political viabilities, none of them were completely off the table. In fact, the options of keeping the GEF as is, as well as reforming it more profoundly, had been tried prior to both conflicts. But the frequent annual reviews and adjustments appeared insufficient to avoid or overcome the two major crises.

8.5.1 Competing Ideas

Should assistance be regarded as justified predominantly based on the present and forward-looking needs of an effective and efficient global response to climate change? Or rather based on historical responsibility for climate change, historical injustice, the goal of equity, and the related local needs of vulnerable countries? Both conflicts have shown that contestation between developed and developing countries over climate finance issues was in crucial parts related to these questions concerning underlying normative ideas and legitimacy (cf. Table 8.2 and Chapter 3).

Climate finance as transfer of capacity from stronger to weaker member countries has co-determined the extent of the overall solidarity of the climate regime (Biermann 1998: 28, 51–55). But the reasons for the general acceptance of assistance we observe here as well as in Chapter 3 have differed between developed and developing countries because of different underlying justificatory ideas across groups (see also Vihma et al. 2011). In a nutshell, developing countries, including Brazil, China, and India, justified their plea for climate finance with reference to the historical responsibility of developed countries for climate change and its adverse effects. Moreover, both conflicts also demonstrated that developing countries regarded a right to development as legitimizing climate finance. On this view, developed countries have an obligation to enable sustainable development. Having failed to erect a 'New International Economic Order' in the 1960s to 1980s, and going beyond the issue of climate change, developing countries also fundamentally justified climate finance as entailing some rectification for historical injustices and the colonial past (Biermann 1998: 45–47, 324–27; Doyle 1983; Golub 2013; Verwey 1990).

Brazil, China, and India saw themselves as Southern leaders and continuously pushed for the concept of historical responsibility to find footing in international agreements. They stood to gain from this approach because it allowed them to remain united with other developing countries in calls for greater developed country contributions. It also facilitated limiting or slowing down their own contributions. Notable among promotions of historical responsibility in the early climate regime was the so-called 'Brazilian Proposal'. It suggested basing differential treatment on the respective contributions of countries to climate change and hence on their historical responsibility (ENB 12/76 of 13 December 1997: 5). Developing countries, chief among them Brazil, China, and India, fought tooth and nail to have the Brazilian Proposal inform the differential treatment mechanisms of the 1997 Kyoto Protocol (cf. Den Elzen et al. 2005; Chapter 3). Further support for the justification based on historical responsibility came from the proposal of India for 'equal and sustainable per capita rights to the atmosphere' (Rajamani 2008b: 919). On matters of financial assistance, technology transfer, and capacity-building, India regarded itself clearly as a developing country with a strong right to development and an entitlement to benefits. India challenged the 'adequacy of commitments', repeatedly argued that 'developed countries' should ramp up their efforts (ENB 12/21 of 10 April 1995: 3, 10; Rajamani 2009), and demanded full-cost funding for any contributions by developing countries (e.g. ENB 12/76 of 13 December 1997: 13).

The examples of incremental costs and additionality are telling with respect to how competing justificatory ideas between developed and developing countries crept into matters of institutional implementation (cf. Table 8.2). A core challenge developing countries have faced is that typical climate finance projects aim at different positive outcomes (such as structural development, capacity- and resilience-building, poverty eradication, economic growth, or technological advances). Project outcomes often only *include* positive climate effects, *among others*. If only some of these effects are regarded as justifying climate finance, projects often fail to receive funds. LDCs and other developing countries therefore tried, but repeatedly failed, to secure a COP decision for 'full cost funding of adaptation' (e.g. ENB 12/260 of 20 December 2004:

14). With respect to additionality, developing countries expressed concern that climate finance justified by global benefits alone would not – additionally – account for remedying historical injustices and could crowd out other transfers. They also worried that, if climate finance was not additional to World Bank (and other) development aid funding, there would be a risk of imposing new 'green' conditionalities on developing countries for receiving World Bank loans in turn (e.g. Streck 2001: 83). Despite attempts by developing countries to prevent counting climate finance as official development aid, some of the inputs into the different climate finance funds indeed fall under this category (cf. Table 8.2) (ENB 12/76 of 13 December 1997: 4). Still, the new funds created after the crisis moments stress their additionality to GEF funding, indicating at least a partial norm expansion (e.g. Dessai 2003; Harmeling and Kaloga 2011).

By contrast, developed countries have regarded differential treatment, including assistance, across both conflicts as justified predominantly by the globally beneficial outcomes it can help achieve. While they accepted the fact that a large part of historical emissions originated on their territory, they were much more reluctant to also accept related and broader understandings of historical responsibility, injustice, or remedial liability. They have continuously rejected formula approaches (such as the 'Brazilian Proposal') to burden-sharing based on historical responsibility. Such formulae would have objectively determined individual shares that could be assigned to both mitigation commitments and obligations in the area of climate finance. From the perspective of developed countries, climate finance thus derives its adequacy first and foremost from effectively and cost-efficiently supporting the overarching goal of preventing dangerous climate change as formulated in Article 2 of the 1992 UN Framework Convention. While equity was also regarded as important, developed country governments tend to relate it to current and prospective rather than to historical differences (cf. Chapter 3). Other climate finance concepts such as voluntariness, additionality, incremental costs, or eligibility criteria are similarly evaluated under this overall proviso (cf. Table 8.2). If effectiveness and efficiency rise by combining climate finance and other international transfers, additionality loses importance. If climate finance is predominantly about global benefits rather than local needs of beneficiaries, funding only incremental costs is easier to justify than full-cost funding. And if countries or projects have greater capacities to produce global benefits effectively and efficiently, their eligibility can rise even if this is suboptimal for local needs of beneficiaries.

From the outset of the climate regime, the UN Framework Convention had acknowledged that climate change was largely brought about by the industrialization and historical emissions of developed countries and that emissions of developing countries should be allowed to rise to enable development out of poverty. Furthermore, the Convention also established a legal link between developing country commitments and the obligation of developed countries to assist (cf. Chapter 3). Together, these acknowledgements have contributed to developing countries holding the normative high ground in negotiations on the legitimacy of climate finance. Developing countries have since regarded assistance in the form of climate finance provided by developed countries as a matter of equity and justice on which they have a legal claim (e.g. Prys-Hansen et al. 2019: 282–283). Given the normative importance of historical responsibility, switching camps from rights-holders to duty-bearers regarding climate finance would have implied an admission of historical responsibility rather than an appealing new status (Buchner et al. 2017; 2019; Clapp et al. 2012; Gray and Gills 2016; OECD 2019; De Renzio and Seifert 2014).

Developing countries remained united in challenging the GEF in both conflicts because, in their view, it did not adequately reflect these justifications enshrined in the UN Framework Convention (Prys-Hansen et al. 2019: 282). These normative considerations cemented Southern unity in both conflicts. However, they also point to a crucial difference between the two climate finance conflicts. As we discussed in Chapter 3, the gap between developed and developing countries' emissions and capabilities had diminished substantially from the first to the second phase, especially regarding rising powers. This meant that the first phase was predominantly characterized by developing countries formulating demands for more assistance based on historical responsibility. In the second phase, developing countries, particularly Brazil, China, and India, increasingly struggled to justify differentiation based on their level of development. Rising powers eventually apparently accepted a package deal. They accepted central obligations in exchange for assistance being expanded and in order to keep the developing country group united. The critique of the new Resource Allocation Framework of the GEF as being too reflective of efficiency-based justifications of developed countries for climate finance, as well as emphasizing the relatively new legitimation of climate finance based on loss and damage, therefore replaced some of the previous backward-looking arguments of developing countries with more forward-looking ideas.

Overall, climate finance negotiations have time and again witnessed clashes between justifications of duty-bearers based on effectiveness and efficiency and normative arguments of rights-holders for remedial responsibility (Coventry 2019: 203; Vanderheiden 2015: 39). As both groups failed to align their competing ideas over the institutional design of climate finance in both conflict preludes, existing institutions came under pressure. Developing countries thus regarded *maintaining the status quo* as unjustified in the preludes and crisis moments of both conflicts and had lost confidence in the option of *incrementally reforming* the GEF or even more in *fundamentally rebooting* climate finance.

8.5.2 Conflicting Interests

Besides the role of ideas and legitimacy concerns, our theoretical framework underlines the importance of power distributions across bargaining coalitions as well as their unity for explaining differential treatment-related conflict dynamics and outcomes (cf. Chapter 1). The perhaps oversimplifying division of the world into developed and developing countries has been rightfully criticized (e.g. Farias 2019). But differential treatment in climate finance has always been and still is very much built around the crude distinction between these two major camps. Major climate agreements as well as all climate finance institutions under the Financial Mechanism continue to work with this distinction, keep it alive, and even reinforce it (Betzold et al. 2012; Castro et al. 2011; Keohane and Oppenheimer 2016; Michaelowa et al. 2014; Rajamani 2008a; 2016). While this masks the substantial diversity within both camps, the differences across groups hold arguably more clout in explaining the climate finance conflicts studied here than those within groups (see also Chapter 3). There is a material, and in this sense non-negotiable, basis to the clear division between these two camps which ultimately stems from the differences in their developmental and economic histories, as well as their differing historical contributions to the phenomenon of climate change (Coventry 2019: 206). Although its significance decreased in phase two, the continued importance of this material divide has lent further support to the Southern unity we observe in both conflicts.

As respective duty-bearers and rights-holders regarding climate finance, developed and developing countries have thus traditionally sat down at opposite ends of the negotiating table. Both country groupings have generally shared an interest in a strong and effective climate regime and accepted assistance as an important instrument towards this end. But related to and informed by the ideas discussed in the previous sub-section, both camps have formed and voiced opposing interests in different bargaining coalitions throughout the history of climate finance. While developed countries sought generally limited amounts of cost-efficient and closely monitored climate finance, developing countries pushed for much higher levels of full-cost funding and stressed the importance of local benefits to protect their interest in economic and social development.

The bargaining power of developing countries in the climate regime has always resulted essentially from their ability to harm the global environment (Biermann 1998: 324–341). On the upper side of the G-77 and China spectrum, the developmental and emissions gap between developed and developing countries has been closing and has even partially disappeared (cf. Chapter 3, Table 3.1). While increasing emissions from the first to the second phase thus implied increasing bargaining power, increasing capabilities simultaneously weakened the claim on assistance of rising powers. This resulted in counteracting influences on differential treatment: one supporting an expansion in favour of all developing countries, the other supporting an end to the unity between developed countries and rising powers. Brazil, China, and India have since been receiving pressure to become contributors from *above* (i.e. developed countries), *below* (i.e. smaller and most vulnerable developing countries), and *within* (i.e. growing domestic environmental awareness) (Barua 2014: 201).

Their response has been to protect and insist upon their right to further development, stave off binding central obligations, and rise without constraints while demanding that developed countries take the lead in mitigation and foot the climate finance bill. Correspondingly, Brazil, China, and India have underlined their view that potentially greater developing country commitments remain dependent upon a corresponding rise in assistance provided by developed countries as originally established in Article 4.7 of the 1992 UN Framework Convention. Based on their interest in selling their eventual contributions to the climate mitigation effort at the highest price, Brazil, China, and India opted for what has been characterized as ‘strategic co-optation’ (Betzold et al. 2012; Kruck and Zangl 2019; Streck 2001; Thompson 2020). All three countries played important roles as ever greater emitters, as Southern leaders, and as GEF ‘recipient donors’ from the start. Given these roles, their influence in restructuring the GEF, as well as the creation of the new funds in both conflicts, was crucial (cf. e.g. Vihma 2011; GEF Trustee 2021: 3). Regarding climate finance, developing countries thus appeared as an increasingly powerful and resiliently united front despite some notable divisions between rising powers and weaker developing countries in other areas of climate negotiations (Prys-Hansen et al. 2019: 283; Streck 2001: 76). Moreover, in stark contrast to climate mitigation where the rising emissions of Brazil, China, and India rendered agreements without their contributions increasingly problematic, smaller developing countries had few incentives to call for a graduation of rising powers in climate finance, too. Such calls would have risked a break-up of Southern unity on this question. Moreover, the graduation of rising powers itself would have reduced the bargaining power of developing countries in negotiations over climate finance: losing the bargaining chip of contributions of rising powers to the mitigation of climate change in exchange for more assistance could have negatively influenced overall funding levels. Together, developing countries thus kept criticizing the GEF and its procedures, and they relentlessly repeated their calls for greater contributions by developed countries (Bodansky et al. 2017: 101; Hallding et al. 2011; Hochstetler 2012; Jamieson 2014: 35; Minas 2013; Qi 2011; Tabau and Lemoine 2012).

The negotiating power of developed countries, in turn, has typically originated in their high emissions combined with their respective capabilities to mitigate climate change and their control over the input dimension of assistance. While Article 4 of the 1992 UN Framework Convention had specified that developed countries have assistance obligations with respect to commitments and adaptation of developing countries, the provisions remained vague and left funding levels to be negotiated. In general, however, developed countries have shared an inherent interest in climate finance carrying the greatest global effect. This meant not only that they prioritized funding for mitigation over funding for adaptation or loss and damage, but also that they prioritized funding for projects that delivered the greatest emissions reductions per unit of investment (Horta et al. 2002: 9). However, developed countries struggled to agree on an exact enough specification of 'global environmental sustainability' indicating that 'the GEF can't tell if it is succeeding because it doesn't know what success is' (Horta et al. 2002: 4). What ensued were relatively vague understandings of what overall levels of climate finance should be regarded as adequate, which institutional rules and structures would best serve these goals, and which concomitant commitments should be demanded from assistance rights-holders. Furthermore, since the US had never ratified the 1997 Kyoto Protocol, it was excluded from crucial negotiations on the structure of the Adaptation Fund in the prelude of the second conflict. Such disagreements, especially between the EU and US, left developed countries exposing an occasionally disoriented and disunited flank in both climate finance conflicts (Coventry 2019: 176–178; Grasso 2011: 363). Additionally, both conflicts contained examples of developed countries expressing openness to expanding and diversifying the institutional landscape of climate finance to better reflect the needs of developing countries.

These power distributions, unity among developing countries, and partial disorientation and disunity among developed countries at crucial points of both conflicts further impaired the viability of *maintaining the status quo*, *incremental reform*, and *completely rebooting climate finance* while *branching out* and *layering* became increasingly appealing as way out of both crisis moments.

8.5.3 Conflicted Institutions

In our theoretical chapter, we further argue that institutional outside alternatives can offer opportunities for exerting pressure on existing structures within a regime (cf. Chapter 1). In climate finance, however, the absence of such outside alternatives appears to have increased pressures on climate finance institutions. In the absence of alternative institutional venues, parties thus faced incentives to establish new alternatives (institutional layering and branching out). Prior to both conflicts, the GEF was either the only or the predominant institution for climate finance. On the one hand, this increased the original bargaining power of contributors as beneficiaries had no or only few substantial alternatives to turn to. On the other hand, it increased pressures from developing countries on the existing institutional set-up to either adapt according to their demands or be ultimately replaced or supplemented. Furthermore, the Convention's respective grouping of developed countries as duty-bearers and developing countries as rights-holders and the simultaneous absence of institutionalized graduation criteria locked in a high degree of unity among rights-holders despite the material rise of Brazil, China, and India.

Out of their stakeholders' conflicting interests and competing ideas, the GEF specifically and the Financial Mechanism more broadly arose as deeply conflicted institutions. When the GEF had completed its process of restructuring in 1994, it reflected an attempt at meeting the interests and ideas of both developed and developing countries. However, it remained torn between too many goal conflicts of too many stakeholders. The absence of graduation criteria and institutional alternatives for more nuanced kinds of climate finance added pressure on negotiators to create new institutions that better reflected the varied landscape of interests and ideas. While the international landscape of climate finance outside of the climate regime had been growing rapidly and continuously, the Financial Mechanism has remained the only venue for climate finance structured by the differential treatment provisions of the climate regime (Buchner et al. 2017; 2019; Gray and Gills 2016; De Renzio and Seifert 2014).

Against this background, the eventual creation of four new climate funds besides and under the GEF supports the argument that when irreconcilable interests and ideas clashed over existing rigid structures, the institutional landscape eventually budged to provide a relief valve. Opening new opportunity structures and further fragmenting the institutional landscape in greater accordance with the varied demands posed to it proved preferable to repeated attempts at restructuring existing institutions or leaving them unchanged.

8.6 CONCLUSION

Neither of the two conflicts studied in this chapter led to an unmaking of differential treatment norms. In fact, both resulted in a modest expansion of differential treatment norms: they led to increased financial transfers from North to South, and they adjusted the ways in which decision-making about such transfers were organized in favour of the interests of rights-holders.

Our analysis illustrates that neither developed nor developing countries alone were able to force institutional change by wielding their respective bargaining power or rhetorically coercing the other side. The observed expansion of differential treatment in both conflicts was instead enabled by a combination of four main factors. First, developing countries were united as simultaneous GEF challengers and defenders of differential treatment. Second, developing countries, and especially rising powers, were increasingly willing to accept and trade in concomitant commitments. Third, alternative institutional opportunity structures that could adequately absorb the varied array of interests and ideas of stakeholders or allow graduation were largely absent. And last, some major developed countries were open to change.

Both conflicts were driven by dissatisfaction of developing countries with existing structures. This had a unifying effect on them and strengthened their request for an expansion rather than an unmaking of differential treatment in climate finance. In the implementation part of the first conflict, the absence of the US from negotiations under the 1997 Kyoto Protocol combined with the independent funding inputs from the CDM help explain the eventually limited influence of the GEF over the Adaptation Fund. In the crisis moment of the second conflict, in turn, openness to change by the US and other developed countries helps explain the creation of the GCF in 2009 and 2010 (Coventry 2019: 206). However, these expansions of climate finance were only granted once the G-77 and China accepted flexible and varied sources of funding and began pledging voluntary mitigation commitments in turn.

Creating the new climate funds at the respective crisis moments represented direct hits to the GEF as the predominant climate finance institution under the UN Framework Convention (Harmeling and Kaloga 2011: 24). Among the available options for institutional change, however, *branching out* and *layering* offered several important advantages compared to the other options. They allowed developed countries to save face as the GEF continued to play an important role after both conflicts. They also promised greater attention to the interests, ideas, and needs of developing countries as the funding levels, funding foci, and operational structures of the new funds differed considerably from those of the GEF. And they promised a diffusion of assistance obligations since the new funds were more open to a 'variety of sources'.

Despite the expansion of differential treatment in climate finance we have sketched out in this chapter, however, criticisms have remained that in practice, climate finance remains inadequate to fulfil the goals of the international climate regime (ENB 12/793 of 16 November 2021). Moreover, the fact that two of the new funds remained under GEF governance meant that the pre-existing problems with the GEF have since also crept into the new institutions. The GCF, too, is characterized by many compromises. Inputs have remained voluntary, the gap between aspired and actual levels of funding has remained wide, and doubts that it will ever be able to rise to the enormous challenges and levels of finance required in the post-2020 climate regime have remained prominent (ENB 12/793 of 16 November 2021; Vanderheiden 2015: 35). Moreover, the relatively loose and indirect reference the GCF makes to the common but differentiated responsibilities (CBDR) principle suggests that, like the overall differential treatment character of the new climate regime, climate finance will be increasingly characterized by binding and ambitious collective targets combined with voluntary nationally determined contributions. Eventually, this may further intensify pressure on rising powers to contribute more as well.

Ultimately, the future of the institutional climate finance landscape will depend on the ability of existing institutions to regain, repair, and maintain the trust of both its duty-bearers and rights-holders. Many developed countries opposed the innovative features of the new funds and were therefore reluctant to increase funding to 'adequate' levels (Harmeling and Kaloga 2011: 26). If this trend persists, the G-77 and China may eventually be hoist with their own petard as the diminishing importance of the GEF may arguably have further dampened the willingness of developed countries to provide adequate, new, and additional funds to an ever more fragmented institutional landscape they never intended. This became apparent during the respective operationalization phases of both conflicts. More recently, COP-26 (2021) in Glasgow has shown once more that trust is a hard currency in climate finance: while the governments of developed countries continue to pledge climate finance, the USD 100bn per year goal announced in Copenhagen in 2009 has yet to be reached.

NOTES

1. We cite official UNFCCC documents according to their UN document number. The documents are available and can be searched based on their official document number at https://unfccc.int/documents (last accessed 6 May 2022).
2. We cite the meeting reports issued by the *Earth Negotiations Bulletin* (ENB) according to their volume (where volume 12 covers international climate negotiations under the UN Framework Convention on Climate Change) and issue number. The reports are available at https://enb.iisd.org/enb/vol12/ (last accessed 6 May 2022).

9. Conflicts over capacity to pay in the health regime

Julian Eckl

9.1 INTRODUCTION

Earlier in this book, Chapter 4 showed that differential treatment plays a key role in global health. In particular, it conceptualized differential treatment in global health financing as capacity, willingness, and need (CWN). Moreover, it concluded that CWN has largely proven resilient while each of its constituent bundles of norms has also seen some change – most notably in the form of graduation and informalization. The present chapter builds on these insights and analyses the specific case of capacity to pay (C2P) further.

From the perspective of the literature on differential treatment (e.g. Rajamani 2006; 2012a), C2P stands out since it comprises the legally binding aspects of CWN. C2P is operationalized through the scale methodology, which specifies and quantifies states' differentiated central obligations (as the first category of differential treatment; cf. Chapter 1; Rajamani 2006, 93–118). This legally sanctionable formula approach to differential treatment is in principle well suited to respond to global economic shifts. Nevertheless, C2P has been subject to intense and detailed contestations.

For each of the two phases (1995–2007 and 2008–2020) covered in Chapter 4, the present chapter on case studies zooms in on a key conflict moment. This allows for a close analysis of the conflict dynamics and complements the general developments covered in Chapter 4. In particular, attention can be paid to the discursive manifestations of the norms studied. This includes both justifications for and criticisms of specific interpretations of these norms. By the same token, it becomes possible to account for the positions of individual countries and of country coalitions. This includes the role of Brazil, China, and India as well as the main lines of conflict. Finally, zooming in generates room to interpret the decisions taken and to discuss potential explanations for them, which will be done in terms of the interplay of ideas, capabilities, and institutions as outlined in Chapter 1.

Such a detailed analysis of C2P is warranted not only from the perspective of the literature on differential treatment but also from the perspective of the literature on the financing of World Health Organization (WHO) and of other international organizations (e.g. Patz and Goetz 2019: 180–196; Reddy et al. 2018; People's Health Movement et al. 2017: 245–262; Browne 2017; Clinton and Sridhar 2017; Goetz and Patz 2017; Graham 2017a; Sridhar and Woods 2013). In particular, this literature's preoccupation with the increasing relevance of voluntary contributions as opposed to assessed contributions has come at the expense of overlooking the contestations around the scale methodology that determines the assessed contributions. A focus on C2P closes this gap.

Moreover, the present chapter makes an important contribution by systematically following policies through levels and fora. In this way, it analyses the complex relations between the United Nations (UN) level and the WHO level. It thereby complements existing research on the scale of assessments that does not go into a detailed analysis of contestations and/or privileges one of the levels (e.g. Koschorreck 2001; Suzara 2002). While UN decisions have usually a formative impact on WHO decisions, this chapter will show that this link has at times been heavily contested and that there is in principle considerable policy space at the WHO level. In particular, implementation flexibilities (as the second category of differential treatment) have proven to be an important policy option.

Finally, the present analysis goes beyond the existing research on financing since it foregrounds the role of norms in the first place. While states certainly prefer to keep their individual financial contributions low, the absolute amounts over which they haggle are often surprisingly small. The distribution of monetary burden appears recurrently as a 'matter of principle' rather than a 'matter of affordability'. For member states, the question of how financial obligations are assigned and legitimized is of fundamental importance.

Regarding C2P, the chapter will show that the norm as such was broadly supported. However, reviewing the scale methodology, which constitutes the operationalization of C2P, and updating data, which constitutes the practical application of the operationalization, have proven contentious. Although reviewing and updating represent in principle two distinguishable sources of change to the scale of assessments, they have often been intertwined in complex contestations. This applies in particular to the first case study that covers a conflict that culminated in 2000 (UN level) and 2001 (WHO level) but had repercussions until 2007 (WHO level). In this first case study, it was mainly the United States of America (USA) who seriously challenged the status quo and demanded modifications to the scale methodology. While the USA's demand to expand an existing restraint on C2P and to lower the maximum ceiling even further was unsuccessfully resisted by essentially all other countries, the G-77 (Group of 77) and China additionally contested changes to the scale of assessments that resulted from updated data and shifted the financial burden from developed to developing countries. For the G-77 and China, the resistance to any changes in the financial burden was very much a question of principle and not linked to an explicitly stated threshold for a justified share. The eventual introduction of implementation flexibilities was a response to the demands of the G-77 and China in particular; at the WHO level, the implementation flexibilities lasted for multiple biennia. This shows that, at the outset, the G-77 and China did not consider graduation a common practice but interpreted it almost as an unmaking of differential treatment – although the ensuing changes to the scale of assessments were marginal in comparison to later developments.

In the second case study, which covers events from 2018 (UN level) and 2019 (WHO level), it was mainly the G-77 and China who seriously challenged the status quo – albeit unsuccessfully. While they had meanwhile accepted changes to the scale of assessments that resulted from updated data, they wanted to modify the scale methodology for two reasons. First, in order to abandon the existing restraint on C2P that came in the form of the aforementioned maximum ceiling. Second, in order to expand the domain of C2P beyond member states, which would have affected the European Union (EU) considerably. While the second case study highlights the general resilience that has characterized C2P ever since the conflict covered in the first case study, the analysis will subsequently put this finding in perspective. It will come back to the graduation of rising powers covered in Chapter 4, and it will show that this graduation can be interpreted as attenuated graduation because the countries' rising assessment rates have not prevented them from remaining beneficiaries of differential treatment. This observation will play an important role in section 9.4, 'Interpreting and Explaining the Cases', where the explanations for the outcomes of the two case studies will be discussed. A related point will be the fact that the G-77 and China have proven a stable coalition over all these years. By contrast, the unique position of the USA has made it difficult for the classic main contributors to find common ground.

Like Chapter 4, the present chapter is based on an analysis of primary sources that was complemented by secondary sources and that has additionally benefited from the insights gained in an ethnographic long-term study of global health governance (e.g. Eckl 2021). In line with Chapter 4, the analysis will focus on a specific set of countries and country coalitions. Firstly, the analysis will focus on Brazil, China, and India, which are the main concern of this book. Secondly, the analysis will focus on the G-77 and China as the most important coalition of developing countries. Thirdly, the analysis will focus on the three classic main contributors to differential treatment in the context of C2P, namely (also in alphabetical order) Germany, Japan, and the USA.

Finally, it should be noted that Germany matters not only because of the size of her assessment rate but also because she is a member of the EU, which is the main formal coalition of developed countries. As a consequence of this constellation, Germany does usually not deliver an individual statement in discussions on the scale of assessments. This means that, in the analysis of the discussions, the focus will be on the EU while the focus will be on Germany when data for individual countries is compared.

9.2 CASE STUDY 1: SERIOUS CONFLICTS OVER CAPACITY TO PAY AT THE UN AND AT THE WHO LEVEL

Contestations of capacity to pay (C2P) manifest commonly in conflicts over the scale of assessments. These conflicts were a constant companion of Phase 1 (1995–2007). They reached a climax in 2000 (UN level) and 2001 (WHO level). Eventually, this led to a modification of the scale methodology. This modification can be interpreted as a further restraint on C2P that favoured the USA. However, changes to individual assessment rates were additionally the result of dynamics in the world economy that the scale reflected through updated data. While the new scale implied changes in central obligations (first category of differential treatment), the compromise solutions for the conflicts also contained implementation flexibilities (second category of differential treatment). Formally, all countries with increasing assessment rates were eligible for implementation flexibilities but, informally, 'developing countries' in particular were meant to use them.

9.2.1 Discussions at the UN Level

A key driver of the conflicts at the UN level were the massive arrears of the USA in combination with her demand that the maximum ceiling should be further decreased. However, the following account will show that the slow emergence of a global economic shift was also important in the sense that it was represented in the updated data applied to the methodology and led to some independent changes to the scale of assessments. The role of these formula-based changes is, however, commonly overlooked. While some of the demands made in the discussions pitted the G-77 and China against specific sets of developed countries, the analysis will also show that, at the UN level, events did not unfold as a clear-cut conflict between developed and developing countries. Rather, the predominant issue was a conflict between the USA and the rest, but the rest did not speak with a unified voice and disagreed on key points.

The scale of assessments had already been a contentious issue in 1999 when the UN General Assembly tasked the Committee on Contributions, which is an advisory body, to prepare a report that would present no less than 12 alternative approaches to calculating the scale of assessments (54/237 D [1999]). Apparently, there had been hope that the Committee on Contributions would not just discuss the 12 alternative approaches but also make a recommendation for a suitable methodology. The committee was, however, not able to provide such guidance. The challenges and internal disagreements that the Committee on Contributions had faced were mentioned by its Chairman when he introduced the requested report to the UN General Assembly's Fifth Committee (A/55/11 [2000] and 1), which is also known as the Administrative and Budgetary Committee.

Following the presentation of the report, the discussion was started by France (A/C.5/55/SR.5 [2000]: 5–6) who spoke on behalf of the EU (and 11 further countries). The delegate pointed out that the EU was the largest contributor to the UN 'and was committed to ensuring that the Organization's expenses were divided fairly among the Member States'. He also said that each member state's contribution 'must reflect as closely as possible its real capacity to pay in the light of its current economic situation and that the scale methodology must be simple, equitable and transparent'. In this context, the speaker highlighted that, in 1998, the EU 'had accounted for 29.5 per cent of world gross national product (GNP), yet it contributed 36.6 per cent of the Organization's regular budget'.

According to the delegate, the 'current scale methodology distorted, rather than reflected, the European Union's capacity to pay for three basic reasons'. First, there was the problem of outdated data and long base periods. The delegate explained furthermore that, second, there were the effects of the relief measures. Debt relief was particularly problematic, not least since interest payments were already deduced when calculating national income. While debt relief was consequently a duplication and should be abandoned, in the case of low per capita income, the gradient should be slightly lowered. The delegate pointed out that, third, there was the maximum ceiling of 25 per cent while the world's largest economy accounted for approximately 29 per cent of the world's GNP. Since the existing maximum ceiling of 25 per cent was already a distorting factor, it should not be lowered further. In terms of lines of conflict, the EU intervention can be summarized as a critique of the insufficient contributions *both* from the growing economies in the developing world *and* from the main contributor (i.e. the USA).

Thereafter, Nigeria spoke on behalf of the G-77 and China (A/C.5/55/SR.5 [2000]: 6). The delegate expressed the group's regret 'that the Committee on Contributions had not provided sufficient guidance' and made clear that '[d]eveloping countries should not be assessed at a rate that exceeded their capacity to pay as a result of adjustments to the scale'. Along these lines, the delegate pointed out that various elements of the methodology should not be changed. This included the 0.01 per cent ceiling for Least Developed Countries and a statistical base period of six years. Moreover, he suggested that some of the elements that are favourable for developing countries had to be further strengthened: the threshold and the gradient for the low per capita income adjustment should be increased and a mitigation mechanism for those countries that passed the threshold should be introduced. Regarding potential changes, the speaker also made it clear that an adjustment of the maximum ceiling 'would be considered only if the burden of payment was redistributed among the major contributors, without affecting the Group of 77 and China'.

Finally, the group rejected the idea that a minimum assessment rate should apply to permanent members of the UN Security Council (UNSC) on the grounds that it would run 'counter to the principle of capacity to pay'. Of note, within the group only China would have been affected by this provision. In terms of lines of conflict, it is important to highlight that, among our focus countries, the demands of the G-77 and China would increase the assessment rates only for Japan and for Germany. First, the G-77 and China did not oppose a lower maximum ceiling as such but were not prepared to share any of the burden that would result from this measure. Second, the proposed enhanced relief measures would increase the burden of countries with a per capita income above the world average, excluding the USA whose rate was in practice fixed by the maximum ceiling.

Following one other speaker, Brazil (A/C.5/55/SR.5 [2000]: 7–8) was next among our focus countries. Brazil endorsed the statement that had been made on behalf of the G-77 and China. In addition to repeating some of the points that had been made in that statement, the delegate contested the GNP data for Brazil on the grounds that the apparent growth of 37 per cent was an artefact of currency conversion while the real growth rate should be 10.3 per cent; consequently, a different conversion method should be used. Also of note, the speaker argued that due to the growing economy of the USA, an adjustment of the maximum ceiling could only lead to its increase. In terms of lines of conflict, this implies an even more dismissive position towards the demands of the USA than the position of the G-77 and China.

The subsequently speaking representative of the USA (A/C.5/55/SR.5 [2000]: 8) put the current debate in a broader historical context and expressed his regrets regarding the arrears of his country. According to him, there was 'growing agreement on the basic elements of a new system' that included 'more up-to-date economic data and broader burden-sharing among Member States' based on 'criteria of real capacity to pay'. Also, the delegate pointed out that additional amendments were necessary in order to account for 'the capacity to pay of the world's powerhouse developing economies'. Moreover, he stated that the 'principle of capacity to pay was not absolute' and that the ceiling modified it 'to avoid dependence on any one Member State'.

In concluding, he pointed out that the USA would – as in the past 55 years – proudly remain the UN's main contributor and that in 2000 it would contribute around three billion, two thirds of which would be voluntary contributions. In terms of conflict lines, it is important to highlight that the US demand to lower the maximum ceiling stood out among the points made and would affect all other countries, with the exception of those who were subject to limits. Countries with high assessment rates such as Japan and Germany would be particularly affected since the 3 per cent reduction would be distributed among member states on a pro ratio basis. Other demands that the USA made would mainly affect some of those countries who benefited from relief measures and/ or from long statistical base periods.

Thereafter, China (A/C.5/55/SR.5 [2000]: 8–9) endorsed the statement by the G-77 and China before pointing out that the 'low per capita income adjustment was the best expression of the principle of capacity to pay' and that it should also be applied to permanent members of the UNSC. Along similar lines, the representative pointed out that in spite of China's relatively high economic growth, her per capita GNP would still be far below the threshold. Generally speaking, the delegate made clear that China's economic growth had to be put in perspective and he pointed at the disruptive side of 'economic globalization' for 'many developing countries'. China also made clear that the financial difficulties of the UN were the result of 'the large arrears accumulated by a small number of countries' and in order to resolve them, payment had to be made on time, in full, and without conditions. With a view to lines of conflict regarding the scale methodology, the position of China could be seen as a defence of the status quo. Unlike the G-77 and China statement, no modifications of the methodology were requested.

After three further delegates had spoken, Japan (A/C.5/55/SR.5 [2000]: 10–11) pointed out that one of the 12 alternatives that had been requested in resolution 54/237 D (1999) was in line with Japan's proposal for a new methodology (cf. Model I in A/55/11 [2000] that will be discussed later in the chapter). While this alternative kept the maximum ceiling at the level of 25 per cent, the delegate did not discuss this aspect. Instead, he focussed on the fact that the model suggested amendments to the low per capita income adjustment that had the intention of better reflecting the capacity to pay of those countries who had a low per capita income but still a large economy. In this context, the delegate stated: 'A limited number of countries with large economies benefited more from the low per capita income adjustments than a larger number of developing countries which truly needed such relief'.

Along similar lines, Japan asked permanent members of the UNSC 'to give up the benefits of per capita income adjustments' as they had 'special responsibilities'. Akin to the argumentation of the EU, Japan pointed at the gap between her assessment rate and her share of world GNP in order to show the deficiencies of the current scale methodology: 'It was very difficult for the Japanese people to understand why Japan's share of the assessed budget was now more than 20 per cent, while its GNP share remained approximately 17 per cent'. In terms of lines of conflict, it is important to highlight that, similar to the EU, Japan criticized the insufficient contributions of the growing economies in the developing world *and* rejected a lowering of the maximum ceiling by supporting Model I.

Following two further delegates, India (A/C.5/55/SR.5 [2000]: 12) associated herself with the statement by the G-77 and China. While India also addressed other issues, including 'the need for an upward revision of the gradient', her focus was on the maximum ceiling: 'Even at its present level, the ceiling represented a departure from the principle of capacity to pay'. India accepted the idea mentioned by the USA that dependence should be avoided but her conclusion was *not* that all member states should contribute more. Rather, the idea was that the other major contributors would increase their share. In terms of lines of conflict, this was fully in line with the statement made by the G-77 and China. Moreover, it was compatible with the demands of the USA to lower the ceiling. However, regarding the other focus countries, it would have increased the assessment rate of Japan and Germany. At the same time, it would have spared Brazil, China, and India.

In the remainder of the discussion, which extended over three meetings of the Fifth Committee, close to 40 individual and group statements were made. For the present purpose it is only important to note that, in line with the preceding account, the other statements by groups of developing countries (Movement of Non-Aligned Countries, Rio Group, ASEAN,[1] and CARICOM[2]) also reinforced the impression of a unified coalition of developing countries that agreed on central positions even if individual speakers foregrounded different aspects.

When all statements had been delivered, key points were summarized and the negotiations were continued informally (A/C.5/55/SR.5 [2000]: 12–14; A/C.5/55/SR.8 [2000]; A/C.5/55/SR.11 [2000]: 2–7). Although it is common practice to continue discussions of the Fifth Committee informally (cf. Sura 2002), there are signs that these discussions were particularly conflictual and lengthy in 2000.[3] When the formal proceedings had resumed, a complex package deal (A/C.5/55/L.36 [2000]) was agreed on by the Fifth Committee and recommended for adaption by the plenary, which considered the report of the committee (A/55/521/Add.1 [2000]) in the afternoon of the same day and adopted the draft resolution contained therein (A/55/PV.89 [2000]: 9–11).

9.2.2 The UN Decision

While resolution A/RES/55/5 B–F (2000) constituted a complex compromise, the aspect that got most of the attention was the highly controversial lowering of the maximum ceiling to 22 per cent. For our purpose, a few more points regarding the scale of assessments are noteworthy, however. Firstly, it is important to note that the individual assessment rates of Brazil, China, and India would have increased even if the maximum ceiling had remained at its previous level. This point will be elaborated on in a moment. Secondly, the relief measures were *neither clearly expanded* (as requested by, for example, the G-77 and China) nor *decisively reduced* (as requested by, for example, the EU). Instead, they remained largely unchanged.[4] Thirdly, a compromise was found in the case of statistical base periods where it was decided to work on the basis of the average of six years (as favoured by quickly growing economies) and three years (as favoured by slowly growing and stagnating economies).

Noteworthy elements of the decision beyond the scale as such are the following. First of all, it contained provisions on implementation flexibilities (second category of differential treatment). For the year 2001, the USA provided a sum equal to 3 per cent of the amount assessed on member states and this amount was distributed among those countries who requested it in order to reduce their individual rates.[5] Of note, the 3 per cent of the USA was, in principle, distributed among both developed and developing countries, but not all countries made use of the opportunity which illustrates the difference between formal eligibility and social expectations. Unclaimed compensations could then be used to increase the compensation for other eligible countries. While the relative increase that each country had experienced can partially explain the volume of the compensation that they received, it was not disclosed how exactly the respective volume for each country was determined and some countries were particularly good at claiming a large compensation. Among Brazil, China, and India, Brazil received the largest compensation (0.5290 per cent, i.e. around one sixth of the overall amount of 3 per cent) followed by China (0.0590 per cent), and India (0.0130 per cent). Finally, Germany also obtained a relatively large compensation (0.3325 per cent) while Japan was one of the countries that did not claim any compensation.

Secondly, the resolution paved the way for less frequent revisions of the scale's methodology by ensuring 'that the elements of the scale of assessments … will be fixed until 2006'. This was, however, subject to another provision which stated that at the end of 2003 the reduced maximum ceiling of 22 per cent would be reviewed – inter alia in light of contributions and arrears. This provision can be understood as a reminder or even as a threat. It makes clear that the USA had to fulfil her part of the package deal and to pay her arrears as well as her future contributions.

Finally, as part of the compromise, the resolution stressed 'that the reduction of the maximum assessment rate ... shall ... have no automatic implication for the apportionment of the expenses of the specialized agencies'. This provision provided a central precondition for the serious conflicts discussed later in the chapter that emerged when WHO became the first UN specialized agency to decide if it would accept the new scale.

In order to contextualize the complex compromise that was found, it is necessary to briefly compare the options that had been suggested, including different statistical base periods. Table 9.1 contains data for the six focus countries.

The table helps to address three sets of questions. Firstly, what independent effect would the application of new data to the old methodology have had? Secondly, what key consequences would each of the main proposals have had? Thirdly, what influence do the base periods have on the results and how does this interpretation of C2P differ from the more complex models?

A comparison between the old scale for 2000 (column #1) and Model A (column #5) shows that, due to economic growth in Brazil, China, and India, the assessment rate for all three countries would have increased from 2000 to 2001 even if the maximum ceiling had remained at 25 per cent. If the finally agreed new scale for 2001 (column #8) is additionally considered, one sees that, as a consequence of the *combined* effect of a maximum ceiling at 22 per cent and of economic growth in Brazil, China, and India, their rates actually increased even further. By contrast, in the case of Germany and Japan, the rates decreased as their share of world income sank. While this effect was reduced due to the lowered maximum ceiling, their rates would have increased above the level of 2000 if the G-77 and China had been exempted from the burden-sharing for the lowered maximum ceiling (column #7). The opposite would have been true if the relief measures had been changed in line with the suggestions made by Japan (column #6).

While the base periods chosen affect the rates of all countries (columns #2 to #4), the difference is particularly striking in the case of Japan, which also explains her relatively high rate in Model A (column #5), which is based on a six-year base period. Regardless of the base period selected in order to calculate national income (columns #2 to #4), the new rate (column #8) for Brazil, China, and India, and for the USA, remains always below their share of world income while Germany and Japan are assessed at a rate higher than their share of world income. The gap between national income and assessment rate is particularly large in the case of China if her income rate of 4.360 per cent for a three-year base period (column #2) is compared with her assessment rate of 1.541 per cent for 2001 (column #8).

Overall, the USA saw her main demand fulfilled although it was against the declared interests of all others.[6] The G-77 and China could neither expand the relief measures nor prevent the lowering of the maximum ceiling but were

Table 9.1 *Actual and potential options for the scale*

Six focus countries	Old scale[i]	Different base periods for calculating each country's share of world income that were considered[ii]			Key alternatives for the methodology that were considered[iii]			New scale[iv]		
	25% max. ceiling and 6ybp[v]	3ybp[vi]	ø3&6y[vii]	6ybp[v]	Model A 25% max. ceiling and 6ybp[v]	Model I 25% max. ceiling, revised relief measures, and 3ybp[vi]	Model J 22% max. ceiling, G-77+ China are exempt, and 6ybp[v]	22% max ceiling, G-77+China are not exempt, and ø3&6y[vii]		
	2000							2001	2002	2003[viii]
	#1	#2	#3	#4	#5	#6	#7	#8	#9	#10
Brazil	1.471%	2.673%	2.549%	2.424%	2.096%	2.600%	2.096%	2.231%	2.093%	2.390%
China	0.995%	4.360%	4.111%	3.862%	1.345%	4.505%	1.345%	1.541%	1.545%	1.532%
India	0.299%	1.308%	1.266%	1.224%	0.315%	0.843%	0.315%	0.343%	0.344%	0.341%
Germany	9.857%	7.658%	7.834%	8.009%	9.585%	8.610%	10.024%	9.825%	9.845%	9.769%
Japan	20.573%	14.805%	15.654%	16.503%	19.750%	16.644%	20.655%	19.629%	19.669%	19.516%
USA	25.000%	27.329%	27.043%	26.757%	25.000%	25.000%	22.000%	22.000%	22.000%	22.000%

Notes:

i Cf. resolution A/RES/52/215 (1997).
ii Cf. report A/55/11 (2000). Data for three years as statistical base period was taken from Model D. Data for six years was taken from Model J. The average was calculated and rounded up by the author.
iii Cf. report A/55/11 (2000).
iv Cf. resolution A/RES/55/5 B–F (2000).
v Six-year base period.
vi Three-year base period.
vii Average of six- and three-year base period.
viii In the resolution, there are five digits after the point.

able to defend key parts of the scale methodology that they valued. Moreover, Brazil, China, and India in particular were able to avoid modifications of the scale methodology that were targeted at increasing their share. Countries like Japan and Germany were neither able to prevent the lowering of the maximum ceiling nor reduce the relief measures but were able to fend off the attempt to make only the classic main contributors (without the USA) compensate the 3 per cent shortfall.

While the concluding section of this chapter will more systematically look into the factors that can explain the outcomes of the conflict moments, it is obvious already at this stage that the unilateral victory for the USA was enabled by her massive arrears while consensual decision-making was a key driver for finding a solution that contained various compromises. With a view to differential treatment, one could argue that C2P as such was not questioned but the maximum ceiling restrained it, and the USA was able to reduce the maximum ceiling further. By the same token, the various other conflicts on the scale of assessments can also be interpreted as disagreements on the operationalization of C2P and its application while calls for a modification of the scale methodology do not necessarily question C2P as such.

9.2.3 Discussions at the WHO Level

While the WHO level inherited conflicts from the UN level, the different institutional context brought up three specific issues. First, there was the question of whether WHO should base its scale of assessments on the new UN scale. This had been common practice but was put in question by UN resolution A/RES/55/5 C (2000) as has been previously explained. A departure from this practice would, in principle, require an alternative procedure or a modification of the UN decision but as will become clear in the following sub-section, much of the discussion addressed this issue in a binary manner and assumed that keeping the old scale was the main alternative. Second, not least since member states wanted to know what the new scale would mean for them in monetary terms, the debate on the scale was eventually linked to the decision on the size of the budget. Third, various procedural questions caused serious conflicts.

The specifics of the negotiation situation led to particular conflict dynamics that differed from the ones at the UN level. Most importantly, with a view to the binary question of whether the package deal from the UN level should be accepted, developed countries tended to take an affirmative position even though they had not uniformly supported the lowering of the maximum ceiling back then. This behaviour, in combination with the fact that the scale decreased for some – but not all – developed countries while many developing countries experienced an increase, led to a situation in which the conflict was perceived as a clash between developed and developing countries, or, more specifically, between the EU and the G-77 and China. In other words, the various nuances regarding country positions, coalitions, and dividing lines that had been relevant at the UN level were no longer visible at the WHO level. By the same token, there was no room to systematically consider the different reasons for which the scale had changed (i.e. the difference between a modified methodology and updated data).

The formal process started at the WHO level when a committee of the Executive Board addressed the issue on the basis of a report by the Director-General (A54/27 [2001]). However, no specific recommendations were made and it was merely concluded that 'the scale of assessments was an important issue' that 'would need to be examined by the ... World Health Assembly' (A54/36 [2001]; see also WHA54/2001/REC/3: 186).

This lack of guidance led immediately to a brief debate between the delegate of Pakistan and the legal counsel when the World Health Assembly started its discussion on the scale of assessments. In this context, the legal counsel confirmed not only that no specific recommendations had been made but also clarified that the current WHO scale would expire at the end of 2001 and that 'a new scale had to be adopted' (WHA54/2001/REC/3: 187). Throughout the subsequent debate, several country delegates contested the assessment of the legal counsel that a new scale was needed. Some even argued that the WHO scale could not be reviewed for procedural reasons, including the very fact that no clear recommendation had been made by the Executive Board.

While another delegation had made a comment before that, the first comprehensive statement was delivered by Cuba on behalf of the G-77 and China (WHA54/2001/REC/3: 187). Cuba said that,

> the proposed new scale of assessments contained in document A54/27 ... would mean that the maximum assessment rate would be reduced from 25% to 22%, with substantial reductions in the contributions of just a few Members, so that the other States Members would have to shoulder the burden of the 3% shortfall. It was apparent from document A54/27 that many major contributors from the developed countries were having their assessments reduced, with a resulting increase in contributions for developing countries. Yet the commitment to international cooperation was incumbent upon the developed, not the developing countries, a point that was particularly relevant to WHO's field of activity.

Cuba also pointed out that the UN resolution had provided that the new UN scale 'should have no automatic implication for the apportionment of the expenses of the specialized agencies'. Moreover, Cuba voiced procedural issues that built, in part, on the points raised by Pakistan and amounted to the criticism that member states had not had enough time to consider the proposal. Overall, 'the Health Assembly should therefore adopt the same scale for the biennium 2002–2003 as for the biennium 2000–2001'. Finally, Cuba requested that, 'before any review of the scale, the Secretariat submit a document showing the real differences in monetary terms in the amount each Member would have to pay'. In terms of lines of conflict, Cuba demanded that the old scale of assessments should be maintained and foregrounded that the proposed changes to the scale were detrimental for developing countries.

Thereafter, Sweden spoke on behalf of the EU (WHA54/2001/REC/3: 187–188). Sweden explained that the present UN scale was the result of a complex package deal and that one element of that deal was that the 22 per cent maximum ceiling should not automatically apply to specialized agencies. At the same time, the present UN scale was also part of the deal. As a consequence, the delegate proposed that the new WHO scale should be based on the present UN scale but 'the concept of capping' in general and the 22 per cent maximum ceiling in particular should *not* be permanently accepted. Thereafter, he pointed out that, collectively, the EU 'was the largest contributor, and its assessed rates exceeded its share of world GNP by almost 25%'. Moreover, he reminded the USA of the other side of the package deal and that the EU 'trusted that the United States administration would expedite the payment of its arrears and assessed contributions to WHO'. In terms of lines of conflict, Sweden proposed to base the new WHO scale on the UN scale while the maximum ceiling should be lowered only temporarily. In contrast to Cuba, who had focussed on the *specific implications of the proposed changes*, Sweden foregrounded the *general effects of the scale methodology*, which made the EU the largest collective contributor and raised its assessment rate above its world income share.

Japan's intervention started with the observation that it was possible to stick to the practice of using UN scales although they 'did not automatically apply to WHO' (WHA54/2001/REC/3: 188). The delegate also pointed out that the latest UN scale had been adopted after intense discussions. All member states, including the G-77 and China, had agreed to it. Moreover, a common scale across the UN system was preferable and re-negotiating the scale would be immensely demanding. Towards the end, he pointed out that even though 'Japan's assessment rate was greater than its share of world GNP ..., it strongly supported the new scale'. In terms of lines of conflict, Japan's position resembled the one that had been expressed by the EU.

Following statements by four other delegations, China pointed out that the scale of assessments 'affected many countries' and had 'implications for other specialized agencies' (WHA54/2001/REC/3: 189). In line with the agreement that had been reached at the UN level, China recommended that the WHO scale should not be based solely on the UN scale. The Chinese delegate also highlighted the following:

> Under the scale proposed in document A54/27, more than 80 Members would have their assessments raised, most of them in developing countries, while decreases would be mostly among developed countries. The burden of developed countries would thus be shifted to developing countries, which would be contrary to the principle of payment according to ability.

At the end of his intervention, the delegate turned to procedural issues, said that more time was needed, and endorsed the proposal by the G-77 and China, which reinforced how China positioned herself in terms of lines of conflict.

Thereafter, Brazil supported the statement on behalf of the G-77 and China and two individual statements, including the one by China (WHA54/2001/REC/3: 189–190). The Brazilian delegate also pointed out that 'Brazil had been making an effort to pay its arrears to various organizations, and it would be a burden to experience an average increase of 40% throughout the United Nations system'. At the same time, 'the United Nations scale of assessments did not automatically apply to other agencies such as WHO' and also this part of the package deal should be respected. 'More time must therefore be allowed for discussions.' In terms of lines of conflict, Brazil, like the G-77 and China, put forward the suggestion 'to adopt the previous year's scale of assessments' for the time being.

More than 100 contributions – ranging from long interventions to brief queries and short statements of support – were made during the subsequent discussions that continued until late in the evening. Countries tended to align themselves with previously made statements and as various members of the G-77 and China spoke, this coalition was often referred to. In contrast to the UN level, no other coalition of developing countries delivered a statement. Among the interventions made later in the debate, two are noteworthy for the present purpose.

India aligned herself with the G-77 and China but made an additional point by considering the current discussions on the scale of assessments in light of the parallel debates on the budget size. The delegate 'noted that maintaining the level of the regular budget while at the same time revising the scale of assessments would adversely affect the developing countries' (WHA54/2001/REC/3: 193). By contrast, the USA pointed at the established practice of using the latest UN scale as a basis for the WHO scale and urged delegates to adopt the proposed scale (WHA54/2001/REC/3: 195) – as had the EU and Japan before.

While the discussions on the first day of the debate (a Friday) ran late into the evening, delegates were not able to come to an agreement. In the course of the discussions, the Director-General increasingly took on a more proactive role and was in the end able to secure the permission to work out a new proposal over the weekend (WHA54/2001/REC/3: 195–204). When the proceedings resumed on Monday, the Director-General presented not only a complex compromise document (A54/49 [2001]) but she had essentially acknowledged the merger of two issues: the scale of assessments and the budget size (WHA54/2001/REC/3: 205–207).

Three drivers had led to this merger. Firstly, and as mentioned above, some countries had demanded that the new scale of assessments should be presented in terms of the actual monetary amount that each member state would have to pay. Secondly and relatedly, countries were wary of the combined effect that a potential budget increase and a new scale of assessment might have on the sum that they would contribute to WHO's assessed budget. Thirdly, the Director-General's new proposal was essentially based on the notion of implementation flexibilities (second category of differential treatment) and contained several relief measures, which led to a financing gap that had to be considered in the budget discussions.

9.2.4 The WHO Decision

While the Director-General had initially requested a budget increase, her compromise document on the scale of assessments (A54/49 [2001]) was based on the assumption that there would be a zero nominal growth budget and spelled out what each member state would have to pay. This illustrates not only that the two issues had by now been linked but also the potential effect of this linking: conflicts over the new scale made member states even more reluctant to accept a budget increase.

The political balancing act that the document achieved was that the UN scale was *not rejected* but its consequences were *radically mitigated*. All those countries whose contributions were reduced by the new scale were assessed according to the new scale; this applied to any country – including the USA. All those countries whose contributions were increased by the new scale could take advantage of relief provisions. The document proposed a 100 per cent relief for the year 2002 – i.e. no member state would have to pay more than in 2001 – and a 75 per cent relief for the year 2003 – i.e. only 25 per cent of the increase would have to be paid for. Additionally, Least Developed Countries received guarantee that they would be assessed according to the old scale if the new scale had led to an increase in their contributions, i.e. they would receive a relief of 100 per cent for both years. Those countries that did not want to take advantage of these provisions were encouraged 'to consider contributing an equivalent amount to miscellaneous income'.

Since various countries had their contributions reduced and since the increases for Non-Least Developed Countries were limited to 12.5 per cent in total (the average of 0 per cent in the first year and 25 per cent in the second year of the biennium), the overall amount assessed on all member states together was actually lower for the biennium 2002–2003 than in the case of the previous biennium 2000–2001.[7] In other words, the relief measures created a funding gap that had to be filled – inter alia with miscellaneous income that would otherwise have gone to priority programmes and other expenditures.[8]

The Director-General's compromise document (A54/49 [2001]) was presented in the morning. Delegates were given time to discuss it amongst themselves until the afternoon when a joint meeting of the two responsible committees was going to address both the scale of assessments and the programme budget, which further reinforced the meanwhile established link between the two issues. With a view to the scale of assessments (WHA54/2001/REC/3: 216–227), there were almost 30 contributions to the debate. While the resolution was adopted with some amendments, the main thrust of the proposal by the Director-General remained intact. This included the prospect that the assessments for the second year of the upcoming biennium would be reviewed in 2002 (WHA54.17 [2001]).

Right after the decision on the scale, the draft resolution on the budget was introduced as the second element of the broader package deal. While the budget had been debated controversially at previous meetings,[9] the proponents of zero nominal growth, which included not only the main contributors (Germany, Japan, and USA) but also developing countries (Argentina and Brazil), had meanwhile prevailed and, following a brief discussion, the draft resolution was adopted without amendments (WHA54/2001/REC/3: 227–230; WHA54.20 [2001]).

Of note, the United Kingdom and the Netherlands stated at the very end of the budget debate that they would forego the right to apply for relief and make a contribution to the miscellaneous income.[10] These announcements, as well as the fact that six more countries from the European Region (EURO) forewent the right to apply for relief, reiterated the potential tension between formal rights and social expectations. On the one hand, the relief measures applied in principle to any country whose contributions were increased by the new scale, and this included developed countries. On the other hand, however, the discussions (and Phase 1 more generally) were marked by a strong sense that developed countries had a moral obligation to support developing countries.[11] This applied even though some of the developing countries had experienced considerable economic growth and it was actually these countries who benefited the most in absolute terms. The top three countries – in terms of the relief they received – were the Republic of Korea, Brazil, and China who received USD (United States dollars) 6 237 746, USD 4 512 412, and USD 3 988 913, respectively. India obtained USD 324 422 (A56/INF.DOC./3 [2003]). Japan and Germany, the remaining focus countries, were not eligible. As discussed earlier, their rates fell (but less than if the maximum ceiling had remained at 25 per cent).

9.2.5 Implementation Flexibilities and Other Repercussions of the WHO Decision

The compromise that was achieved in 2001 was not questioned when the Executive Board and the World Health Assembly reviewed the scale in 2002.[12] Quite to the contrary, the compromise had set a successful precedent and its key elements also characterized the rest of Phase 1. First, the UN scale continued to serve as the basis of the WHO scale. Second, the impact of changes to the scale was also later reduced through implementation flexibilities (second category of differential treatment). Third, scale, budget, and implementation flexibilities were often addressed as part of a package deal. We will look at each of the three elements in turn.

With a view to the first element, the World Health Assembly decided in 2003 that it would, from now on, accept the latest UN scale as the basis for its own scale (WHA56.33 [2003]).[13] While this decision is not irrevocable (WHA56/2003/REC/3: 173), it still put the compromise from 2001 on a more permanent basis. In particular, the decision implied that the WHO would not make use of the leeway that had been created by the UN General Assembly (A/RES/55/5 C [2000]).[14] This formal reaffirmation of previous practice has proven consequential for subsequent discussions on the scale of assessments and it has repeatedly been referred to in later documents (e.g. A58/30 [2005]).[15]

The commitment to accept the UN scale was, however, hedged by the second element of the compromise, namely implementation flexibilities that were implemented through the so-called 'adjustment mechanism'. The adjustment mechanism was demanded by developing countries in particular, while critics highlighted that it was contrary to C2P.[16] The adjustment mechanism was introduced in 2003 and would operate during the two subsequently following biennia (WHA56.34 [2003]).

The mechanism's mode of operation was similar to the relief measures agreed in 2000. The baseline was the WHO scale for the biennium 2000–2001. Member states who saw a scale-induced increase of their monetary contributions in comparison to that baseline were eligible for a compensation. The compensation was limited to a maximum share of the increase that was experienced in each year. These maximum shares receded in the course of the four years covered: they were 60 per cent for 2004, 40 per cent for 2005, 40 per cent for 2006, and 30 per cent for 2007. No special provisions for Least Developed Countries were made this time. Table 9.2 displays the combined

Table 9.2 Sequential application of 'relief' (2002–2003) and 'compensation' (2004–2007)

Year	2002	2003	2004	2005	2006	2007
Maximum share by which the theoretical increase of individual country contributions can be reduced	100%	75%	60%	40%	40%	30%
Remaining share of the theoretical increase that becomes the actual increase	0%	25%	40%	60%	60%	70%

implementation flexibilities that were provided through the sequential application of 'relief' (as decided in 2001) and 'compensations' (as decided in 2003).

As Table 9.2 shows, the changes that were made to the scale of assessments at the UN level were phased in at the WHO level over the course of six years (2002–2007). This demonstrates the strong resistance to these changes. Moreover, since the old WHO scale for the 2000–2001 biennium served as the baseline, not only were the consequences of the UN decision from 2000 delayed but also the changes to the UN scale that emerged thereafter due to updated data.

Regarding the adjustment mechanism, countries did not receive the compensation to which they were eligible automatically. They had to claim a sum up to the eligible maximum amount from a limited common pool that was resourced in the budgeting process.[17] As a consequence, the actual sum received was going to be influenced by the degree to which the resources transferred to the adjustment mechanism could cover the total costs of the claims made. In the case of the biennium 2004–2005, USD 12.7 million was claimed while USD 12.4 million was available, which led to a slight reduction of the individual compensations. For example, China claimed its maximum amount of USD 3 204 855 but was credited USD 3 082 792; Brazil claimed its maximum amount of USD 2 460 220 but was credited USD 2 451 582; and India claimed its maximum amount of USD 324 935 but was credited USD 310 501 (EB115/INF.DOC./8 [2005]).[18] As in the case of 'relief', Japan and Germany were not eligible.

While these numbers show that almost half of the total sum available went to Brazil, China, and India, it is noteworthy that, due to its quickly growing economy, the United Kingdom was another country that was eligible for a substantive compensation. Unlike the position that it had taken in 2001 when it decided to forego its right to apply for relief and to make a contribution to the miscellaneous income, it did claim a compensation this time – in order to express its opposition to the adjustment mechanism (WHA56/2003/REC/3: 191),[19] which, as mentioned before, others had also criticized as being contrary to C2P. Of note, a year later India in turn criticized the adjustment mechanism on the basis that it might eventually run out of funds if not only developing countries but also major developed countries (presumably the United Kingdom) received compensation from it (WHA57/2004/REC/3: 190).

This brings us to the third and final element of the consequential compromise of 2001, namely the joint consideration of scale, budget, and the relevant implementation flexibilities. While a detailed analysis of these discussions would go beyond the scope of this chapter, it is essential to foreground that changes in the scale of assessments drove wedges into the coalition of developing countries, reinforced the norm of budget moderation, and contributed to the increasing weight of willingness to contribute (W2C). In particular, countries with an increasing assessment rate often proved critical of parallel increases of the regular budget.

This was particularly obvious in the discussions in 2003 that covered the scale, the budget, and the adjustment mechanism (WHA56/2003/REC/3: 33–42, 166–174, 190–192, 218).[20] The proposal of the Director-General to opt for a zero real growth budget met strong opposition from various countries including Japan and Germany but also China and Brazil who argued in favour of zero *nominal* growth. The USA's and the EU's positions pointed in the same direction even though they did not explicitly refer to zero nominal growth. By contrast, India was among the countries who took a different position and 'emphasized the importance of ensuring that the regular budget did not shrink in real terms' (WHA56/2003/REC/3: 38). The budget size that was agreed on in the end was at the level of zero real growth but covered a lower level of cost increases than the Director-General had originally hoped for.

Interestingly, once a package deal had been agreed on, Thailand made a retrospective statement on behalf of the G-77 (without China) that was contrary to the positions of China and Brazil – but in line with the position of India – in the sense that it argued against a zero nominal growth budget (WHA56/2003/REC/3: 174). Also of note since it is unlike the position that it will take in Phase 2, China highlighted twice in the discussions that the UN scale should *not* automatically apply to the WHO (WHA56/2003/REC/3: 38–39, 191).[21]

9.2.6 Brief Summary

In summarizing the various developments, one can assert that C2P as such was not questioned but there were conflicts over its interpretation, operationalization, and application as well as over the restraints that had been put on it. The conflicts reached a climax at the UN level in 2000 and at the WHO level in 2001; moreover, they induced further decisions at the WHO level in 2003 and had repercussions until 2007, which was the last year of the adjustment mechanism. The overall conclusion from these developments is that while the most important change to the scale methodology that occurred during Phase 1 was a unilateral victory for the USA, Phase 1 saw *generally* a massive resistance to *any* increases in the assessment rates for developing countries. Regardless of the origins of the change (modified methodology or updated data), agreement was only made possible by repeatedly postponing the increases through different forms of implementation flexibilities (second category of differential treatment). The way in which these were arranged, however, had the effect that some implementation flexibilities applied to certain developed countries – even when they had originally opposed them. This formal eligibility did not necessarily lead to actual claims and when these claims were made, they were at times criticized by some developing countries. This shows that the formal rules of the implementation flexibilities did not align with the social expectations regarding differential treatment.

9.3 CASE STUDY 2: CONTINUOUS AND NEWLY EMERGING CONFLICTS OVER CAPACITY TO PAY

During Phase 2 (2008–2020), contestations of C2P also manifested in conflicts over the scale of assessments. However, the contestations did not result in a modification of the scale methodology that had, in principle, remained unchanged since the events in the year 2000. On the other hand, there were still changes to individual assessment rates that resulted from dynamics in the world economy that the scale reflected through the routine application of updated data to the existing methodology. Moreover, towards the end of Phase 2, the G-77 and China became more assertive in their criticism of the methodology and reassessed the boundaries of C2P. The controversies reached a temporary climax during the scale negotiations in 2018 when the demands of the G-77 and China would have increased the contributions by the USA and by the EU in particular. The second case study zooms in on these conflicts at the UN level and looks into the sparse reactions at the WHO level.

9.3.1 Discussions at the UN Level

While in 2000 key drivers for the conflicts had been the USA's arrears and demands, in 2018 it was the G-77 and China that challenged the status quo most clearly and tabled eventually a draft resolution reflecting their demands. The discussions on the scale of assessments were initiated by the Chair of the Committee on Contributions who introduced the committee's report (A/C.5/73/SR.1 [2018]: 8–9). While the report (A/73/11 [2018]) contained a large amount of background information and came forward with various conclusions and recommendations, the more controversial issues had been postponed until additional guidance was provided by the General Assembly.

The first statement was made by Egypt who spoke on behalf of the G-77 and China (A/C.5/73/SR.1 [2018]: 9–10). The delegate highlighted that assessed contributions should be paid in full, on time, and without conditions and added later that the group 'rejected the unilateral withholding of contributions in order to put pressure on the United Nations, which ran contrary to the letter and spirit of the Charter'. Moreover, he reaffirmed the role of 'capacity to pay' and 'rejected any changes in the elements of the current methodology aimed at increasing the contributions of developing countries'; he made clear that the core elements of the methodology 'were not negotiable'. The only exception was the maximum ceiling.

While these were long held positions of the G-77 and China, the delegate also mentioned a new line of argument that had emerged in recent years and called for an expansion of the domain of C2P:[22] 'Organizations with an enhanced observer status at the United Nations that enjoyed rights and privileges usually granted only to observer States should have the same financial obligations as such States'. While the speaker did not mention it directly, the EU is the international organization that would have been affected by this proposal. Moreover, the delegate pointed at the practical consequences of the current methodology: 'The share of the regular budget scale of assessments borne by States members of the Group of 77 and China would increase to 25.477 per cent – approximately three times the Group's share for the 2007–2009 period – while the scale of assessments for developed countries would continue to decrease'.

He ended his statement with a comment on the negotiation process, which 'should be open, inclusive and transparent'; the comment reaffirmed at the same time the unity of the G-77 and China, which opposed 'decision-making in small groups'. In terms of lines of conflict, it can be summarized that the demands would have affected the USA and the EU in particular.

Of note, the other country coalitions who could claim to speak on behalf of developing countries were more prominent in 2018 than in 2000 since they intervened early in the debate and immediately after the G-77 and China. Broadly speaking, the other developing country coalitions were in line with the demands of the G-77 and China but there was some variation in the degree to which they wanted to modify the current methodology. While the statement by Uganda (on behalf of the Group of African States), the statement by El Salvador (on behalf of CELAC),[23] and the statement by Antigua and Barbuda (on behalf of CARICOM) can in the main be interpreted as a rejection of any changes to the methodology that would increase the contributions of developing countries (A/C.5/73/SR.1 [2018]: 10–12), the statement by Singapore (on behalf of ASEAN) made demands beyond the status quo and followed the G-77 and China in this regard (A/C.5/73/SR.2 [2018]: 2).

Following the Group of African States, CELAC, CARICOM, and ASEAN, the fifth statement by a country coalition whose membership overlapped with the G-77 and China was delivered by South Africa, who spoke also on behalf of Brazil, the Russian Federation, India, and China. In a comparatively concise statement, the delegate made particularly clear that 'with the exception of the maximum assessment rate', the 'elements of the current scale methodology were not open to negotiation' (A/C.5/73/SR.2 [2018]: 2). Regarding lines of conflict, it was in the main in line with the demands of the G-77 and China but silent on the financial obligations of international organizations with enhanced observer status.

The observer for the EU (who spoke also on behalf of seven more countries) made clear that the current scale methodology would not accurately reflect member states' 'capacity to pay' and that the report of the Committee on Contributions would elucidate to some degree why this was the case (A/C.5/73/SR.2 [2018]: 2–3). The member states of the EU were 'the largest collective financial contributors' and they emphasized the need

> for the General Assembly to ensure a more equitable and balanced distribution of financial responsibilities among Member States, in accordance with the principle of the capacity to pay. The current scale methodology could be improved to better reflect that principle. For instance, while an essential element of the methodology, the low per capita income adjustment did not entirely fulfil its intended purpose as a form of targeted relief for countries with low per capita income. Any changes to the low per capita income adjustment must be based on reliable data and should represent a technical enhancement of the methodology.

He continued his statement by pointing out that 'the methodology must not deviate from Article 17 of the Charter' which could be interpreted as a rejection of the proposal that international organizations like the EU could be assessed, since Article 17(2) stipulates that the 'expenses of the Organization shall be borne by the Members as apportioned by the General Assembly'. In the concluding part, he made clear that 'Member States had a fundamental duty to pay their assessed contributions in full, on time and without conditions'. Regarding lines of conflict, the EU's comment on the scale methodology can be interpreted as an indirect criticism of the fact that countries like India and China benefit from the low per capita income adjustment.

The statement by the USA (A/C.5/73/SR.2 [2018]: 3) called for a preservation of the status quo. It can essentially be summarized as a defence of the existing maximum ceiling and of the principle that the UN should not rely 'on the contributions of a single Member State'. The delegate of Japan pointed out in his statement (A/C.5/73/SR.2 [2018]: 3–4) that the 'updated scale contained in the report of the Committee on Contributions (A/73/11) accurately took into account the recent changes in the economic situation of each Member State' but made also clear that the scale could still be improved 'to more equitably reflect each Member State's capacity to pay'. In other words, there were only vague hints regarding lines of conflict.

China's statement (A/C.5/73/SR.2 [2018]: 4) highlighted that states' 'capacity to pay' was 'ultimately determined by their per capita income' and supported longer statistical base periods as they would be a more stable and sustainable measure of capacity to pay that 'reduced the negative impact of short-term economic fluctuations'. At the same time, the delegate took up an issue that can be considered a classic concern of contributors, namely the quality of data. Moreover, he argued that there was an 'inappropriate blurring of the distinction between developed and developing countries' that was demonstrated by the 'increase in the assessed contributions owed by developing countries and the decrease in those owed by developed countries'. Consequently, the 'debt burden adjustment and the low per capita income adjustment should be strengthened' and criticisms of these elements 'were unacceptable'. Finally, the delegate elaborated on the situation of China where he did not only reiterate that China remained a developing country but also followed the tradition of major contributors to evoke the perspective of their taxpayers who would watch the increase closely. Regarding lines of conflict, China called mainly for strengthening of the relief measures.

After two other interventions, the delegate of India started his statement (A/C.5/73/SR.2 [2018]: 4–5) by pointing out that 'all Member States must fulfil their financial obligations to the Organization in full, on time and without conditions'. Furthermore, he made it clear that India supported the continued use of the current scale methodology even though it 'would result in a significant increase in the assessed contributions owed by India'. While India 'believed that organizations with an enhanced observer status should have the same financial obligations as observer States', the delegate was also explicit regarding the elements of the methodology that should not change: 'The principle of the capacity to pay and the low per capita income adjustment were not open to negotiation, and such core elements as the base period, GNI, conversion rates, the gradient, the floor and the debt-stock adjustment must also be retained'. Regarding lines of conflict, India was in agreement with the G-77 and China but silent on the maximum ceiling.

Thereafter, Brazil made a brief statement (A/C.5/73/SR.2 [2018]: 5) in which she emphasized inter alia that 'the principle of capacity to pay should not be undermined by arbitrary considerations and political concerns, and developing countries, including least developed countries, should not be overburdened by assessed contributions'. Moreover, the Brazilian delegate stated that 'the Fifth Committee must conduct open, inclusive and transparent deliberations'. Regarding lines of conflict, the statement can be read as a support for the status quo. After two more interventions, the formal discussion on the scale of assessments was suspended and continued informally.

As in the first case study, the long duration and repeated extension of the informal discussions can be seen as some evidence for the challenging negotiations.[24] Even more striking and highly unusual, however, is the fact that two competing draft resolutions were tabled at the end of the informal part: one by Egypt on behalf of the G-77 and China (A/C.5/73/L.6 [2018]) and one by the chair (A/C.5/73/L.8 [2018]). This means not only that the delegates were not able to use the informal discussions to reach an agreement but also highlights that consensual decision-making is not a legal requirement and that competitive voting can always be used as a threat by those who are able to mobilize a majority. However, while there were competing draft resolutions on the table, there was no competitive vote. Rather, Egypt withdrew the G-77 and China's draft resolution for the regular scale (and the one for the peacekeeping scale). Subsequently, the chair's draft resolution could be adopted by consensus and the UN scale was formally adopted in resolution A/RES/73/271 (2018) that followed the recommendations of the Fifth Committee (A/73/421/Add.1 [2018]).[25]

9.3.2 The UN Decision

The resolution reaffirmed 'the fundamental principle that the expenses of the Organization shall be apportioned broadly according to capacity to pay' and that the scale of assessments shall be based on a methodology that had, in principle, remained unchanged since the events in the year 2000 that have been analysed above. In spite of the stasis at the level of the scale methodology, there were considerable changes in the practical consequences of the methodology, in particular for China whose assessment rate rose from 7.921 per cent to 12.005 per cent which made her the second largest contributor while Japan had moved to the third position (8.564 per cent). Of note, China was among the countries who commented on the decision taken and highlighted that she would 'from 2019, be the second largest contributor to the regular budget, which would represent a significant amount for a developing country with a population of 1.4 billion' (A/C.5/73/SR.26 [2018]: 10).

Not least in light of the contestations that preceded the decision, this raises the question of what changes the alternative draft resolution would have brought about. The proposal by Egypt on behalf of the G-77 and China (A/C.5/73/L.6 [2018]), contained, among other differences, two noteworthy elements. First, the proposal would have abolished the 22 per cent maximum ceiling; that is, it would have abolished this restraint on C2P's scope. Second, it would have set a 'notional assessment rate of 21.152 per cent' for the EU. In other words, it would have expanded the domain of the norm to international organizations with enhanced observer status.

If these provisions had been agreed on, they would have altered the distributions of costs considerably. Firstly, as displayed in Table 9.3 below, an abolishment of the maximum ceiling would have affected the individual scales of all six focus countries. While the scale of the USA would have changed the most and would have increased (+5.260 per cent points), it is noteworthy that the decrease for Germany (-0.514 per cent points) and for Japan (-0.717 per cent points) would have been larger than the decrease for China (-0.298 per cent points) as the – by then – second largest contributor. The reason for this is that an abolishment of the maximum ceiling would not only mean that the gap between the US income and the US rate would no longer be redistributed; rather, it would also imply that the USA would *additionally* contribute to absorbing the relief measures and the Least Developed Countries ceiling. This would disburden countries like Germany and Japan who traditionally carry the largest share while the G-77 and China tend to be beneficiaries of these elements. By the same token, also collectively, these traditional major donors, Germany and Japan, would have seen a larger reduction (-1.231 per cent points) than Brazil, China, and India (-0.480 per cent points).

Secondly, previous practice in the case of states suggests that if the EU had been treated as a participating non-member, the bloc would initially have been assessed through a 'flat annual fee' at 50 per cent of its notional assessment rate, i.e. at 10.576 per cent. This 'fee' would have been considered as an element of the UN's general income and would not have been credited to the regular budget.[26] However, from the perspective of the EU and its member states it would have constituted an additional financial obligation. Among our focus countries only Germany is an EU member and would have been affected by this decision.

Conceptually speaking, the attempt to expand C2P to the EU is highly interesting since it would create stronger expectations than willingness to contribute (W2C), whose social dimension merely encourages actors to make unspecific amounts of voluntary contributions to the budget of international organizations. 'Fees' that follow from an expanded scope of C2P would generate specific and predictable amounts of flexible and reliable resources whose character comes closer to assessed contributions than to voluntary contributions.

The 'fee' for the EU is also included in Table 9.3 but three things should be noted. First, the 'fee' is payable in addition to the amount assessed on member states, i.e. it does not reduce the obligations of member states. Second, while the EU contributes to other international organizations to which it is a contracting party, there is no comparable precedence for this specific constellation. It is consequently unclear if the proponents of this arrangement would have been

Table 9.3 *Comparison of the implications of the two draft resolutions regarding the scale of assessments and payable fees*

	Previous assessment rates (2016–2018) as decided in A/RES/70/245 (2015)	Draft resolution by the chair (A/C.5/73/L.8 [2018]) that was eventually adopted	Draft resolution by Egypt on behalf of the G-77 and China (A/C.5/73/L.6 [2018])
	#1	#2	#3
Brazil	3.823%	2.948%	2.787%
China	7.921%	12.005%	11.707%
India	0.737%	0.835%	0.814%
Germany	6.389%	6.090%	5.576%
Japan	9.680%	8.564%	7.847%
USA	22.000%	22.000%	27.260%
European Union (fee)*	0.000%	0.000%	10.576%

Note: *As calculated by the author on the basis of a notional assessment of 21.152 per cent and a flat annual fee percentage of 50 per cent.

able to introduce it at the WHO level as well where the EU's special status is based on an exchange of letters.[27] In any event, the attempt would certainly have sparked considerable discussions. Third, the 'fee' would be considerably higher (or lower) if the General Assembly set a flat annual fee percentage above (or below) 50 per cent.

While a comparison of column #1 and column #2 shows the independent effect of the application of updated data to the scale methodology, a comparison between column #2 and column #3 shows the different effects of the two draft resolutions. Obviously, the financial implications on the USA and on the EU would have been considerable if the draft resolution by the G-77 and China had been accepted. By tabling a controversial draft resolution, the G-77 and China were much more assertive than previously. In light of their majority of the votes, they demonstrated that they would, in principle, be able to get what they wanted – at least at the level of rule-making; those who were voted down could still have withheld, delayed, or reduced payments. On the other hand, it has to be noted that as long as the G-77 and China did not break the procedural norm of consensual decision-making, the chances for radical change remained small.

9.3.3 The WHO Level, the WHO Decision, and China's New Self-understanding

A few weeks after the UN decision, a report by the Director-General of WHO (EB144/44 [2019]) proposed to accept the new UN scale as the basis for a new

WHO scale. The proposal was supported by the responsible committee of the Executive Board (EB144/4 [2019]). Also, when the Executive Board itself addressed the agenda item it proved uncontroversial. The only country that spoke on the issue during the meeting was China 'who expressed support for the draft resolution' (EB144/2019/REC/2: 213) Of note, the delegate also 'hoped that countries whose assessed contributions had been lowered would continue to support the Organization by increasing their voluntary contributions'.

A further report by the Director-General (A72/38 [2019]) recapitulated the position of the Executive Board and explicitly pointed at the decision from 2003 (WHA56.33 [2003]) that UN scales should determine WHO scales. Based on this report, the World Health Assembly adopted the WHO scale of assessments along the lines that the Director-General had suggested. In the case of Brazil, China, and India, the scales were set at the following levels: Brazil 2.9482 per cent, China 12.0058 per cent, and India 0.8341 per cent; and, in the case of the classic main contributors, they were: Germany 6.0904 per cent, Japan 8.5645 per cent, and USA 22.0000 per cent (WHA72.12 [2019]). During the discussions prior to the decision only three countries spoke. One of them was China whose representative stated 'that her Government was committed to paying its assessed contributions in accordance with the draft resolution' (A72/B/PSR/3 [2019]: 6). The delegate also mentioned that China had made voluntary contributions since 2017.

Only in light of the historical conflicts, and in comparison to the continuous conflicts at the UN level, the course of events at the WHO level becomes noteworthy. In other words, without these two comparative cases it is difficult to appreciate the relevance of the situation as it presented itself at the WHO level at the end of Phase 2. Firstly, there are the affirmative position and the new self-understanding of China. She commented on rather than fundamentally criticized her rising assessment rate. Moreover, she no longer took issue with the fact that the WHO scale was based on the UN scale. Secondly, also with a view to the other countries, it is striking that there was a general absence of open conflicts while hardly any comments were made.

9.3.4 Behavioural Compliance with and Contestation of Capacity to Pay

While the previous sub-section suggested that developing countries in general and China in particular have increasingly accepted the idea that their economic growth leads to increasing assessment rates, we still have to assess to what degree the focus countries actually fulfil their financial obligations. The key question is whether the operationalization of C2P through the UN scale methodology and its practical consequences are also accepted at this level – or if member states contest them through non-payment.

According to the financial regulations of the WHO that were in place at the end of Phase 2, instalments of 'assessed contributions shall be due and payable as of 1 January of the year to which they relate' but it will only be as of 1 January of the following year that 'the unpaid balance of such assessed contributions shall be considered to be one year in arrears' (WHO 2020: 140). Moreover, only once a member state 'is in arrears in an amount that equals or exceeds the amount of contributions due from it for the preceding two full years, the Health Assembly takes a decision on suspension of the Member's voting privileges in accordance with resolution WHA41.7 (1988)'.[28]

Against this background, it has become common practice for a minority of countries to pay in advance (i.e. before 1 January), a majority pay between 1 January and 31 December, and a second minority pay in the subsequent following year or even later, i.e. they go into arrears. Moreover, it has become common for countries to make partial payments. Finally, in analogy to the provisions regarding Article 19 of the UN Charter, countries who are unable to fulfil their financial obligations due to exceptional circumstances can negotiate special arrangements (usually multiyear payment plans) to settle their arrears and to avoid losing their right to vote.[29]

While payments after 1 January can, in principle, pose a challenge to the liquidity of WHO, 31 December has become the threshold on which countries focus since they fall in arrears only thereafter. This threshold is also referred to by the WHO secretariat in its annual reports on the status of collection of assessed contributions that are presented at every World Health Assembly. Data from these reports has been used to assess the degree to which the six focus countries did or did not fulfil their financial obligations during Phase 2.[30] For the purpose of this analysis, unmet financial obligations were expressed as a percentage share of countries' assessed contributions.[31] Thus, if a country had paid all assessed contributions, the percentage share would be zero. A value between zero and 100 would indicate the share of the assessed contributions that was still owed for the previous year while a value above 100 would indicate that arrears for more than one year had accumulated.

The analysis showed that four of the six countries fulfilled their obligations reliably (within the grace period of one year after which delayed payments become arrears). Germany never fell in arrears while the other three did so only once and to a small degree: 1 per cent in the case of India, 10 per cent in the case of Japan, and 30 per cent in the case of China. By contrast, Brazil and the USA were much less reliable as shown in Table 9.4.

While the arrears of the USA are a problem because of their sheer size, it is still noteworthy, that, in relative terms, the arrears of Brazil were often even larger. At the same time, Brazil did not fall into arrears during the early years

Table 9.4 *Unmet financial obligations of Brazil and the US at the end of each calendar year*

	2008	2009	2010	2011	2012	2013	2014	2015	2016	2017	2018	2019	2020
Brazil	0%	0%	0%	0%	100%	5%	100%	176%	82%	75%	91%	100%	200%
USA	40%	103%	23%	33%	23%	53%	33%	53%	17%	102%	52%	117%	169%

of Phase 2 when, as will be discussed below, she was still a clearer beneficiary of (but also a contributor to) differential treatment. It should also be noted that the situation in 2020 was very specific: the USA decided to leave WHO, and Brazil threatened to do so – in both cases due to conflicts over COVID-19 policies and recommendations.

What these observations come down to is, first of all, that, as repeatedly announced, China did indeed follow up on her obligations. While Germany, India, and Japan also commonly fulfilled their financial obligations by the end of each calendar year, India was the only one of the six focus countries that had made any advance payments.[32] Moreover, the specific status of Brazil as a country that no longer benefits much from differential treatment is further reinforced by the observation that from 2012 it has continuously fallen into arrears albeit at varying levels. In 2015 her arrears came close to two annual payments and in 2020 they amounted to two annual payments. Finally, even though the maximum ceiling had been lowered during Phase 1, the USA has not abandoned the practice of falling into arrears.

9.3.5 Brief Summary

As in the previous case study, one can assert that C2P as such was not questioned. However, there were conflicts over its interpretation, operationalization, and application as well as over the restraints that had been put on it. Moreover, the following points are noteworthy. First, the scale of assessments remains a contentious issue but the conflicts are currently limited to the UN level. Secondly, there is a strong resistance against making any modifications to the methodology that could increase the financial contributions of developing countries. Nevertheless, the routine application of new data has – generally speaking – the effect of reducing the contributions of those countries that used to be the major contributors and of increasing the assessments on growing economies such as Brazil, China, and India. We will discuss the details of this graduation below which will show that it actually comes in an attenuated form. Thirdly, the maximum ceiling of 22 per cent remains a point of contention but the G-77 and China have additionally developed a new line of argument in order to increase the assessments on actors outside of their group and have started to demand a financial contribution from the EU on top of the assessments on the EU's individual member states. The events of 2018 are significant in the sense that the G-77 and China introduced a draft resolution that mirrored their demands. While consensual decision-making is common practice, the presentation of the draft resolution can also be interpreted as a threat since the G-77 and China would in principle have had enough votes to pass the resolution by a two-thirds majority of the members present and voting.

9.4 INTERPRETING AND EXPLAINING THE CASES

A key particularity of WHO-channelled health financing is the way in which differential treatment has been institutionalized. Paying tribute to this particularity, this concluding discussion of the interplay of explanatory factors will start off with the institutional factors. Thereafter, we will turn to ideas followed by coalitions and capabilities.

9.4.1 Institutional Arrangements

In terms of institutional arrangements, three noteworthy issues warrant closer inspection. First, the way in which they enable and hinder change. Second, the different fora and contexts in which decisions are taken. Third, the question of whether the scale of assessments is dealt with individually or in combination with other issues.

Turning to the first point, the institutional arrangements are both a source of stability and of change. A central stabilizing factor is the procedural norm of consensual decision-making that makes it difficult to alter the status quo in the absence of broad support as became obvious in the second case study. Qualifications to this observation will be discussed in sub-section 9.4.3 on capabilities, which addresses inter alia the specific role of the USA that became visible in the first case study. The most important institutional source of change is the fact that differential treatment is based on a formula approach. C2P is operationalized through the scale methodology and the scale of assessments is regularly revised on the basis of updated data. To be sure, this updating is not necessarily uncontroversial and it was heavily contested during Phase 1, including in the first case study; however, it is an institutional set-up that enables change. The institutional arrangement is also responsible for a further, albeit much more contested, path that change typically takes, namely the modification of individual elements of the scale methodology.

A second particularity of the institutional arrangements is that discussions and decisions take place in multiple fora and in different contexts. Most importantly, decisions made at the UN level have a formative impact on decisions made at the WHO level but the mere need to formally accept the UN scale as the basis of the WHO scale also gives, in principle, the possibility to deviate from this practice. From this perspective, resolution WHA56.33 (2003) is a revocable affirmation of this practice. But even if the formative role of the UN level is accepted, the institutional set-up gives the opportunity to introduce additional layers of differential treatment such as implementation flexibilities at the WHO level. Moreover, the obligation to pay assessed contributions to the WHO is monitored and enforced at this level while the long grace period that is given before the 'voting privileges and services to which a Member is entitled' are suspended, means that enforcement is a continuous challenge (cf. Table 9.4).

This brings us to the third point, which, like the previous one, also points to the relevance of the context in which discussions and decisions take place. Historically, the scale of assessments has for the most part been discussed individually and rarely in combination with the budget. This institutional separation matters since, in the time period covered in this study, the lines of conflict were generally less complex in the case of the scale of assessments than in the case of the budget. By staying away from budget-related conflicts, it was easier to hold large coalitions together in discussions on the scale of assessments. In particular, as will be elaborated on in sub-section 9.4.3 on coalitions, it was possible to secure a unity between rising powers and other developing countries on the scale of assessments while rising powers proved reluctant to support other developing countries when they, in discussions on the budget, called for an increase in assessed contributions. This is illustrated by the fact that the G-77 and China have not played a visible role in budgeting debates in the time period covered.

9.4.2 Ideas Regarding Legitimacy and Identity

In terms of ideas, there are two aspects that matter for the present purpose: first, the overall legitimacy of C2P; second, the self-understanding that countries communicated about themselves in this context.

Regarding the first point, C2P as such was never questioned but specific aspects of its operationalization were contested. Moreover, some of the criticisms changed over time. Most importantly, during Phase 1 (and in the first case study), developing countries contested any increase of their assessment rates. They criticized the mere fact that there was change at all. They did not discriminate continuously between sources of change (modified methodology or updated data), neither did they elaborate what threshold would define a justified share. The particularity of this structural and static approach, as well as the concomitant notion of legitimacy, becomes visible if a comparison is made with Phase 2 (and the second case study). In this more recent time period, developing countries, including Brazil, China, and India, paid a larger share in absolute terms but had accepted the general idea that dynamics in the world economy would lead to changes in the scale of assessments. The changes were increasingly seen as evidence for the mounting relevance of developing countries and the contestation focussed on defending the existing scale methodology (except for the maximum ceiling) and, towards the end of Phase 2, on expanding the domain of C2P to the EU.

Also, Japan and the EU continuously affirmed the legitimacy of C2P but they questioned both the specific arrangements for the relief measures in its operationalization and the restraints that had been put on it through the maximum ceiling. The USA was assertive in demanding a restraining of C2P but did not question the norm as such. Moreover, the USA's criticism of the operationalization overlapped with some of the criticisms raised by Japan and the EU.

When it comes to self-understandings, the most striking change can be observed in the case of China. While China long proved critical of both increases for developing countries and of an automatic application of the UN scale to the WHO scale, she has increasingly taken on an affirmative position and foregrounds now that she has become the second largest contributor. As mentioned in Chapter 4, this does, however, not imply that she feels subject to willingness to contribute (W2C), too. In particular, her voluntary contributions remain – in relative terms – small and are earmarked for specific purposes. This dual take on financing is made possible by the fact that both C2P and W2C matter for WHO-channelled financing. In the case of China, it has resulted in partial graduation since C2P applies to a much smaller part of the budget than W2C. It is also noteworthy that China continuously highlights her status as a developing country and hence her links to the developing world.

The self-understandings of India and Brazil have been more constant and clear-cut in the sense that India continues to point at increases in her assessment rate without claiming a new role and that Brazil has long foregrounded that she is a contributor to differential treatment and that she finds it challenging to meet her concomitant financial obligations. Similarly, Japan and the EU accept, in principle, the notion that they should contribute more than others but dispute the gap between their share of world income and their assessment rates. The USA foregrounds her status as main contributor while also warning against dependence on a single member state.

What should be noted for both kinds of ideas is the observation that the discussions deal with the distribution of monetary burden as a 'matter of principle' rather a 'matter of affordability'. For member states, the question of how financial obligations are assigned and legitimized is of fundamental importance, although the actual amounts over which they haggle are usually relatively small. Moreover, if a country was really unable to fulfil its financial obligations, special arrangements due to exceptional circumstances could be negotiated (as mentioned in sub-section 9.3.4 above). The fact that countries consider financial contributions to be a 'matter of principle' foregrounds the importance of analysing financial questions through a norms lens and the usefulness of taking multiple explanatory factors seriously.

9.4.3 Coalitions and Capabilities

With a view to coalitions and capabilities, there are two sets of issues that warrant closer inspection. First, the continuous role of the G-77 and China at the UN level – including the alignment of rising powers with them – which shows the ability of developing countries to form a stable coalition. Second, the specific role of the USA, which is noteworthy for both the USA's capabilities in the form of (withheld) contributions and for the detrimental effect of the USA's position on the unity of the classic major contributors. We will take each of these sets of issues in turn.

In order to understand the strong support of Brazil, China, and India for differential treatment and their continuous alignment with the other developing countries, one has to take a closer look at the complex way in which they have been both beneficiaries of and contributors to differential treatment. While all three benefited less from differential treatment at the second conflict moment than at the first one, they still do benefit to some degree. This applies to India and China in particular. Since the rising powers remain beneficiaries of differential treatment in spite of some graduation, one can speak of attenuated graduation in the case of C2P and, as promised in Chapter 4, the present discussion of coalitions will therefore have to elaborate on what 'being a beneficiary' implies. In particular, it will discuss five ways to determine the extent to which a country benefits from differential treatment.

If we take the equal burden-sharing alternative of 0.52 per cent (cf. Chapter 4) as the starting point, then India is the only country among Brazil, China, and India that was a pure beneficiary at the outset of the analysis. Even at the end of Phase 1, her assessment rate remained below the threshold when it reached 0.45 per cent at the UN level (A/RES/61/237 [2006]). India went past the threshold only in 2010 at the UN level (A/RES/64/248 [2009]) when she was assessed at 0.534 per cent and consequently one year later at the WHO level (WHA63.5 [2011]). Secondly, if we look at measures that lower a country's assessment rate below its share of world income, the following observations can be made. During both phases, Brazil, China, and India have all benefited from differential treatment in the form of the first relief measure, namely debt adjustment, for which even Brazil continues to be eligible. By contrast, only India and China have benefited from the second relief measure, namely low per capita income adjustment, throughout both phases. Thirdly, Brazil, China, and India have all benefited from differential treatment in the form of implementation flexibilities but they did so 'only' in the six years after the first conflict moment while none were agreed on during Phase 2. Fourthly, both India and China benefited from the operationalization of differential treatment regarding statistical base periods that delayed the visibility of the continuous economic growth of the countries. The situation is more ambiguous in the case of Brazil as her economy proved more volatile. Fifthly, there is the question of to what extent the assessment rates for Brazil, China, and India have increased and if they have become one of the main contributors. Due to increases, all three were contributing more to differential treatment by the end of Phase 2 than previously (i.e. their assessment rate had increased visibly). However, only China has seen a steep increase in her rate and thereby moved into the group of main contributors.

In other words, in various ways and to varying degrees, Brazil, China, and India were simultaneously beneficiaries of and contributors to differential treatment by the end of Phase 2. When it comes to the question of which of the five ways to capture the status of the three countries as beneficiaries of differential treatment explains their common position on the scale methodology best, the second one sticks out which looks at the ratio between a country's share in world income and its assessment rate. Based on data contained in document A/73/11 (2018), Figure 9.1 illustrates this assertion by showing the practical consequences of the scale methodology on the rates of the six focus countries.

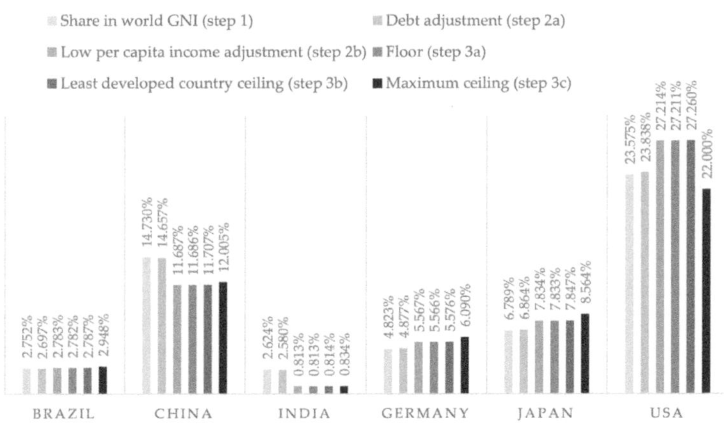

Figure 9.1 *Impact of each element of the methodology on the 2019–2021 assessment rates of the six focus countries*

A comparison of Brazil, China, and India with each other shows that it is China and India in particular who continue to benefit from relief measures while Brazil sees only a small reduction for 'debt adjustment' and pays overall more than her share of the world income. Moreover, it is noteworthy that the

Least Developed Countries ceiling is not among the 'costliest' elements of the scale methodology. This makes differential treatment for this sub-group of developing countries unproblematic for those of our focus countries who contribute in different degrees to its financing (Brazil, China, India, Germany, and Japan) while the maximum ceiling exempts the USA from burden-sharing in any event.

If this snapshot is put into the broader context of Phase 2 as a whole, a very similar picture emerges.[33] The individual assessment rates for China and India have been consistently lower than their respective shares of the world economy. The same applies for the USA but for different reasons. Moreover, Germany and Japan have continuously faced assessment rates above their shares of the world economy. Only the case of Brazil is more complex. At the outset of Phase 2, Brazil was assessed at a rate below her share of the world economy but this changed later on, i.e. she moved from being an overall beneficiary to being an overall contributor. The central tipping point for Brazil was when she was no longer eligible for the low per capita income adjustment and had to share the burden of absorbing the redistributive effects of this element of the scale. However, more recently her assessment rate has moved closer to her share of world income again.

With a view to the unity of developing countries in general and the alignment of rising powers with the G-77 and China in particular, the following observation becomes apparent. It is not surprising that China and India align with other developing countries and remain supportive of the current scale methodology. The interpretation (or operationalization) of differential treatment that underlies the scale methodology is particularly favourable for these two countries since they have large populations. While the self-understanding of China and India as developing countries, as well as their alignment with the other developing countries, is not undermined by financial incentives, the situation is less clear-cut in the case of Brazil who has become an overall contributor to differential treatment and has long mourned her assessment rate.

Despite her more ambiguous position, Brazil supports the other developing countries in the negotiations on the scale methodology. At the same time, she contests the current arrangement through her arrears and, in budget debates, by her reluctance to support an increase in assessed contributions. This reluctance is at times explicitly shared by China while India tends to be more supportive of it – and WHO's African member states are traditionally particularly vocal in their support for such increases. It is in this sense that the institutional separation of scale and budget makes it easier to hold a broad coalition of developing countries together. Also of note, the status of Brazil, China, and India as beneficiaries was at times criticized by developed countries but not by developing countries, who do not lose anything by having them in their coalition. In terms of capabilities, the sheer membership size of the G-77 and China coalition dwarfs all other coalitions in terms of the votes they can mobilize.

However, in the context of coalitions and capabilities, the USA holds a unique position and she has been able to capitalize on it in order to negotiate a restraining of C2P. Paradoxically, the USA argued that a maximum ceiling was needed in order to avoid dependence on a single member state but she has only been able to achieve her goals due to this very dependence. By not paying her assessed contributions across various UN organizations, including the WHO, the USA has been able to coerce all others to agree to her suggestions while, on the surface, the decisions were taken by consensus. In this context, it is also important to note that the specifics of the USA's political system made the threats particularly credible and that the US Congress was a driving force for the pressures that the USA put on the UN (Koschorreck 2001; Mackey and Novotny 2012). Nevertheless, specific presidents were not irrelevant, and during the conflict moment in 2000 the looming change of president might have contributed to the finding of an agreement since the incoming president appeared to be even more critical of the UN.

The specific position of the USA matters not only since it can explain the tailored rules that the USA secured for herself. Additionally, it explains why the classic main contributors have struggled to unite around a common cause. Counterfactually speaking, a coalition of these countries would probably have been able to develop a more targeted response to the global economic shifts than the USA's strategy of reducing her own assessment rate. More specifically, proposals along the lines of Model I that was discussed in the context of the first conflict moment, and that was strongly supported by Japan, could have given more responsibilities to countries with large economies while preserving differential treatment for all other developing countries. As indicated earlier in the chapter, Model I would have increased the assessment rate for Brazil, China, and India in particular. By contrast, the present, unilaterally enforced, arrangement not only increased the rates of 'the world's powerhouse developing economies' (A/C.5/55/SR.5 [2000]: 8), but also meant that the majority of countries have to share the burden of closing the gap between the USA's national income and her assessment rate. Additionally, countries who do not benefit from the relief measures have to compensate their redistribution effects without the support of the USA. Only those countries who are subject to one of the other two limits (i.e. the floor or the Least Developed Countries ceiling) are not affected by the special arrangements for the USA that restrain C2P.

9.5 CONCLUSION

From the perspective of the literature on differential treatment, C2P is a prototypical, but understudied, norm of differential treatment. It is operationalized through the scale methodology and leads to legally binding obligations for all member states. C2P has even been overlooked in the literature on WHO financing, which has been preoccupied with the role of voluntary contributions. This neglect in the literature stands in contrast to the time and energy that member states spend on this topic. Actually, they see financing issues often as a 'matter of principle' and haggle over tiny details and small monetary amounts. To them, the question of how financial obligations are assigned and legitimized is of fundamental importance. The present chapter paid tribute to the perspective of member states by foregrounding the role of norms in financing debates and it rectified the previous neglect of C2P in the literature.

More specifically, the present chapter analysed two key moments during which C2P was contested. The analysis showed that the norm as such was broadly supported. However, reviewing the scale methodology, which constitutes the operationalization of C2P, and updating data, which constitutes the practical application of the operationalization, have proven contentious. Reviewing and updating represent, in principle, two distinguishable sources of change to the scale of assessments, but the degree to which they have been intertwined in complex contestations tells us something about changing notions of legitimacy.

In the first case study, the G-77 and China were opposed to any changes that would redistribute financial obligations from developed to developing countries. At the WHO level, the contestations resulted in implementation flexibilities that eventually expanded over three biennia and implied a loss in income for WHO. In the second case study by contrast, the idea had been accepted that such change was a legitimate consequence of the global economic shift – as long as it was only induced by updated data and not by modifications to the scale methodology. This altered understanding is particularly noteworthy if one considers that the volume of the changes to the scale of assessments had become much larger during Phase 2 than what it used to be during Phase 1.

The increasingly sharp distinction between reviewing the methodology and updating data has also made it clearer that C2P has been adjusted in different ways. In spite of continuous contestations, the operationalization of the norm through the scale methodology has proven resilient ever since the massive conflict that was analysed in the first case study. The application of the methodology by contrast has given rise to a considerable dynamic and led to graduation, although the discussions on the methodology itself remain deadlocked by a combination of substantive disagreement and consensual decision-making. From the perspective of Brazil, China, and India, who continue to benefit from differential treatment, this graduation comes, however, in an attenuated form. This applies to India and China in particular.

Regarding the question of who challenged the status quo in each case, it is noteworthy that, in the first conflict moment, the USA was the main challenger and, in the second conflict, the G-77 and China were the main challengers. The USA was able to lower the maximum ceiling further and thereby restrain C2P even more. The G-77 and China were not able to abandon the maximum ceiling and to expand the domain of C2P to the EU. While the G-77 and China have for the time being not been able to modify the scale methodology along their desired lines, they have been able to defend and preserve all those elements that they value. More generally, it is also noteworthy that, especially at the UN level, the G-77 and China have proven a stable coalition over an extended period of time – a coalition that continues to include rising powers. A common identity as developing countries, the institutional separation of the discussions on the scale methodology, and attenuated graduation have all contributed to this stability.

NOTES

1. Association of Southeast Asian Nations.
2. Caribbean Community.
3. Cf. Koschorreck 2001 and consider also that the Fifth Committee was originally expected to conclude its work by 1 December 2000 (A/55/PV.9 [2000]: 2) while the first formal meeting after the informal meetings was only on 23 December 2000.
4. Regarding change, the new scale relied on debt-stock for calculating debt as had been favoured by developing countries. The previous scale had used both debt-flow (for 1998) and debt-stock (for 1999–2000).
5. Actually, the sum was not paid by the US administration but by a private individual, Ted Turner (Koschorreck 2001; Mackey and Novotny 2012).
6. Even though the USA got very much what she wanted, it should still be noted that in previous years her representatives had announced that they were aiming for a maximum ceiling of 20 per cent (A/C.5/52/SR.9 [1997]: 9).
7. This sum did not appear in the appropriation resolution, however, but was calculated retrospectively (A54/INF.DOC./10 [2001]).
8. There was a transition from casual income to miscellaneous income at WHA54 in 2001 and documents referred to both accounting approaches. For the original proposals regarding miscellaneous income, cf. A54/6 (2001); A54/6 Corr. 1 (2001); WHA54/2001/REC/3: 32; see also A54/25 (2001) on casual income.
9. WHA54/2001/REC/3: 15–37; see also A54/5 (2001); A54/5 Corr.1 (2001); A54/37 (2001); PB/2002–2003 (2001).
10. For their announcements, their eligibility, and their non-application, cf. WHA54/2001/REC/3: 230; A54/49 (2001); A56/INF.DOC./3 (2003).
11. On this point, consider, for example, two statements by Cuba (WHA54/2001/REC/3: 187, 225–226).
12. EB109/2002/REC/2: 172–173; A55/29 (2002); WHA55/2002/REC/3: 158.
13. The wording of the resolution suggests that the latest UN scale will only be accepted as long as the maximum ceiling and the floor remain unchanged.
14. See also paragraph 8 in A56/51 (2003) on this matter.
15. This has consistently been interpreted to imply that the availability of a new UN scale results in the adoption of a new WHO scale even if the old (biennial) WHO

scale was still valid (e.g. A57/23 [2004]; WHA57.15 [2004]). This also applies for ad hoc adjustments to the UN scale (cf. WHA56.12 [2003] in particular).

16. For a statement along these lines by Canada, cf. WHA56/2003/REC/3: 191.
17. On the volume and financing of the adjustment mechanism, cf. WHA56.32 (2003) and WHA56.34 (2003).
18. It should be noted that the adjustment mechanism was revised in 2004 when a new UN scale resulted in a new WHO scale (A57/23 [2004]; WHA57.15 [2004]). This explains why the anticipated amounts of contributions and compensations (A56/51 [2003]; A56/51 Corr. 1 [2003]) did not necessarily overlap with actual amounts of contributions and compensations (EB115/INF.DOC./8 [2005]).
19. The United Kingdom could have claimed the maximum amount of USD 3 039 350 out of which it claimed and received USD 1 222 890 (EB115/INF.DOC./8 [2005]).
20. See also PB/2004–2005 (2003); A56/35 (2003); A56/51 (2003); A56/51 Corr. 1 (2003); A56/INF.DOC./3 (2003); WHA56.12 (2003); WHA56.33 (2003); WHA56.34 (2003).
21. In 2004, the scale proved controversial for a final time during Phase 1 (WHA57/2004/REC/3: 180–191, 223–225; A57/23 [2004]; WHA57.15 [2004]). In 2005, the controversies were focussed on the budget (WHA58/2005/REC/3: 64–80, 107–110, 311; WHA58.4 [2005]; WHA58.19 [2005]; A58/30 [2005]; A58/INF.DOC./1 [2005]).
22. While the report of the Committee on Contributions (A/73/11 [2018]: 51–52) mentions that it had been an issue once in 1999, it was from 2015 onwards that it became a recurrent concern and developed into a concrete demand. See also A/54/11 (1999): 13; A/70/11 (2015): 48; A/71/11 (2016): 37; A/72/11 (2017): 36.
23. Community of Latin American and Caribbean States.
24. On the repeated extension that eventually also impacted the recess date of the General Assembly, cf. A/73/PV.3 (2018): 1; A/73/PV.52 (2018): 29; A/73/PV.65 (2018): 5.
25. This eventual agreement was reached under considerable time pressure. Having resumed its formal proceedings on 22 December 2018, the Fifth Committee concluded its work at 20:25 hours on the same day (A/C.5/73/SR.26 [2018]: 11) while the plenary meeting concluded at 23:45 hours, i.e. soon after the Fifth Committee and 15 minutes before the repeatedly postponed date of recess would have expired.
26. On the way in which the notional assessment for non-members is translated into annual fees, cf. A/73/11 (2018): 51. On the way in which payments by non-members are included in the budget, cf., for example, A/74/6 (Income sect. 2) (2019).
27. *Official Journal of the European Communities*, 2001/C 1/04, 4 January 2001.
28. While this is a recurrent wording in WHO documents, the wording here was taken from A69/48 (2016): 2.
29. For an example, cf. WHA64.20 (2011).
30. Based on A62/30 (2009); A63/33 (2010); A64/31 (2011); A65/30 (2012); A66/30 (2013); A67/44 (2014); A68/39 (2015); A69/48 (2016); A70/41 (2017); A71/31 Rev1 (2018); A72/37 (2019); A73/26 (2020); A74/31 (2021).
31. As decided in 2013 (WHA66.16), countries with assessments above USD 200 000 pay half of their dues in USD and the other half in CHF (Swiss franc).

Consequently, the final numbers are the average of the USD and the CHF account.

32. From 2010 onwards, the documents also account for advance payments and since then India has made several of them. For the years 2010 and 2015 the advance payments covered the full amount that was assessed in regard to India. Actually, the payment for 2015 covered 102 per cent. For 2018 and 2019, India made advance payments of 1.7 per cent each while these payments amounted to 1.5 per cent for 2020.
33. Cf. the documents for the four scales negotiated during Phase 2: A/64/11 (2009); A/67/11 (2012); A/70/11 (2015); A/73/11 (2018), as well as resolutions A/RES/64/248 (2009); A/RES/67/238 (2012); A/RES/70/245 (2015); A/RES/73/271 (2018).

10. Conclusion

Clara Weinhardt, Julian Eckl, and Klaus Dingwerth

10.1 INTRODUCTION

The growing economic importance of emerging powers alters the balance of power in international politics. In view of this development, scholars and practitioners have paid much attention to what this means for a declining West. How, they asked, do the power shifts towards rising powers challenge the Western norms at the heart of the liberal international order (Lake et al. 2021; Ikenberry 2018)? In the preceding chapters, we have examined global power shifts from a different angle. Instead of focussing on 'Western' norms, we have asked what the rise of Brazil, China, India, and other emerging markets in the Global South means for a major set of norms – international norms of differential treatment – to the construction of which developing countries have strongly contributed.

So, when and how have states contested and adjusted international norms of differential treatment for developing countries as a group in the wake of global power shifts? In this concluding chapter, we summarize, compare, and reflect upon the most relevant observations we have made in the preceding chapters. We proceed in four steps. In section 10.2, we discuss our results in relation to two main findings: that systems of differential treatment for developing countries as a group are increasingly unmade, but that significant pockets of resilience remain. In section 10.3, we revisit the main theoretical expectations we have formulated in Chapter 1 and discuss how we can best account for the pattern of unmaking and resilience we observe. In section 10.4, we discuss our third main finding: that both the unmaking and the resilience we observe occur in a variety of distinct forms. Finally, section 10.5 concludes with reflections on what implications that the patterns we observe and the ways in which we may theorize them have for various aspects of the (liberal) international order.

Taken together, this concluding chapter demonstrates that shifting the perspective from 'Western' norms to those that explicitly sought to benefit developing countries – and hence various countries within the Global South –

pays off. Our reconstruction of major regime-level developments, as well as of key conflicts in each regime, confirms our assumption that this specific part of the international normative order has increasingly come under pressure, too. The consequences of this pressure are not uniform within and across regimes. However, it is possible to identify some general developments as well as their implications.

10.2 ON BALANCE, SYSTEMS OF DIFFERENTIAL TREATMENT ARE INCREASINGLY UNMADE – BUT SIGNIFICANT POCKETS OF RESILIENCE REMAIN

In the preceding chapters, we provided a fine-grained reconstruction and analysis of the – at times complex and contradictory – developments around norms of differential treatment for developing countries as a group. In this concluding chapter, we start by using a broader brush in order to provide a clear picture of general developments. At the outset, we will provide a tabular answer to the following binary question: Which of our empirical cases qualifies as a case of either unmaking or resilience? Furthermore, is there a systematic difference before (Phase 1) and after the onset of global power shifts (Phase 2)? Answering these questions helps us to fill a gap in the existing literature on global power shifts that is primarily interested in implications for 'the West'. As we demonstrate, systems of special rights for developing countries have also become subject to contestation and adjustments in response to the rise of Brazil, China, India, and others. Our findings allow us to specify not only when normative change has occurred, but also how an unmaking of the mid-1990s' status quo has unfolded.

The findings that are summarized in Table 10.1 relate to the general developments that we want to address. The table shows that prior to the recent global power shifts (Phase 1), differential treatment norms remained resilient in all eight cases we examine. This resilience is noteworthy since the preceding chapters have clearly demonstrated that this outcome emerged against the background of significant contestations. For example, in the climate regime, the United States (US) and some of its allies fiercely contested the exemption of 'major emitters' early on. In the health regime, the classic main contributors such as the US, the European Union (EU), and Japan criticized the manner in which the financial burden-sharing was organized. In both cases, however, the contestations did not lead to major adjustments that would qualify as an unmaking.

After the onset of the recent global power shifts (Phase 2), the picture changes. Here, we observe an unmaking of special rights for developing countries (or of the corresponding special obligations for developed countries)

Table 10.1 Overview of outcomes in Phase 1 and Phase 2

Regime / Issue	Main outcome in Phase 1 (1995–2007/2008)	Main outcome in Phase 2 (2008/2009–2020)
Trade		
Regime-level developments	Resilience	Unmaking
Agricultural trade	Resilience	Unmaking
Intellectual property rights	Resilience	Unmaking
Climate		
Regime-level developments	Resilience	Unmaking
Climate mitigation	Resilience	Unmaking
Climate finance	Resilience	Resilience
Health		
Regime-level developments	Resilience	Resilience
Capacity to pay	Resilience	Resilience

in five of our eight cases. Most importantly, this includes two regime-level studies (trade and climate), which gives these two outcomes particular weight. The other three are conflict-level studies (agricultural trade, intellectual property rights, and climate mitigation). This pattern thus confirms a key assumption we formulated at the outset of our study (cf. Chapter 1). Like previous global transformations, the rise of Brazil, China, India, and others does indeed affect the ways in which the international community organizes differential treatment for its 'disadvantaged' members.

What are the key changes that tilt the balance towards unmaking after the rise of Brazil, China, India, and others in more recent times? The clearest case of unmaking is climate change mitigation, which has become subject to an unmaking of differential treatment of developing countries as a group. Here, we observe that repeated contestation has led to clear-cut legal adjustments that unmake the pre-existing system of differential treatment. What was the status quo and how has it changed? At the outset, differential treatment had been straightforward. The 1995 Berlin Mandate and the 1997 Kyoto Protocol formally exempted all developing countries from legal commitments to limit their greenhouse gas emissions. By contrast, the formal exemption of developing countries could no longer be upheld in more recent years (Phase 2) in light of a long-lasting contestation of differential treatment norms by some industrialized states. Following a process that began after the 2007 Bali Climate Change Conference and reaching a climax in the 2015 Paris Agreement, it is now *all countries* who individually define their own nationally determined contributions (NDCs) – although 'in the light of different national circumstances'. The fact that developing countries are no longer exempt from obligations suggests that the 'common' element in the definition of 'common but differentiated responsibilities' (CBDR) has gained traction in comparison to the earlier emphasis on the 'differentiated' element. In other words, there is now more 'symmetry' between the commitments of developed and developing countries.

In the trade regime, the unmaking of differential treatment of developing countries as a group is less clear-cut than in the climate regime but still considerable. Formal adjustments of the overarching legal framework of differential treatment are still missing, and, in principle, special rights continue to be reserved for developing countries as a group. Yet, (some) regime members have begun to vote with their feet: the reluctance of key developed countries to grant differential treatment to developing countries as a group has resulted in the de facto unmaking of special rights. The most striking development in light of ongoing contestation of the legal framework is the shrinking range of (new) beneficiaries: revised and newly negotiated provisions of special and differential treatment (SDT) tend to be restricted to Least Developed Countries (LDCs). Over time, for instance, longer transition periods regarding intellectual property rights apply to LDCs only (cf. Chapter 6). Part of this trend is that differential treatment as it used to exist becomes less central, as differential treatment for LDCs gains in importance. Conversely, if negotiation proposals continue to treat developing countries as a homogenous group, World Trade Organization (WTO) members in more recent years have become reluctant to close a deal. The unmaking of differential treatment thus partly manifests itself in the stalemate of negotiations. Despite the promises attached to the Doha Development Round negotiations at the WTO, few new provisions on differential treatment that cover all developing countries as a group have been forthcoming. This became apparent in negotiations on agricultural subsidies (cf. Chapter 5). The stalemate on agriculture at the Ministerial Conference in Buenos Aires in 2017 was fuelled by China's and India's insistence to uphold differential treatment for developing countries as a group – despite their increasingly large role as providers of agricultural subsidies.

Yet, while we observe significant unmaking after the rise of Brazil, China, and India, we do not witness an unmaking across the board. Instead, some differential treatment schemes remain resilient even if the world around them changes significantly. Notably, this refers to developments in the field of global health financing, where both the regime-level chapter and our conflict case studies point to resilience, and to the subfield of climate finance (cf. Table 10.1). The resilience in the case of World Health Organization (WHO)-channelled health financing can be demonstrated best by taking a closer look at capacity to pay (C2P) which constitutes its legally binding pillar (cf. Chapter 4). C2P is operationalized through the scale methodology that calculates the assessed contributions of each member state. While the rules for the scale methodology have been contested by those who wanted to expand differential treatment and by those who wanted to reduce differential treatment, they have, in the end, remained unchanged since 2000 (United Nations (UN) level) and 2001 (WHO level). Even the rising powers continue to benefit from differential treatment as it is operationalized through the scale methodology – this applies to China and India in particular. Moreover, the formal and informal rules that underpin the practice of voluntary differentiation – the willingness to contribute (W2C) – have in the main proven resilient.

In addition, our analysis of international negotiations on climate finance also reveals stability (cf. Chapter 8). Here, we have seen that developing countries were able to defend differential treatment, and even partially expand it, in light of global power shifts. In particular, developing countries appreciated the addition of the Green Climate Fund as yet another financing channel. They had perceived the previous arrangements as driven by donor interests and thus requested a greater say in the allocation of international assistance for climate mitigation and adaptation. Moreover, the overall amount of international assistance increased markedly during Phase 2, thus adding further weight to the differentiation between contributors (notably Annex II states) and beneficiaries (developing countries).

Finally, we also observe some resilience in the regime-level chapter on trade (cf. Chapter 2), where attempts to reform the legal framework of differential treatment remains unchanged – despite increasing contestation and efforts to reform it. However, this resilience of the legal framework has not prevented the incremental unmaking that we observe at the level of negotiations and that was discussed above as the dominant trend in the trade regime.

To sum up, normative change in response to global power shifts goes beyond 'Western' norms. Beyond human rights, democracy, or liberal trade rules, special rights for developing countries have also become subject to contestation. Even though significant pockets of resilience remain, we observe unmaking as the dominant trend.

10.3 INTERESTS, IDEAS, AND INSTITUTIONS: ACCOUNTING FOR UNMAKING AND RESILIENCE

What explains the instances of unmaking and resilience after the onset of recent global power shifts? In the introduction to this book, we formulated some theoretical expectations in this regard. When we look at the three conflicts in the post-2008/2009 phase that resulted in unmaking, we find strong support for the expectations we derived from rationalist and constructivist approaches. Regarding institutional opportunity structures we find that they matter, albeit not always in the ways we expected (see also section 10.4). Taken together, our findings illustrate the added value of a comprehensive explanatory framework that integrates insights from rationalist, constructivist, and institutional perspectives.

10.3.1 Accounting for Unmaking

10.3.1.1 Interest-based coalitions

Before we elaborate on our explanation for the unmaking we observe, it is important to recap a point that we made in the introduction to this book regarding coalition (dis)unity: in line with rationalist accounts, we expected that systems of special rights are more likely to be unmade when the coalitions that share an interest in maintaining them fall apart and become weaker (cf. Chapter 1). In the case of differential treatment norms for developing countries, a central question hence was whether or not 'Southern' coalitions would remain united in their demands for special rights – even if the rise of Brazil, China, India, and other rising powers has increased the economic heterogeneity among coalition members. Coalition unity in turn is influenced by diverging or converging material interests.

In the trade and climate conflict case studies, the unmaking of differential treatment has indeed gone hand in hand with the breaking up of Southern coalitions. In the conflict over climate mitigation, the Southern coalition behind developing country exemptions became more divided over time. In the end, the small island states, members of the LDC Group, and members of the African Group shared an interest in a new and comprehensive global agreement 'applicable to all parties'. A central motive for these countries was climate change itself: as countries that were highly vulnerable to global warming, they had an interest in achieving the strongest net reductions in greenhouse gas emissions at the fastest pace. At the same time, the Northern coalition united around the request for commitments from 'major emitters'. This newly found unity is difficult to understand without considering the increasing economic competition these countries faced from rising powers. In the conflict over agricultural trade, like in the climate mitigation case, the Southern coalition that had supported such rights in Phase 1 was unable to maintain its unity in Phase 2. Here, disagreement emerged among the rising powers. Notably, the growing ability of China and India to subsidize their agricultural production became increasingly costly for Brazil as a major agricultural exporter. As a result, Brazil sided with the EU in proposing a curtailment of the provisions that allowed developing countries to make such subsidies. Similarly, the unmaking of differential treatment in the case of negotiations over implementation flexibilities related to the protection of intellectual property rights was partly driven by disunity. A division between developing countries and LDCs became apparent when the LDCs submitted their own proposal on transition periods. This fragmentation of Southern coalitions arguably limited their chances of success, given the

Global North remained relatively united in their opposition to both proposals. As a result, transition schedules for developing countries were not extended.

10.3.1.2 The (contested) legitimacy of differential treatment norms

Our conflict case studies show, moreover, that shifting constellations of interests – and resulting coalition patterns – were not the only driving forces of the unmaking we observe. In all cases of unmaking, we observe long-standing processes of contestation of the status quo of differential treatment. The reluctance of a growing number of regime members to continue to grant special rights to developing countries as a group has not only undermined the legitimacy, but has also contributed to shifting coalition patterns. In climate mitigation, a common trend in the more recent years is that those justifications that were based on historical emissions became less widely accepted as attention shifted to contemporary emissions. This draws more attention to fast-growing economies among Global South countries. This emphasis further undermined the unity of Southern coalitions: climate change was no longer imagined primarily as a 'North-South challenge' but rather as a 'global collective action problem' (Bäckstrand and Lövbrand 2019: 523). While exemptions from mitigation commitments lost some of their legitimacy, the call for 'major developing countries' to contribute to the global mitigation effort enjoyed strong discursive support.

In trade, the rise of India and China to the ranks of major subsidizers in agriculture has similarly undermined the legitimacy of their calls to continue to grant special rights to all developing country members. By the time of the 2017 Buenos Aires Ministerial Conference, the narrative of an unjust agricultural system – biased in favour of the developed world – lost traction once China and India had become major subsidizers. As a result, contestation of special rights in agriculture increasingly cuts across 'North–South' terms (cf. Hopewell 2019). The African Group, for instance, demanded a reduction of *all* subsidies at the Buenos Aires Conference, while India and China only focussed on those that were prevalent in developed countries. At a more general level, we also observe that increasing contestation of the status quo that allows rising powers to self-declare as developing countries has paved the way for an unmaking. WTO members have become reluctant to grant new differential treatment provisions to developing countries as a group, as long as rising powers do not (voluntarily) graduate from access to these rights. In contrast to the climate case, contestation is, however, primarily 'pressure from above', with the US playing the most vocal role in pushing for reform. Smaller developing countries so far tend to remain reluctant to openly speak out against China, India, or other rising powers that defend their access to special rights.

10.3.1.3 Institutional opportunity structures

Lastly, we also presumed that institutional factors play a role in accounting for an unmaking of special rights. We expected that systems of differential treatment would be adjusted in line with the challengers' demands if the existing institutional structure within or outside the regime's focal institution provides opportunities for change that challengers may exploit. These include both forum shopping opportunities outside a regime as well as institutional path dependencies within a given governance structure.

What we found was, first, that in a majority of the conflicts examined, forum shopping opportunities within the larger regime complex either did not exist or were not meaningful enough to have an effect on outcomes. For the issue of domestic support in agriculture negotiations, there exist no real possibilities for forum shifting to increase pressure in the core regime at the multilateral level. Domestic support is usually excluded from negotiations of bilateral or regional free trade agreements. Regarding climate mitigation, alternative institutional options outside the United Nations Framework Convention on Climate Change (UNFCCC) framework did not exist in 1995 and only played a marginal role in 2011. In climate finance negotiations, alternative institutions for channelling finance in principle exist, but could neither adequately absorb the varied array of interests and ideas of stakeholders nor allow developed countries to push for the graduation of rising powers.

That forum shopping opportunities can nonetheless play a role became apparent in the case of intellectual property rights. Here, both developed and developing countries made use of alternative institutional fora in the wider regime complex, such as the World Intellectual Property Organization, to lend support for their respective positions in the WTO – and vice versa. Yet, in the end the effect of forum shopping was to reinforce the North–South conflict lines in the core trade regime. In global health financing, we also find that the loose coupling of WHO financial contributions with the UN scale of assessments created opportunities to deviate from the UN practice. The institutional set-up – and the fact that WHO members need to formally accept the UN scale – thus made it possible to introduce additional layers of differential treatment such as implementation flexibilities at the WHO level. While not a conventional case of forum shopping, this case illustrates that specific forms of regime complexity may shape outcomes.

Second, however, we find strong evidence that prior institutionalizations of systems of special rights for developing countries 'within' a given regime shaped the *timing* of unmaking that we find across the different issue-area-specific conflicts. The sunset clause of the Kyoto Protocol, for instance, was decisive for the timing of the unmaking we observed at Conference of the Parties (COP)-17 (2011) in Durban. It forced states to devise a 'post-2012' regime, which is why unmaking unfolded during COP-17.

Conversely, the special rights of developing countries in agriculture are, in principle, designed in such a way that they are valid indefinitely – unless they are re-negotiated. This helps to explain why the unmaking occurred only at a later stage – in 2017 – and has remained partial so far.

10.3.2 Accounting for Resilience

The main instances of resilience that we observe pertain to differential treatment that comes in the form of finance: climate finance and financing for global health. Here, developing countries have tended to remain beneficiaries of differential treatment, while developed countries are commonly major contributors. The explanations for these cases in which we observe resilience largely correspond to the ones we have provided for the cases of unmaking but point in the opposite direction: the resilient cases display a unity of Southern coalitions not only before the onset of global power shifts (Phase 1), but also afterwards (Phase 2). Contestation of the legitimacy of the special rights of developing countries was also less strong in the realm of finance compared to the other issue-specific conflicts. This, in turn, facilitated the prevalence of North–South conflict lines. Finally, institutional factors, especially with regard to institutional opportunity structures 'within' the regimes, complement these explanations.

In the health financing case, unlike in other regimes, the fact that rising powers had become economically more powerful did not give rise to strong financial conflicts. First of all, developing countries that qualify for the relief measures of the scale methodology do not lose anything if rising powers benefit from them, too. Second, states decide on the volume of the WHO budget independently from the scale of assessments. In other words, conflicts over the size of the budget do not necessarily undermine coalition unity regarding the scale methodology. While there were consequently no factors that radically undermined the unity of Southern coalitions, the specific case of the US as the only country to which the maximum ceiling applies undermined the formation of a unified Northern coalition. Moreover, rising powers continued to define themselves as developing countries, and this self-description was largely accepted by other developing countries. Contestation of the legitimacy of differential treatment was thus less pronounced.

In the climate regime, the material interests of developing countries became more heterogenous overall. Yet, they shared a common interest in climate finance, and like in the health case, there is still a shared understanding that developed countries have financial responsibilities towards developing countries. To be sure, the poorer developing countries could have benefited from excluding rising powers from the list of countries eligible for climate finance and even more so if the rising powers contributed financial assistance.

However, they also needed the support of these countries in climate finance negotiations. Because emerging economies made their acceptance of mitigation commitments conditional on a significant increase in international climate finance, there was something to gain for all developing countries. Moreover, it is not considered legitimate that developing countries formulate serious financial demands from rising powers.

Lastly, the resilience of the C2P norm in global health illustrates that pre-existing institutionalizations of differential treatment matter. In contrast to what we witnessed in climate mitigation or agriculture negotiations, it facilitated resilience. Due to the formula approach that underlies the scale methodology, its starting point had always been different to the other two regimes. It combines a treatment of (a large part of) developing countries as a group with an individual treatment of countries: while the relief measures are intended to benefit developing countries in particular, each country's assessment rate is in principle calculated on an individual basis. Here, the share of world income provides the starting point. The institutional specifics of the scale methodology thus imply that the economic rise of countries does have some impact on burden-sharing even if they continue to benefit from differential treatment. The preservation that we observe went hand in hand with graduation. Economies that grow faster than others will eventually see some increase in their assessment rates.[1] This more individualized system of differential treatment has thus faced less pressure to adjust in light of global power shifts – even though it has become contested as well.

Taken together, our case studies suggest that (changing) constellations of interests but also collective identities, most notably as 'developing countries', are key for understanding the strength and unity of the coalitions of states that challenge (or support) existing systems of differential treatment. Whenever 'developing countries' have become less united in their coalitions over time, and special rights less legitimate in light of global power shifts, we observed the unmaking of the status quo. Moreover, institutional factors not only affected the timing of unmaking, but also shaped the extent to which existing systems of differential treatment were under pressure to adjust to changing realities. The more rigid a pre-existing approach, the more likely that it became subject to contestation.

10.4 THE UNMAKING AND THE RESILIENCE OF SPECIAL RIGHTS COME IN A VARIETY OF DISTINCT FORMS

We started this concluding chapter with a broad brush meant to provide a clear picture of general developments. They were covered in the preceding two sections where we had essentially coded all cases along a binary unmaking/

resilience distinction. In this sub-section, we use a finer brush and draw on our rich empirical material in order to account for the various forms of unmaking and resilience we identify. This will add nuance to the discussion. In terms of the concepts used, we draw on the introduction to this book (cf. Chapter 1 and Figure 1.1) where we discuss four forms of unmaking (*erosion, curtailment, individualization*, and *fragmentation*) and two forms of resilience (*preservation* and *expansion*) that can emerge with or without *graduation* of rising powers. In addition to these concepts from the introduction, our case studies foregrounded the ambiguous role of processes of *informalization* that occur in combination with both unmaking and resilience. We will group the subsequent elaboration around the regimes studied. In terms of explanations for the specific forms that unmaking and resilience take, we see a clear link to institutional factors.

In the trade regime, the dominant form of unmaking is fragmentation. While it had long been taken for granted that developing countries as a group are the legitimate beneficiaries of differential treatment, this expectation no longer holds from the perspective of all countries. Differential treatment and the concomitant special rights are increasingly limited to sets of beneficiaries that are smaller than the group of developing countries. More precisely, they are usually limited to LDCs and, by extension, they exclude rising powers. An illustrative case in point is the TRIPS Agreement where only LDCs have received a further extension of the transition schedule. While this is a clear unmaking of the status quo ante, it implies also that if we look at it from the perspective of LDCs only, there is an additional element of preservation to it. At the same time, the Doha Development Round has not delivered on its promises regarding differential treatment of developing countries as a group. What has complicated the negotiations is that rising powers in principle continue to count as beneficiaries of differential treatment, which has become highly contested. In the absence of new provisions along these lines, newly negotiated differential treatment becomes increasingly restricted to the less controversial sub-group of LDCs. Unmaking in the form of individualization only occurs at the margins. The 2014 Trade Facilitation Agreement (TFA) is the best illustration. In this case, developing countries were no longer treated as a group but instead of putting them in new sub-groups, differential treatment varied for each country individually. This approach has allowed emerging economies to take on more substantial liberalization commitments compared to others without giving up their status as developing country members at the WTO. The TFA also goes hand in hand with an informalization of differential treatment: developing country members decide by themselves what length of transition periods and reliance on financial assistance they consider necessary given their own capacities to implement the agreement.

Finally, these forms of unmaking go hand in hand with a certain degree of preservation, namely the 'survival' of the legal framework of differential treatment in the WTO. Foundational documents of the system of special rights do not come with a sunset clause. This has made it difficult to reform the self-declaration approach that, in principle, allows rising powers to continue to claim developing country status in the WTO. Given that decisions are taken by consensus, rising powers and other developing countries have so far successfully blocked reform attempts and defended the status quo.

In the climate regime, the dominant trend is unmaking in the form of individualization, often driven by informalization in relation to climate mitigation, paired with some expansion in relation to climate finance. Similar to the trade regime, the notion that developing countries should be treated as a homogeneous group no longer receives broad support among developed countries and is partly contested by developing countries as well. In particular, support for the idea that they should be formally exempted from legal commitments to limit their greenhouse gas emissions has eroded.

The differences in form that can be found within the trade regime partly relate back to the sunset clause that set an expiration date to the differential treatment system that the Kyoto Protocol had institutionalized. This sunset clause facilitated a form change in the institutionally enshrined rules of differential treatment. Thus, while the Kyoto Protocol's interpretation of differential treatment formally excluded developing countries from mitigation commitments, its successor – the Paris Agreement – introduced a more informal regime of differentiation that in principle extends the Kyoto Protocol's template of individualized goals for Annex I countries to 'all parties', including developing countries.

The price developed countries paid for this unmaking was a slight expansion of differential treatment in the field of climate finance. The conflict-level chapter on climate finance foregrounds this important opposing development that constitutes a case of the broader concept of resilience. Climate finance has witnessed an increase in funding, and it has seen some changes in the institutional arrangements along the lines that had been demanded by developing countries who continue to be seen as rightful beneficiaries of differential treatment in the field of climate financing. Since the expansion of differential treatment in climate financing was part of a regime-wide package deal in which developing countries accepted unmaking of special rights in the field of emission reduction commitments in exchange for expansion in the field of financing, it seems likely that the ambitions of developing countries will remain dependent on developed countries' financial support.

In the health regime, the most noteworthy observation is that the original approach to differential treatment has in the main seen preservation over time. This applies to its legally binding pillar, namely C2P in particular. Akin to the institutional context in the other regimes, the formal rules of the scale methodology can only be changed by consensus which made formal revisions very difficult. In contrast to the other regimes, however, a deadlock in formal negotiations does not imply that an informal workaround has to be developed since the scale of assessments can still be changed on the basis of updated data. In the context of C2P, there have been more instances of attenuated graduation of rising powers in the past decade than before, but they simultaneously remain beneficiaries of differential treatment. This applies to China and India in particular.

When it comes to the second pillar of differential treatment in WHO-channelled health financing, namely W2C and voluntary contributions, the formal rules have also remained unchanged. Yet, in this case, social expectations and informal rules are much more relevant. Two points are noteworthy. First of all, voluntary contributions have generally become increasingly important and currently play a larger role than assessed contributions. This contributes to a general informalization of differential treatment as a whole in the case of health financing.

Secondly, W2C has actually the potential to expand differential treatment. It comes without any formal monetary obligations and makes responsibilities more diffuse by basing them on an (ad hoc) self-declaration approach. As long as it is mainly developed countries (and private actors) who feel subject to it, it can preserve or even expand differential treatment. This theoretical potential does, however, not play out at present. The main problem is that the massively expanding volume of voluntary contributions has led to a problematic dependence on a less reliable financing source. Moreover, voluntary contributions are often earmarked for specific purposes. This situation allows for informal influence and exposes global health work to the vagaries of contributors and non-contributors alike.

This problematic aspect is closely linked to another aspect of informal differential treatment that rising powers seem to cherish. W2C leaves graduation at the discretion of the countries concerned. In this context, it is noteworthy that Brazil, China, and India so far do not really feel subject to it. In other words, there has been no real graduation of these countries in this case which makes their overall graduation attenuated (due to the scale methodology) as well as partial. What these developments come down to is that the formal core of differential treatment in WHO-channelled health financing has been preserved but was accompanied by a certain degree of graduation of rising powers and by informalization.

Table 10.2 provides a comprehensive account of the various forms in which unmaking and resilience of differential treatment have occurred in the three regimes we study.

Table 10.2 Variation in the forms of unmaking and resilience across the regimes

Regime	Dominant trend	Form of unmaking or resilience of differential treatment
Trade	Unmaking	• Fragmentation as dominant trend: shift towards LDCs as beneficiaries • Some forms of individualization and informalization at the margins • Preservation at the level of the overarching legal framework
Climate	Unmaking	• Individualization and informalization of differential treatment • Some forms of expansion regarding climate finance
Health	Resilience	• Preservation regarding assessed contributions (C2P) • Informalization through the increasing importance of voluntary contributions (W2C) • Moreover, there was attenuated and partial graduation of rising powers

This section has drawn on our rich empirical material to add some nuance to the observations that were made in the preceding two sections. In this context, we would like to make a final note on our sources: beyond the common basis in terms of primary sources – the official outcomes of international meetings as well as on the existing records of negotiations – our conflict-level case studies were complemented by a case-specific variety of additional sources. This variation in the types of sources may have allowed us to see things we could not otherwise see. For instance, the reliance on UN reports in the case of conflicts over financing for global health has allowed us to reconstruct the practical consequences of the scale methodology on the assessment rates of the six focus countries (cf. Chapter 9). Similarly, the use of interviews with trade officials has nuanced our assessment of the driving forces of unmaking in the case of agriculture negotiations, as it has allowed us to uncover contestation of China's and India's use of special rights that has not necessarily made it into the public discourse. Contestation may, for instance, come in the form of (less visible) negotiation practices (cf. Stimmer and Wisken 2019) or nascent discontent.

At the same time, the use of diverse kinds of sources also comes with risks. The reliance on additional types of sources in one case but not in others may have introduced bias. For instance, processes of contestation may appear more prominently in cases in which we relied on interviews to uncover them (primarily trade), as compared to others; in the global health case study, however, we also relied on informal exchanges with experts from the field to counteract this potential bias. In the climate cases, there was ample documentation available of both discursive processes of contestation and negotiation positions adopted, which rendered reliance on interviews less crucial. Despite our attempts to carefully select and triangulate our sources, some biases may have persisted. With these caveats in mind, the reminder of this conclusion is devoted to a discussion of the implications of our findings.

10.5 IMPLICATIONS

The case studies in this book provide ample evidence for the ways in which systems of differential treatment of developing countries shape international politics in light of the rise of Brazil, China, India, and others. In the discipline of international relations (IR), however, the discussions of the implications of global power shifts are commonly linked to 'Western' norms and principles of global order. What, then, does our focus on differential treatment of developing countries as a global ordering principle imply for debates in the field of IR? What does it mean to say that special rights for developing countries are unmade in many (but by no means all) areas? If they are unmade, what new forms of differential treatment emerge in global politics? In this final section, we zoom out again and examine these questions along the following lines: first, debates on global power shifts and international institutions; second, debates on global order and Global South countries; and, third, we offer insights from our comparative perspective on (nascent) debates on differential treatment in international politics. In doing so, we also discuss avenues for future research.

10.5.1 Debates on Global Power Shifts and International Institutions

The literature on power shifts and international institutions has been a growth industry in recent years. Our results add nuance to several assumptions made in this literature. For instance, our case studies provide empirical illustrations for the notion that, when it comes to global power shifts, rising powers are not always the challengers of international institutions. Instead, they can also become the target of adjustment challenges (Kruck and Zangl 2020; Schöfer and Weinhardt 2022). This is an aspect the existing literature has largely overlooked in its focus on the high-profile challenges to major international economic organizations like the International Monetary Fund, the World Bank, or the WTO by rising powers (Zangl et al. 2016).

Next, our findings support and qualify the previous observations that 'power shifts often create an impetus for institutional adjustment, but they do not automatically lead to institutional adaptation' and that, while power shifts 'may affect the overall distribution of power', the dynamics associated with them will often be 'issue area specific' (Kruck and Zangl 2020: 6). With regard to both aspects, our case studies help to see why. Power shifts may fail to lead to institutional adjustments where Global South coalitions remain united, either because the interests of developing countries and rising powers continue to converge or because solidarity remains strong. As our case studies demonstrate, Global South coalitions have been more likely to remain united on issues of finance, but less so when it came to climate mitigation or domestic support in agriculture where rising powers joined the ranks of 'major emitters' or 'major subsidizers'. In addition, dynamics are likely to '[differ] from one issue area to another' because the institutional playing field may vary greatly (see also Lipscy 2015). The presence or absence of sunset clauses, for instance, helps to explain why power shifts often create an impetus for change, but do not always lead to such change.

Moreover, the differences that we observe across regimes shed new light on the evolving, multifaceted principles of global order as multilateral institutions adjust to global power shifts. In what Acharya (2017) refers to as a 'multiplex world order', global governance becomes more fragmented and decentred. The variation we find across the unmaking of special rights in different issue areas confirms that global order is indeed becoming more fragmented. Yet, our findings also nuance the lines of conflict that shape the nascent contours of a multiplex world order. While the baseline assumption is that global governance is becoming less Western-centric, we show that contestation and change does not inevitably reflect such 'West' vs. 'Non-West' conflict lines. For instance, in agriculture negotiations in the late 2010s, Brazil sided with the EU, rather than with China and India, in debates on special rights and subsidies. Conversely, unity of the developing country G-77 (Group of 77) coalition and China was crucial for preserving and expanding differential treatment in financing for global health and climate finance. This suggests that the resulting fragmentation of the evolving global order (cf. also Stephen 2017) reflects patterns of contestation that cut across 'North–South' conflict lines in some cases, while reinforcing them in others.

Taken together, future research on global power shifts and international institutions should be wary of falling into the trap of simple binaries: rising powers do not automatically act as challengers of existing international institutions, nor do these institutions always adjust in ways that reflect so-called 'Global South' (or 'Non-Western') preferences. Fine-grained, empirical analyses are needed to uncover the multifaceted ways in which international institutions are adjusting to global power shifts across different issue areas. Lastly, research on the future of the so-called liberal international order could benefit from explicitly taking into account how contestation over differential treatment may threaten multilateralism. As the trade case illustrates, the inability of WTO members to reform special rights for developing countries contributes to the organization's ongoing crisis and negotiation deadlocks.

10.5.2 Debates on Global Order and Global South Countries

A related set of implications from our study concerns debates on the changing nature of global order (Lake et al. 2021; Ikenberry 2018). In contrast to the existing literature that tends to ask what global power shifts mean for 'the West', we show that changes in global order are not limited to 'Western' norms and principles but affect a wider set of global rules that Global South countries have been pushing for. Once we acknowledge the contributions developing countries have made in the process of establishing the international order, however, we can also see why and how the unmaking of special rights is a potential loss for developing countries. At the same time, our findings also go a step further since we have not only mapped challenges to norms that are traditionally valued by developing countries; rather, we have also come across challenges to the very notion of 'developing countries'.

The unmaking of special rights may only be a first sign that the categories of 'developed' and 'developing' countries are gradually losing their constitutive roles in the international order. In all three regimes we examine in this study, the distinction between developed and developing countries remains central up until now. But it is hard not to interpret the increasing contestation of differential treatment norms – including the contestation of their validity as such – as a contestation of the developed–developing dichotomy, as well. Our findings thus speak to those scholars that claim that the economic rise of Brazil, China, India, and others has begun to erode the distinction between the 'North' and the 'South', or 'developed' and 'developing' countries, as a central structuring principle (Farias 2019; Alami and Dixon 2020: 3; Haug et al. 2021: 1928; Weinhardt and Schöfer 2022; see also Eckl and Weber 2007).

Adding to this research that questions the binary distinctions between 'North' and 'South', our findings help to shed light on different groups of countries within the Global South. The patterns of normative change that we observe affect different (political) groups of developing countries within the Global South differently. With regard to country categories, an at least tripartite division is emerging in relation to special rights: first, the group of LDCs stands out as the most marginalized among developing countries and it is often these countries only that benefit from novel differential treatment provisions. A second group are the rising powers that are increasingly seen as a group by itself that stands out as 'large developing countries' or 'developing countries with special capabilities' compared to others. In spite of this recognition of special capabilities, rising powers have retained at least some of the differential treatment benefits that stem from their status as developing countries. Third, the unmaking of differential treatment for developing countries as a group will hit countries that are neither LDCs nor rising powers hardest. In contrast to LDCs, these countries have lost (and are likely to continue to lose) some of their access to differential treatment. In contrast to rising powers, they may (still) lack the resources to adapt to a new international order with fewer and weaker special rights for developing countries.

More research is thus needed to analyse and explore what political labels and categories are emerging as the Global South itself becomes more heterogeneous; moreover, follow-up research could unpack what the implications of changes in systems of differential treatment are for different countries across different international regimes. While our findings hinted at variegated implications, the focus of our study has been on mapping and explaining patterns of change – and not on the winners and losers of these changes. Here, political economy analyses are conceivable, as well as approaches that assess how new political labels and divisions (re)create multilateral hierarchies (cf. Waisbich et al. 2021: 2090; Fehl and Freistein 2020). Moreover, such assessments of distributional consequences open the door to ethical debates: is providing fine-grained differential treatment on the basis of individual country capacities necessarily less equitable compared to according special rights to developing countries as a group?

10.5.3 Differential Treatment of Developing Countries in International Politics

Existing scholarship on changing norms of differential treatment as a global ordering principle remains scarce and is often confined to legal perspectives (Ukpe and Khorana 2021; Cullet 2016; Rajamani 2006). When changes in systems of differential treatment have been examined, studies tend to remain issue-area-specific with a primary focus on the climate, or environmental and trade regimes (Pauwelyn 2013; Lamp 2017; Farias 2023; Farias and Roger 2023; Castro and Kammerer 2021; Weinhardt and Schöfer 2022; Dingwerth 2023). What does our comparative perspective that comprised climate, trade, and global health financing add to existing scholarship? We show that while differential treatment is changing in various ways, a common trend is that it is, on average, becoming more fragmented, more individualized, and more informal. We address the implications of each trend in the following paragraphs.

First, a trend that is cross-cutting is the increasing layering of differential treatment provisions for different (sub-groups of) developing countries within each regime. This trend is particularly pronounced in trade and climate, but also exists to some extent in global health. Sub-groups such as the LDCs or small island states increasingly compete with developing countries as a group for special rights. As a result, developing countries that do not fit these newly founded sub-groups are likely to lose out. At a more general level, the tendency to introduce additional layers of differentiation within the group of developing countries is likely to make it more difficult for 'Southern' coalitions to remain united – in contrast to what Johnson and Urpelainen (2020) find. Debates that pit different sub-groups of developing country against each other – and not only against 'developed' countries – are increasingly layered over the historically informed, unifying arguments about anti-hegemonic struggles against the 'Global North' (cf. Haug et al. 2021: 1929) that originally informed the calls for differential treatment.

Second, the trend towards individualized differential treatment suggests an even more fine-grained manner in which we are moving away from differential treatment of developing countries as a group. Arguably, this trend is most pronounced in global health, where the scale methodology calculates individual assessment rates and where individualized differential treatment has a long tradition. Across all cases, however, we observe that individualization increases. Notably, it goes hand in hand with what scholars refer to as the 'politics of numbers' (Broome and Quirk 2015: 819): the benchmarks and indicators chosen for assessing individualized contributions to differential treatment – and thresholds for graduation – are not neutral and highly politicized.

At the WTO, rising and established powers, for instance, push for different economic indicators – ranging from per capita to aggregate income measures – to assess who should have access to special rights. The climate cases show that it does not just matter which economic indicators are chosen, but also whether or not they are complemented by non-economic ones. Indicators in the climate regime could, for instance, include historical emissions, current emissions, and/or capacities measured by gross domestic product, the Human Development Index, or some other measure. Finally, in the context of the scale of assessments in global health the definition of statistical base periods and the calculation of debt are among the seemingly technical issues that attract contestation. These 'numbers games' illustrate the political contestation that formula approaches towards the individualization of differential treatment come with. Maybe unsurprisingly, our findings indicate that whenever an individualized approach towards differential treatment is added to a regime at a later stage, it is more likely that it remains informal – as discussed in the final paragraphs below.

The trend towards informalization, third, is something that we did not foresee but that nonetheless fits into a more general trend in global governance (cf. Roger 2020). Our comparative analysis suggests that the effects of informalization are likely to be issue-area-specific. In the health case, informalization has the potential to expand differential treatment by downplaying 'common' responsibilities and foregrounding 'differentiated' ones (but it comes at the price of dependence and informal governance as discussed earlier in this chapter). Thus, it has given rising powers the possibility to deny major financial responsibilities in the context of voluntary contributions. Conversely, informalization in the case of climate and, to some extent, trade has foregrounded the element of 'common responsibilities', as it has allowed rising powers to increasingly act as contributors to differential treatment. While China is unlikely to formally renounce its access to special rights in the trade regime, it has voluntarily opted out of the recent COVID-19 related TRIPS waiver for developing country members (Mercurio and Upreti 2022).

Finally, to further unpack the changing contours of special rights for developing countries in light of global power shifts, future research should move beyond the three regimes that we examined. How prevalent is the recent fragmentation, individualization, and informalization of differential treatment that we observe in other regimes? What trends emerge, for instance, in other environmental regimes in which differential treatment is common (Farias 2023), or with regard to 'scale of assessments' for the financing of UN peacekeeping missions (Coleman 2020)? Have special rights of developing countries been adjusted in the UN deep seabed mining regime in light of global power shifts, and if so how?

Overall, our comparative study of differential treatment across three regimes has allowed us to highlight common trends and to assess their implications. Looking into the future, and returning to a more broad-brush perspective, we can imagine at least two scenarios. In one scenario, the general trend of unmaking continues and new agreements with provisions for differential treatment will focus mainly on LDCs. This scenario of further unmaking includes, however, the possibility that rising powers retain some benefits in some areas. In a second scenario, differential treatment would actually make a comeback. If an intensified strategic competition between two poles, for example China and the US, develops and if each side starts to work on alternative institutions, developing countries (and other rising powers) might increasingly demand differential treatment in exchange for remaining active members of existing multilateral institutions.

Ultimately, however, our central message is rather straightforward: differential treatment is what international society makes of it while the forms it will take are neither fully pre-determined nor entirely open. Our hope is as bold as it is simple: by providing a comprehensive account of differential treatment and the manner in which it has changed in the past quarter of a century, we do not only show where we are and how we got there; rather, we also provide ample material to reflect on a key question that concerns all those who have a stake in differential treatment: Where do they want to go from here and how will they make their goals a reality?

NOTES

1. In the case of China and India in particular, it is important to reiterate, however, that this graduation was attenuated in the sense that the countries nevertheless

continued to benefit from differential treatment as it is operationalized in the scale methodology.

References

Abdel-Latif, Ahmed. (2005). Developing Country Coordination in International Intellectual Property Standard-Setting (Trade-Related Agenda Development and Equity Working Papers 24). South Centre.

Acharya, Amitav. (2017). After Liberal Hegemony: The Advent of a Multiplex World Order. *Ethics & International Affairs*, *31*(3), 271–285.

Adaptation Fund. (n.d.). All Funded Projects. Projects & Programmes. https://www.adaptation-fund.org/projects-programmes/

Adaptation Fund Board. (2017). Operational Policies and Guidelines for Parties to Access Resources from the Adaptation Fund (Amended in October 2017). Adaptation Fund. https://www.adaptation-fund.org/document/operational-policies-guidelines-parties-access-resources-adaptation-fund/

Agence France Press. (2011, 15 December). Brazil Hails Europe Leadership in Climate Talks.

Agreement on Agriculture. [AoA]. (1994). https://www.wto.org/english/docs_e/legal_e/14-ag.doc

Agreement on Trade-Related Aspects of Intellectual Property Rights [TRIPS]. (1994).

Alami, Ilias, and Adam Dixon. (2020). The Strange Geographies of the 'New' State Capitalism. *Political Geography*, *82*, 1–12.

Alessandrini, Donatella. (2010). *Developing Countries and the Multilateral Trade Regime: The Failure and Promise of the WTO's Development Mission*. Oxford: Hart Publishing.

Alter, Karen J., and Sophie Meunier. (2009). The Politics of International Regime Complexity. *Perspectives on Politics*, *7*(1), 13–24.

Arrow, Kenneth J. (1962). Economic Welfare and the Allocation of Resources for Invention. In National Bureau of Economic Research (ed.), *The Rate and Direction of Inventive Activity: Economic and Social Factors* (pp. 609–626). Princeton: Princeton University Press.

Arts, Bas, and Wolfgang Rüdig. (1995). Negotiating the 'Berlin Mandate': Reflections on the First 'Conference of the Parties' to the UN Framework Convention on Climate Change. *Environmental Politics*, *4*(3), 481–487.

Atal, Maha Rafi. (2016, 7 April). View on Private Sector: Pharma Shift Won't Help Poorest. *SciDev.Net*. https://www.scidev.net/global/column/private-sector-pharma-poor-gsk/

Bäckstrand, Karin, and Ole Elgström. (2013). The EU's Role in Climate Change Negotiations: From Leader to 'Leadiator'. *Journal of European Public Policy*, *20*(10), 1369–1382.

Bäckstrand, Karin, and Eva Lövbrand. (2019). The Road to Copenhagen: Contending Climate Governance Discourses in the Post-Copenhagen Era. *Journal of Environmental Policy & Planning*, *21*(5), 519–532.

Baker, Dean, Arjun Jayadev, and Joseph E. Stiglitz. (2017). Innovation, Intellectual Property, and Development: A Better Set of Approaches for the 21st Century (AccessIBSA Paper Series).

Ballesteros, Athena, Smita Nakhooda, Jacob Werksman, and Kaija Hurlburt. (2010). Power, Responsibility, and Accountability: Rethinking the Legitimacy of Insitutions for Climate Finance. *Climate Law*, *1*(2), 261–312.
Barua, Mintu. (2014). India's Environmental Strategy in the Global Climate Negotiations. *International Studies*, *51*(1–4), 195–211.
Bauchmüller, Michael. (2011, December 12). Inhalte? Nebensache; Auf der Klimakonferenz feilschen Taktiker bis zur letzten Minute um Termine – Substanz muss nachgeliefert werden. *Süddeutsche Zeitung*, p. 2.
Beach, Derek, and Rasmus Brun Pedersen. (2019). *Process-Tracing Methods: Foundations and Guidelines*. Ann Arbor: University of Michigan Press.
Bernstein, Steven. (2001). *The Compromise of Liberal Environmentalism*. New York: Columbia University Press.
Betzold, Carola, Paula Castro, and Florian Weiler. (2012). AOSIS in the UNFCCC Negotiations: From Unity to Fragmentation? *Climate Policy*, *12*(5), 591–613.
Bevir, Mark, and Jason Blakely. (2020). *Interpretive Social Science: An Anti-Naturalist Approach*. Oxford: Oxford University Press.
Bhala, Raj. (2000). Enter the Dragon: An Essay on China's WTO Accession Saga. *American University International Law Review*, *15*(6), 1469–1538.
Biermann, Frank. (1998). *Weltumweltpolitik zwischen Nord und Süd. Die Neue Verhandlungsmacht der Entwicklungsländer*. Baden-Baden: Nomos Verlag.
Blatter, Joachim, and Markus Haverland. (2012). *Designing Case Studies: Explanatory Approaches in Small-N Research*. Basingstoke: Palgrave Macmillan.
Blaxekjær, Lau Øfjord, and Tobias Dan Nielsen. (2014). Mapping the Narrative Positions of New Political Groups under the UNFCCC. *Climate Policy*, *15*(6), 751–766.
Bodansky, Daniel. (1993). The United Nations Framework Convention on Climate Change: A Commentary. *Yale Journal of International Law*, *18*, 451–558.
Bodansky, Daniel. (1994). Prologue to the Climate Change Convention. In I. M. Mintzer and J. A. Leonard (eds.), *Negotiating Climate Change: The Inside Story of the Rio Convention* (pp. 45–74). Cambridge: Cambridge University Press.
Bodansky, Daniel, Jutta Brunnée, and Lavanya Rajamani. (2017). *International Climate Change Law* (1st ed.). Oxford: Oxford University Press.
Bode, Ingvild, and Hendrik Huelss. (2018). Autonomous Weapons Systems and Changing Norms in International Relations. *Review of International Studies*, *44*(3), 393–413.
Boltanski, Luc, and Laurent Thévenot. (2016). *On Justification: Economies of Worth*. Princeton: Princeton University Press.
Borione, Delphine, and Jean Ripert. (1994). Exercising Common but Differentiated Responsibility. In I. M. Mintzer and J. A. Leonard (eds.), *Negotiating Climate Change: The Inside Story of the Rio Convention* (pp. 77–96). Cambridge: Cambridge University Press.
Boyte, Rachel. (2010). Common but Differentiated Responsibilities: Adjusting the Developing/Developed Dichotomy in International Environmental Law. *New Zealand Journal of Environmental Law*, *14*, 63–102.
Breidenich, Clare, Daniel Magraw, Anne Rowley, and James W. Rubin. (1998). The Kyoto Protocol to the United Nations Framework Convention on Climate Change. *The American Journal of International Law*, *92*(2), 315–331.
BRICS. (2011, 14 April). Sanya Declaration. https://web.archive.org/web/20170406064302/http://infobrics.org/document/9_

BRICS. (2012, 28 March). The 2nd Meeting of the BRICS Trade and Economic Ministers: Joint Press Release. https://web.archive.org/web/20170404075933/http://infobrics.org/document/5/
BRICS. (2016, 13 October). The 6th Meeting of the BRICS Trade Ministers on 13 October 2016 at New Delhi: Trade Ministers Communique. https://web.archive.org/web/20170404080314/http://infobrics.org/files/pdf/95.pdf
Brink, Lars, and David Orden. (2017). The United States WTO Complaint on China's Agricultural Domestic Support: Preliminary Observations (Paper presentation, subsequently updated). International Agricultural Trade Research Consortium's (IATRC's) 2016 Annual Meeting (12 December 2016), Scottsdale, Arizona.
Brink, Lars, and David Orden. (2020). Taking Stock and Looking Forward on Domestic Support under the WTO Agreement on Agriculture (IATRC Commissioned Paper 23).
Broome, André, and Joel Quirk. (2015). The Politics of Numbers: The Normative Agendas of Global Benchmarking. *Review of International Studies*, *41*(5), 813–818.
Broude, Tomer. (2006). The Rule(s) of Trade and the Rhetos of Development: Reflections on the Functional and Aspirational Legitimacy of the WTO. *Columbia Journal of Transnational Law*, *45*(1), 221–261.
Browne, Stephen. (2017). Vertical Funds: New Forms of Multilateralism. *Global Policy*, *8*(S5), 36–45.
Buchner, Barbara K., Padraig Oliver, Xueying Wang, Cameron Carswell, Chavi Meattle, and Federico Mazza. (2017). Global Landscape of Climate Finance 2017. Climate Policy Initiative. https://www.climatepolicyinitiative.org/publication/global-landscape-of-climate-finance-2017/
Buchner, Barbara K., Alex Clark, Angela Falconer, Rob Macquarie, Chavi Meattle, Rowena Tolentino, and Cooper Wetherbee. (2019). Global Landscape of Climate Finance 2019. Climate Policy Initiative. https://www.climatepolicyinitiative.org/publication/global-landscape-of-climate-finance-2019/
Bukovansky, Mlada, Ian Clark, Robyn Eckersley, Richard Price, Christian Reus-Smit, and Nicholas Weeler. (eds.) (2012). *Special Responsibilities: Global Problems and American Power*. Cambridge: Cambridge University Press.
Bull, Hedley. (1977). *The Anarchical Society: A Study of Order in World Politics*. London: Macmillan.
Bush, George W. (2001, 13 March). Letter from US President Bush to Senators Hagel, Helms, Craig, and Roberts. https://georgewbush-whitehouse.archives.gov/news/releases/2001/03/20010314.html
Bushey, Douglas, and Sikina Jinnah. (2010). Evolving Responsibility? The Principle of Common but Differentiated Responsibility in the UNFCCC. *Berkeley Journal of International Law*, *28*(6), 1–10.
Buzdugan, Stephen, and Anthony Payne. (2016). *The Long Battle for Global Governance*. London and New York: Routledge.
Buzdugan, Stephen, and Anthony Payne. (2020). The Long Battle for Global Governance Continued. In E. Vivares (ed.), *The Routledge Handbook to Global Political Economy: Conversations and Inquiries* (pp. 328–342). London and New York: Routledge.
Castro, Paula, and Marlene Kammerer. (2021). The Institutionalization of a Cleavage: How Differential Treatment Affects State Behavior in the Climate Negotiations. *International Studies Quarterly*, *6*(3), 683–698.
Castro, Paula, Lena Hörnlein, and Katharina Michaelowa. (2011). Path Dependence of Negotiation Structures in International Organizations: The Impact of Annex

I Membership on Discussions within the UNFCCC (CIS Working Paper 67, University of Zurich).
Cheng, Wenting. (2019). China Engages with the Global Intellectual Property Governance: The Recent Trend. *Journal of World Intellectual Property*, *22*(3–4), 146–161.
Chorev, Nitsan. (2012). *The World Health Organization between North and South*. Ithaca: Cornell University Press.
Christensen, Thomas J. (2015). *The China Challenge: Shaping the Choices of a Rising Power*. New York: W.W. Norton & Company.
Chung, Jane, and Joori Roh. (2019, 25 October). South Korea to Give Up Developing Country Status in WTO talks. *Reuters*. https://www.reuters.com/article/us-southkorea-trade-wto/south-korea-to-give-up-developing-country-status-in-wto-talks-idUSKBN1X401W
Clapp, Jennifer. (2006). WTO Agriculture Negotiations: Implications for the Global South. *Third World Quarterly*, *27*(4), 563–577.
Clapp, Christa, Jane Ellis, Julia Benn, and Jan Corfee-Morlot. (2012). Tracking Climate Finance: What and How? (OECD/IEA Climate Change Expert Group Papers, No. 2012/01). Paris: OECD Publishing.
Clark, Ian. (2007). *Legitimacy in International Society*. Oxford: Oxford University Press.
Clark, Pilita. (2011, 15 December). The Great Regrouping. *Financial Times* (London edition), p. 13.
Clinton, Chelsea, and Devi Sridhar. (2017). Who Pays for Cooperation in Global Health? A Comparative Analysis of WHO, the World Bank, the Global Fund to Fight HIV/AIDS, Tuberculosis and Malaria, and Gavi, the Vaccine Alliance. *The Lancet*, *390*(10091), 324–332.
Cogan, Jacob Katz. (2016). Financing and Budgets. In J. K. Cogan, I. Hurd, and I. Johnstone (eds.), *The Oxford Handbook of International Organizations* (pp. 903–919). Oxford: Oxford University Press.
Coleman, Katharina P. (2020). United Nations Peacekeeping Decisions: Three Hierarchies, Upward Mobility and Institutionalised Inequality among Member States. *Global Society*, *34*(3), 318–334.
Correa, Carlos. (2002). Public Health and Intellectual Property Rights. *Global Social Policy*, *2*(3), 231–278.
Correa, Carlos, and Xavier Seuba. (eds.) (2019). *Intellectual Property and Development: Understanding the Interfaces*. Singapore: Springer.
Cost, Frank, and Stanley Wildrick. (2007). *Emerging Global Markets: A Five-Country Comparative Study*. Rochester: Printing Industry Center.
Coventry, Philip. (2019). North-South Division and Injustice in the UNFCCC Climate Finance Policy Process: A Historical Institutionalist Perspective [PhD Thesis, University of Reading]. Central Archive at the University of Reading.
Cullet, Philippe. (1999). Differential Treatment in International Law: Towards a New Paradigm of Inter-State Relations. *European Journal of International Law*, *10*(3), 549–582.
Cullet, Philippe. (2003). *Differential Treatment in International Environmental Law*. Aldershot: Ashgate.
Cullet, Philippe. (2016). Differential Treatment in Environmental Law: Addressing Critiques and Conceptualizing the Next Steps. *Transnational Environmental Law*, *5*(2), 305–328.

Dasgupta, Chandrashekhar. (1994). The Climate Change Negotiations. In I. M. Mintzer and J. A. Leonard (eds.), *Negotiating Climate Change: The Inside Story of the Rio Convention* (pp. 129–148). Cambridge: Cambridge University Press.

De Menezes, Henrique Z. (2018). South-South Collaboration for an Intellectual Property Rights Flexibilities Agenda. *Contexto Internacional, 40*(1), 117–138.

De Renzio, Paolo, and Jurek Seifert. (2014). South–South Cooperation and the Future of Development Assistance: Mapping Actors and Options. *Third World Quarterly, 35*(10), 1860–1875.

Death, Carl. (2012). A Predictable Disaster for the Climate – but Who Else Won and Lost in Durban at COP17? *Environmental Politics, 21*(6), 980–986.

Deere Birkbeck, Carolyn. (2009). *The Implementation Game: The TRIPS Agreement and the Global Politics of Intellectual Property Reform in Developing Countries.* Oxford: Oxford University Press.

Deere Birkbeck, Carolyn. (2016). WIPO's Development Agenda and the Push for Development-Oriented Capacity-Building on Intellectual Property: How Poor Governance, Weak Management, and Inconsistent Demand Hindered Progress (GEG Working Paper, 105).

Dehmer, Dagmar. (2011, 13 December). Klimagipfel: Neue Weltordnung. *Der Tagesspiegel*, p. 1.

Deitelhoff, Nicole, and Lisbeth Zimmermann. (2020). Things We Lost in the Fire: How Different Types of Contestation Affect the Robustness of International Norms. *International Studies Review, 22*(1), 51–76.

Deleuil, Thomas. (2012). The Common but Differentiated Responsibilities Principle: Changes in Continuity after the Durban Conference of the Parties. *Review of European Community and international Environmental Law, 21*(3), 271–281.

Den Elzen, Michel G. J., Michiel Schaeffer, and Paul L. Lucas. (2005). Differentiating Future Commitments on the Basis of Countries' Relative Historical Responsibility for Climate Change: Uncertainties in the 'Brazilian Proposal' in the Context of a Policy Implementation. *Climatic Change, 71*, 277–301.

Depledge, Joanna. (2009). The Road Less Travelled: Difficulties in Moving between Annexes in the Climate Change Regime. *Climate Policy, 9*(3), 273–287.

Dessai, Suraje. (2003). The Special Climate Change Fund: Origins and Prioritisation Assessment. *Climate Policy, 3*(3), 295–302.

Diakosawas, Dimitris. (2001). *The Uruguay Round Agreement on Agriculture in Practice: How Open Are OECD Markets?* Paris: OECD Publishing.

Dingwerth, Klaus. (2023). Multi-Layered Differentiation in the Climate Regime: The Gradual Path from Rio to Paris. *Environmental Politics.* Advance online publication. https://doi.org/10.1080/09644016.2023.2210488

Doty, Roxanne Lynn. (1996). *Imperial Encounters: The Politics of Representation in North-South Relations* (Vol. 5). Minneapolis: University of Minnesota Press.

Doyle, Michael W. (1983). Review: Stalemate in the North-South Debate: Strategies and the New International Economic Order. *World Politics, 35*(3), 426–464.

Dreyfuss, Rochelle C. (2009). *The Role of India, China, Brazil and Other Emerging Economies in Establishing Access Norms for Intellectual Property and Intellectual Property Lawmaking* (IILJ Working Paper 2009/5).

Dubash, Navroz K., and Lavanya Rajamani. (2015). Multilateral Diplomacy on Climate Change. In D. M. Malone, C. R. Mohan, and S. Raghavan (eds.), *The Oxford Handbook of Indian Foreign Policy* (pp. 663–678). Oxford: Oxford University Press.

Dunmore, Charlie. (2011, 13 December). Durban Talks a Victory for Europe's Climate Chief. *Reuters*. https://www.reuters.com/article/us-eu-climate-hedegaard-idINTRE7BC1NQ20111213
DW (Deutsche Welle). (2021, 9 August). German Floods: Up to €30 Billion Needed for Recovery. *DW News*. https://www.dw.com/en/german-floods-up-to-30-billion-needed-for-recovery-fund/a-58807147
Eckl, Julian. (2021). Focal Times and Spaces: How Ethnography Foregrounds the Spatiotemporality of International Organizations and Global Governance. *Global Policy*, *12*(S7), 34–44.
Eckl, Julian, and Ralph Weber. (2007). North: South? Pitfalls of Dividing the World by Words. *Third World Quarterly*, *28*(1), 3–23.
Efstathopoulos, Charalampos. (2012). Leadership in the WTO: Brazil, India and the Doha Development Agenda. *Cambridge Review of International Affairs*, *25*(2), 269–293.
Eglin, Michaela. (1997). China's Entry into the WTO with a Little Help from the EU. *International Affairs*, *73*(3), 489–508.
Ella, Doron. (2017). China and the United Nations Framework Convention on Climate Change: The Politics of Institutional Categorization. *International Relations of the Asia-Pacific*, *17*(2), 233–264.
European Commission. (1980). Speech [on the Multilateral Trade Negotiations] by Heinrich von Moltke, Deputy Head of Delegation, Delegation of the Commission of the European Communities, at the Washington International Conference 1980 [Speech transcript]. University of Pittsburgh, Archive of European Integration. http://aei.pitt.edu/12545/
European Commission. (2018a). Economic Partnership Agreements (EPAs) [Factsheet]. https://www.eeas.europa.eu/sites/default/files/epas_factsheet_september_2018.pdf
European Commission. (2018b). WTO Modernisation – Introduction to future EU proposals [Concept paper]. https://www.wita.org/atp-research/eu-concept-paper-on-wto-reform/
European Union – The Council. (1995). Community Strategy on Climate Change: Preparation of the First Conference of the Parties to the UN Framework Convention on Climate Change (Berlin, 28 March To 7 April 1995) – Council Conclusions (Council Document No. 5681/95 of 16 March 1995). Brussels: European Union.
FAO (Food and Agriculture Organization). (2000). *Agriculture, Trade and Food Security: Vol. II.* Country Case Studies. Rome: FAO.
Farge, Emma. (2021, 10 December). Exclusive: Envoy Says China Will Forego Many 'Developing Country' Benefits at WTO. *Reuters*. https://www.reuters.com/markets/commodities/exclusive-envoy-says-china-will-forego-many-developing-country-benefits-wto-2021-12-10/
Farias, Déborah Barros Leal. (2019). Outlook for the 'Developing Country' Category: A Paradox of Demise and Continuity. *Third World Quarterly*, *40*(4), 668–687.
Farias, Déborah Barros Leal. (2023). Country Differentiation in the Global Environmental Context: *Who* is 'Developing' and According to *What*? *International Environmental Agreements: Politics, Law and Economics*, *23*(3), 253–269.
Farias, Déborah Barros Leal, and Charles Roger. (2023). Differentiation in Environmental Treatymaking: Measuring Provisions and How They Reshape the Depth-Participation Dilemma. *Global Environmental Politics*, *23*(1), 117–132.
Fehl, Caroline, and Katja Freistein. (2020). Organising Global Stratification: How International Organisations (Re)Produce Inequalities in International Society. *Global Society*, *34*(3), 285–303.

Finnemore, Martha, and Kathryn Sikkink. (1998). International Norm Dynamics and Political Change. *International Organization*, *52*(4), 887–917.
Flåm, Karoline Hægstad, and Jon Birger Skjærseth. (2009). Does Adequate Financing Exist for Adaptation in Developing Countries? *Climate Policy*, *9*(1), 109–114.
Forst, Rainer. (2017). *Normativity and Power: Analyzing Social Orders of Justification*. Oxford: Oxford University Press.
G-90. (2005). G-90 Declaration (ACP/61/057/05 Rev.2). https://caricom.org/documents/9779-g90_declaration_on_the_sixth_wto_ministerial_conference.pdf
GATT. (1979). Decision on Differential and More Favourable Treatment, Reciprocity and Fuller Participation of Developing Countries (Enabling Clause) [Decision of 28 November 1979 (L/4903)]. https://www.wto.org/english/docs_e/legal_e/enabling1979_e.htm
GATT General Council. (1971). Minutes of Meeting – Held in the Palais des Nations, Geneva, on 25 May 1971 [C/M/69]. https://docs.wto.org/gattdocs/q/GG/C/M69.PDF
Gautier, Lara, Andrew Harmer, Fabrizio Tediosi, and Eduardo Missoni. (2014). Reforming the World Health Organization: What Influence Do the BRICS Wield? *Contemporary Politics*, *20*(2), 163–181.
GCF (Green Climate Fund). (n.d.-a). Countries: Areas of Work. https://www.greenclimate.fund/countries
GCF (Green Climate Fund). (n.d.-b). Resource Mobilisation. https://www.greenclimate.fund/about/resource-mobilisation/irm
GEF (Global Environment Facility). (1994). Report by the GEF to the Intergovernmental Negotiating Committee for a Framework Convention on Climate Change on the Restructured Global Environment Facility [A/AC.237/89, Annex I]. New York: UNGA / INC.
GEF (Global Environment Facility). (2019). Instrument for the Establishment of the Restructured Global Environment Facility. New York: GEF.
GEF (Global Environment Facility). (2021a). Funding. https://www.thegef.org/about/funding
GEF (Global Environment Facility). (2021b). Who We Are. https://www.thegef.org/who-we-are
GEF Independent Evaluation Office (IEO). (2014). Midterm Evaluation of the System of Transparent Allocation of Resources (Evaluation Report No. 94). https://doi.org/10.13140/RG.2.2.21357.08163
GEF Secretariat. (2006). Summary of Negotiations on the 4th Replenishment of the GEF Trust Fund [GEF/A.3/6].
GEF Secretariat. (2018). Summary of Negotiations of the 7th Replenishment of the GEF Trust Fund [GEF/C.54/19/Rev.03].
GEF Trustee. (2021). Eighth GEF Replenishment: Overview of Financial Structure [GEF/R.8/04].
Gehring, Thomas, and Sebastian Oberthür. (2009). The Causal Mechanisms of Interaction between International Institutions. *European Journal of International Relations*, *15*(1), 125–156.
Geiger, Christophe. (2012). Weakening Multilateralism in Intellectual Property Lawmaking: A European Perspective on ACTA. *The WIPO Journal*, *3*(2), 166–178.
General Agreement on Tariffs and Trade [GATT]. (1947). United Nations Treaty Series 64, 30 October 1947, p. 187.

General Agreement on Tariffs and Trade [GATT]. (1994). Annex 1A, Marrakesh Agreement Establishing the World Trade Organization, United Nations Treaty Series 1867, 15 April 1994, p. 33.
Glauber, Joseph W., Jonathan Hepburn, David Laborde, and Sophia Murphy. (2020). What National Farm Policy Trends Could Mean for Efforts to Update WTO Rules on Domestic Support (IISD Report). Winnipeg: International Institute for Sustainable Development.
Gobierno de Guatemala. (2021). Statement by His Excellency Mr Mario Roberto Rojas Espino, Minister of Environment and Natural Resources of Guatemala at the 26th Session of the Conference of the Parties to the UN Framework Convention on Climate Change, 09 November 2021 [Speech transcript]. https://unfccc.int/sites/default/files/resource/GUATEMALA_cop26cmp16cma3_HLS_EN.pdf
Goetz, Klaus H., and Ronny Patz. (2017). Resourcing International Organizations: Resource Diversification, Organizational Differentiation, and Administrative Governance. *Global Policy*, *8*(S5), 5–14.
Goldemberg, José. (1994). The Road to Rio. In I. M. Mintzer and J. A. Leonard (eds.), *Negotiating Climate Change: The Inside Story of the Rio Convention* (pp. 175–186). Cambridge: Cambridge University Press.
Goldemberg, José. (1995). Energy Needs in Developing Countries and Sustainability. *Science*, *269*(5227), 1058–1059.
Golub, Philip S. (2013). From the New International Economic Order to the G20: How the 'Global South' Is Restructuring World Capitalism from Within. *Third World Quarterly*, *34*(6), 1000–1015.
Goswami, Urmi A. (2011, 13 December). India in Durban to Find a Solution to Climate Change: Natarajan. *The Economic Times*.
Graham, Erin R. (2014). International Organizations as Collective Agents: Fragmentation and the Limits of Principal Control at the World Health Organization. *European Journal of International Relations*, *20*(2), 366–390.
Graham, Erin R. (2015). Money and Multilateralism: How Funding Rules Constitute IO Governance. *International Theory*, *7*(1), 162–194.
Graham, Erin R. (2017a). Follow the Money: How Trends in Financing Are Changing Governance at International Organizations. *Global Policy*, *8*(S5), 15–25.
Graham, Erin R. (2017b). The Institutional Design of Funding Rules at International Organizations: Explaining the Transformation in Financing the United Nations. *European Journal of International Relations*, *23*(2), 365–390.
Grasso, Marco. (2011). The Role of Justice in the North–South Conflict in Climate Change: The Case of Negotiations on the Adaptation Fund. *International Environmental Agreements*, *11*(4), 361–377.
Gray, Kevin, and Barry K. Gills. (2016). South–South Cooperation and the Rise of the Global South. *Third World Quarterly*, *37*(4), 557–574.
Groombridge, Mark A. (1999). The TRIPS Trade-Off: Reconciling Competing Interests in the Millennium Round. *Journal of World Intellectual Property*, *2*(6), 991–1013.
Grubb, Michael, Christian Vrolijk, and Duncan Brack. (1999). *The Kyoto Protocol: A Guide and Assessment*. London: The Royal Institute for International Affairs.
Gupta, Joyeeta. (1995). The Global Environment Facility in Its North-South Context. *Environmental Politics*, *4*(1), 19–43.
Gupta, Joyeeta. (2014). *The History of Global Climate Governance*. Cambridge: Cambridge University Press.

Gütschow, Johannes, Annika Günther, and Mika Pflüger. (2021). *The PRIMAP-hist National Historical Emissions Time Series (1750–2019) v2.3.1* [Data set]. Zenodo. https://doi.org/10.5281/zenodo.5494497

Gütschow, Johannes, M. Louise Jeffery, Robert Gieseke, Ronja Gebel, David Stevens, Mario Krapp, and Marcia Rocha. (2016). The PRIMAP-hist National Historical Emissions Time Series. *Earth System Science Data*, *8*(2), 571–603.

Hale, Thomas N., David Held, and Kevin Young. (2013). *Gridlock: Why Global Cooperation Is Failing When We Need It Most.* Cambridge: Polity Press.

Hallding, Karl, Marie Olsson, Aaron Atteridge, Antto Vihma, Marcus Carson, and Mikael Román. (2011). *Together Alone: BASIC Countries and the Climate Change Conundrum* [TemaNord 2011:530]. Copenhagen: Nordic Council of Ministers.

Hannah, Erin, James Scott, and Rorden Wilkinson. (2018). The WTO in Buenos Aires: The Outcome and Its Significance for the Future of the Multilateral Trading System. *The World Economy*, *41*(10), 2578–2598.

Hanrieder, Tine. (2015). *International Organization in Time: Fragmentation and Reform*. Oxford: Oxford University Press.

Harmeling, Sven, and Alpha O. Kaloga. (2011). Understanding the Political Economy of the Adaptation Fund. *IDS Bulletin*, *42*(3), 23–32.

Haug, Sebastian, Jacqueline Braveboy-Wagner, and Günther Maihold. (2021). The 'Global South' in the Study of World Politics: Examining A Meta Category. *Third World Quarterly*, *42*(9), 1923–1944.

Hedegaard, Connie. (2011, 15 December). EU Will Continue to Lead on Kyoto. *Reuters*.

Hein, Wolfgang, and Suerie Moon. (2013). *Informal Norms in Global Governance: Human Rights, Intellectual Property Rules and Access to Medicines*. Farnham: Ashgate.

Heinrich Böll Stiftung and ODI (Overseas Development Institute). (2019a). Adaptation Fund. Climate Funds Update. https://climatefundsupdate.org/the-funds/adaption-fund/

Heinrich Böll Stiftung and ODI (Overseas Development Institute). (2019b). Green Climate Fund. Climate Funds Update. https://climatefundsupdate.org/the-funds/green-climate-fund/

Heinrich Böll Stiftung and ODI (Overseas Development Institute). (2019c). Least Developed Countries Fund. Climate Funds Update. https://climatefundsupdate.org/the-funds/least-developed-countries-fund-2/

Heinrich Böll Stiftung and ODI (Overseas Development Institute). (2019d). Special Climate Change Fund. Climate Funds Update. https://climatefundsupdate.org/the-funds/special-climate-change-fund/

Heldt, Eugénia. (2017). Shaping Global Trade Governance Rules: New Powers' Hard and Soft Strategies of Influence at the WTO. *European Foreign Affairs Review*, *22*, 19–36.

Heron, Tony. (2013). *Pathways from Preferential Trade: The Politics of Trade Adjustment in Africa, the Carribean and Pacific.* New York: Palgrave Macmillan.

Hindley, Brian V. (1971). *The Economic Theory of Patents, Copyrights, and Registered Industrial Designs: Background Study to the Report on Intellectual and Industrial Property.* Ottawa: Economic Council of Canada.

The Hindu BusinessLine. (2011, 13 December). Changed Climate in Durban.

Hochstetler, Kathryn. (2012). The G-77, BASIC, and Global Climate Governance: A New Era in Multilateral Environmental Negotiations. *Revista Brasileira de Política International*, *55*, 53–69.

Hochstetler, Kathryn, and Manjana Milkoreit. (2015). Responsibilities in Transition: Emerging Powers in the Climate Change Negotiations. *Global Governance*, *21*(2), 205–226.
Hoda, Anwarul. (2009). Special and Differential Treatment of Developing Countries. In T. P. Stewart (ed.), *Opportunities and Obligations: New Perspectives on Global and US Trade Policy* (pp. 35–46). Alphen aan den Rijn: Kluwer Law International.
Honkonen, Tuula. (2009). The Principle of Common but Differentiated Responsibilities in Post-2012 Climate Negotiations. *Review of European Community and International Environmental Law*, *18*(3), 257–268.
Honma, Masayoshi. (2004). WTO Negotiations and Other Agricultural Trade Issues in Japan (Hi-Stat Discussion Paper Series No. 54).
Hopewell, Kristen. (2016). *Breaking the WTO: How Emerging Powers Disrupted the Neoliberal Project.* Stanford: Stanford University Press.
Hopewell, Kristen. (2019). US–China Conflict in Global Trade Governance: The New Politics of Agricultural Subsidies at the WTO. *Review of International Political Economy*, *26*(2), 207–231.
Hopewell, Kristen. (2020). *Clash of Powers: US–China Rivalry in Global Trade Governance*. Cambridge: Cambridge University Press.
Hopewell, Kristen. (2022). Heroes of the Developing World? Emerging Powers in WTO Agriculture Negotiations and Dispute Settlement. *The Journal of Peasant Studies*, *49*(3), 561–584.
Horta, Korinna, Robin Round, and Zoe Young. (2002). *The Global Environment Facility: The First Ten Years – Growing Pains or Inherent Flaws?* Environmental Defense and the Halifax Initiative.
Huang, Yanzhong. (2020). Emerging Powers and Global Health Governance: The Case of BRICS Countries. In C. McInnes, K. Lee, and J. Youde (eds.), *The Oxford Handbook of Global Health Politics* (pp. 301–324). Oxford: Oxford University Press.
Hudec, Robert E. (2010). *Developing Countries in the GATT Legal System.* Cambridge: Cambridge University Press.
Hurrell, Andrew, and Sandeep Sengupta. (2012). Emerging Powers, North–South Relations and Global Climate Politics. *International Affairs*, *88*(3), 463–484.
Hyder, Tariq Osman. (1994). Looking Back to See Forward. In I. M. Mintzer and J. A. Leonard (eds.), *Negotiating Climate Change: The Inside Story of the Rio Convention* (pp. 201–226). Cambridge: Cambridge University Press.
ICTSD (International Centre for Trade and Sustainable Development). (2017). Negotiating Global Rules on Agriculture Domestic Support: Options for the WTO's Buenos Aires Ministerial Conference [Issue paper]. Geneva: ICTSD.
IHME (Institute for Health Metrics and Evaluation). (2011). *Financing Global Health 2011: Continued Growth as MDG Deadline Approaches*. Seattle, WA: IHME.
IHME (Institute for Health Metrics and Evaluation). (2020). *Financing Global Health 2019: Tracking Health Spending in a Time of Crisis.* Seattle, WA: IHME.
Ikenberry, G. John. (2018). The End of Liberal International Order? *International Affairs*, *94*(1), 7–23.
IPCC (Intergovernmental Panel on Climate Change). (2007). *Climate Change 2007 – Mitigation of Climate Change: Contribution of Working Group III to the Fourth Assessment Report of the IPCC* [B. Metz, O. R. Davidson, P. R. Bosch, R. Dave, L. A. Meyer (eds.)]. Cambridge: Cambridge University Press.

Jacobson, Harold K. (1973). WHO: Medicine, Regionalism, and Managed Politics. In R. W. Cox and H. K. Jacobson (eds.), *The Anatomy of Influence: Decision Making in International Organization* (pp. 175–215). New Haven: Yale University Press.

Jamieson, Dale. (2014). *Reason in a Dark Time*. New York: Oxford University Press.

Jinnah, Sikina. (2017). Makers, Takers, Shakers, Shapers: Emerging Economies and Normative Engagement in Climate Governance. *Global Governance*, *23*(2), 285–306.

Johnson, Tana, and Johannes Urpelainen. (2020). The More Things Change, the More They Stay the Same: Developing Countries' Unity at the Nexus of Trade and Environmental Policy. *The Review of International Organizations*, *15*(2), 445–473.

Kanungo, Anil Kumar. (2011). The Process of China's Accession to the World Trade Organization: Obstacles and Implications. *International Studies*, *48*(3–4), 305–316.

Kates, Jennifer, and Rebecca Katz. (2011). The Role of Treaties, Agreements, Conventions, and Other International Instruments in Global Health. *Infectious Disease Clinics of North America*, *25*(2), 455–475.

The Kathmandu Post. (2011, 15 December). Decoding Durban Deal.

Keohane, Robert O., and Michael Oppenheimer. (2016). Paris: Beyond the Climate Dead End through Pledge and Review? *Politics and Governance*, *4*(3), 142–151.

Kessie, Edwini. (2007). The Legal Status of Special and Differential Treatment Provisions under the WTO Agreements. In G. A. Bermann and P. C. Mavroidis (eds.), *WTO Law and Developing Countries* (pp. 12–35). Cambridge: Cambridge University Press.

Khor, Martin. (2004). Comments on the WTO's Geneva 'July 2004 Package' (TWN Briefing Paper 22). Penang: Third World Network.

Khor, Martin. (2020a). Strange Outcome of Cancun Climate Conference. In M. Khor and M. Raman (eds.), *A Clash of Climate Change Paradigms: Negotiations and Outcomes at the UN Climate Convention* (pp. 71–84). Penang: Third World Network.

Khor, Martin. (2020b). Durban Conference Launches Negotiations for New Global Deal. In M. Khor and M. Raman (eds.), *A Clash of Climate Change Paradigms: Negotiations and Outcomes at the UN Climate Convention* (pp. 85–94). Penang: Third World Network.

Khor, Martin, and Meenakashi Raman. (2020). Introduction. In M. Khor and M. Raman (eds.), *A Clash of Climate Change Paradigms: Negotiations and Outcomes at the UN Climate Convention* (pp. 1–8). Penang: Third World Network.

Kim, Hyung Jin. (1995). The Strategy for the Republic of Korea in the Negotiations of the United Nations Framework Convention on Climate Change. *Korean Journal of Comparative Law*, *23*, 71–98.

Kjellén, Bo. (1994). A Personal Assessment. In I. M. Mintzer and J. A. Leonard (eds.), *Negotiating Climate Change: The Inside Story of the Rio Convention* (pp. 149–174). Cambridge: Cambridge University Press.

Kleimann, David, and Joe Guinan. (2011). The Doha Round: An Obituary (Global Governance Programme Policy Brief 1/2001). European University Institute, Robert Schuman Centre for Advanced Studies.

Koschorreck, Wilfried. (2001). Ted Turner als Deus Ex Machina. *Vereinte Nationen*, *49*(2), 65–70.

Krägenow, Timm. (1995). *Verhandlungspoker um Klimaschutz: Beobachtungen und Ergebnisse der Vertragsstaatenkonferenz zur Klimarahmenkonvention in Berlin.* Freiburg i.B.: Öko-Institut.

Krook, Mona Lena, and Jacqui True. (2012). Rethinking the Life Cycles of International Norms: The United Nations and the Global Promotion of Gender Equality. *European Journal of International Relations*, *18*(1), 103–127.

Kruck, Andreas, and Bernhard Zangl. (2019). Trading Privileges for Support: The Strategic Co-Optation of Emerging Powers into International Institutions. *International Theory*, *11*(3), 318–343.

Kruck, Andreas, and Bernhard Zangl. (2020). The Adjustment of International Institutions to Global Power Shifts: A Framework for Analysis. *Global Policy*, *11*(S3), 5–16.

Kumar, Mohan. (2018). *Negotiation Dynamics of the WTO.* Singapore: Palgrave Macmillan.

Kurtz, Jürgen. (2004). Developing Countries and Their Engagement in the World Trade Organization: An Assessment of the Cancun Ministerial. *Melbourne Journal of International Law*, *5*(1), 280–297.

Kyoto Protocol to the United Nations Framework Convention on Climate Change. (1997, 11 December).

Lake, David A., Lisa L. Martin, and Thomas Risse. (2021). Challenges to the Liberal Order: Reflections on International Organization. *International Organization*, *75*(2), 225–257.

Lamp, Nicolas. (2017). The 'Development' Discourse in Multilateral Trade Lawmaking. *World Trade Review*, *16*(3), 475–500.

Lee, Hoesung, and Jin-Gyu Oh. (2002). Mitigation Initiatives: Korea's Experiences. *Climate Policy*, *2*(2–3), 197–209.

Lee, Joo-Young. (2015). *A Human Rights Framework for Intellectual Property, Innovation and Access to Medicines.* London: Routledge.

Lee, Kelley. (2009). *The World Health Organization (WHO)*. London: Routledge.

Lighthizer, Robert. (2017). Opening Plenary Statement of United States Trade Representative Robert Lighthizer at the WTO Ministerial Conference [Speech transcript]. https://ustr.gov/about-us/policy-offices/press-office/press-releases/2017/december/opening-plenary-statement-ustr

Lipscy, Phillip Y. (2015). Explaining Institutional Change: Policy Areas, Outside Options, and the Bretton Woods Institutions. *American Journal of Political Science*, *59*(2), 341–356.

Lipscy, Phillip Y. (2017). *Renegotiating the World Order: Institutional Change in International Relations*. Cambridge: Cambridge University Press.

Mackey, Timothy K., and Thomas E. Novotny. (2012). Improving United Nations Funding to Strengthen Global Health Governance: Amending the Helms–Biden Agreement. *Global Health Governance*, *6*(1), 1–19.

Maguire, Rowena. (2013). The Role of Common but Differentiated Responsibility in the 2020 Climate Regime. *Carbon & Climate Law Review*, *7*(4), 260–269.

Mano, Ana. (2019, 20 March). Brazil's New Status Would Not Affect Prior AG Commitments: WTO Chief. *Reuters*. https://www.reuters.com/article/us-brazil-trade-idUSKCN1R12NW

Maswood, S. Javed. (2007). Developing Countries and the G20 in the Doha Round. In L. Crump and S. J. Maswood (eds.), *Developing Countries and Global Trade Negotiations* (pp. 41–62). London: Routledge.

May, Christopher. (2007). The World Intellectual Property Organization and the Development Agenda. *Global Governance*, *13*(2), 161–170.

McGee, Jeffrey, and Jens Steffek. (2016). The Copenhagen Turn in Global Climate Governance and the Contentious History of Differentiation in International Law. *Journal of Environmental Law*, *28*(1), 37–63.
Mearsheimer, John J. (2019). Bound to Fail: The Rise and Fall of the Liberal International Order. *International Security*, *43*(4), 7–50.
Mercurio, Brian, and Pratyush Nath Upreti. (2022). From Necessity to Flexibility: A Reflection on the Negotiations for a TRIPS Waiver for COVID-19 Vaccines and Treatments. *World Trade Review*, *21*(5), 633–649.
Michaelowa, Katharina, Paula Castro, and Lena Ho. (2014). Constructed Peer Groups and Path Dependence in International Organizations: The Case of the International Climate Change Negotiations. *Global Environmental Change*, *25*, 109–120.
Michalopoulos, Constantine. (2000). The Role of Special Differential Treatment for Developing Countries in GATT and the World Trade Organization (Policy Research Working Paper 2388). Washington, D.C.: World Bank.
Minas, Stephen. (2013). FPC Briefing: BASIC Positions – Major Emerging Economies in the UN Climate Change Negotiations. The Foreign Policy Centre. https://fpc.org.uk/fpc-briefing-basic-positions-major-emerging-economies-in-the-un-climate-change-negotiations/
Ministry of External Affairs – Government of India. (2007). PM's Intervention on Climate Change at the Heiligendamm Meeting. https://eoi.gov.in/kabul/?pdf0179?000
Ministry of Industry and Commerce – Government of India. (2017). India's Duty Free Tariff Preference (DFTP) Scheme for Least Developed Countries (LDCs). https://commerce.gov.in/wp-content/uploads/2020/02/MOC_636434269763910839_international_tpp_DFTP.pdf
Ministry of Trade and Industry – Government of Singapore. (2019). Singapore Reaffirms Commitment to Work with Like-Minded Partners to Strengthen the World Trade Organization [Press release]. https://www.mti.gov.sg/-/media/MTI/Newsroom/Press-Releases/2019/09/SDT-press-release.pdf
Moon, Suerie. (2011, 16–19 March). Rising Powers, Emerging Markets: Implications of Multipolarity for Intellectual Property Rules, Access to Medicines and Global Health [Conference paper]. International Studies Association Convention, Montreal, Canada.
Morin, Jean-Frédéric, and Chantal Blouin. (2019). How Environmental Treaties Contribute to Global Health Governance. *Globalization and Health*, *15*, 47.
Morin, Jean-Frédéric, Omar Serrano, Mira Burri, and Sara Bannerman. (2018). Rising Economies in the International Patent Regime: From Rule-Breakers to Rule-Changers and Rule-Makers. *New Political Economy*, *23*(3), 255–273.
Morse, Julia, and Robert O. Keohane. (2014). Contested Multilateralism. *The Review of International Organizations*, *9*(4), 385–412.
Moschini, GianCarlo. (2003). Intellectual Property Rights and the World Trade Organization: Retrospect and Prospects (Working Paper 03-WP 334). Iowa State University, Center for Agricultural and Rural Development (CARD).
Müller, Benito. (2006). Montreal 2005: *What Happened and What It Means* (OIES Paper). Oxford: Oxford Institute for Energy Studies.
Müller, Benito. (2014). *Performance-Based Formulaic Resource Allocation – a Cautionary Tale* (OIES Paper). Oxford: Oxford Institute for Energy Studies.
Murphy, Craig N. (1994). *International Organization and Industrial Change: Global Governance since 1850.* Cambridge: Polity Press.

Musungu, Sisule F., and Cecilia Oh. (2006). The Use of Flexibilities in TRIPS by Developing Countries: Can They Promote Access to Medicines? South Centre, and World Health Organization. https://apps.who.int/iris/handle/10665/43503

Muzaka, Valbona. (2019). India and Brazil in Pursuit of the Competitive Knowledge Economy. *Review of International Studies*, *45*(2), 345–364.

Muzaka, Valbona, and Matthew Louis Bishop. (2015). Doha Stalemate: The End of Trade Multilateralism? *Review of International Studies*, *41*(2), 383–406.

Narlikar, Amrita. (2006). Fairness in International Trade Negotiations: Developing Countries in the GATT and WTO. *The World Economy*, *29*(8), 1005–1029.

Narlikar, Amrita. (2020). *Poverty Narratives and Power Paradoxes in International Trade Negotiations and Beyond.* Cambridge: Cambridge University Press.

Narlikar, Amrita, and Diana Tussie. (2004). The C20 at the Cancun Ministerial: Developing Countries and Their Evolving Coalitions in the WTO. *The World Economy*, *27*(7), 947–966.

Narlikar, Amrita, and Rorden Wilkinson. (2004). Collapse at the WTO: A Cancun Post-Mortem. *Third World Quarterly*, *25*(3), 447–460.

New, William. (2013). At WTO, LDC Fight for Extension of TRIPS Transition Continues. Third World Network Intellectual Property Watch. https://www.twn.my/title2/intellectual_property/info.service/2013/ipr.info.130509.htm

Noland, Marcus. (1995). China and the International Economic System (Working Paper 95-6). Peterson Institute for International Economics.

Nullmeier, Frank. (2021). *Kausale Mechanismen und Process Tracing: Perspektiven der qualitativen Politikforschung*. Frankfurt and New York: Campus.

Oberthür, Sebastian. (1993). *Politik im Treibhaus: Die Entstehung des internationalen Klimaschutzregimes.* Berlin: Edition Sigma.

Oberthür, Sebastian, and Hermann Ott. (1995). UN/Convention on Climate Change: The First Conference of the Parties. *Environmental Policy and Law*, *25*(4/5), 144–156.

Oberthür, Sebastian, and Hermann Ott. (2000). *Das Kyoto-Protokoll: Internationale Klimapolitik für das 21. Jahrhundert.* Opladen: Leske + Budrich.

Odagiri, Hiroyuki, Akira Goto, Atsushi Sunami, and Richard R. Nelson. (2010). *Intellectual Property Rights, Development and Catch-Up: An International Comparative Study.* Oxford: Oxford University Press.

OECD (Organisation for Economic Co-operation and Development). (2011). Africa Fact Sheet. https://www.oecd.org/investment/investmentfordevelopment/47452483.pdf

OECD (Organisation for Economic Co-operation and Development). (2019). *Climate Finance Provided and Mobilised by Developed Countries in 2013–17*. Paris: OECD Publishing.

Ott, Hermann. (1994). Tenth Session of the INC/FCCC: Results and Options for the First Conference of the Parties. *Environmental Law Network International Newsletter*, *2*, 3–7.

Pal, Parthapratim. (2001). *Implementation Issues of the Agreement on Agriculture and Its Implications for Developing Countries*. New Delhi: Economic Research Foundation (ERF). https://www.networkideas.org/focus/sep2002/AOA.pdf

Park, Walter G., and Douglas C. Lippoldt. (2008). Technology Transfer and the Economic Implications of the Strengthening of Intellectual Property Rights in Developing Countries (OECD Trade Policy Papers, No. 62). Paris: OECD Publishing.

Patel, Khadija. (2011, 12 December). While COP17 Hailed 'a Success', Country Slammed as Mediator. *AllAfrica*.

Paterson, Matthew. (1996). *Global Warming and Global Politics*. London: Routledge.
Patz, Ronny, and Klaus H. Goetz. (2019). *Managing Money and Discord in the UN: Budgeting and Bureaucracy*. Oxford: Oxford University Press.
Paul, Thazha Varkey, Deborah Welch Larson, and William C. Wohlforth. (eds.). (2014). *Status in World Politics*. Cambridge: Cambridge University Press.
Pauw, Pieter, Kennedy Mbeva, and Harro van Asselt. (2019). Subtle Differentiation of Countries' Responsibilities under the Paris Agreement. *Palgrave Communications*, *5*, 86.
Pauwelyn, Joost. (2013). The End of Differential Treatment for Developing Countries? Lessons from the Trade and Climate Change Regimes. *Review of European Community and international Environmental Law*, *22*(1), 29–41.
People's Health Movement, Medact, Third World Network, Health Poverty Action, Medico International, and ALAMES. (2017). *Global Health Watch 5: An Alternative World Health Report*. London: Zed Books.
Percy, Sarah V., and Wayne Sandholtz. (2022). Why Norms Rarely Die. *European Journal of International Relations*, *28*(4), 934–954.
Pratap, Ravindra. (2004). WTO and Tariff Preferences: India Wins Case, EC the Law. *Economic and Political Weekly*, *39*(18), 1788–1790.
Preeg, Ernest H. (2012). The Uruguay Round Negotiations and the Creation of the WTO. In M. Daunton, A. Narlikar, and R. M. Stern (eds.), *The Oxford Handbook on the World Trade Organization* (pp. 122–138). Oxford: Oxford University Press.
Pritchard, Bill. (2009). The Long Hangover from the Second Food Regime: A World-Historical Interpretation of the Collapse of the WTO Doha Round. *Agriculture and Human Values*, *26*(4), 297–307.
Prys-Hansen, Miriam, Kristina Hahn, Malte Lellmann, and Milan Röseler. (2019). Contestation in the UNFCCC – The Case of Climate Finance. In M. D. Stephen and M. Zürn (eds.), *Contested World Orders: Rising Powers, Non-Governmental Organizations, and the Politics of Authority Beyond the Nation-State* (pp. 272–302). Oxford: Oxford University Press.
Qi, Xinran. (2011). The Rise of BASIC in UN Climate Change Negotiations. *South African Journal of International Affairs*, *18*(3), 295–318.
Rajamani, Lavanya. (2003). From Stockholm to Johannesburg: The Anatomy of Dissonance in the International Environmental Dialogue. *Review of European Community and International Environmental Law*, *12*(1), 23–32.
Rajamani, Lavanya. (2006). *Differential Treatment in International Environmental Law*. Oxford: Oxford University Press.
Rajamani, Lavanya. (2008a). Differentiation in the Post-2012 Climate Regime. *Policy Quarterly*, *4*(4), 48–51.
Rajamani, Lavanya. (2008b). From Berlin to Bali and Beyond: Killing Kyoto Softly? *International & Comparative Law Quarterly*, *57*(4), 909–939.
Rajamani, Lavanya. (2009). India and Climate Change: What India Wants, Needs, and Needs to Do. *India Review*, *8*(3), 340–374.
Rajamani, Lavanya. (2010). The Making and Unmaking of the Copenhagen Accord. *International & Comparative Law Quarterly*, *59*(3), 824–843.
Rajamani, Lavanya. (2012a). The Changing Fortunes of Differential Treatment in the Evolution of International Environmental Law. *International Affairs*, *88*(3), 605–623.
Rajamani, Lavanya. (2012b). The Durban Platform for Enhanced Action and the Future of the Climate Regime. *International & Comparative Law Quarterly*, *61*(2), 501–518.

Rajamani, Lavanya. (2013). Differentiation in the Emerging Climate Regime. *Theoretical Inquiries in Law, 14*(1), 151–172.
Rajamani, Lavanya. (2016). Ambition and Differentiation in the 2015 Paris Agreement: Interpretative Possibilities and Underlying Politics. *International & Comparative Law Quarterly, 65*(2), 493–514.
Raustiala, Karl, and David G. Victor. (2004). The Regime Complex for Plant Genetic Resources. *International Organization, 58*(2), 277–309.
Reddy, Srikanth K., Sumaira Mazhar, and Raphael Lencucha. (2018). The Financial Sustainability of the World Health Organization and the Political Economy of Global Health Governance: A Review of Funding Proposals. *Globalization and Health, 14*, 119.
Robbins, Carol A. (2009). Measuring Payments for the Supply and Use of Intellectual Property in National Bureau of Economic Research. In M. Reinsdorf, and M. J. Slaughter (eds.), *International Trade in Services and Intangibles in the Era of Globalization* (pp. 139–171). Chicago: University of Chicago Press.
Roger, Charles. (2020). *The Origins of Informality: Why the Legal Foundations of Global Governance Are Shifting, and Why It Matters*. Oxford: Oxford University Press.
Rowlands, Ian H. (1995a). Explaining National Climate Change Policies. *Global Environmental Change, 5*(3), 235–249.
Rowlands, Ian H. (1995b). *The Politics of Global Atmospheric Change*. Manchester: Manchester University Press.
Saez, Catherine. (2013). LDC Request for Waiver of IP Obligations Meets Conditions from Developed Countries. Intellectual Property Watch. https://web.archive.org/web/20131016001206/https://www.ip-watch.org/2013/05/09/ldc-request-for-waiver-of-ip-obligations-meets-conditions-from-developed-countries/
Saez, Catherine. (2015). LDC Pharma IP Waiver until 2033 Approved by WTO TRIPS Council. Intellectual Property Watch. https://web.archive.org/web/20151213001302/https://www.ip-watch.org/2015/11/06/ldc-pharma-ip-waiver-until-2033-approved-by-wto-trips-council/
Sandholtz, Wayne, and Kenneth Stiles. (2008). *International Norms and Cycles of Change*. New York: Oxford University Press.
Schmid, Lisa Katharina, Alexander Reitzenstein, and Nina Hall. (2021). Blessing or Curse? The Effects of Earmarked Funding in UNICEF and UNDP. *Global Governance: A Review of Multilateralism and International Organizations, 27*(3), 433–459.
Schöfer, Till, and Clara Weinhardt. (2022). Developing-Country Status at the WTO: The Divergent Strategies of Brazil, India and China. *International Affairs, 98*(6), 1937–1957.
Sebenius, James K. (1994). Towards a Winning Climate Coalition. In I. M. Mintzer and J. A. Leonard (eds.), *Negotiating Climate Change: The Inside Story of the Rio Convention* (pp. 277–320). Cambridge: Cambridge University Press.
Sell, Susan. (2011). TRIPS Was Never Enough: Vertical Forum Shifting, FTAs, ACTA and TPP. *Journal of Intellectual Property Law, 18*(2), 447–478.
Sengupta, Sandeep. (2020). Deciphering India's Foreign Policy on Climate Change: The Role of Interests, Institutions, and Ideas. In J. Plagemann, S. Destradi, and A. Narlikar (eds.), *India Rising: A Multilayered Analysis of Ideas, Interests, and Institutions* (pp. 167–194). New Delhi: Oxford University Press.

Serrano, Omar. (2016). China and India's Insertion in the Intellectual Property Rights Regime: Sustaining or Disrupting the Rules? *New Political Economy*, *21*(4), 343–364.

Shalal, Andrea, and Emma Farge. (2022, 16 March). US, EU, India, S.Africa Reach Compromise on COVID Vaccine IP Waiver Text. *Reuters*. https://www.reuters.com/business/healthcare-pharmaceuticals/us-eu-india-s-africa-reach-tentative-pact-covid-vaccine-ip-waiver-sources-2022-03-15/

Sharma, Sachin Kumar, and Abhijit Das. (2018). EU–Brazil Proposal on Farm Support: Strengthening: Agricultural Reforms or Undermining Them? *Agricultural Economics Research Review*, *31*(1), 75–86.

Sharma, Shalendra D. (1996). Building Effective International Environmental Regimes – The Case of the GEF. *Journal of Environment & Development*, *5*(1), 73–86.

Sharma, Shalendra D. (2004). Going beyond Cancun: Realizing the Development Promise of the Doha Agenda. *Global Economic Review*, *33*(2), 17–38.

Sharma, Sudhir, and Denis Desgain. (2013). *Understanding the Concept of Nationally Appropriate Mitigation Action*. Roskilde: UNEP Risø Centre.

Sheinbaum, Claudia, and Omar Masera. (2000). Mitigating Carbon Emissions while Advancing National Development Priorities: The Case of Mexico. *Climatic Change*, *47*, 259–282.

Sidaway, James D. (2012). Geographies of Development: New Maps, New Visions? *The Professional Geographer*, *64*(1), 49–62.

Sinha, Aseema. (2021). Understanding the 'Crisis of the Institution' in the Liberal Trade Order at the WTO. *International Affairs*, *97*(5), 1521–1540.

Sjöberg, Helen. (1999). Restructuring the Global Environment Facility (Working Paper 13). Washington, D.C.: Global Environmental Facility.

Sridhar, Devi, and Ngaire Woods. (2013). Trojan Multilateralism: Global Cooperation in Health. *Global Policy*, *4*(4), 325–335.

Srivastava, Sanjay. (2008). Negotiation Analysis: The Cancun Ministerial of the WTO. *International Studies*, *45*(1), 23–43.

Stephen, Matthew D. (2017). Emerging Powers and Emerging Trends in Global Governance. *Global Governance*, *23*(3), 483–502.

Stimmer, Anette. (2019). Beyond Internalization: Alternate Endings of the Norm Life Cycle. *International Studies Quarterly*, *63*(2), 270–280.

Stimmer, Anette, and Lea Wisken. (2019). The Dynamics of Dissent: When Actions Are Louder Than Words. *International Affairs*, *95*(3), 515–533.

Streck, Charlotte. (2001). The GEF – A Role Model for International Governance? *Global Environmental Politics*, *1*(2), 71–94.

Sura, Vikram. (2002). The Process of Informals in the Fifth Committee. *UN Chronicle*, *1*, 59–63.

Suzara, Felizardo B. (2002). A Study on the Formulation of an Assessment Scale Methodology: The United Nations Experience in Allocating Budget Expenditures among Member States. *Journal of Official Statistics*, *18*(3), 481–510.

Syam, Nirmalya. (2014). Transition Period for TRIPS Implementation for LDCs: Implications for Local Production of Medicines in the East African Community (Research Paper 59). South Centre.

Tabau, Anne-Sophie, and Marion Lemoine. (2012). Willing Power, Fearing Responsibilities: BASIC in the Climate Negotiations. *Carbon & Climate Law Review*, *6*(3), 197–208.

Thompson, Alexander. (2020). Emerging Powers and Differentiation in Global Climate Institutions. *Global Policy*, *11*(S3), 61–72.

Tu, Xinquan, and Robert Wolfe. (2021). Reviving the Negotiation Function of the WTO: Why the Onus Falls on the Three Major Powers. In B. Hoekman, X. Tu, and D. Wang (eds.), *Rebooting Multilateral Trade Cooperation: Perspectives from China and Europe* (pp. 29–44). London: CEPR Press.
TWN (Third World Network). (2008). *Bali News Updates and Climate Briefings*. Penang: Third World Network.
TWN (Third World Network). (2009). *Poznan News Updates*. Penang: Third World Network.
TWN (Third World Network). (2010). *Copenhagen News Updates and Climate Briefings*. Penang: Third World Network.
TWN (Third World Network). (2011a). *Cancun News Updates and Climate Briefings (November/December 2010)*. Penang: Third World Network.
TWN (Third World Network). (2011b). Bangkok News Update No. 10: New Direction in Kyoto Protocol Talks (April 2011). https://www.twn.my/title2/climate/news/bangkok03/bkk3_news_up10.pdf
TWN (Third World Network). (2011c). Bonn News Update No. 22: Strong Disagreements Over Way Forward on Legal Options Group (June 2011). https://www.twn.my/title2/climate/news/Bonn08/TWN_bonn8.up22.pdf
TWN (Third World Network). (2011d). *Panama Climate News Update (October 2011)*. Penang: Third World Network.
TWN (Third World Network). (2012). *Durban News Updates and Climate Briefings*. Penang: Third World Network.
TWN (Third World Network). (2013). *Doha News Updates and Climate Briefings*. Penang: Third World Network.
TWN (Third World Network). (2014). *Warsaw News Updates and Climate Briefings*. Penang: Third World Network.
TWN (Third World Network). (2017, 13 December). WTO, from Negotiating to 'Litigation-Centred' Body, Complains US. https://www.twn.my/title2/wto.info/2017/ti171222.htm
Ukpe, Aniekan, and Sangeeta Khorana. (2021). Special and Differential Treatment in the WTO: Framing Differential Treatment to Achieve (Real) Development. *Journal of International Trade Law and Policy*, *20*(2), 83–100.
UNAIDS (Joint United Nations Programme on HIV/AIDS). (2011). DOHA+10 TRIPS Flexibilities and Access to Antiretroviral Therapy: Lessons from the Past, Opportunities for the Future [Technical brief]. https://www.unaids.org/sites/default/files/media_asset/JC2260_DOHA+10TRIPS_en_0.pdf
UNFCCC. (2022a). Adaptation Fund. https://unfccc.int/Adaptation-Fund
UNFCCC. (2022b). Green Climate Fund. https://unfccc.int/process/bodies/funds-and-financial-entities/green-climate-fund
UNFCCC. (2022c). Introduction to Climate Finance. https://unfccc.int/topics/climate-finance/the-big-picture/introduction-to-climate-finance
United Nations Framework Convention on Climate Change [UNFCCC]. 9 May 1992.
US Congress. (1997). S.Res.98 [Report No. 105-54] Expressing the Sense of the Senate Regarding the Conditions for the United States Becoming a Signatory to any International Agreement on Greenhouse Gas Emissions under the United Nations Framework Convention on Climate Change. Washington, D.C.: 105th Congress (1997–1998). https://www.congress.gov/105/bills/sres98/BILLS-105sres98ats.pdf
Vanderheiden, Steven. (2015). Justice and Climate Finance: Differentiating Responsibility in the Green Climate Fund. *The International Spectator*, *50*(1), 31–45.

VanGrasstek, Craig, and Pierre Sauvé. (2006). The Consistency of WTO Rules: Can the Single Undertaking Be Squared with Variable Geometry? *Journal of International Economic Law*, *9*(4), 837–864.

Verheyen, Roda. (2005). *Climate Change Damage and International Law: Prevention Duties and State Responsibility*. Leiden: Brill.

Verwey, Wil D. (1990). The Principles of a New International Economic Order and the Law of the General Agreement on Tariffs and Trade (GATT). *Leiden Journal of International Law*, *3*(2), 117–142.

Vihma, Antto. (2011). India and the Global Climate Governance: Between Principles and Pragmatism. *Journal of Environment & Development*, *20*(1), 69–94.

Vihma, Antto, Yacob Mulugetta, and Sylvia Karlsson-Vinkhuyzen. (2011). Negotiating Solidarity? The G77 through the Prism of Climate Change Negotiations. *Global Change, Peace & Security*, *23*(3), 315–334.

Waisbich, Laura Trajber, Supriya Roychoudhury, and Sebastian Haug. (2021). Beyond the Single Story: 'Global South' Polyphonies. *Third World Quarterly*, *42*(9), 2086–2095.

Weinhardt, Clara. (2020). Emerging Powers in the World Trading System: Contestation of the Developing Country Status and the Reproduction of Inequalities. *Global Society*, *34*(3), 388–408.

Weinhardt, Clara, and Till Schöfer. (2022). Differential Treatment for Developing Countries in the WTO: The Unmaking of the North–South Distinction in a Multipolar World. *Third World Quarterly*, *43*(1), 74–93.

Weinhardt, Clara, and Tobias ten Brink. (2020). Varieties of Contestation: China's Rise and the Liberal Trade Order. *Review of International Political Economy*, *27*(2), 258–280.

White House. (2019). Memorandum on Reforming Developing-Country Status in the World Trade Organization [Presidential memorandum]. https://trumpwhitehouse.archives.gov/presidential-actions/memorandum-reforming-developing-country-status-world-trade-organization/

WHO (World Health Organization). (1948). *Summary Report on Proceedings, Minutes and Final Acts of the International Health Conference Held in New York from 19 June to 22 July 1946* (Official Records of the World Health Organization, No. 2). New York and Geneva: WHO.

WHO (World Health Organization). (2020). *Basic Documents, Forty-Ninth Edition, Including Amendments Adopted up to 31 May 2019*. Geneva: WHO.

WHO Evaluation Office. (2016). Evaluation of WHO's Presence in Countries [Evaluation brief]. https://www.who.int/docs/default-source/documents/evaluation/whos-presence-in-countries-eval-brief-2016.pdf

Wiener, Antje. (2008). *The Invisible Constitution of Politics: Contested Norms and International Encounters*. Cambridge: Cambridge University Press.

Wiener, Antje. (2009). Enacting Meaning-in-Use: Qualitative Research on Norms and International Relations. *Review of International Studies*, *35*(1), 175–193.

Wiener, Antje. (2018). *Contestation and Constitution of Norms in Global International Relations*. Cambridge: Cambridge University Press.

Wiener, Antje, and Uwe Puetter. (2009). The Quality of Norms Is What Actors Make of It – Critical Constructivist Research on Norms. *Journal of International Law and International Relations*, *5*(1), 1–16.

Wilkinson, Rorden, Erin Hannah, and James Scott. (2016). The WTO in Nairobi: The Demise of the Doha Development Agenda and the Future of the Multilateral Trading System. *Global Policy*, *7*(2), 247–255.

WIPO (World Intellectual Property Organization). (2020, 7 April). China Becomes Top Filer of International Patents in 2019 amid Robust Growth for WIPO's IP Services, Treaties and Finances [Press release 2020/848]. https://www.wipo.int/pressroom/en/articles/2020/article_0005.html

Wiseman, Geoffrey. (2010). 'Polylateralism': Diplomacy's Third Dimension. *Public Diplomacy Magazine*, *2*, 24–39.

World Bank. (2022). World Bank Development Indicators. The World Bank Group. https://databank.worldbank.org/source/world-development-indicators

WTO (World Trade Organization). (n.d.-a). Ministerial Conferences. https://www.wto.org/english/thewto_e/minist_e/minist_e.htm

WTO (World Trade Organization). (n.d.-b). Who Are the Developing Countries in the WTO? https://www.wto.org/english/tratop_e/devel_e/d1who_e.htm

WTO (World Trade Organization). (2001). Meeting of the Working Party on the Accession of China: Statement by H.E. Vice Minister LONG Yongtu, Head of the Chinese Delegation, at the Sixteenth Session of the Working Party on China [Speech transcript]. https://www.wto.org/english/news_e/news01_e/china_longstat_jul01_e.htm

WTO (World Trade Organization). (2006). Transparency Mechanism for RTAs. https://www.wto.org/english/tratop_e/region_e/trans_mecha_e.htm#:~:text=On%2014%20December%202006%2C%20the,and%20notification%20to%20the%20WTO

WTO (World Trade Organization). (2014). World Trade Report 2014. https://www.wto.org/english/res_e/booksp_e/world_trade_report14_e.pdf

Yu, Peter K. (in press). TRIPS Wars: Developing Countries Strike Back. In A. George (ed.), *Flashpoints: Changing Paradigms in Intellectual Property and Technology Law*. New Orleans, Louisiana: Quid Pro Books.

Zangl, Bernhard. (2008). Judicialization Matters! A Comparison of Dispute Settlement under GATT and the WTO. *International Studies Quarterly*, *52*(4), 825–854.

Zangl, Bernhard, Frederick Heußner, Andreas Kruck, and Xenia Lanzendörfer. (2016). Imperfect Adaptation: How the WTO and the IMF Adjust to Shifting Power Distributions among their Members. *The Review of International Organizations*, *11*(2), 171–196.

Zelicovich, Julieta. (2022). Are There Still Shared Values to Sustain Multilateralism? Discourse in World Trade Organization Reform Debates. *Third World Quarterly*, *43*(2), 332–351.

Zhuawu, Collin, and Teddy Y. Soobramanien. (2017). WTO Ministerial Conference in Buenos Aires: What's at Stake for Small, Least Developed, and sub-Saharan African countries? *Commonwealth Trade Hot Topics*, *144*, 1–8.

Index